Management Learning

Management Learning

Integrating Perspectives in Theory and Practice

edited by

John Burgoyne and Michael Reynolds

SAGE Publications

London ● Thousand Oaks ● New Delhi

SAGE Publications Ltd
6 Bonhill Street
London EC2A 4PU

SAGE Publications Inc
2455 Teller Road
Thousand Oaks, California 91320

SAGE Publications India Pvt Ltd
32, M-Block Market
Greater Kailash - I
New Delhi 110 048

British Library Cataloguing in Publication data

A catalogue record for this book is available from the British Library

ISBN 0 8039 7643 7
ISBN 0 8039 7644 5 (pbk)

Library of Congress catalog card number 97–068756

Typeset by Photoprint, Torquay, Devon
Printed in Great Britain by The Cromwell Press Ltd, Broughton Gifford, Melksham, Wiltshire

Contents

Contributors

Richard Boot, independent writer, researcher and consultant, UK.

John Burgoyne, Professor, Department of Management Learning, Lancaster University, UK.

Robert Chia, Senior Lecturer, Department of Accounting, Finance and Management, University of Essex, UK.

Ian Cunningham Chairman, Centre for Self-Managed Learning, London, UK.

Graham Dawes, Centre for Self-Managed Learning, London, UK.

Mark Easterby-Smith, Professor, Department of Management Learning, Lancaster University, UK.

Norman Fairclough, Professor, Department of Linguistics, Lancaster University, UK.

Stephen Fox, Senior Lecturer, Department of Management Learning, Lancaster University, UK.

Ginny Hardy, Lecturer, Department of Management Learning, Lancaster University, UK.

Vivien Hodgson, Senior Lecturer, Department of Management Learning, Lancaster University, UK.

Brad Jackson, Associate Professor, Faculty of Continuing Education, The University of Calgary, Canada.

Monica Lee, Lecturer, Department of Management Learning, Lancaster University, UK.

Anna Lorbiecki, Lecturer, Department of Management Learning, Lancaster University, UK.

Judi Marshall, Professor, School of Management, University of Bath, UK.

Victoria Marsick, Professor, Department of Organization and Leadership, Teachers College, Columbia University, USA.

David McConnell, Reader, Centre for the Study of Networked Learning, Division of Adult Continuing Education, University of Sheffield, UK.

Mike Pedler, Revans Professorial Fellow, Revans Centre for Action Learning and Research, University of Salford, UK.

Peter Reason, Senior Lecturer, School of Management, University of Bath, UK.

Michael Reynolds, Senior Lecturer, Department of Management Learning, Lancaster University, UK.

Robin Snell, Associate Professor, Department of Management, City University of Hong Kong.

Morgan Tanton, Lecturer, Department of Management Learning, Lancaster University, UK.

Richard Thorpe, Professor, Faculty of Management and Business, Manchester Metropolitan University, UK.

Karen Watkins, Professor, Department of Adult Education, University of Georgia, USA.

Hugh Willmott, Professor, Manchester School of Management, UMIST, UK.

Introduction

Management learning is an area of both professional practice and theoretical inquiry, and has as a special concern the linking of these two domains in a way that advances both. Professional practice adds to management learning theory, and theoretical insights add to practitioners' activities. What kinds of theory relate to practice, and what kinds of practice are open to theoretical insight?

Practice, at the end of the day, needs theories to shape it. Theory, on the other hand, is tested and developed through practice. These practical and academic pursuits, while different, can mutually support and contribute to each other. The normative theories of practitioners, and the observation of the consequences of implementing them, can contribute to the descriptive, interpretative and critical theories that are of interest to academics. These more 'academic' formulations can in turn suggest ways of 'improving' normative theories, though rarely or never in ways that are definitive or final.

This mutually supportive interplay of the theoretical and the practical, we contend, is a particular feature or aspiration of the theory and practice of management learning, as is the dilemma of understanding how these two areas relate to each other. This book is our first systematic attempt to deal with these issues across the broad range of areas within management learning. This introduction discusses types of practice and theory in the world of management learning, its history, and a variety of ways of mapping the field, as well as explaining the structure of the book.

Types of Practice

Different types of practice, which are increasingly accessible to development through interaction with theory, can be distinguished as *effective practice*, *reflective practice* and *critically reflective practice*. In most or all management development and management education settings there exists practice that is regarded as effective and successful. Such effectiveness is often judged as objective – the clear and reliable achievement of outcomes that are incontrovertibly judged to be good. In other ways such attributions of effectiveness can (and many theorists would prefer this formulation) be seen as a consensus of subjective views among those people who matter in a given situation.

Within the field of action, both practice and practitioners are labelled as effective whether or not the practitioners can render an account of how they perform. If practitioners are regarded as effective, even though they cannot explain their 'success', they are producing *effective practice* and are simply *effective practitioners*. Such practitioners know that they perform, but may regard their skill as intuitive, unconscious, tacit.

Where practitioners can render some plausible account of how they perform, in other words articulate a theory of their practice, they become *reflective practitioners* producing *reflective practice*. Among the advantages of being a reflective practitioner is the ability to transfer skills – through the teaching and learning of a conscious normative theory – to others, and the possibility of working out how to adapt the theory and practice to a changed circumstance rather than relying on intuition and trial and error – the only route available to the effective practitioner. Reflective practitioners, in other words, have a working theory of their practice, which will tend to be normative in that it suggests what should be done and why it should work.

Producing *critically reflective practice* has another layer of theory behind the working normative theory. This is likely to be a rich and diverse mixture of descriptive, interpretative and critical theories, and also an understanding of a range of rival normative theories to a 'preferred' one. This second layer of theory serves as a resource for practitioners to question continuously and revise their working theory, and to make sense of experiences that do not 'fit' current working theories. Critically reflective practice will be more sophisticated not only in its understanding of the instrumental aspects of the work – what actions lead to what outcomes in what circumstances – but also in the valuing, ethical and moral aspects of practice. It reveals a deeper concern with the purposes that the practice is or might be serving. Critically reflective practitioners can also interpret practice and its immediate organizational context as part of the broader economic, political and social context, and to have an understanding of the kind of society that their work is reproducing or changing.

Critically reflective practitioners are aware that with every practical action they take they are 'fixing (temporarily) their belief' and acting on their current best working theory, but they realize that this may also be open to challenge and improvement. This attitude applies both to the instrumental (how to achieve an outcome) and moral (how to decide what outcomes are 'good') components of their practice. Critically reflective practitioners operate what they judge to be the best 'working idea' available to them at all times, but they also have a commitment continually to search for a better one. The second layer of theory is the major resource for this, giving the practitioner a richer set of ideas and concepts with which to think about these issues. The critically reflective practitioner of management learning has access to the most sophisticated process of learning that we are capable of, given our current state of understanding.

Types of Theory

What kinds of theory might we look for in dealing with management learning? We suggest that there are four 'pure types' which allow us to understand what is available from the world of theory that can contribute to critical reflective practice:

1 Normative theories that propose an answer to the question: What should be done?
2 Descriptive theories that offer an answer to the question: What is going on?
3 Interpretative theories that try to explain *why* things happen the way they do.
4 Critical theories that examine such in-depth questions as: What assumptions are we making in analysing things as we do? What aspects are we leaving out? What value judgements are built into positions taken? What larger social processes are our theory and practice part of? What contradictions and paradoxes are there between these various values, assumptions, agendas, omissions? What would it take to resolve them?

Normative theories tell us what to do. For example, to say that teaching or training should (a) describe a procedure; (b) demonstrate it; (c) give learners practice in doing it themselves; and (d) give feedback on the effectiveness of their actions, is a prescription of how to teach or train, and has embedded in it a normative theory of how people learn.

A *descriptive theory* represents what is thought to happen regularly or normally. The differing roles that people are observed to take on in team-work, as in the work of Belbin (1981), can be taken as an example of this kind of theory. If, however, this typology is taken, as it often is, as a description of what people in teams *should* or *must* do, as well as what they do do, then it has been turned back into a normative theory. When practitioners explicitly or implicitly use the descriptive as normative they take on a conservative role – normalizing deviants and newcomers to the conventions of the situation.

An *interpretative theory* attempts to answer the question 'Why is this happening?' For example, the way people behave towards each other and the effects they have on each other can be interpreted in terms of Freudian psychoanalytic theory or Jungian theory. Interpersonal behaviour can also be interpreted in terms of transactional analysis (Barker, 1980), neurolinguistic programming (Brandler and Grinder, 1979), the manifestation and inter-action of personality types like those described by the Myers-Briggs Inventory, or in terms of larger social processes and tensions that manifest through people in interpersonal situations (Reynolds, 1994). Gendered behaviour, for example, can be interpreted as a manifestation of the habits, attitudes, beliefs or personalities of individuals, but also in terms of the larger social processes that shape their role, and create these attitudes and beliefs in the first place.

For any given phenomenon that may be described there is usually a whole range of available interpretative theories, as this example shows. Interpretative theories attempt to be descriptive of a deeper level of reality, that which is presumed to generate phenomena. They can provide the basis for a normative conclusion if a value judgement is made about how things should be, in terms of the interpretative theory. If it is judged that someone has difficulties in dealing with certain kinds of problem because of their defence mechanisms, and that this is a bad thing, then a psychodynamic interpretative theory can be used to deduce a normative course of action to deal with it, such as proposing an intervention that would help the person reduce the use of that particular defence mechanism.

Critical theories continuously question all the claims, assumptions, contradictions, omissions and value judgements that are built into normative, descriptive and interpretative theories. An intention behind critical theory is the strengthening of normative, descriptive and interpretative theories by searching out their weak points, and what it would take to overcome these. Critical theory also turns this discipline on itself, in a search for some basis of truth, value, logic or argument to provide a point from which to critique other theories. Examples of some of the kinds of issues and questions that have been raised by a more critical perspective in management learning are:

- Are the principles of openness, honesty and trust, as advocated in some management learning activities as good for satisfaction and efficiency, really just serving these ends, or are they exposing people to ever tighter discipline and control?
- In encouraging managers to think of themselves as having learning styles, team or personality types, do we help them to 'know themselves' as they are but discourage them from thinking of themselves as adaptable, having personal choice over their behaviour?
- Are the currently fashionable business concepts disseminated in management learning – mission, vision, empowerment, self-managed teams – as liberating and efficiency-generating as they are said to be? Do they represent what is really happening, or do they sweeten the pill of a tightening, 'downsizing' organization, which undermines job security, retaining a more demanding style of conventional organization and management?
- Is there a tendency in management learning practice to encourage managers to think of their problems or choices as technical and instrumental ones – having the 'right approach' to achieve some given but unquestioned end – which obscures or distracts the manager from an awareness of having moral and ethical choices to make?

Critical theory encourages us not to bury or ignore the difficult issues and problems which may be hidden in management development practice.

Aim of the Book

This book is intended as a resource to understand and think in-depth about management learning, both as an area of professional and vocational practice and as an area of academic inquiry. Most of the material in the book is conceptual and theoretical, but it none the less intends to present this area of theory and practice in a way that is accessible to readers with little prior reading on the subject. It is also our intention to take the reader near to the 'frontiers' of practice and thinking. To span from 'origins' to 'frontiers' in one volume would be unrealistic in many fields of study. It is only the relative youth of the management learning field that justifies this attempt.

As Willmott points out in Chapter 9, there are at least two ways of understanding the term 'management'. If it is regarded as an activity of organizing people and things to create and achieve purposes, then it can be seen as a universal activity in space and time. Ancient books on politics, the church, war and the state can be examined for what we would now call management principles, even though the term 'management' would not be used in them. This is the 'universal' meaning of the term. In what we will call the 'social' meaning of the term, we are interested in what is actually called and labelled management, managers, managing and managerialism. We note that the term really came into use with the industrial revolution and the rise in the form of capitalism that supported it. 'Managing agents' were the people whom the owners of the new factories hired to run things for them as they expanded or 'retired' to try to live like wealthy landowners (see Child (1969) for an interpretation of the history of management and management thought). As a socially defined activity we note that the 'existence' of management and managerialism varies with place and time. Management learning is concerned with management in both senses. The *learning* part of management learning refers to both what is acquired and how this acquisition takes place, when individuals and social groupings acquire the ability to manage.

These remarks inevitably make some initial assumptions and distinctions that underpin what is to come. Among these is the distinction between theory and practice, and the link between them which is of pervasive concern in management learning. Management learning refers to the activities of people variously labelled management trainers, educators, developers, human resource development specialists, organization development practitioners, and those working in career management. Also under the heading of 'practice' belong those forms of management learning that are labelled natural, incidental, informal, non-contrived, learning that takes place in the course of ongoing work and activity, without any deliberate or explicit attempt to make it happen (see Marsick and Watkins, this volume).

The theory of management learning refers to all the conceptual formulations that describe, interpret or create these activities. Embedded in the management learning idea is the proposition that theory and practice are deeply intertwined – all practice 'implements' some theory or constructs practice out of it, and all theory actually or potentially shapes or creates reality through its practice. The continuous mutual influence of theory and practice is one description of the learning process itself, which surfaces another primary characteristic of management learning: its *reflexivity*. Management learning changes as it applies the principle of learning to itself.

The final initial formulation to be highlighted here is the territorial metaphor of introducing management learning from its origins to its frontiers of knowledge. While we hope it is helpful to say something of our intention for this book, the metaphor is an example of a useful idea that we later want to challenge and move on from as part of the learning process – a formulation that creates an initially useful meaning, which then has to be challenged and changed to move understanding on. In this case we have to point out that management learning does not have clear beginnings, clear-cut 'known territory' or a well-marked frontier. The beginnings are many, the known territory is always available for re-examination from different perspectives, and the frontiers are multiple and unclear, or at least contested and open to debate.

The underlying metaphor of progress through the conquest of unknown territory and its transformation into known territory implies a modernist view of progress which is much challenged in management learning and other fields of social science, since what is to count as progress is not clear and open to critical examination. What counts as progress is another core issue in management learning. While the idea of straightforward 'progress' implied in the metaphor is commonly embedded in the language of the practice of management learning, in phrases like 'current best practice', 'the latest theory' and 'progressive organizations', it is very much part of management learning to question the basis for such claims.

This introduction has discussed the types of practice that we may seek to influence through our vocational education activities, and the types of theory available to help with this and with the study of management learning as a field. We have made some initial remarks about the nature of management learning and will proceed by sketching something of its *history*. Next we describe our structuring of this volume, which is one way of mapping the field. Following this there are descriptions of other attempts which have been made to 'characterize the field' of management learning by producing frameworks within which substantive issues, theories and practices can be located.

History of Management Learning

Our history of management learning is very much based on our work and experience at Lancaster University over 22 years, and is therefore explicitly partial in reflecting our own particular strand of history.

The 1960s saw an expansion of management education in the UK with the adoption of the largely American idea of business schools. At the same time private and public sector companies and other organizations began to take management training and development seriously as internal activities. Today, about a quarter of university students are involved in management and business studies in some way, and all large organizations have substantial management training and development activities, going as far as to create self-styled 'internal universities'. Management training and development is now a major industry in itself. There are at least 80 university-related management schools in the UK, and several independent colleges with multi-million pound turnovers. All the major consultancy firms offer a broad range of management development services, and there is an army of individual independent consultancies, small partnerships and companies, and networks of providers, all seeking to help individuals and organizations through processes of management learning. Substantial professional bodies exist for individuals engaged in management education, training and development. Unfortunately, these represent the split between theorists and practitioners, which in the UK context are the British Academy of Management – constituting the main meeting point for academics – and the Association for Management Education and Development – the body largely serving corporate employees and consultants.

One of the apparent paradoxes of the management learning industry is its continuing success and growth in material terms, which has taken place against a background of continuing criticism and doubt about its aims, methods and effectiveness. Our explanation for this is that it is a problem-based area of activity, rather than a solution-based one. Some activities, such as AIDS research and treatment, exist because there is a problem. Others, perhaps like the mobile phone and fax machine industries and markets, exist because there is a solution. There is much to be said for the argument that management learning is a problem-generated (rather than a solution-generated) area of activity. This makes sense not only of the co-existence of growth and criticism in the field, but also of the great variety of approaches and methods used in management education and development.

In content terms, the field covers everything from self-awareness and interpersonal skills to sophisticated financial, marketing and statistical techniques. In process terms, management learning embraces everything from formal educational lecturing, MBA programmes, instruction, all kinds of information technology applications, outdoor management development, sophisticated simulations and business games to the full range of esoteric experiential learning methodologies. It may not be far from the truth to argue that any new activity, whether it be the latest 'adrenalin' hobby like bungee jumping or the most recent advance in chaos theory, is likely to be tried out as a contribution to management development. This suggests a field that is so uncertain about its solutions that anything is worth a try.

This situation has led to a continuing preoccupation with evaluation, the attempt to investigate and demonstrate what is of value in management education and development (see Hesseling, 1966; Burgoyne, 1973; Hamblin

1974; Easterby-Smith, 1986, for attempts to formulate methods to deal with this problem). It can be argued that management learning as a field of study was created in response to two main influences. These were the continuing doubts and criticisms of management education and development, and the shortage of management educators, teachers, trainers and developers. The first created a demand for research, with evaluation as the prime methodology, and the second created the need for teaching, the creation of which was based on the hope that a management learning research programme would create an appropriate design and curriculum for this.

Early management learning research was concerned with an attempt to create a rational framework for understanding the purposes, processes and effects of management education training and development (see Burgoyne and Stuart, 1978). It took an interest in the interpersonal behaviour and skills of training and teaching (Snell and Binstead, 1981, 1982), the dynamics of learning groups (see Reynolds, 1994, for a summary) and the beginnings of the use of information technology and open and distance learning in management learning (Hodgson et al., 1987). Later research took more of an interest in the context of these processes: for example, national and corporate management learning policies and strategies, social issues and processes addressed in management learning, career management, organizational learning ethics and social responsibility (Maclagan and Snell, 1992).

Another trend in management learning research has been a move from the pragmatic – closely linked to problems and issues as experienced by practitioners – to the more theoretical and philosophical approach. This trend, paradoxically, opens up the gap between the theoretical and the practical in management learning, with the result that much management learning writing will seem esoteric to the practitioner. We take this seemingly paradoxical development to be a sign of maturation of the field of management learning, since it enables it to engage more fully with the worlds of both theory and practice. The difference is needed so that each can contribute to the other, but a consequence of the difference is that the effort necessary to keep theory and practice connected, and to translate between them, has to be greater.

Various of the chapters in this book, particularly the first two, also give historical perspectives on management learning.

The Structure of the Book

Continuing our historical analysis, the inception of management learning can be located as an attempt to question and redirect the growing field of management education, training and development which grew rapidly in the 1960s on the basis of the belief that an improvement in management would restart the stalled improvement in the social and economic performance of managed organizations after the initial period of post-war reconstruction.

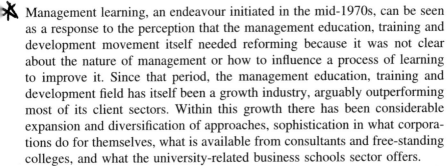

Management learning, an endeavour initiated in the mid-1970s, can be seen as a response to the perception that the management education, training and development movement itself needed reforming because it was not clear about the nature of management or how to influence a process of learning to improve it. Since that period, the management education, training and development field has itself been a growth industry, arguably outperforming most of its client sectors. Within this growth there has been considerable expansion and diversification of approaches, sophistication in what corporations do for themselves, what is available from consultants and free-standing colleges, and what the university-related business schools sector offers.

Despite this, it is not obvious that an increase in the quality of economic and social life has resulted from better management, creating more satisfying organizational performance for stakeholders. There is an argument for the need of a third stage or level of reform. A major aim for this book is to establish the broader understanding of management learning from which priorities for this third stage of reform might emerge. The sequence of sections in this volume reflects our view of what is necessary to make this possible.

First, we need to take the broadest possible view about what management learning might be, and how it might be conceived in terms of the broad spectrum of intellectual resources available to us towards the end of the millennium. Part I, *Making Sense of Management Learning*, offers a rich variety of ways of thinking about management learning and its underpinnings. Our underlying proposition for finding a basis for a third stage of reform for management through learning is to dig deeper into interpretative and critical theory, and advance critical reflective practice and the critically reflective practitioner in the hope of finding better bases for normative theory and practice. Part II, *Being Critical*, introduces a variety of critical perspectives, including critical activists (Cunningham and Dawes) as well as critical academics.

Much critical thinking, with its commitment to digging ever deeper into underlying assumptions, internal contradictions and the form of its own roots and justifications, stays in critical analytical mode, and hence tends to become disempowered in terms of being influential outside the realm of its own specialist discourse. To return to the fray of broader social action, the issues of *Values and Purposes* must be addressed, as they are in Part III, by authors who, in their different ways, seek to define justifications for ways forward in the light of different kinds of critical thinking.

Finally, Part IV, *Developments in Design*, takes us towards the necessary issue of implementation, and back to a traditionally high-profile preoccupation in management learning. Our hope is that design that is underpinned more thoroughly than it has been in the past by critical analysis and justification of value and purpose will lead to forms of management education, training and development that are more deeply thought through and with more profound effects than has been the case so far.

Ways of Characterizing the Field

'Making Sense', 'Being Critical', 'Values and Purposes' and 'Developments in Design' provide one way of dividing up the field of management learning, which makes sense of its current stage of development. Other frameworks for dividing the field have emerged at different points in its history, and we end this introduction by summarizing them.

The MLml framework

Perhaps the simplest management learning framework is the one implied by the phrase itself – issues and practices to do with the nature of management and those to do with the processes of learning associated with it. Stephen Fox (1994a, 1994b) adds another to this distinction – that between formalized, institutionalized practices of management (M) and learning (L) and the equivalent practices in informal, naturally occurring management (m) and learning (l).

'M' are those activities formally labelled as Management in organizational settings, for example jobs with this term in their titles. 'L' are events, courses and so forth, explicitly and deliberately designed and labelled as existing to bring about learning. 'm' are the everyday processes of 'managing' to get things done, and all the informal processes that go alongside the formal ones in organizations. Management learning[1] research has long acknowledged 'l'. Burgoyne and Stuart (1976) concluded that the great majority of managerial expertise comes from informal, uncontrived processes. Marsick and Watkins (1990) have reported an extensive study of this phenomenon, the implications of which they discuss in this volume. Organizational expertise is being increasingly conceptualized as existing in 'communities of practice', where it is situationally specific and acquired largely through informal processes (Lave and Wenger, 1991, discussed by Fox, this volume). These distinctions are then developed by Fox to indicate a number of phenomena that can be seen as part of management learning, and worthy of investigation (see Figure 1).

Multiple perspectives and integration

Burgoyne (1994) has developed the argument that management learning is maturing into an integrated area of study and practice via a number of perspectives. These are (see Figure 2):

1   Professional practices, where management learning is described as a set of practitioner activities: setting up and running learning events, processes of career management, defining competencies, evaluating and implementing organizational change programmes and so on.
2   The multi-disciplinary approach, where a set of theoretical ideas are selected from different disciplines which can be used to 'make sense' of

M	L
formal, explicit, deliberate management	formal, explicit, deliberate learning
m	**l**
informal managing	informal learning

Categories generated:

MM Formal attempts to 'manage management' – e.g., formally define a new corporate management philosophy.

mM The informal, personal and private strategies that individuals and groups employ to deal with formal management systems.

Mm Formal management attempts to control informal management processes – e.g., attempts to manage culture.

mm The interplay of informal management processes on each other.

LL Formal research on and study of deliberate and explicit learning processes as in courses, etc.

Ll Formal research on and study of informal learning.

lL Learning to cope with formal learning experiences and situations.

ll Informal understandings of informal learning processes.

Figure 1   *The MLml Framework*

(1). For example: the psychology of learning, the sociology of knowledge, disciplines of design from engineering, and other ideas from linguistics and information technology.

3 Management learning as an integrated area of study, which fuses the concepts from (2) into a unified conceptual framework. Burgoyne (1994) suggested that one such synthesis could encompass the linked concepts of *learning, managing, organizing, exchanging* and *wealth creation*.

4 Management learning as an applied philosophy in the sense that managing and learning to manage involves arranging all that exists to create and define purposes for doing so. In that sense management learning raises all the big questions of what exists, how does it behave, how can it be organized, how can purposes be chosen and defined? The challenge of formulating a theory and practice, drawing on all fields of knowledge in the multi-disciplinary approach in (2) above to formulate a coherent an integrated understanding and practice (the aim of (3) above) poses all the traditional problems of philosophy – what can be known (ontology), how it can be known (epistemology), what can be regarded as good or desirable states of affairs (ethics and aesthetics), and the nature of action

and praxis, moving from understanding to doing things on the basis of available understanding to bring about desirable states of affairs. Digging back to the philosophical roots of understanding and action is therefore part of the management learning agenda (see Chia, this volume).

5   Finally, management learning can be interpreted as an applied ideology, picking up on the point about ethics. Management learning theory has been strongly influenced by the humanistic ethic of adult education (androgogy – the practice of helping adults learn, see, for example, Knowles, 1980). The values associated with this position are that with appropriate organization (created by good management and learning) human beings can be emancipated (made free through a full knowledge of their situation) so that they can formulate and achieve their highest needs and potential. In this optimistic or utopian view the humanistic ideology is often extended to one that can be labelled 'holistic', to include the idea that humans, thus emancipated, will look after each other, future generations and the environment (meaning the rest of animate and inanimate nature), taking an attitude of 'stewardship', since the well-being of the other contributes to the well being of the self.

Practitioners of management learning will be aware of this ideology as it is embodied in various approaches to self-development, self-managed learning (see Cunningham and Dawes, this volume), and various approaches to team-work and team-building based on notions of openness, trust and honesty. These are practices that not only create satisfying modes of work but also create efficiency. Practitioners will also be aware how naive and impractical such approaches can seem given that many or even all organizational and managerial situations seem to work on the basis of power, calculation and politics.

These doubts have their theoretical parallels in the view that management is intrinsically about the exercise of power on behalf of the powerful, the owners of resources. Many of the practices of openness and trust can be compellingly reinterpreted as rendering people accessible to even greater degrees of control, and incorporating them into control systems as self-policing and self-subjectifying.

Many current theoretical developments associated with critical thinking and the postmodern construction of reality seriously question the notion of the autonomous good self, the utopian optimism and aspiration to progress embodied in the humanist/holist ideology. However, much of this criticism can be interpreted as being itself driven by an emancipatory agenda, and hence ultimately seeking the same goals. The debate rages on in both theory and practice, and it is not clear whether and how this can be resolved. The most that can be said at this juncture is that this debate is itself central to management learning, and the struggle with it can be argued to be management learning's most important contemporary project.

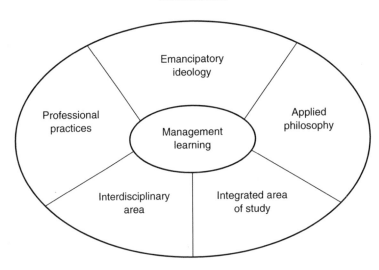

Figure 2 *Multiple perspectives and integration*

Two further frameworks, while not mapping such a variety of theoretical and practical issues, add useful extra perspectives on the field of management learning.

Domains and decisions

As both Easterby-Smith and Thorpe (Chapter 2) and Fox (Chapter 1) point out, management learning activity tends to have two localities: educational institutions (business and management schools and departments in, and associated with, universities) and work organizations (public and private sector) and the consultancy firms and activities that support them. The former tend to be described in terms of education, and also to be the location of formal academic research on the topic. In the latter, the terminology is usually of training and development.

Within each of these domains activities and decisions span from the operational to the strategic and policy-oriented. Outside these domains there are national and international policies directly about or affecting management learning, usually concerned with economic development, training and international aid. Some of these policies are implemented through governmental and intergovernmental bodies, for example Training and Enterprise Councils in the UK and the International Labour Office internationally. This way of looking at management learning suggests that its domains of activity can be mapped, as in Figure 3.

Corporate management development policy and practices

Management learning processes in work organizations (rather than educational settings) has been further elaborated as part of the process of organizational strategy formation and implementation. It has been argued

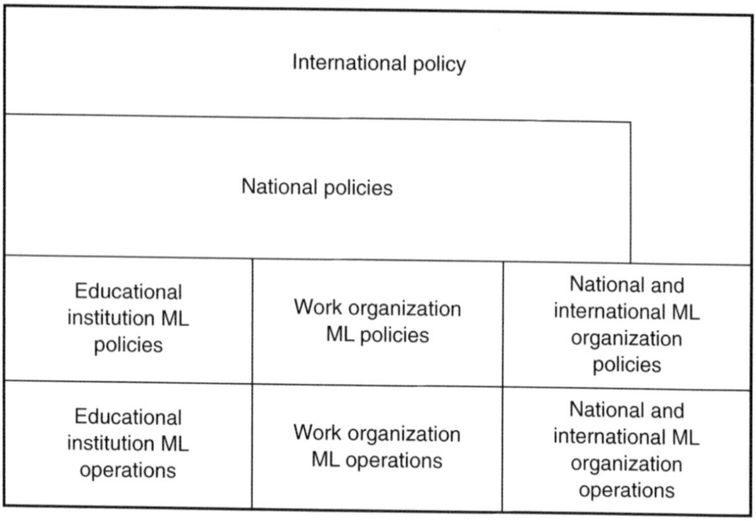

International policy		
National policies		
Educational institution ML policies	Work organization ML policies	National and international ML organization policies
Educational institution ML operations	Work organization ML operations	National and international ML organization operations

Figure 3   *Domains of management learning (ML) activity*

that corporate management development can be usefully defined in terms of career theory (Burgoyne, 1988). Briefly, a career can be seen as a series of 'deals' or psychological contracts between a person and one, or a number of, organization(s), with each career move being a new deal or negotiation. The psychological contract covers both *structural* (what the person does) and *developmental* (how the person changes and develops) issues.

Management development as a corporate activity can be thought of as dealing with this psychological contract from the organizational end. Corporate management learning activities at the operational level fall into the two categories of *structural* and *developmental*. Structural activities are exemplified by succession planning, assessment centres, and the methods and techniques used to place managers in jobs. Developmental activities are those intended to help people change and develop through learning (i.e., courses, mentoring, etc.). Corporate management development consists of these two kinds of activity and the formulation of a management development policy which links the structural and developmental tactics with the implementation and informing of corporate policy.

This view of corporate management development policy and practice as an aspect of management learning broadens the domain of the latter to deal with organizational processes of career management and structuring. In suggesting that management learning activities are involved in both improving and developing corporate policy in a process linked to individual development, it also provides a link to the concept of the *learning organization*, since it suggests how organizational and individual change can be reciprocally linked. Figure 4 shows the schema implied by this career theory-based formulation of management development policy.

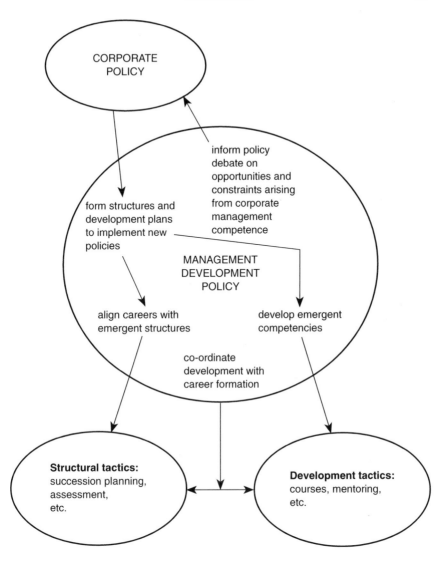

Figure 4   *Corporate management development policy and practices*

The 'no map' approach

The final point of view concerned with defining or mapping the field of management learning is the view that it is not helpful to propose a map, because this will inevitably leave something out and inhibit development of the field. In this view, management learning is better thought of as the combination of the ideas and practices of all those who associate themselves with management learning as practitioners and academics. This approach has obvious attractions, but also poses the problem of who are management learning practitioners and academics. If this is to be centrally defined, then some model will be needed to define who is in and who is out. The alternative, more liberal point of view is that individuals who want to identify themselves as being involved in management learning can do so, and what management learning is becomes the activities and ideas of this 'open club'.

Note

1 In continuing to use the abbreviation 'management learning' we need to point out that it incorporates M, L, m and I in the senses used here.

References

Bandler, R. and Grinder, J. (1979) *Frogs into Princes*. Moab, UT: Real People Press.

Barker, D. (1980) *TA and Training: The Theory and Use of Transactional Analysis in Organisations*. Aldershot: Gower.

Belbin, R.M. (1981) *Management Teams: Why They Succeed or Fail*. London: Heinemann.

Burgoyne, J.G. (1973) 'An action research experiment in the evaluation of a management development course', *Journal of Management Studies*, 10: 8–14.

Burgoyne, J.G. (1988) 'Management development for the individual and the organisation', *Personnel Management*, June: 40–4.

Burgoyne, J.G. (1994) 'Managing by learning', *Journal of Management Learning*, 25 (1): 35–55.

Burgoyne, J.G. and Stuart, R. (1976) 'The nature, use and acquisition of managerial skills and other attribute', *Personnel Review*, 5 (4): 19–29.

Burgoyne, J.G. and Stuart, R. (1978) *Management Development: Context and Strategies*. Aldershot: Gower.

Child, J. (1969) *British Management Thought: A Critical Analysis*. London: Allen and Unwin.

Easterby-Smith, M.P.V. (1986) *Evaluation of Management Education, Training and Development*. Aldershot: Gower.

Fox, S. (1994a) 'Debating management learning: I', *Management Learning*, 25 (1): 83–93.

Fox, S. (1994b) 'Debating management learning: II', *Management Learning*, 25 (4): 579–97.

Hamblin, A. (1974) *Evaluation and Control of Training*. Maidenhead: McGraw-Hill.

Hesseling, P. (1966) *Strategy in Evaluation Research*. Assen, Netherlands: Van Gorcum.

Hodgson, V.E., Mann, S.J. and Snell, R.S. (eds) (1987) *Beyond Distance Teaching Towards Open Learning*. Milton Keynes: Societies for Research into Higher Education/Open University Press.

Knowles, M.S. (1980) *The Modern Practice of Adult Education: From Pedagogy to Androgogy*. Chicago: Follett.

Lave, J. and Wenger, E. (1991) *Situated Learning: Legitimate Peripheral Participation*. Cambridge: Cambridge University Press.

Maclagan, P. and Snell, R. (1992) 'Some implications for management development of research into managers' moral dilemmas', *British Journal of Management*, 3 (3): 157–68.

Marsick, V.J. and Watkins, K.E. (1990) *Informal and Incidental Learning in the Workplace*. London and New York: Routledge.

Reynolds, M. (1994) *Groupwork in Education and Training*. London: Kogan Page.

Snell, R.S. and Binsted, D.S. (1981) 'The tutor–learner interaction in management development, part 2: Games tutors play: How covert tutor manoeuvres affect management learning', *Personnel Review*, 10 (4): 3–13.

Snell, R.S. and Binsted, D.S. (1982) 'The tutor–learner interaction in management development, part 4: The facilitation of learning by discussion', *Personnel Review*, 11 (2): 3–14.

PART I
MAKING SENSE OF MANAGEMENT LEARNING

The different approaches to describing the field, which were summarized in the Introduction, reflect the growing interest in understanding management learning as an emergent area of inquiry and practice. In different ways these descriptions take account of location (educational institutions, the workplace, staff colleges); research directions and methodologies; ideas, concepts and theoretical frameworks that have been newly developed or incorporated from parent disciplines; and the processes and procedures which characterize practice within the different sites (accreditation, membership of professional networks, associations).

Description raises further questions. What do the differentiations into sites, methods or theoretical perspectives signify, educationally and socially? What principles and interests are implied in distinctions of practice or concealed within conceptual selectivity? Are particular choices of training methods or of learning theories based only on research findings or practical considerations? These questions are of particular interest given the positioning of management learning at the boundary of two communities of practice – management and academia – each with its distinct sense of purpose and tradition. Choices among theory and method both reflect and reinforce these differences and the characteristics of management learning as a boundary discipline. The social and institutional context of this field is therefore complex, incorporating systems of values and beliefs which sometimes diverge, and whose divergence can bestow a degree of marginality on its members.

Management Learning as an Emergent Field

What are the main ideas in learning and managing and how have they changed over time? What do changes and development in theory and practice signify? Choices made in management learning practice, like those in education generally, are never value-free. Changes in ideas about learning and in designs for learning are likely to reflect shifts in balance between conflicting positions which have always been present, representing tensions between, for example, pragmatic concerns for harnessing rational, scientific thought in the service of effective management, and a more politicized inquiry into how definitions of 'effective management' are constructed, by whom, and in whose interests.

Particular ideas about managing and learning which become established may do so as a response to the perceived limitations of theory and practice in the light of research findings, or they may represent the search for an approach which will prove more relevant to managers' day-to-day experience of the workplace, and so be more likely to enable them to engage with situations competently as well as with some sense of personal reward. But the selection of ideas and methods is not based solely either on scholarship or on professional wisdom. It is just as likely to be an expression of values which enjoy general popularity at the time or which have gained the approval of more powerful coalitions or particular interest groups.

This thesis has been explored in the context of organizational design by Harrison (1972) and later Handy (1976) – who extended Harrison's concept of 'organizational ideology' – and developed in depth in the work of Burrell and Morgan (1979), who described the different philosophical positions underlying thinking and practice in the study of organizations. Similar observations can be made in relation to management learning. There are many ideas to choose from, some becoming well established and others barely acknowledged – sometimes regardless of the status given them in their root disciplines. Furthermore, the ideas about learning which are especially influential in management learning are drawn from different and sometimes – on the face of it at least – contradictory schools of thought.

So, for example, more traditional origins in cognitive psychology are reflected in the importance attached to psychometrics, particularly in their application to assessment centres and development centres, and in the pivotal position given to learning-styles theory. In management development in particular, however, there has been an influence of equal strength from humanistic psychology, and from this source the theory and practice of self-directed or student-centred learning has been introduced into management learning as an alternative to more traditional educational methods.

These 'holistic' approaches, with their emphases on understanding the whole person as mediated through experience, have come to be seen as providing more connectedness to daily personal and professional life and, in avoiding the passivity thought to be associated with more conventional educational methods, as offering managers more opportunity for development than seemed possible in focusing exclusively on the acquisition of knowledge and skills. Proponents of experiential learning theory have exercised considerable influence within management learning for similar reasons. Authors like Kolb (1984) and Schön (1983), continuing in the tradition of pragmatism associated with the American educator John Dewey, have offered a concept of learning which has more immediacy for managers in enabling them to situate their learning in everyday professional experience.

So as with different ideas about organizational design, ideas about learning and learning design can indicate different value positions as much as distinct schools of research. Interpretation of values and beliefs as well as of theoretical foundations is therefore a necessary part of the task of making sense of management learning as a field of practice, and provides material for understanding its history, what it has become, and what might be its future possibilities.

The Chapters in this Section

In the first chapter *Stephen Fox* acknowledges the professional realms whose activities contribute in different, and sometimes overlapping, ways to the field as a whole. In exploring the interrelationship between management education and management development, and the ways this may be changing, he draws on a perspective on learning which is more social in inclination than has been traditional in management learning. By this means Stephen Fox accounts for the current situation in the field by observing its recent history as well as its current purposes and organizational settings.

As with the educational approach, research in management learning varies in scope, methodology, purpose, scale and situation. The chapter by *Mark Easterby-Smith* and *Richard Thorpe* takes account of where research is situated, whether primarily in academia or in organizations, and how its focus is defined, ranging from policy concerns to interest in learning processes. As with the other contributions in this section, their chapter illustrates the way management learning reflects important debates within the wider research context in support of distinct methodologies. The authors explore how differences in research methodology can be explained by the type of purpose and the nature of the stakeholder.

In their account of the 'arena thesis' *John Burgoyne* and *Brad Jackson* describe a way of conceptualizing action and analysis in management learning which provides an alternative to the unitarist perspective of organization and management that has been dominant for much of the twentieth century. Their thesis is based on the inevitability of diversity which they regard as a potential source of development in ideas and practice within management learning. The arena thesis acknowledges the importance of working creatively with conflicts between different interest groups, rather than denying or suppressing them.

In the first two chapters, authors locate developments in the field of management learning in its early beginnings. *Robert Chia* goes even further back to identify different and competing philosophical traditions which can be seen to influence distinct schools of theory and practice in the present day. By tracing these origins we can better understand the educational and social significance of the differences in the ways we design and carry out management education and development work. Though the schools of thought which Robert Chia compares lie deep in the history of social and intellectual development, they are very much ingrained in current interpretation and practice in the work of management learning professionals.

As a prominent area within management learning, groupwork has played a central part in the formal education and development of managers, reflecting an emphasis on participation more generally in management thinking. *Richard Boot* and *Michael Reynolds* describe different dimensions which can be used to make sense of the proliferation of group-based methods as applications of experiential learning theory. Why has there been such an emphasis on groups and groupwork? Why have some theories of groups been adopted and others ignored? Are there limitations in remaining preoccupied with groups in management education and development?

Taken together, the accounts of management learning in this section introduce different perspectives for describing and interpreting the range of sites, activities, purposes, methods and philosophies which characterize this emerging field of theory and practice. In doing so, different ideas are developed which in themselves add to its growing knowledge base.

References

Burrell, Gibson and Morgan, Gareth (1979) *Sociological Paradigms and Organizational Analysis*. London: Heinemann Educational Books.

Handy, Charles B. (1976) *Understanding Organizations*. Harmondsworth: Penguin.

Harrison, Roger (1972) 'How to understand your organization', *Harvard Business Review*, September–October: 119–28.

Kolb, David A. (1984) *Experiential Learning*. Englewood Cliffs, NJ: Prentice-Hall.

Schön, Donald (1983) *The Reflective Practitioner*. New York: Basic Books.

1

From Management Education and Development to the Study of Management Learning

Stephen Fox

> The world in which we live is an emergent world, it is humankind on the move. . . . Humanity is in a great collective learning process. . . . The difficulties people seem to have when they are asked to perceive the world, and thus also human society – and, not least, themselves – as processes in the making, are possibly connected with the difficulty of seeing themselves as precursors of an unknown and, in part, completely inconceivable future.
>
> (Elias, 1995: 40)

Two contrasting approaches to management education and development have emerged since the 1960s. On the one hand, there is management education, a subset of higher education (HE), largely provided by university business and management schools and subject to the critical rigours of the wider academic and research community. On the other hand, there is management development, a subset of human resource development (HRD), which is largely provided by the private sector in the form of in-house management development, training and development, and/or HRD departments of organizations assisted by numerous freelance consultants, small and large training businesses, as well as a few charitable foundations. Management education tends to be more theoretical, emphasizing a body of knowedge, whereas management development tends to be more practical, emphasizing a repertoire of skills – in Quinn's (1992) terms: 'know-what' and 'know-why' in contrast to 'know-how'.

In the first section of this chapter, I will discuss the emergence of the study of management learning. This section will argue that despite their historic differences, management education and management development are increasingly overlapping professions. It will suggest that whether or not they finally become one professional field of practice, both share some common features which privilege theory over practice and the individual over the social. In the second section, I will outline what is at stake in this privilege, paying attention to the 'situated learning' approach (Lave and Wenger, 1991) as an illustrative example which highlights the practical and the social. Lave and Wenger's work is taken from recent turns in the direction of learning theory and the social psychology of cognition which represent a challenge to orthodoxy in these fields. The third section discusses the situated learning approach as applied to the study of management learning and the consequences for management education and development.

The Emergence of Management Learning

Management learning began as a subject area by seeking to bridge the gap between the theory and practice of management education and development, the MA in Management Learning at Lancaster University (launched in 1981) being the first masters programme in the subject area. Since the late 1980s several programmes have been established in other UK universities, some using 'management learning' as the title, others preferring 'training and development', 'HRD' or 'change consultancy'. Management learning began by applying learning theory, psychology, educational research and sociology to the processes by which managers learned in action or in training-rooms and business school classrooms, contributing to these 'root' disciplines but also to management and organization theory.

Although the worlds of management education and management development are increasingly overlapping, they are also distinct (see Figure 1.1). They differ in the following ways:

1 In content: management development tends to develop personal knowledge, repertoires and skills (e.g., time management, stress management, assertiveness, team work, presentations, influencing, negotiating, selling, personal development, counselling, interpersonal skills), whereas management education tends to develop analytical and critical skills in the academic disciplines relevant to management (e.g., economics, operations management and research, accounting, finance, marketing, organization theory and behaviour, strategic management).
2 In teaching methods: management education is predominantly delivered by traditional methods (e.g., lecture, tutorial and seminar), whereas management development uses a much wider range of methods (see Huczynski, 1983; and Reynolds, this volume).
3 In organization: management development is largely supplied by market mechanisms, whereas most management education, especially at undergraduate level, is supplied by the public education system.

Management education straddles the natural and social sciences; operations management relies on many of the statistical methods developed in the natural and applied sciences (forecasting and engineering, for example), whereas organization theory relies on the social and human sciences (such as sociology and psychology). The other management disciplines fall between these two extremes. The polar orientation within management education goes back to its inception in the UK, when Noel Hall (1964) noted the difference between quantitative and sociological orientations in the then

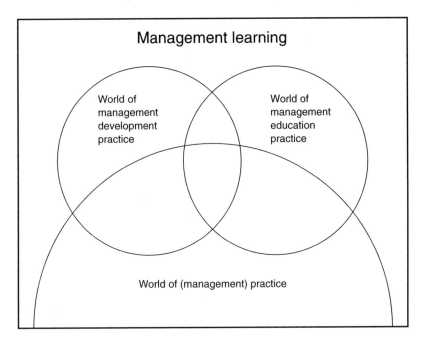

Figure 1.1   *Management learning: the scope of study*

newly founded business schools. This quantitative–sociological continuum broadly maps on to the technical–critical continuum. Management research and education attempts to research and disseminate technical and functional ways of increasing management and organizational efficiency (both in terms of business operations and human behaviour), but it also raises critical issues concerning the moral, cultural, social and political aspects of managing and organizing.

Overall, it appears that, in the UK, the weight of the syllabus is tipped in the direction of the technical rather than the critical end of the continuum (see Fox, 1989, 1992a; Willmott, 1994; Grey and Mitev, 1995). In the USA, the same polarity is visible although the weight of the field is tipped even further in the direction of the technical and functional rather than the critical (see Fox (1994b) for further discussion of these points, and Fox (1992b) for the pattern in the European Union). Paradoxically, it is the technical and functional orientation to management education, with its reductionist approach, which is most criticized by practising managers in both the USA and the UK for being least relevant to their problems. It would appear that managers want management schools to offer more than technical trouble-shooting; rather, they want them to offer theories and ideas which address wider problems.

Despite the distinctions discussed above, in the UK at least management education and development are increasingly overlapping and this has come about as a result of many interweaving pressures. First is the impact of cultural changes. In the UK, management had not quite been regarded as a respectable middle-class occupation prior to the 1980s and the universities were still rather hostile and sneering about the new subjects of management studies and business administration (Thomas, 1980). This was in marked contrast with the USA where management was seen as a perfectly good occupation and where universities had been teaching business and management studies since the 1880s. The Thatcher–Reagan years changed the situation in Britain, where enterprise and management gained in cultural cachet and management education became one of the fastest-growing subjects in higher education. At the same time, the competency movement, originating in the USA, led to the integration of interpersonal and practical skills within the management education curriculum. This took the management curriculum in directions which corporate management developers had been pursuing for years and blurred the boundary between management education and management development.

Secondly, funding pressures have meant that management schools are increasingly under pressure from their host universities to generate revenues, some of which subsidize more general university-wide activities. This is because the numbers of students going though the higher education system in the UK have nearly doubled since the late 1980s, bringing the UK system at last closer to its major competitors (Handy et al., 1988). In common with US universities, UK institutions are increasingly seeking funding from other sources than government (Trow, 1989), and management schools are strategically significant in this attempt.

A third pressure comes from the availability of new offers. Management schools are gearing up to provide post-experience courses as well as post-graduate programmes. Therefore they compete in the management development as well as the management education market. They are also differentiating the MBA 'product', the market for full-time programmes having peaked in the late 1980s, by launching part-time (Executive) MBAs, company-MBAs, consortial-MBAs, regional-MBAs and new alternatives to the MBA genre, such as Masters in International Management, Management with Languages and Critical Management. These types of provision required management schools to move closer to corporate expectations about customer care (using hotels instead of campus), the syllabus (negotiating the content with corporate clients), and 'teaching methods' (less reliance on lectures, for example), while striving to maintain academic standards.

Fourthly, the net result of the expansion of management education was to produce more academically qualified managers in organizations who in turn expected management development practitioners to be appropriately qualified. This pressure has increased demand in the subject area of management learning, training and development and HRD which has led to a proliferation of programmes and research projects in the late 1980s and early 1990s.

Finally, there is the pressure from shakeout. Many organizations 'shook out' managers from all levels in the 1980s and 1990s. Many of them entered the independent consultancy business (especially in areas such as training and development, management development, HRD and change management), engendering a more competitive market place. As a consequence, many practitioners in these fields, even the ones with strong client bases, decided to take one of the new masters degrees as a way of maintaining their competitive edge and professionalism.

A consequence of these changes is that the new 'disciplinary' area of knowledge and practice, which we call management learning, has begun to emerge in the academy. This is both a subject area and a research community which studies management education and development, HRD and training and development, as well as informal managing and learning processes (Fox, 1994a, 1994b). Management learning is not the same as HRM, or personnel management, but is wider in the sense that the *learning and managing processes*, which it seeks to understand and better manage, are more pervasive human processes than the management of employees in large organizations, the activity upon which personnel and human resource managers have built their professional identity. Management learning studies the whole range of professional attempts to manage learning, including the narrower case of learning to manage (Fox, 1994a, 1994b).

One of management learning's points of academic departure was the recognition that educating managers is a different proposition from educating school-leavers or undergraduate students. Adult education recognizes that adults learn differently and that this difference is compounded when they learn part-time about subjects which are relevant to their professional practice. Consequently, management learning takes a research interest in the wide variety of teaching methods used in management development and advocates that management schools should widen their repertoires of teaching methods. A second point of departure was the recognition that formal education and development activities are merely the tip of a *learning iceberg*. People, including managers and professionals of all kinds, learn in their everyday working lives and this 'natural learning' may be augmented (Burgoyne and Hodgson, 1983). The 'self-development' movement of the 1970s and 1980s was one attempt to augment natural learning. However, it is possible that 'self-development' was used as a convenient rhetoric for the low spending on education and training by corporations and government in the UK which Handy, Gordon, Gow and Randlesome (1988) identified.

The next section of this chapter outlines new thinking in educational research which advocates new research attention upon natural learning. The new thinking is called 'situated learning theory' and stands in contrast to 'traditional cognitive theory' by emphasizing the *practical and social dimension* of learning. I want to outline some of this work and, in conclusion, to relate it back to management education and development. To introduce the idea of social learning it is useful to consider some of Norbert Elias's ideas on 'technization' and 'civilization'. These terms roughly map on to the technical–critical continuum outlined above. The idea is that technical advances are followed by cultural and social adjustments which domesticate the new technologies but, at the same time, prepare the ground for new technical innovations.

Elias (1995) shows that there is a discernible *civilizing process*, related to a process he calls 'technization', which moves in a specifiable direction but which presumes no ultimate end-point. It only 'advances' relative to where it has been; it does not advance towards any final or inevitable end, but it does advance on many disparate fronts all at once. For instance, many individual inventors dispersed across many countries struggled over the centuries to construct a vehicle in which a human being could fly. Before it became possible no one really knew whether it could *ever* become possible, because this research, like all pure research, was a fundamentally open-ended quest. Ordinary people, including the business community, ignored the inventors, so much so that when the Wright brothers flew the first successful flight in 1903, few of their contemporaries took note. It was only later, when they began to put on displays and carry passengers at fairgrounds in Europe, that some sections of the public, especially the war ministries, became aware of the breakthrough (Elias, 1995: 32). In the early twentieth century, human flight was the project of a very small, geographically dispersed community of people who, over generations, had accumulated and shared ideas precipitating the eventual success of the brothers Wright.

That is how technization advances, by groups of people working competitively and collaboratively over time. Then the rest of the population begins to realize their achievement and its potential uses, and then adapts them, in this case building aerodromes, factories, runways and working out how to use the invention for disparate social purposes – dropping bombs, carrying mail and passengers, spying, 'shuttle diplomacy', tourism and so on. All this required specialized social regulations, the marking out of national 'air-space', international 'flight-paths' and the training of pilots, ground staff, air-traffic controllers, cabin crew – a whole new series of industries and occupations which did not exist before. A new etiquette developed of how to behave on an aeroplane – what to do in an emergency, how to respond to the customer-care trained cabin staff – a new aspect of 'civilization' and 'civilized manners'.

Elias's view of the development of social processes such as these is similar to Mintzberg and Waters's (1985) understanding of 'emergent' corporate strategies, which are the unplanned product of many interweaving strands of activity, only discernible after the fact, looking back. The world manifests an overall pattern which nobody planned deliberately but which is nevertheless highly organized and has arisen out of many particular threads of highly planned activity. Some would see the unplanned overall pattern as ultimately dangerous for humans. For example, they might argue that the development of many particular threads, separately from each other, aggregates into phenomena like 'ozone depletion', possibly at a rate which humanity as a whole will never learn to arrest, no matter how fast it moves down the learning curve. Others would see this newly named phenomenon – 'ozone depletion' – as a sign that the problem has been spotted and therefore will be remedied – scientists are learning what it is, assessing the danger and in due course how to solve it. But both these views project too far into the future beyond what we can tell.

The Situated Social Learning Approach

As Elias (1995) showed, many planned but unrelated activities become part of a wider unplanned collective learning process. While his analysis addressed global processes, Lave and Wenger (1991) have discussed *situated learning* in more local terms. Their approach is new for educational research, cognitive psychology and learning theory because it proceeds by applying many relevant insights from sociology and anthropology to *practical* and *social* learning processes going on outside classrooms, processes which educational research and cognitive psychology have tended to ignore. They argue that: 'any complex system of work and learning has roots in and interdependencies across its history, technology, developing work activity, careers, and the relations between newcomers and old-timers and among co-workers and practitioners' (Lave and Wenger, 1991: 61). Lave and Wenger point out that nearly all the research ignores these pervasive social learning processes, which not only accompany, but are actually integral to, many work and other social activities, by focusing instead largely upon schooling. Even where psychologists have accepted the importance of social processes to learning, as in the case of Vygotsky's followers (see Wertsch, 1991, for a recent account), their research tends to be based on accounts and descriptions relating to the formal settings of 'schooling' – formal, institutionalized learning rather than everyday, incidental, informal or 'natural' learning (Lave and Wenger, 1991: 47–9). As they later say:

> At the very least, schooling is given a privileged role in intellectual development. Because the theory and institution have common historical roots (Lave, 1988), these school-forged theories are inescapably specialized: they are unlikely to afford us the historical–cultural breadth to which we aspire. It seems useful, given these concerns, to investigate learning-in-practice in situations that do not draw us in unreflective ways into the school milieu. (1991: 61)

To understand learning-in-practice leads us to an alternative, apparently far-removed literature of ethnographic field studies, exploring non-schooling forms of everyday learning, such as apprenticeship, which can be informal as well as formal. In Yucatan, for example, Jordan (1989) has studied the 'apprenticeship' of Yucatec Mayan midwives who do not even use the term to describe the process whereby some Maya girls become midwives. Rather 'apprenticeship happens as a way of, and in the course of, daily life' (1989: 932, quoted in Lave and Wenger, 1991: 68), for girls who have mothers or grandmothers who are midwives. These girls hear stories in the course of their elders' activities as midwives, run errands for them such as collecting appropriate herbs, and generally help out. Eventually, after such a girl has had a child herself, she might 'come along to a birth, perhaps because her ailing grandmother needs someone to walk with . . .' (Lave and Wenger, 1991: 68) and thus she might find herself helping out at the scene of the birth. At some later point,

> . . . she may decide she actually wants to do this kind of work. She then pays more attention, but only rarely does she ask questions. Her mentor sees their association primarily as one that is of some use to her ('Rosa already knows how to do a massage, so I can send her if I am too busy'). (1991: 69)

Gradually Rosa takes on more and more of the work load, 'starting with the routine and tedious parts, and ending with what is in Yucatan the culturally most significant, the birth of the placenta' (1991: 69).

Such studies form the basis of Lave and Wenger's key concept, the idea of 'legitimate peripheral participation'. Rosa at first did not even know what she was participating in, she was so *peripheral* to the activity of midwifery. However, despite that, she had a *legitimate* part to play: she was running errands, collecting herbs, doing things that were, unbeknown to her, part of being a midwife. She was of 'some use' to her grandmother, even before she decided actively to learn from the older woman, turning her into a mentor.

Key elements of situated learning

At this point it will be useful to summarize five of the key elements in situated learning according to Lave and Wenger (1991):

1   People who perform some practice, usually conceived as a 'work' practice, belong to a community of practice, which is Lave and Wenger's term for how most people learn 'naturally' in their (work) communities (cf. Burgoyne and Hodgson, 1983). However, conceptions of 'work' vary by culture. It is unlikely, for example, that midwifery in Yucatan is regarded as work in the Western sense, yet feminist readings of this Yucatec Mayan practice may label it a form of 'invisible work'. Communities of practice do not necessarily overlap with more specific communities of practitioners. It is possible that Mayan midwives operating in different villages never meet or communicate and do not belong to the same community of practitioners, while they do belong to the same community of practice. The same might be true of many 'professional communities' in the West. We generally use the term 'community of practice', which is the wider concept, to cover also the idea of a 'community of practitioners'.

2   The (work) practice at the core of any community of practice typically follows a cycle with a beginning, middle and end, which might be spread over minutes, hours, days or months, depending on the nature of the task – delivering a child, navigating a ship's voyage, diagnosing an illness or running an advertising campaign, for example.

3   The community of practice socially reproduces itself typically over a longer time cycle than the work practice cycle itself and does so by an apprenticeship system which can be highly informal, as in the case of becoming a Mayan midwife, or highly formal, as in the case of

becoming a stone mason or naval quartermaster. Communities of practice are reproduced via communities of practitioners. In apprenticeship systems, however informal, the novices begin participating in a legitimate way by assisting the more experienced members of the community. That is to say they are regarded as 'legitimate', if 'peripheral', participants. The position of peripherality is crucial since it allows them to observe skilled practitioners' *practise*, then copy and learn. This is in marked contrast with formal education in which pupils' and students' work is not regarded as making a legitimate contribution to the community of scholars in a discipline or research community until masters or doctoral level, and they are not even able to see skilled researchers and scholars practising.

4   Each community of practice is marked by asymmetrical power relations between old-timers (who are masters of the practice) and newcomers (who are apprenticed to the masters). In such apprenticeship-learning the apprentice learns by copying the master, usually by doing some peripheral, low-risk, minor but necessary parts of the process and gradually and centripetally trying to do the more central, more difficult parts of the process. The process of learning to copy a master is not without tensions, however. For example, consider the tensions between replication and change, clones and heretics, and between continuity and discontinuity.

5   Communities of practice are not wholly independent or self-sufficient; they are dependent on other communities of practice which require their services or products or supply their materials and resources. They are also dependent upon a supply of suitable newcomers/apprentices who in traditional cultures are frequently the children of the 'masters'. Communities of practice are therefore part of a network of overlapping and tangential communities of practice which trade with each other in either the official or convivial economy.

It may be appreciated from the above five points that Lave and Wenger are not putting the idea of situated learning forward as 'an educational form, much less a pedagogical strategy or a teaching technique', rather they see it 'as an analytical viewpoint on learning, a way of understanding learning' and they make 'a fundamental distinction between learning and intentional instruction' (1991: 40). The latter includes teaching and training, whereas their approach offers a kind of framework for analysing the work practices of any community of practice – formal or informal.

Situated learning's critique of 'schooling'

Lave and Wenger do claim 'that rethinking schooling from the perspective afforded by legitimate peripheral participation (LPP) will turn out to be a fruitful exercise' (1991: 41). They critique formal education, which would include most training and educational contexts, and there are several interrelated parts to their critique of 'schooling' from a situated learning perspective. Three of these interrelated parts will be relevant to our discussion in the final section of this chapter.

1   Schooling does not produce practitioners of some practice. Rather it produces schooled adults, people who are able *to talk about* practice rather than belong to a community of practice (know-what without know-how).

2   Schooling effectively cuts students and teachers off from other communities of practice. It sequesters them and it can alienate learners because the link between talking about and performing a practice is not there.

3   Teaching and learning in the institutions of schooling are mediated by discourse rather than by observing a skilled performance and imitating it, which is more often the medium for learning in apprenticeship systems as varied as midwifery, karate, or carrying out doctoral research in the sciences. Schooling produces what might be called 'communities of discourse' rather than communities of practice, and necessitates the separation of abstract knowledge (know-what and know-why) from knowing in practice (know-how and care-why) (Quinn, 1992). This separation makes it possible to differentiate 'talking about' from 'talking within' a practice: the former tends to be more descriptive, explanatory and systematic, whereas the latter tends to be more performative and *ad hoc*.

It may appear that situated learning theorists are anti-schooling, but this is not Lave and Wenger's position at all. On the contrary, their point is that despite its great accomplishments, formal 'schooling' has endemic problems which can be thrown into relief and understood all the better when contrasted with 'communities of practice'. Some researchers of management development and education recognize that a considerable amount of learning occurs outside formal learning events and programmes (e.g., Burgoyne and Hodgson, 1983; Mumford, 1989; Marsick and Watkins, this volume). However, there are very few detailed studies of these 'natural' or 'everyday' learning processes, partly because they are less easy to investigate than classrooms and other formal settings. By drawing together and analysing several ethnographic studies of apprenticeship, Lave and Wenger (1991) have begun to show what research into natural learning might find and to provide frameworks for finding patterns in the data.

Discussion: Management Learning and Situated Learning

In the second section of this chapter we examined the shift in perspective which follows from adopting a situated learning approach. Here we return to the question of management learning as a programme and project in order to draw out the implications of situated learning for this field. If communities of practice are crucial to everyday natural learning processes and achievements and if we emphasize practice over theory and the social over the individual, what might the consequences be for management learning?

First, we have to recognize that management learning is itself a research community which is embedded within and is part of wider communities of practice – management education, management development and HRD. These practitioners are not separate from the management learning research community, but rather they belong to it when they switch hats and *practise as researchers* of management education and development and HRD. They do this whenever they conduct some research to help with their practice – for example, when carrying out a 'training needs analysis' or conducting an evaluation, or when researching some new materials or ideas with which to design a learning programme or event. Research in the sense just described is an everyday activity which is already part of many practitioners' working lives. Such informal research skills are complemented by the growing number of professional researchers conducting formal research in the area of management learning.

Having said that management learning is a research community embedded in the management education and development and HRD communities, the main point of this chapter so far has been to say that these communities of formal practice represent the tip of a 'learning iceberg'. Situated learning theorists draw our attention to everyday, 'natural' learning processes which are inherent in many diverse working communities of practice. Orr's doctoral thesis and other publications (1990a, 1990b), for example, provide ethnographies of service technicians both in training and at work in a large corporation. The work of these technicians is described in training manuals and in job descriptions, but Orr's ethnographic description is far richer. Suchman's (1987, 1990) ethnographies of cognitive scientists and systems designers, who used whiteboards to develop their designs collaboratively, is particularly revealing. Her work, like Orr's and Elias's, shows the open-endedness of performing activities which, even if they are planned or programmed in advance (via the training manual, business plan, or job description, for example), are ultimately dependent upon tacit and embodied skills which defy the plan.

Suchman (1990) explains the open-endedness of tacit know-how by analogy with canoeing down a series of rapids. For instance, before the descent one might plan one's approach, thinking something like this:

'I'll get as far over to the left as possible, try to make it between those two large rocks, then backferry hard to the right to make it around that next bunch.' A great deal of deliberation, discussion, simulation, and reconstruction may go into such a plan and to the construction of alternate plans as well. But in no case – and this is the crucial point – do such plans control action in any strict sense of the word 'control.' . . . When it really comes down to the details of getting the actions done, *in situ*, you rely not on the plan but on whatever embodied skills of handling a canoe, responding to currents and the like are available to you. (Suchman, 1990: 310)

It is the same with any planned course of action from running a work-shop according to a design for learning, to any management of change initiative.

The aim in this chapter has been to highlight that the situated learning approach raises the stakes for practitioners of management education and development, HRD and management learning. The main point is that this approach places emphasis on *management learning* processes rather than on management educational and developmental processes. The latter are a narrower, and formal, set of practices which are frequently *done to* people by professionals to make them learn, whereas management learning processes cover these and the rest of the learning iceberg – the everyday processes whereby people manage learning and learn to manage (Fox, 1994a, 1994b).

Theory and practice

If management learning has a message for management education and development and HRD practitioners based on situated learning theory, it is that they/we are subject to the 'critique of schooling' levelled by Lave and Wenger (1991), that we produce 'schooled' or 'trained' adults rather than improve existing learning communities of practice in the numerous varieties of managerial work. Related to this critique is the criticism that management education and development and HRD practitioners are more expert in 'talking about' than in 'talking within' managerial practices, producing communities of discourse rather than contributing directly to communities of managerial practice. As a result, our efforts are bedevilled by the 'transfer of learning' problem which raises questions over the 'value-added' of formal training in the eyes of communities of top-managerial practice, as well as line management communities.

There are several defences to these accusations but, arguably, there is also a need to respond and the situated learning approach can offer some ways forward. The first defence is that although management education and development are increasingly becoming a single area of practice – as argued in the first part of the chapter – this area actually does have within it two distinct communities of practice, which we have called 'management development' and 'management education', which should not become total substitutes. The latter has a primary duty to produce new generations of scholars and researchers capable of producing original knowledge and insights, just as do other fields of higher education (the natural sciences, arts and humanities, and social sciences). Management education should not become a substitute for management development but either a preparation for, or time-out from, a managerial career. Management development and HRD, on the other hand, should be useful to managerial communities of practice in organizational settings and career structures. If we accept that there is a legitimate difference between management education and management development, then any consequences we draw from the situated learning approach should be different in the two cases. We should therefore accept that management education is about reproducing *research communities of practice* which are reliant upon schooled adult communities of discourse. In *academic disciplines* 'talking-about' is an essential part of *research practice* – producing, discussing and evaluating theories is an essential part of the job. *Talking about* is *talking within* the practice of theory building and critique. Therefore management education should maintain the difference between pure and applied research, education and professional training, or it will endanger its *raison d'être*.

The second defence to the accusation that developers do not generally understand how learners work and learn socially in everyday situations is to argue that they are not alone. Top management also can be blind to organizational sub-cultures and the tacit knowledge within them. In fact organizations' espoused or official accounts of work practices (found in training manuals, job descriptions, procedural guidelines, and the like) are very often too abstract, offering little understanding of actual working-learning practices. Management development and HRD practitioners are not the only managers who need to pay attention to situated learning communities of practice. It could be argued that situated learning offers management development and HRD a rationale for extending their professional scope, and a methodology for doing so. This prospect is discussed below.

Individual and social learning

Individuals are often credited by educators, developers and trainers with possessing many ideal capacities: for experiencing the world in a unique way; for independent thought; for deciding freely; for taking independent action; for being personally responsible for their actions; for knowing right from wrong; and for differentiating between true and false. Because educators, developers and trainers see people in such ways, they design educational, developmental and training processes which turn people into individuals. Frequently, this involves taking people out of the fabric of their everyday working-learning contexts into the context of some kind of classroom. The consequence is that educators', developers' and trainers' designs for learning often individualize people in ways which separate them from their conventional roles, behaviours, streams of activity and working relationships. Such individualizing designs can be very useful for facilitating learners' self-awareness, or for disseminating information to populations of learners, or for demonstrating alternative behaviours and skills, but they are not good for understanding how learners work and learn socially in everyday situations.

One implication of Lave and Wenger's (1991) research is that the learning done in the course of everyday work can be highly significant for communities of practice, but that educators, developers and trainers are almost blind to it. One consequence of this is that trainers and developers often do not know what their participants know, but only know what they themselves can teach. In recent years Nonaka (1991) has pointed out that communities of practice (he prefers the term 'communities of interaction') actually store invaluable tacit knowledge which 'knowledge creating companies' can use to improve their competitive advantage, but only if they can first find ways of making the tacit knowledge explicit. Brown and Duguid (1991) follow Lave and Wenger directly and, like Nonaka, argue that communities of practice should be accessed by the organizations in which they exist. They warn that formal Organizational Development-style initiatives (involving task forces and new project groups, for example) for intervening in the workplace to install TQM, JIT, or other 'branded' OD interventions, can actually damage the tacit knowledge which is already there, either by overwhelming it, ignoring it, dismissing it, or translating it into the language of some universal change-programme so that its essence is lost.

The fact that organizations are made up of many different overlapping cultures was widely recognized in the 1980s, but the focus then was how to impose a model corporate culture upon the whole organization. The fashion for designer corporate cultures frequently involved external consultants in facilitating tiny groups of top managers to produce 'mission' or 'value' statements, followed by various top-down 'culture change' initiatives to 'win hearts and minds' and even to change behaviour. Top managers talked about the 'Hewlett Packard Way', for instance, and tried to make a culture out of slogans and 'corporate belief statements'. In the 1990s, the work of Nonaka, Quinn, and Brown and Duguid among others, points to a different, more low-key approach, one which does not try to change corporate cultures until it has first understood them. These approaches work with the grain of the different cultures, within the firm rather than with top-team fantasies. The aim frequently is still to introduce changes which will improve corporate performance, but the emphasis is upon 'learning with' as opposed to telling communities of practice how to change. One way that trainers and developers could enhance and develop their professional role is by learning to do 'field-work' inside communities of practice, learning to translate tacit knowledge into explicit knowledge. The skills for doing this are similar to those of anthropological field-workers. Such skills need to be learned 'in the field' but initially with the help of more experienced ethnographers.

Field-work would involve trainers and developers in learning more about the communities whose practices they ultimately want to improve. The easiest way to accomplish this shift of professional emphasis is to begin by spending more time on training needs analysis, but also to conduct these in ways which go with the grain of the culture and requires field-work skills, rather than questionnaire design and personal appraisal interviewing.

Summary and Conclusion

I have argued in this chapter that management education is distinct from management development and that both of these areas of activity contribute in different ways to the theory and practice of management. I have also argued that management learning is the study of the management of learning processes, especially those which contribute to the practice of management, *including* both management education and development. The chapter subsequently offered an appreciative account of situated learning theory (SLT), drawing out implications for management learning.

SLT draws our attention to the fact that formal management education and development are but the tip of a learning iceberg and that most learning to manage, and managing to learn (Fox, 1994a), occurs 'on-job' in tacit, culturally embedded ways through people's work practices within organizations, groups and other communities of practice. In common with writers on situated learning, some writers on management learning have studied learning in action. For example, they have studied learning in action in the context of everyday managerial work (Burgoyne and Hodgson, 1983; Davies and Easterby-Smith, 1984) and in the context of business school life (Fox, 1990b).

I have suggested that the situated learning approach offers a way to extend the professional scope and skills of management developers, enabling them to understand the situated learning communities of practice which already exist in organizations. This would enable management and HRD practitioners to understand better the tacit knowledge which the sub-cultures of the organization possess and to make this more explicit for the organization. Nonaka (1991), among others, argues why this could be of great benefit to organizations, and the work of Orr (1990a, 1990b) and Suchman (1987, 1990), as well as of Lave and Wenger (1991), provides illuminating illustrations of how this might be so.

Annotated Bibliography

For those who would like to pursue the idea of situated learning further, I recommend: J. Lave (1991) 'Situating learning in communities of practice', in L.B. Resnick, J.M. Levine and S.D. Teasley (eds), *Perspectives on Socially Shared Cognition.* Washington, DC: American Psychological Association; and J. Lave (1993) 'The practice of learning', in Seth Chaiklin and Jean Lave (eds), *Understanding Practice: Perspectives on Activity and Context.* Cambridge: Cambridge University Press. These give concise summaries of the approach, and the book by Chaiklin and Lave collects a number of studies which use the approach. The paper by Brown and Duguid (1991), cited in the references, provides an excellent application of situated learning theory to the organizational world. For those wanting more organizational applications, I recommend Nonaka (1991), cited in the references, and C.K. Prahalad and G. Hamel (1990) 'The core competence of the corporation', *Harvard Business Review*, May–June: 79–91. Neither of these papers refer to the 'communities of practice' idea directly, but the issues they discuss are very similar.

References

Brown, J.S. and Duguid, P. (1991) 'Organizational learning and communities of practice: toward a unified view of working, learning, and innovation', *Organization Science*, 2 (1): 40–57.

Burgoyne, J.G. and Hodgson, V.E. (1983) 'Natural learning and managerial action: a phenomenological study in the field setting', *Journal of Management Studies*, 20 (3): 387–99.

Davies, J. and Easterby-Smith, M. (1984) 'Learning and developing from managerial work experiences', *Journal of Management Studies*, 21 (2): 169–83.

Elias, N. (1995) 'Technization and civilization', *Theory, Culture & Society*, 12 (3): 7–42.

Fox, S. (1989) 'The panopticon: from Bentham's obsession to the revolution in management learning', *Human Relations*, 42 (8): 717–39.

Fox, S. (1990a) 'Strategic HRM: postmodern conditioning for the corporate culture', *Management Education and Development*, 21 (3): 192–206.

Fox, S. (1990b) 'The ethnography and the problem of social reality', *Sociology*, 24 (3): 431–46.

Fox, S. (1992a) 'What are we? The constitution of management in higher education and human resource management', *International Studies of Management & Organization*, 22 (3): 71–93.

Fox, S. (1992b) 'The European learning community: towards a political economy of management learning', *Human Resource Management Journal*, 3 (1): 70–91.

Fox, S. (1994a) 'Debating management learning: I', *Management Learning*, 25 (1): 83–93.

Fox, S. (1994b) 'Debating management learning: II', *Management Learning*, 25 (4): 579–97.

Grey, C. and Mitev, N. (1995) 'Management education: a polemic', *Management Learning*, 26 (1): 73–90.

Hall, N. (1964) 'Education and management', *Journal of Management Studies*, 1 (2): 105–15.

Handy, C., Gordon, C., Gow, I. and Randlesome, C. (1988) *Making Managers*. London: Pitman.

Huczynski, A.A. (1983) *Encyclopedia of Management Development Methods*. Aldershot: Gower.

Jordan, B. (1989) 'Cosmopolitan obstetrics: some insights from the training of traditional midwives', *Social Science and Medicine*, 28 (9): 925–44.

Lave, J. (1988) *Cognition in Practice: Mind Mathematics and Culture in Everyday Life*. Cambridge: Cambridge University Press.

Lave, J. and Wenger, E. (1991) *Situated Learning: Legitimate Peripheral Participation*. Cambridge: Cambridge University Press.

Mintzberg, H. and Waters, J.A. (1985) 'Of strategies, deliberate and emergent', *Strategic Management Journal*, 6: 257–72.

Mumford, A. (1989) *Management Development: Strategies for Action*. London: Institute of Personnel Management.

Nonaka, I. (1991) 'The knowledge-creating company: how Japanese companies create the dynamics of innovation', *Harvard Business Review*, November/December: 96–104.

Orr, J. (1990a) 'Talking about machines: an ethnography of a modern job', PhD dissertation, Cornell University, Ithaca, NY.

Orr, J. (1990b) 'Sharing knowledge, celebrating identity: war stories and community memory in a service culture', in D.S. Middleton and D. Edwards (eds), *Collective Remembering: Memory in Society*. Beverley Hills, CA: Sage. pp. 169–89.

Quinn, J.B. (1992) *Intelligent Enterprise*. New York: Free Press.

Suchman, L.A. (1987) *Plans and Situated Actions: The Problem of Human–Machine Communication*. New York: Cambridge University Press.

Suchman, L.A. (1990) 'Representing practice in cognitive science', in J. Lynch and S. Woolgar (eds), *Representation in Scientific Practice*. Cambridge, MA: MIT Press. pp. 301–21.

Thomas, A.B. (1980) 'Management and education: rationalization and reproduction in British business', *International Studies of Management & Organization*, 10 (1–2): 71–109.

Trow, M. (1989) 'American higher education – past, present and future', *Studies in Higher Education*, 14 (1): 5–22.

Wertsch, J.V. (1991) 'A sociocultural approach to socially shared cognition', in L.B. Resnick, J.M. Levine and S.D. Teasley (eds), *Perspectives on Socially Shared Cognition.* Washington, DC: American Psychological Association. pp. 85–100.

Willmott, H. (1994) 'Management education: provocations to debate', *Management Learning*, 25 (1): 105–36.

2

Research Traditions in Management Learning

Mark Easterby-Smith and Richard Thorpe

The main aim of this chapter is to provide a review of the dominant research trends in management learning. This is done through examining examples of research that tackle different kinds of problems and topics within the field. As an initial organizer we have developed a matrix with two dimensions. These differentiate respectively between the educational and corporate sectors and between policy and operational concerns (Figure 2.1). The *educational–corporate* dimension provides a distinction according to the main location of management learning: whether it takes place within the 'walls' of educational establishments, or whether it takes place at, or under the control of, employer organizations. The term corporate is used to include any employing organization which contains a management function. The *policy–operational* dimension provides a distinction with implications of scale: the policy level concentrating on general issues and principles often at a national level; the operational level implying a local focus and an emphasis on techniques and methods used within particular institutions. Within each of the quadrants thus created we provide typical illustrations of the content

	Education sector	Corporate sector
Policy level	Evolution of education in the UK and USA. Key reports and debates. Growth and the Management Charter Initiative.	Establishment of competencies as alternative to academic education. Rise of vocational qualifications and role of government and corporate institutions.
Operations level	Effectiveness of management education methods. Processes in teaching and learning. Development of new and innovative forms of management teaching/ learning.	Evaluation of corporate training methods. Investigating natural learning at work. Mentorship. Organizational learning. Effectiveness of management development and HRM.

Figure 2.1 *Examples of research traditions in management learning*

of research conducted into management learning. We also comment on the different methods used because there are distinct methodological traditions within each quadrant. These are also affected by the type of problem and the nature of the stakeholders involved. For example, at the policy level where the focus is on matters of principle, considerable reliance is placed on the views of opinion-formers. There is less reliance on 'rigorous' research in the corporate sector than in the educational sector, and at the operations level there is greater reliance on empirical research, individual cases and the accounts of individuals.

Before embarking on the review of research traditions in management learning it is also worth highlighting a fundamental debate about the appropriate means by which knowledge should be derived and the weight that should be placed on such knowledge. The debate is often characterized as being between positivism on the one hand and phenomenology on the other, although there are a great number of compromise positions between these two approaches to research, such as action research, which draw, to some extent, on both traditions. Management emerged as a field of study in the late nineteenth century,[1] and as a relatively new discipline it was obliged to follow the research methods associated with related disciplines, such as economics and psychology. At the time these took a strongly positivist approach with a reliance on quantitative measures, statistical analysis and the search for universal (causal) laws. This trend was reinforced by the major review of management education conducted by Gordon and Howell (1959) in the USA. Not only did they advocate much more rigorous training for management academics, they also recommended that the curriculum taught in business schools should have a much greater reliance on quantitative and analytic methods. This not only affected the mainstream research traditions of management, but also sub-specialisms like management training and education.

However, the quantitative approach was not without its critics. Mintzberg (1973) and Kotter (1982) claimed that they could find little evidence to support the view that managers behaved in the way the traditional theories suggested. Their research adopted a more phenomenological approach, using qualitative techniques, observation and the accounts of managers themselves. Other academics, supported by employers and using qualitative research techniques (Livingston, 1971; Hayes and Abernathy, 1980; Peters and Waterman, 1982), argued that the teaching of quantitative techniques of analysis for managers was of limited value and that there were factors less amenable to quantification that were more important, such as an ability to lead, persuade, identify problems, create vision and manage 'culture'. These findings were endorsed by the Porter and McKibbin (1988) report for American Association of Collegiate Business Schools (AACSB) in response to falling MBA numbers in the USA.

These two traditions, the quantitative/positivist and the qualitative/ constructivist, now co-exist within US management research, and the tension between the two is also evident in other countries, such as the UK. In the following sections of this chapter we will comment on how they are implicated in research into different forms of management learning.

Research into Management Education Policy

We have referred to some of the policy level debates in the USA above, with regard to how they influence views of research methods in management education in general. In this section we focus on examples of policy-oriented research conducted in the UK. The reason for focusing on just one national system is that we wish to illustrate in some depth both the substance and process of policy research in management education. However, one can note that although the focal issues may vary by country, the underlying procedures are similar in the USA and other European countries (Locke, 1989).

A debate still to be resolved followed a highly controversial paper published by two professors from the City Business School (Griffiths and Murray, 1985). This suggested that parts of management education, especially those at postgraduate level, should be privatized. Like the Mant Report (BIM, 1971) which preceded it, the Griffiths and Murray Report was not based on any research as such, but it quickly gained 'research' status and was extremely influential, setting in train an upheaval in management education policy that is with us today. Its proposals would mean the withdrawal of much government funding from the sector and in the political climate of the time it had to be taken seriously. The response was rapid and concerted. At a meeting in the offices of the British Institute of Management attended by the Secretary of State for Education, Sir Keith Joseph, it was agreed that these ideas should be resisted and that this could best be done by authoritative reports which could demonstrate that industry needed more management education, that it could fund only a part of it, and that in comparison to international competitors the UK was very backward in the training and education provided for managers. Accordingly, two senior professors, John Constable and Charles Handy, were commissioned to lead studies looking respectively at the demand/supply of management education in the UK and at the provisions made by international competitors. Funding was provided by the Confederation of British Industry (CBI), the British Institute of Management (BIM) and the National Economic Development Office (NEDO).

Handy and his colleagues carried out case studies on management education systems in France, Germany, the USA and Japan which enabled statistical comparisons to be made with the UK on matters such as participation rates, the approach being fairly inductive and intuitive initially, moving to quantitative comparisons later. Constable collected statistics on courses run by higher education, companies and consultants. Some of the figures, they admit, were dubious since no comprehensive databases existed at the time on matters such as faculty numbers and short-course provision. However, the seductive nature of the quantitative presentation made it appear definitive. Both reports were published on the same day and this added to their impact (Constable and McCormick, 1987; Handy et al., 1987).

Both reports recommended expansion. Constable and McCormick recommended increasing the number of degrees at all levels. This might have been expected as a consequence of the methodology used which collected 'facts' about numbers and levels; but also highlighted was the need to develop the educational infrastructure, increase the training of teachers and introduce tax incentives for students. Handy's recommendations in contrast pointed to the complexity of management development. His research had studied the context in which management development took place in different countries and his findings reflected these qualitative insights. Central to his recommendations was the establishment of a central body to drive through the initiatives, supported by an appropriate information base. Handy offered a 10-point plan which included expanding the educational base to encourage work experience. He also suggested encouraging leading organizations to set the standard for in-company training and advocated co-operation between organizations and business schools.

Although most stakeholder groups accepted the argument for expansion, there has been a continuing debate about the form(s) it should take and the structures that are needed to support it. Proposals to set up a Chartered Institute of Management, implying full professionalization of management, were dropped after vigorous opposition from academics, consultants and managers; a number of leading companies signed up for commitment to a code of good management development practice, which is still supported by the Management Charter Initiative organization (MCI); and a major push was established to introduce 'competency' certification of managers at all levels as opposed to the traditional academic and vocational qualifications. The latter is the only one of these three proposals that has had much impact on management education, and then primarily at the lower levels due to the availability of government funding. The higher levels, both undergraduate and postgraduate degrees, still remain firmly under the control of universities. Meanwhile, student numbers increased very rapidly in the five years after the two reports, but more as a result of increased awareness and market pressures than as a result of deliberate planning and action.

More recently, assessments of research and teaching quality in British business and management schools have evoked a range of critical responses (Taylor, 1994; Berry et al., 1995). Taylor, from the Department of Economics at Lancaster University, produced a detailed statistical analysis of the 1992 research assessment results from the 85 Business and Management departments in the UK. Developing a regression model from a set of quantitative indicators of research outputs and inputs, he showed it was possible to make comparisons between schools and showed how these regressors could be used as predictive/control variables to explain the variations between departments. Among the variables discovered in the model were the size of the department, the articles in refereed academic journals and research income. From his work the possibility exists that these variables might be able to be used to determine research rating in future exercises.

An example of a more qualitative study was that conducted into the Higher Education Funding Council for England (HEFCE) teaching quality assessment by Berry, Lock and Easterby-Smith (1995). This report included reflections on their own experiences as assessors and assessees. The main focus of the research was a content analysis (essentially a qualitative method) of the visit reports examining the positive aspects and issues offered by the assessors which supported the judgement made on each establishment visited. In addition, in order to gain some insights into the context of each visit and report, the background of each specialist assessor and the nature of the role of each lead assessor were considered. From this essentially qualitative approach, the conclusions were that the scope of activities that were actually assessed differed markedly between institutions. They found a strong correlation between teaching and research excellence, suggesting content was a major factor in judgements about the quality of teaching, but they also noted that student quality was an important contributing factor.

Summary of methods

From a research point of view the patterns that are evident for the UK and the USA are also repeated in other countries (Locke, 1989; Tanton and Easterby-Smith, 1989). Research into management education policy is an 'establishment' activity. It is controlled by powerful interest groups who determine what will be researched and how. Occasionally, mavericks such as Griffiths and Murray enter the fray. But despite being senior professors whose ideas matched political thinking at the time, their impact was only indirect: their paper provided the stimulus for a stream of activity that had the opposite effect in some respects to what they had proposed.

Both in the UK and USA the researchers act as the handmaids of interest groups and it often seems that personal credibility is more important than mastery of the latest research methods. Questionnaire surveys supported by interviews are the favoured data collection methods, backed up by demographic statistics, where available. If hard data is not available, then intelligent guesses seem more acceptable than no statistics. Informants will carry more credibility if they too are senior and influential, and they will often be selected, often unconsciously, to reflect the opinions favoured by the sponsors of the research. The Porter and McKibbin report mentioned earlier is one example of a survey which attempted to provide new solutions to a recognized problem, but then gathered data from people who were a part of the initial problem. The Handy Report in the UK overcame this particular limitation by studying other countries, but even then the sponsors already knew that management education was more advanced in the comparator countries, so the results were likely to favour their case for expansion in the UK.

The timeliness of studies and linkage to current agendas and debates are essential if anyone is to take note of suggestions, interpret results and take consequent action. Researchers may attempt to anticipate such action and lay down arguments in favour of or against different courses. Improvements in data storage and handling capacity mean that future studies will become more grounded in reliable statistics but it will still be necessary to seek the views of influential stakeholders.

Research into Corporate Development Policy

In this quadrant we consider research which bears on the general frameworks that surround corporate management learning. Thus we are primarily concerned here with government and national institutional policy on corporate training and development, including both public and private sector organizations in the discussion. Many of the debates on the corporate side parallel those in the educational sector, and research methods have similar requirements – the need for relevance and timeliness, the importance of stakeholder agendas and opinion-formers.

We focus here primarily on the development of competency models which are being used for the selection and training of managers. This originated with a study by the American consultants, McBer (Boyatzis, 1982), which defined a set of 18 competencies that they claimed were needed by most managers. They surveyed over 2,000 managers in 12 organizations using behaviour event interviews and projective tests, and the competencies were identified from extensive factor analysis of the data collected. American business schools were unmoved by this research, despite an earlier study by the AACSB (Porter, 1983). In the early 1980s the American Management Association made an attempt to introduce its own competency-based MBA (Powers, 1983), but this failed. New attempts are afoot to introduce competency frameworks for senior managers and directors into British business schools based on the MCI level three standards, although there appears to be a similar lack of enthusiasm not least because of criticism of the research methods on which these standards are based.

Within companies, however, there has been far greater interest, on both sides of the Atlantic. Competencies are now widely used in appraisal systems and in the identification of development needs. Some apply a generic model on the assumption that there are a limited number of core competencies which are relevant to most managers in most situations. This has been the approach favoured by government-sponsored research in the UK where a rigid methodology known as Functional Analysis has been used to identify competence. This involves breaking any job down into its constituent elements and identifying the skills and abilities associated with their effective performance. In this approach we see the positivistic influences in the methods used to classify and determine training needs for students and managers (Thorpe and Holman, 1993).

Cockerill (1989) and others have argued against the use of standardized competencies. They see competencies as being dependent on the context of a particular organization. Boddy, Paton and MacDonald (1995) report that many organizations are moving towards more highly devolved systems where different parts of the same organization define different competencies in order to reflect their distinct value systems and operational problems. Similarly, there is a view that different sets of competencies are appropriate for different levels of managers. Most sets start with the Boyatzis or MCI model and then modify categories through research methods such as the repertory grid or critical incident technique. These two techniques are good at assessing the tacit elements of a job which individuals recognize as important to performance, yet find hard to articulate. This social constructionist approach enables the competency framework to be based on how the managers of a particular organization see competence.

The political undertones of policy research in the 'corporate' sector can easily come to the surface. Thus, a few years ago Richard Thorpe and his colleague Ardha Danieli (formerly Best) were asked to investigate high drop-out rates on the national Employment Training Scheme. They chose to use a qualitative methodology and based their research on interviews with a sample of those who had dropped out. The result showed a high level of dissatisfaction among trainees. They felt that the training provision was very inflexible, that many of the courses were of low quality and that their participation in the scheme was very unlikely to lead to permanent employment (Thorpe and Best, 1989). But when these results were presented to the representatives of the sponsoring body it was clear that there were few surprises. They were already aware of most of the issues raised and the data merely served to confirm what was already known. The researchers felt that they had done their work and that their conclusions would probably become buried in the bureaucracy of their sponsor, but there was a new twist. Someone (not the researchers) leaked the report to the press on the grounds that it was in the public interest that a critical report should not be suppressed. This led to a flurry of damage limitation activity from the sponsors, until the issue lost its political immediacy. The sponsors were most annoyed, and the researchers were most embarrassed.

Summary of methods

Once again, from the examples presented here, the funding, interpretation and implementation of research findings cannot easily be separated from politics. The same issues may have very different salience and significance in the two sectors, particularly the concept and application of 'competencies'. In addition, the role of researchers and the processes of research are different. Most of the policy research in the corporate sector relies on funding from sponsors; in the educational sector much of it is unfunded, because it is often in the interests of academics to carry out research for nothing if it is likely to have a direct impact on their livelihood. Given the funding emphasis, it is not surprising that much of the work in the corporate sector is oriented towards implementing, and improving existing policies, rather than subjecting them to independent and critical evaluation. On the other hand, when policies are driven by central government and associated quangos, the statistical reporting about their implementation tends to be systematic because of the implications for public accountability. This provides a potential advantage over those working in the educational sector where statistics are harder to interpret because of the greater diversity of institutions and provision, and many of them are not available at the levels of desegregation that would make them useful (as in the difficulty found by Constable and McCormick (1987) in estimating the number of management teachers in the UK when numbers had initially to be inferred from the general category of 'social sciences and business studies').

Research into Operational Management Education

The most interesting research in this area has been in the process and outcomes of management education methods. Although it has not had such a high profile as some of the studies discussed above, some have created internal debate and controversy. The research methods used have relied more on practice within educational research and many of the studies have used evaluation methods. In order to demonstrate some of the trends we have used examples from a number of studies that have been conducted over the last 25 years.

There has always been a great deal of interest in the efficacy of traditional methods such as lectures and case studies. Bligh (1971) was able to review nearly 100 experiments that compared the effectiveness of lecturing with other teaching methods. These had used tests applied before and after the session in question. This enabled him to conclude that, with the exception of programmed learning, the lecture method is as effective as any other method for transmitting information, that most lectures are not as effective as more active methods for the promotion of thought, and that lectures were not an effective means of changing attitudes. This study points to one of the major problems in conducting research into educational outcomes: the difficulty of deciding which particular criterion to accept.

A study by Partridge and Scully (1979) examined the relative merits of the case method and business games for teaching business policy at an introductory level. In this study a class of 38 students was divided into eight sub-groups matched in terms of academic attainment up to that point in the course; four groups were taught by case method and the other four participated in a business game. All students completed a series of open questions designed to test their understanding of business policy before their course and 12 weeks afterwards, and the answers were evaluated by an independent judge who knew neither the identity of the student nor which answers were 'before' and which were 'after'. The result showed improvement for all groups between the two administrations of the test, but all the of 'game' groups showed greater improvement in the quality of their answers than the 'case' groups.

Although the Partridge and Scully study was conducted very carefully, it has been criticized on methodological grounds. First, their business policy test focused on understanding and did not cover other potential areas of learning, such as knowledge or attitudes. Secondly, although they tried to control for the 'teacher effect' by removing the tutor from the business game and handling the cases in as neutral a manner as possible, one might argue that this removes the realism from the comparison. And thirdly, even if the study is methodologically flawless, it does not tell us why one method is superior to another.

These considerations have led to some disenchantment with experimental designs, and more interest in the use of qualitative methods that look at the processes of courses. One classic example carried out by Argyris (1980) was a study of the methods used by 'star performers' when teaching executives with the case method. He interviewed all of the faculty before the course started about their teaching philosophies and then observed the sessions that they taught on the course. Through an analysis of the number of questions and comments during classroom discussions he was able to test whether their behaviour bore out the espoused aims of the faculty: these being to make it clear that there were no right or wrong answers for each case, and to reduce student dependency on the teacher. His results showed that in all but one case the behaviour of faculty was contrary to their espoused theories and that they used a variety of techniques such as progressively giving out hints to a class about the 'right' solution, in order to maintain control of the process and outcomes of the case.

Recent work that has examined the process within computer-supported courses has used discourse analysis to examine the interactions between participants which are recorded in electronic conference exchanges. In this case the technology provides natural access to electronic conversations which can be printed off by participants and the researcher at the touch of a button. This method has enabled researchers to examine issues such as power in tutor/student interactions and the effects of gender on learning with a level of detail and rigour formerly unavailable (Hardy et al., 1994).

The second major area of research at the operational level is about appropriate content of undergraduate management courses and MBAs. There are a number of stands – whether 'management' is a subject that can be taught at all, whether the subject can be broken down into discrete disciplines (Raelin, 1994), and whether emphasis should be placed on the application of ideas rather than knowledge for its own sake. This debate ties in with the arguments already discussed about the value of competency-based approaches to management education. Exchanges have taken place about whether management is a subject that ought to be taught, because of the political interests that are automatically subsumed, and hence for the need for management courses to make managers aware of the broader political structures within which they operate (Willmott, 1994; Grey and

Mitev, 1995). Those people who view management learning in behavioural terms will look for links between desired end behaviour and suitable instructional processes. Their view is that knowledge and skills are content dependent and, as a consequence, reliance is placed on 'correct' methods of analysis and instruction – the research methods so often favoured by those who subscribe to this view are positivist. Those who believe managers learn from experience take the view that much significant management learning emanates from work-related events. They also believe that many aspects of management can only be addressed through action and involvement, for example, the development of influencing skills, political awareness and an understanding of the moral dilemmas that exist. As a consequence for those with this perspective a phenomenological approach to research is likely to be one to which they will subscribe.

Yet a third perspective on management is a social constructionist one. Here the manager is seen as 'practical author' (Shotter, 1993). Reality is vague and only partially specified and always unstable. One of the ways of gaining greater clarity is through discussion with others and through negotiated meaning – as a consequence, language is important. Through the process of negotiation and articulation, moral and ethical dimensions can be addressed and new meaning and understanding generated. The research process or methodology necessary in understand this view of management development is social constructionism.

Summary of methods

We see a trend from quantitative to qualitative research over the last two decades, particularly in relation to specific educational methods. To some extent research approaches have varied according to the substantive focus of interest. During this period there have been shifts of focus from measuring the outcomes of methods to investigating how they work in practice, and from looking at individual methods to looking at the impact of broad programmes and educational philosophies. In these cases many questions cannot be answered just through empirical studies, and it is often necessary to consider them as part of the wider social context. As such they become the subject of broader debates about matters of principle and policy.

Research into Operational Corporate Development

Within corporate settings it is hard to distinguish clearly between learning and other aspects of the manager's work. Managers usually recall having learnt more from their experiences at work than from any formal education and training (Davies and Easterby-Smith, 1984; Marsick and Watkins, 1990), and it is often difficult to isolate single causes from the whole range of interests, anxieties and experiences that shape managerial roles and identities. However, for the purposes of organization we will discuss three typical research topics which fall into this quadrant: research into the methods of corporate training and development; research into 'natural' processes of learning at work; and research into the wider learning processes that may go on at systemic or structural levels of the organization.

Research into corporate *training and development* has usually focused on new and controversial programmes. Thus in the 1960s and 1970s T-Groups attracted a great deal of interest because they were seen as a radical way of changing individual values and behaviour. Subsequently, the T-Group movement became incorporated into organization and development (OD) which was seen as more closely linked to organizational objectives and less tough on individuals.

Early research into organizational development suffered from the 'insider perspective': most of it was based on single cases of interventions written by the key players which demonstrated how successful their work had been (e.g., Blake et al., 1964). That is why Mirvis and Berg (1977) made an important contribution with their collection of a range of case studies where OD interventions had failed. During the 1980s OD attracted less comment, possibly because its radical agenda of democratizing and humanizing the workplace had been assimilated into performance-related objectives (Reynolds, 1979).

An example of a major initiative of this kind, which took place in a European multinational during the 1980s, was evaluated by Easterby-Smith and Tanton. The programme involved putting over 600 middle managers through 10-day residential courses which included three-day experiential workshops. Evaluation took the form of 60 interviews with a stratified sample of participants and a questionnaire that was completed by 93 per cent of the participants. The interviews were semi-open and helped identify some of the issues and successes associated with the programme and provided the structure for the multiple-choice items in the main questionnaire. An attempt was also made through the interviews to track down specific people who were rumoured to have been harmed by the group workshop, but the researchers were unable to find a single example. Survey results showed that the group workshops were considered the most valuable part of the programme, especially in comparison with the conventional parts which used lectures, cases and discussions (Easterby-Smith, 1990) The significance of this study was that it was conducted by outsiders who were neither involved in the sponsorship nor provision of courses, and the research involved an effort to disprove the view of the clients that the training had been highly beneficial in corporate terms and had not harmed individuals.

Another corporate training activity that has attracted much attention is outdoor management development (OMD). Most of the published work on this was produced by providers of OMD, and hence there is very little work that is independent and critical. The question that has dominated research and publications on OMD is whether it is more or less effective as a means of development than other forms of training and development, and subsidiary questions then follow, such as whether it is better at serving individual or organizational development needs. Donnison (1993) points

those working in the field have to adopt a defensive position because both 'management' and 'education' are often regarded as inferior subjects by academics in more established disciplines.

Nevertheless, there are also grounds for optimism. Management as a discipline is becoming much better organized (and rather more respected) in academia, and the significance of market demands and external funding gives it much political weight in all but the most traditional of universities. This maturity is mirrored by those involved in research. The use and value of qualitative approaches and the insights that these have yielded in recent years has begun to remove the questions that have previously surrounded the legitimacy of this approach. Similarly, the field of management learning is becoming more self-conscious and better organized as an area of study; it is also drawing interest from academics with distinguished records in related disciplines, which must be some recognition of its strategic significance. These, however, are but indicators of available opportunities; they still have to be taken. And that is a matter for the initiative and determination of the research community in this field.

Note

1 The first major centre to be established in the USA was the Warton School of Business in 1881, although in some European countries there are foundations which predate this, such as the Ecole Supérieure de Commerce de Paris which was founded in 1819.

Annotated Bibliography

For an overview of methods available for evaluating management development, in both industrial and educational settings, see Mark Easterby-Smith (1994) *Evaluating Management Development, Training and Education* (2nd edn). Farnborough: Gower. The book is critical of 'scientific' methods of evaluation, and stresses the political nature of the process, and hence the importance of identifying the interests of relevant stakeholders. Christopher Grey and Robert French (1996) *Rethinking Management Education*. London: Sage, is an edited collection of papers which take a 'critical' stance towards management education. Contributions raise questions about the content and purposes of management education and about whose interests it is serving. Charles Handy, Ian Gow, Colin Gordon and Collin Randlesome (1988) *Making Managers*. London: Pitman, is an interesting study which compares UK provision of management education and development with that in four other countries (Germany, France, Japan and the USA). This external focus both is interesting in itself and raises some challenging questions about the nature of provision in the UK. For a classic study reviewing the provision of US management education based on surveys of business schools, their alumni and corporate clients, see Lyman W. Porter and Lawrence E. McKibbin (1988) *Management Education and Development: Drift or Thrust into the 21st Century?* New York: McGraw-Hill. Although intended to lead to a radical shake-up of the system, the results turn out to be rather conservative, possibly because substantially they are based on views of 'insiders' who may have a stake in maintaining the *status quo*.

References

Argyris, Chris (1980) 'Some limitations of the case method: experiences in a management development program', *Academy of Management Review*, 5 (2): 291–8.

Berry, Tony, Lock, Andy and Easterby-Smith, Mark (1995) 'Learning from assessment – reflections on the assessment of quality of education in business and management', paper presented to the British Academy of Management Conference, Sheffield.

Blake, Robert R., Mouton, Jane S., Barnes, Louis B. and Greiner, Larry E. (1964) 'Breakthrough in organization development', *Harvard Business Review*, November–December: 133–55.

Bligh, Donald (1971) *What's the Use of Lectures?* Harmondsworth: Penguin.

Boddy, David, Paton, Robert and MacDonald, Sylvia (1995) 'Competence-based management awards in higher education?', *Management Learning*, 26 (2): 179–92.

Boyatzis, Richard E. (1982) *The Competent Manager: A Model for Effective Performance*. New York: Wiley.

British Institute of Management (1971) *Business School Programmes: The Requirements of British Manufacturing Industry*. London: British Institute of Management.

Cockerill, Tony (1989) 'The kind of competence for rapid change', *Personnel Management*, 21 (9): 51–6.

Constable, John and McCormick, Roger (1987) *The Making of British Managers: A Report for the BIM and CBI into Management Training, Education and Development*. London: British Institute of Management and Confederation of British Industry.

Davies, Julia and Easterby-Smith, Mark (1984) 'Learning and developing from managerial work experiences', *Journal of Management Studies*, 21 (2) 169–84.

Donnison, Philip (1993) 'The effect of outdoor management development on self-efficacy'. Unpublished MSc dissertation, Birkbeck College, University of London, London.

Easterby-Smith, Mark (1990) 'Creating a learning organization', *Personnel Review*, 19 (5): 24–8.

Easterby-Smith, Mark, Braiden, Elizabeth and Ashton, David (1980) *Auditing Management Development*. Farnborough: Gower.

Easterby-Smith, Mark, Thorpe, Richard and Lowe, Andy (1991) *Management Research: An Introduction*. London: Sage.

Fox, Steve and McLeay, Stuart (1992) 'An approach to researching managerial labour markets: HRM, corporate strategy and financial performance in UK manufacturing', *International Journal of Human Resource Management*, 3 (3): 523–54.

Freedman, Richard D. and Stumpf, Stephen A. (1980) 'Learning style theory: less than meets the eye', *Academy of Management Review*, 5 (3): 445–7.

Gordon, Robert A. and Howell, James E. (1959) *Higher Education in Business*. New York: Columbia University Press.

Grey, Christopher and Mitev, Natalie (1995) 'Management education: a polemic', *Management Learning*, 26 (1): 73–90.

Griffiths, Brian and Murray, Hugh (1985) *Whose Business? A Radical Proposal to Privatise British Business Schools* (Hobart Paper 102). London: Institute of Economic Affairs.

Handy, Charles, Gow, Ian, Gordon, Colin, Randlesome, Collin and Moloney, M. (1987) *The Making of Managers*. London: National Economic Development Office.

Hardy, Virginia, Hodgson, Vivien E. and McConnell, David (1994) 'Computer conferencing: a new medium for investigating issues in gender and learning', *Higher Education*, 28: 403–18.

Hayes, Robert H. and Abernathy, William J. (1980) 'Managing our way to economic decline', *Harvard Business Review*, 58: 67–77.

Honey, Peter and Mumford, Alan (1982) *The Manual of Learning Styles*. Maidenhead: Peter Honey.

Kolb, David A., Rubin, Irwin M. and McIntyre, James M. (1984) *Organizational Psychology: An Experiential Approach to Organizational Behaviour* (4th edn). Englewood Cliffs, NJ: Prentice-Hall.

Kotter, John P. (1982) *The General Managers*. New York: Free Press.

Livingston, J. Sterling (1971) 'The myth of the well-educated manager', *Harvard Business Review*, 49: 79–89.

Locke, Robert R. (1989) *Management and Higher Education since 1940*. Cambridge: Cambridge University Press.

Mangham, Ian and Silver, M. (1986) 'Management training: context and practice'. Research report, University of Bath, Bath.

Marsick, Victoria J. and Watkins, Karen E. (1990) *Informal and Incidental Learning in the Workplace*. London: Routledge.

Mintzberg, Henry (1973) *The Nature of Managerial Work*. London and New York: Harper and Row.

Mirvis, Philip H. and Berg, David N. (1977) *Failures in Organization Development and Change*. New York: Wiley.

Partridge, S.E. and Scully, D. (1979) 'Cases versus gaming', *Management Education and Development*, 10 (3): 172–80.

Peters, Tom J. and Waterman, Robert H. (1982) *In Search of Excellence: Lessons from America's Best Run Companies*. London and New York: Harper and Row.

Porter, Lyman W. (1983) 'Teaching managerial competencies: an overview', *Exchange*, 8 (2): 8–9.

Porter, Lyman W. and McKibbin, Lawrence E. (1988) *Management Education and Development: Drift or Thrust into the 21st Century?* New York: McGraw-Hill.

Powers, E.A. (1983) 'The AMA management competency programs: a development process', *Exchange*, 8 (2): 16–20.

Raelin, Joe A. (1994) 'Whither management education: professional education, action learning and beyond', *Management Learning*, 25 (2): 301–18.

Reason, Peter and Rowan, John (1981) *Human Inquiry: A Sourcebook of New Paradigm Research*. London: Wiley.

Reynolds, Michael (1979) 'Experiential learning: a declining force for change', *Management Education and Development*, 10 (2): 89–99.

Shotter, John (1993) *Cultural Politics of Everyday Life*. Buckingham: Open University Press.

Tanton, Morgan and Easterby-Smith, Mark (1989) 'Management development: is the western model inevitable?', in Julia Davies, Mark Easterby-Smith, Sarah Mann and Morgan Tanton (eds), *The Challenge to Western Management Development*. London. Routledge.

Taylor, Jim (1994) 'Measuring research performance in business and management studies in the United Kingdom: the 1992 research assessment exercise', *British Journal of Management*, 5 (4): 275–88.

Thorpe, Richard and Best, Ardha (1989) 'A study into early learning of participants in employment training in the South Yorkshire area', unpublished research report, Manchester Polytechnic, Manchester.

Thorpe, Richard and Holman, David (1993) 'MCI management competencies: observable, measurable, generalisable and universal, but still flawed', paper presented to the British Academy of Management Conference, Bath University, Bath.

Weil, Susan (1992), 'Creating capability for change in higher education: the RSA Initiative', in R. Barnett (ed.), *Learning to Effect*. Buckingham: Open University Press.

Willmott, Hugh (1994) 'Management education: provocations to a debate', *Management Learning*, 25 (1): 105–36.

3

The Arena Thesis: Management Development as a Pluralistic Meeting Point

John Burgoyne and Brad Jackson

Many conventional explanations of learning activities within organizations assume a unitarist perspective. That is, they assume that at a theoretical or practical level, any particular learning activity can or should be tied to a specific purpose. However, as is discussed in Chapter 1 by Stephen Fox and Chapter 6 by Ian Cunningham and Graham Dawes, management learning is a considerably more complex, uncertain and multi-faceted process. While the predominately unitary perspective has enabled researchers and practitioners to make some progress in advancing management learning, for example the articulation of learning theories shaping interventions (Burgoyne and Stuart, 1977), it has ultimately limited our efforts to make a real and full contribution to management theory and practice for several related reasons.

First, a unitary perspective oversimplifies the process of management learning and excludes critical elements in that process. Consequently, organizations have become overly preoccupied with the behavioural aspects of management, devoting considerable energy to develop rigorous competency measures while important cognitive and symbolic elements are left ignored. Secondly, with this incomplete conception, the unitarist perspective has proven to be ultimately impractical. Too many management development initiatives have foundered because they have addressed the wrong issues based on some idealized rational analysis of what 'should' be going on, rather than the complexities affecting the people involved. Thirdly, unitarism ignores the political dimension of organizations. If individuals are genuinely concerned with making management learning central to the organization's ongoing success, they need to better understand its political dynamics and with that understanding, incorporate political dynamics into the implementation of organized management learning initiatives. The 'arena thesis' presents an alternative pluralist conception of management learning designed to expose the weaknesses of the prevailing unitarist paradigm as well as present a viable alternative which can guide both theory and practice in the field.

This chapter is organized into five sections. In the opening section, we draw on the work of institutional theorists to describe how management learning has become a progressively institutionalized field that is dominated by a unitarist perspective. The second section provides the context for the arena thesis by looking briefly at the origins of the pluralist perspective from which the thesis has been developed. The pluralist perspective will be compared to two other competing perspectives within organizational theory – the traditional unitary perspective and the considerably less mainstream radical perspective. In the third section we describe the arena thesis, outlining the principal terms and concepts and indicating how the thesis may help our understanding and practice of management learning. The fourth section elaborates upon some specific processes and techniques for opening up and revitalizing the arena of management learning within particular organizations. In the final section we consider the implications that the arena thesis has for theory and practice. We will lay out an agenda for further research that will take the arena thesis from its current embryonic state to a more fully realized, and ultimately, more useful and insightful form.

The Institutionalization of Management Learning

In the past decade, the study of institutions has experienced something of a renaissance. The 'new institutionalism', as it is frequently referred to, has been created by a loose collection of American organizational theorists in reaction to the sustained supremacy of behavioural over cognitive processes and functionalist over individualist perspectives in organizational theory (Powell and DiMaggio, 1991). Institutional theory is concerned with the forces of institutionalization found outside the organization and the internal processes of institutionalization. Writers in this field distinguish the 'technical' from the 'institutional' organizational environment. The former consists of the instrumental elements of production and exchange of goods and services that are the traditional concern of organizational theorists. The latter is characterized by the elaboration of rules and regulations unrelated to the technical and instrumental efficacy of the organization (Meyer et al., 1983).

While the term 'institutional' has perhaps been over-zealously applied to a seemingly indiscriminate collection of organizational phenomena, Zucker identifies two defining elements that are shared: '(a) a rule-like, social fact quality of an organized pattern of action (exterior), and (b) an embedding in formal structures, such as formal aspects of organizations that are not tied to particular actors or situations (nonpersonal/objective)' (Zucker, 1987: 444).

The starting point for new institutionalism is to flip the conventional concern with organizational difference and variation on its head by raising the intriguing yet rarely asked question of why so much empirical work suggests that practices and arrangements within organizations are remarkably similar? Two of the leading figures in this field, Meyer and Rowan (1983), have suggested that one of the major reasons for this state of affairs

is that organizations are driven to incorporate practices and procedures that
are defined by the prevailing rationalized concepts of organizational work
and institutionalized in society. The quest for legitimacy with external and
internal stakeholders encourages managers to adopt practices and procedures
which may have limited or, in some cases, negative instrumental efficacy in
the short term but, in gaining the confidence of these stakeholders, might
improve the organization's long-term survival prospects. The net result of
this process of institutionalization is that 'formal structures of many organizations in post-industrial society dramatically reflect the myths of their
institutional environments instead of the demands of their work activities'
(Meyer and Rowan, 1983: 340). The 'myths' that generate formal and
organizational structure have two key properties. First, they tend to be
rationalized and impersonal prescriptions that identify various social purposes as technical ones. Secondly, because they are highly institutionalized
they are considered to be 'taken-for-granted' or 'objectified' and, therefore,
well beyond the discretion of any individual participant or organization
(Berger and Luckmann, 1991).

Institutional theory has been applied in a number of institutional settings
such as schools and hospitals (Meyer et al., 1983), as well as numerous
institutional fields such as personnel administration (Baron et al., 1986),
standards-making (Olshan, 1993) and computerization (Prasad and Prasad,
1994). Of particular relevance to this chapter are two studies that have
looked at corporate training programmes from an institutional perspective.
Specifically, these studies were interested in the prevalence and uniformity
of corporate training programmes in all sectors of industry, as well as the
recent broadening of scope of these programmes to include personal growth
and self-management programmes in addition to the traditional technical and
human relations training. Previous approaches to analysing the role of
training in the organization have tended to focus upon its contributions to
productivity, human capital, organizational socialization and the promotion
of organizational change and development.

In a study of training programmes that was conducted in a single, urban
county in northern California, Monahan, Meyer and Scott found that the
efficacy of training tended to be taken on faith and was, in effect, a 'set of
legitimated ideas with virtues that are taken for granted' (1994: 263).
Moreover, the training programmes that were implemented were not
typically created in a specific organization but were taken from a favourable
institutional environment. Organizations adopted institutional training
packages that were, echoing the words of Selznick (1957), a pioneer in
institutional research, 'infused with value' from far beyond the local
situation they were studying. Scott and Meyer (1994) argue that the
institutionalization of training is part of a much broader and considerably
more established institution of instruction which connotes a widely accepted
set of arrangements, norms and assumptions about how to facilitate learning
(i.e., one person showing another or others how to do something). They
conclude that, 'contrary to the notion that corporate training operates in a

manner quite distinctive to instruction in more conventional educational settings' (Scott and Meyer, 1994: 240), training programmes continue to 'reflect the continuing influence and power of the institutional beliefs and patterns associated with the traditional educational sector' (ibid.: 252).

How have training programmes become so isomorphic? DiMaggio and Powell (1991) have identified three mechanisms through which institutional isomorphic change occurs. First, organizations are subjected to 'coercive pressures' from other organizations upon which they are dependent, such as the state, customers, suppliers and regulatory bodies. In the case of training, this would include government funding or tax breaks for certain forms of training and health and safety legislation that requires certain forms of training to be carried out.

A second mechanism producing isomorphism which is particularly relevant to management learning is 'mimetic process', through which organizations seek to enhance their legitimacy by modelling themselves on other organizations that are perceived to be successful and innovative. The past decade has witnessed corporate North America being gripped on a grand scale by a rapid succession of organizational improvement techniques such as total quality management, business process re-engineering and the learning organization (Gill and Whittle, 1993; Huczynski, 1993; Jackson, 1996). These techniques, more commonly referred to as 'fads', 'flavours of the month' and 'magic bullets', have brought in their wake rafts of institutionally sanctioned training programmes designed to spread the word throughout the organization.

The third isomorphic mechanism is a collection of 'normative pressures' that are exerted by the increased professionalization of the workplace. Formal education plays an important role in legitimating the cognitive base of training. As individuals move into the workplace, this cognitive base is further institutionalized through professional networks such as the American Society for Training and Development, and the Institute of Personnel and Development (in the UK). Human resource development and training professionals legitimize their status within their field and their organizations by demonstrating that they are *au courant* with the latest technologies and developments within the training field.

The institutional perspective challenges our thinking not just about the efficacy of training, but also management learning. A considerable portion of management learning activities, particularly those which fall under the 'organized' category described in Chapter 6 of this volume, currently take place under the general rubric of training programmes. In many organizations the distinction between the two fields is not made either because it is not recognized or not deemed significant. Institutional theory provides a valuable theoretical framework for understanding why the unitarist perspective has been institutionalized within the management learning field. While the unitarist nature of our management learning activities are overtly tied to advancing the organization's instrumental and technical objectives, in reality it has as much, if not more, to do with helping the organization achieve the far more critical goal of institutional legitimacy. The problem with institutionalism is that, although the organization may achieve its highly prized legitimacy, it ultimately promotes widespread mediocrity and mimicry in its management practice. Local initiative and ingenuity that is far more closely attuned to the organization's immediate environment and considerably more efficacious is quashed in favour of practices that have been developed 'out there'. Unfortunately, the new institutional theory only hints at what needs to be done to reverse the process. For example, DiMaggio and Powell suggest that:

> A theory of institutional isomorphism may help to explain the observations that organizations are becoming more homogeneous and that elites often get their way, while at the same time enabling us to understand the irrationality, the frustration of power, and lack of innovation that are so commonplace in organizational life. (1991: 79)

Along the same lines, DiMaggio (1988) has asserted the potential for individual action within institutionalized environments with his discussion of the role of 'institutional entrepreneurs' in drawing on personal resources to disrupt old institutions and initiate new ones. Institutional entrepreneurs recognize that institutionalism is essentially a taken-for-granted political process in which certain groups of actors from within and beyond the organization can exert power over others without having to confront them overtly. The key to reverse institutionalization, therefore, is to find ways to make this political process more explicit and more inclusive. The next section will explore political models of organization that aim to do just this.

Pluralist Models of Organization

The idea that organizations are political systems in which individuals and sub-groups vie for power has long been recognized by organizational theorists (e.g., Dalton, 1959; Cyert and March, 1963). Most organizational theorists have, however, endeavoured to treat organizational politics as a supplement or complement to traditional lines of work on organizations. Organizational politics thus remains a relatively neglected and somewhat marginal field. As Lawler and Bacharach observe, 'efforts to clearly distinguish political from non-political spheres and to interweave the political with existing foci have implicitly retained the connotation that "politics" in organizations is limited, irrational, unfair or illegitimate' (Lawler and Bacharach, 1983: 84).

In the absence of a well-developed theory of organizational politics, Morgan (1986) likens the organization to a political system, within which the organization can be understood as mini-states where the relationship between the individual and society is paralleled by the relationship between the individual and organization. In making this parallel, he identifies three frames of reference (as shown in Table 3.1) that have been developed to

Table 3.1   *Summary of the three political models of organization*

	Unitarist	Radical	Pluralist
Interests	Common organizational objectives.	Contradictory 'class' interests.	Diversity of individual and group interests.
Conflict	Rare and transient. Can be removed through appropriate managerial action.	Inevitable part of wider class conflict.	Inherent and ineradicable but potentially positive.
Power	Largely ignored in favour of concepts such as authority, leadership and control.	Unequally distributed. Part of power relations of society at large.	Crucially variable – plurality of power-holders drawing power from a plurality of sources.
Role of management learning	Serves organization's instrumental goals.	Maintains status quo by reproducing social relations.	Serves plurality of goals for individuals, groups and the organization.
Organizing metaphor	Parade	Battleground	Arena

Source: Adapted from Morgan, G. (1986) *Images of Organization*. Newbury Park, CA: Sage. pp. 188–9

analyse politics at the society-wide level and applies them to the organization. These frames of reference can serve as both analytical tools and as 'organizational ideologies' that can be used by managers to shape the character of their organization. The 'unitary' frame of reference sees society as an integrated whole where the interests of individuals and society are ultimately synonymous. The state is sovereign and individuals subordinate themselves to serve the state and, in the process, satisfy their own true interests and the common good. Applied to the organization, the unitarist perspective focuses on the achievement of common objectives for the organization. Conflict tends to be rare, temporary and viewed as the product of marginal or rebellious elements who are not 'properly playing the game' but can be handled by appropriate managerial action. This perspective predominates in traditional organizational theory, which portrays organizations as being naturally co-operative systems and largely ignores the role of power in organizational life, in favour of concepts such as authority, leadership and control.

At the other end of the political spectrum, Morgan describes the 'radical' frame of reference which, being influenced by a Marxist perspective, 'views society as comprising [*sic*] antagonistic class interests, characterised by deep-rooted social and political cleavages held together as much by coercion as by consent' (Morgan, 1986: 186). The organization is portrayed as a particular kind of institutional venue in which the class struggle is played out and in which conflict is an inevitable part of a much wider class conflict that can only be suppressed, not productively channelled. In contrast to the unitarist perspective, power is a key feature of organization which is a reflection of the uneven power relations in the wider society.

The term 'pluralism' is used in political science to characterize idealized kinds of liberal democracy where potentially authoritarian tendencies are held in check by the free interplay of interest groups that have a stake in government (Bullock and Stallybrass, 1977). The 'plural society' which develops is contrasted with a society that is dominated by a single elite and within which no such competition is free to develop. The 'pluralist' frame of reference within organizations emphasizes the diversity of individuals and group interests in the organization. The organization is seen as a kind of loose coalition which has only a passing interest in the formal goals of the organization. Like the radical perspective, conflict is viewed as being an inevitable fact of life, but differs in that it is viewed as being something that can have potentially positive aspects which, if properly handled, can be functional to both the individual and organization. Power is the crucial medium through which conflicts of interest are alleviated and resolved.

If we were to think of a metaphor that might aptly capture the essence of each frame of reference, the unitarist organization might best be characterized as a 'parade' of individuals who are marching purposely forward in step in one direction to the same tune. The organization from the radical perspective, on the other hand, might best be seen as Burrell and Morgan (1979) suggest, as a 'battlefield' where rival forces such as management and trade unions strive to achieve ends which are ultimately incompatible. Pluralism's basic willingness to acknowledge that, while difference is inevitable, conflict is inherently not, can perhaps best be metaphorically illustrated by the 'carnival'. Within the carnival, a dazzling array of seemingly unrelated activities are being simultaneously undertaken by individuals and groups with diverse agendas seeking to satisfy diverse needs and desires. This frenzied activity, however, invariably takes place with more synergy than conflict, and with a dynamic complexity that is beyond the intelligence of any single agent to understand. The organizational context within which this carnivalesque activity is played out might best be metaphorically described as an 'arena'. *The Concise Oxford Dictionary* defines the word 'arena' as being a 'central part of an amphitheatre, in which combats take place; a scene of action, sphere of action'. The critical element of this definition is the word 'action', in particular, a specific type of purposive action that is undertaken by actors within a formalized social context.

Max Weber portrayed organizations as arenas of political struggle in which sub-groups with incompatible interests based primarily on their power and status competed. The structure of organizations is a social control mechanism created by the calculative decisions of organizational actors (individuals or sub-groups) as a means to deal with continual conflict. In addition to structure, Weber (1947) identified authority that was legitimated on 'rational', 'traditional' or 'charismatic' grounds as the major means for controlling actors in the organization and, in the process, constraining the boundaries of conflict between interest groups.

Expanding upon Weber's conception of social action in organizations, Silverman (1970) has advanced an 'action frame of reference' for analysing organizations. The essential element in this approach is to view organizations as the outcome of interaction of motivated people who are attempting to resolve their own problems and pursue their own ends. Silverman is critical of traditional organizational analysis for exclusively trying to answer questions posed by those who control the operation of organizations, namely managers. Instead, he suggests that organizational structure and processes become less taken-for-granted and be more open to discussion to all interested parties, not just management. The environment for Silverman is a source of meanings for organizational members who are defining the situation in ways which allow them to defend their own actions and make sense of the actions of others. Some actions are given significance, others are not, but actions are entirely subjective – they have no other meaning than those given to them by actors. It is this action frame of reference which informs our conception of management learning as an arena for social action which we describe as the 'arena thesis'.

The Arena Thesis

The arena thesis is an alternative pluralist perspective that views management learning as a domain within which conflicting purposes and values within an organization meet to be reinforced, reconciled or proliferated. The arena concept, as it is to be used here, implies a number of important features. First, it is a place where differences 'meet', are fought over, and reconciled and reconfigured into new groupings, factions and alliances. Secondly, the arena is visible. Other parties can observe, and become aware of differences and their sources. Thirdly, it is accessible. Other observers can become participants as they become aware of issues they want to be involved in. Fourthly, the arena recognizes that the element of performativity, that individuals taking on 'roles' and 'scripts', is an inevitable and not always unfortunate quality of conflict identification and resolution. Fifthly, it acknowledges that the staging of such activities in terms of time and location can have an important bearing on its outcome.

Finally, and most contentiously, the arena can, to a degree, be managed. Management can serve to make the arena work by increasing the chances that important differences are aired and that opportunities for compromise and synergy are not lost where these can be better than win or lose. The 'management' of arena is, however, problematical, because it implies a unitary purpose, a structure which, by definition, enables some possibilities and disables others. Any treatment of a pluralistic situation has the strong potential to become an attempt to turn it back in to a unitarist one. With or without this tendency, however, any approach which at least acknowledged pluralism or purpose, with or without an agenda to depluralize it, may be welcomed.

Implicit in the arena thesis is the proposition that management learning activities, even when externally legitimized by the processes described in institution theory, serve this 'meeting point' function more than any other activity. Such an argument could, of course, be mounted for any organization activity: the design of an IT system, the formation of the product/service portfolio, even the formulation of a car-parking policy. Why might the 'arena' process be particularly located in management learning activities? The theoretical argument is that management learning activities, as that set of human resource 'management' practices that reflexively turns on management itself, is continuously the locus for dealing with the essential ambiguities of the employment contract for managers. It is this special feature which, Townley (1993) argues, gives HRM its distinctive dynamics. Management learning is the arena in which the diverse desires and interests of managers confront any current dominant unitarist rationale for organizational activity.

More empirically, management learning activities are the locus in which non-standard thoughts are given some legitimacy. It is common practice for discussions in management learning events to be defined as 'brainstorming' – talking openly and confidentially, exploring the personal as well as the professional, values as well as technical issues. This is arguably a manifestation of the above argument, that the ambiguity of the employment contract – what people want and what they are formally constrained to do – has to be dealt with somewhere. It is this that gives management learning activities their special quality. They live in the continual tension between being the space for the emancipatory process of giving divergent views a voice and exposing 'deviant' thoughts to surveillance, monitoring and control in the way that Foucault (1980) suggests. The management learning arena lives, arguably, in continual tension between being the place in which organizational revolutions of thought and practice can be formulated between people and the space in which incipient revolution can be spotted and suppressed by dominant coalitions supporting current unitarist agendas.

To help clarify how the arena thesis is played out, we have taken a hypothetical management development activity, such as a new competency-based leadership programme, and shown in Table 3.2 how the 'same' management development activity can either be supported or blocked by different interested parties for very different reasons. The rationales that are provided in Table 3.2 are by no means complete, but they are typical of the explicit and implicit rationales that we have come across in our work with organizations. The constituency of the parties varies according to the particular initiative that is presented. The constituencies presented in the table reflect classic hierarchically defined stakeholders. Constituencies are essentially political alignments of individuals who coalesce around a particular issue or group of issues. Some of the rationales portrayed in Table 3.2 converge between the different parties, whereas others are divergent. Differ-

Table 3.2   *Comparison of organizational stakeholders' rationales for supporting or blocking a management learning initiative*

Stakeholder	Rationale for supporting	Rationale for blocking
Participants	Personal development; recognition of importance to the organization; reward; improved marketability; break from routine.	Waste of time and money; denies possibility of preferred alternative activity; reluctant to take on new responsibilities implied by the activity.
Subordinates	Recognition of importance of their unit to organization; demonstrates commitment to education; improved supervision.	Waste of time and money; wrong activity prescribed; resistance to change; not there to supervise.
Peers	Recognition that perhaps they too will be given opportunity to participate in a programme; solves performance problem.	Waste of time and money; wrong activity prescribed; stops them from participating; creates workload problems.
Line managers	Short-term skilling; performance problem solution; reward and incentive; measure of commitment by organization to their department.	Waste of time and money; wrong activity prescribed; organization out of touch with reality; creates line problems.
Human resource professionals	Opportunity to demonstrate contribution to organization's effectiveness; professional knowledge; strengthens political ties within organization.	By-passed in decision-making process; prevents possibility of implementing desired alternative; weakens political position within the organization.
Senior managers	Mechanism to convey a message (e.g., commitment to quality or mission); demonstrating action to other stakeholders; improved financial performance.	No obvious link to the bottom line; runs contrary to message; doesn't adequately convey action to other stakeholders.
Boards or other overseers	Concrete means to demonstrate support for employees; communicate messages throughout organization; improved financial performance.	Only contributes to bloated overhead; doesn't adequately demonstrate action to other stakeholders; may be disruptive.
External consultants	Financial opportunity; builds customer base; potential for further opportunities within organization.	Inadequate financial opportunity; will not build customer base; no potential further opportunities; failure undermines credibility.
Government funding agencies	Demonstrates action in support of management development policy.	Initiative not visible enough; may attract negative publicity.
Academic researcher	Potential to advance knowledge about management learning.	Doesn't generate significant new knowledge of management learning.

ing rationales are not necessarily divergent in their action or behavioural implications. Different factions can support the same action for entirely different reasons. Support for a particular initiative can be garnered from a plurality of purposes and, therefore, does not have to conform to the same unitarist definition of its purpose.

The arena thesis portrays management learning as an arena in which these different purposes, values and agendas meet, are fought over and are reconciled. Our hypothetical example highlights how the planning and setting up of a formal management development programme, particularly in negotiating the programme's legitimacy with its multiple stakeholders, is in itself a kind of organizational development work in which internal conflicts and differences can be dealt with developmentally or destructively. Frequently, the latter is the case. Organizations are littered with the remnants of past organizational improvement initiatives that have come unstuck not because they were technically unsound or inappropriate to the organization's context, but because they were not formulated to win support among the diverse stakeholders in the arena of management learning. Such an approach emphasizes the political nature of management development work and the political skills involved in carrying it out. It is somewhat ironic and problematic, therefore, to find that many human resource management and organizational development education programmes tend to be preoccupied with the techniques of management development and organizational change and not the political dimension (Kakabadse and Parker, 1984). If formal educational programmes are genuinely interested in fostering institutional entrepreneurship in the management learning field, they need to inculcate sensitivity to the political environment and instil the appropriate political skills to work effectively within the arena.

Legitimacy is a concept of recurring importance within this chapter. Within new institutionalism, organizational legitimacy is a set of constitutive beliefs that are the primary driver for institutional processes. Within Weber's notion of social action, legitimacy is the major means of controlling actors in the organization and constraining conflict between interest groups. Legitimacy is also central to the arena thesis. Unfortunately, in common with many widely used and discussed concepts, legitimacy is not well defined. In an attempt to gain some clarity around the term, Suchman offers a broad but helpful definition of legitimacy as 'a generalised perception or assumption that the actions of an entity are desirable, proper, appropriate within some socially constructed system of norms, values, beliefs and definitions' (Suchman, 1995: 574). He distinguishes three types of organizational legitimacy: 'pragmatic', which rests on the self-interested calculations of an organization's most immediate audiences; 'moral', which rests not on what will benefit the constituent but what is seen to be the 'right thing to do'; and 'cognitive' legitimacy which is based on what the constituent understands rather than what it will gain or believes to be right. Pragmatic legitimacy is the peculiarly Machiavellian brand of legitimacy that is most widely recognized and practised, yet also widely abhorred. However, Suchman notes that, 'as one moves from the pragmatic to the moral to the cognitive, legitimacy becomes more subtle, more profound' (ibid: 585). Cognitive legitimacy is achieved with great difficulty when a particular entity is widely understood and taken-for-granted, or institutionalized. This has important implications for management learning researchers and practitioners who work primarily with the cognitive realm of the organization.

In common with institutional researchers, Suchman is critical of strategic researchers such as Pfeffer (1981) and Pfeffer and Salancik (1978) who have tended to depict legitimacy as an 'operational resource' that can be controlled by managers for instrumental purposes. However, unlike the institutional researchers, Suchman suggests that managers can do something about legitimacy but are constrained by the cultural environments within which they work, pointing out that 'managers do enunciate supportive myths and prescribe culturally congruent rituals; however, managers rarely convince others to believe much that the managers do not believe themselves' (Suchman, 1995: 577). The disastrous effects of this tendency have been graphically demonstrated in organizations where non-believing line managers are coerced into implementing centrally sanctioned organization-wide improvement techniques that have ultimately come to grief as a result.

Given the centrality of legitimation in preserving and institutionalizing organizational practices and beliefs, the critical task within the arena of management learning will be to find ways to persuade organizational actors to identify, discuss and constructively question the appropriateness of these prevailing legitimized structures. Those structures that do not withstand the scrutiny of multi-stakeholders should be de-legitimized and replaced by alternative structures, recognizing that these too have to become legitimized if they are to receive widespread support and commitment. The irony is certainly not lost on us that all of this will be for nought if the instigators fail to legitimize the arena as a viable and relevant entity in its own right! While this chapter has somewhat predictably focused on the cognitive legitimacy of the arena thesis, both moral and pragmatic legitimation strategies will also need to be developed if the thesis is to become an organizational reality. The following section will examine some guiding principles and techniques for doing that.

Implications for Practice: Protecting and Facilitating Dialogue within the Arena

The distinction was made in the introduction between normative, descriptive, analytical and critical theories. While normative and critical theories are in one sense at the different ends of this spectrum, from 'base practice' to 'high theory', they are also similar, and differ from descriptive and interpretative theory in that they deal overtly with ethical, evaluative issues of what can be judged to be right. Descriptive and interpretative theory, on the other hand, tends to be presented as more neutral, even though critical interpretations will reveal implicit normative assumptions in them. Normative theories may simply follow unquestioned assumptions of their own, or the values of the performative power structure in which they operate. On the other hand, normative theories can potentially also be critical, with an orientation similar to that proposed by Willmott (1994) for 'critical action learning'. Critical normative theory would both commit to action on the basis of an existential choice of the best available option, but also be available for continuous critical reflection on the possibility that the choice might be 'wrong', on either value/ethical or instrumental grounds, and hence subject to alteration and revision.

Such thinking suggests an extension of Argyris and Schön's (1974) well-known argument for the 'reflective practitioner' into a suggestion of the three possibilities discussed in the introduction: the unreflective or pragmatic practitioner who reflects relatively little; the reflective practitioner who attempts to understand his or her practice at the level of descriptive and interpretative theory; and the critical reflective practitioner who would reflect additionally on the very criteria by which any action can be judged as 'working', recognizing the moral and ethical choice involved. Against this background it can be reflected that the arena thesis itself has strong emancipatory undertones. It implies the opening up of organizational processes to minority or low-power voices, but within an understanding of the power dynamics concerned. From this perspective a number of practical propositions can be put forward, deliberately expressed in normative terms with critical qualifications:

1   Management learning practitioners should reframe and renegotiate their understanding of their work from providing a technical HRD function for managers to creating, protecting and operating the 'arena' as a space for exploring and building on difference.

2   Processes that tend to be seen as the necessary but wasteful and time-consuming preliminaries to management learning activities, like lobbying for support for programmes, should be seen as part of the *important* work, since the very process of negotiating the acceptable conditions for a programme is part of the 'arena' process.

3   The general purpose of creating and protecting 'arenas', that is to say, any setting, event or process that allows ideas to be explored and shared between people and interest groups, can be seen as a general purpose worth pursuing.

4   Apply the theory and practice of dialogue (Blantern and Belcher, 1994) in terms of facilitating processes directed at the creation, questioning and development of joint meanings in organizations.

5   Within this, particularly pursue the facilitation of meta-dialogue (Burgoyne, 1995), the aim of which is to explore the epistemological, ontological and ideological underpinning of substantive beliefs as a possible aid to learning constructively from substantive differences of view.

Implications for Theory

The underlying theoretical orientation of the arena thesis is that organizations are, and are part of, multi-stakeholder situations, to be understood in terms of stakeholder analysis (Burgoyne, 1994) as arrangements based on continually reformulating joint understandings created by dialogue that represent an evolving set of operating agreements between stakeholders. Such a process sets up a mutual learning process between the collective and the parts which constitute the definition of a learning company (Pedler et al., 1996).

Management learning is a major arena for this process, and this is because, as Townley (1993) argues, it is the organizational activity that centrally addresses the indeterminacy of the arrangements between the collective entity of the organization and those – the managers – who most centrally create it. Institutional theory offers an explanation of why organizations none the less tend to adopt management learning practices that are unitarist in their rhetoric and attempted practices, which arguably prevents them making the kind of contribution to organizational development that the above analysis implies they should.

This formulation makes sense as far as it goes, but does not go so far as to address the issue of how the differing desires between stakeholders are constructed in the first place, though it can be inferred that they are both transferred and moderated in the interactions between people in organizational settings. Further understanding of the origination or formulation of desires as they come to bear in organizational settings is one of the theoretical frontiers of this approach. Similarly, advocating the usefulness of dialogue and its attendant concern with power within the organizational arena brings to the fore the debate between the possibility of the ideal emancipatory knowledge community as articulated by Habermas (1987) and the critique that this is not possible due to the embeddedness of power in language (Foucault, 1980). A fuller development of the arena thesis requires a resolution of this issue, probably along the lines suggested by Foucault, that it may be possible to find conditions within which the use of power can be morally and ethically defined as positive.

Summary

We began this chapter by arguing that the field of management learning had, through the process of institutionalization, become dominated by a unitarist perspective. In the quest for legitimacy from both their external and internal stakeholders, many organizations have sought to constrain their management learning activities so that they conform with institutional norms and do not stand apart from activities conducted by their competitors within their institutional field. The net result has been a field that has become homogeneous, mediocre and under-realized. In an effort to counter these isomorphic (standardizing) tendencies, we have put forward a metaphorically based alternative which we dub the 'arena thesis'.

The arena thesis suggests that management learning should be analysed from a pluralist perspective that emphasizes the diversity of frequently conflicting interests and stakeholders within the organization. It also recognizes that management learning can serve as an excellent arena within which these conflicting purposes and values can meet to be reinforced, reconciled or proliferated. To facilitate this process, whoever takes the initiative to activate the arena within their organization, be they managers or learning professionals, they must learn to hone their own political sensitivity and be especially attuned to the complex legitimizing dynamics that prevail within their organizations. Some of these skills and techniques for opening dialogue have been reviewed in this chapter. The arena thesis is, however, just a thesis. It is a proposition that, while having potentially appealing face value, will need to be put to the test through a systematic programme of action-based research if it is to have any significant and lasting impact on the theory and practice of management learning.

Annotated Bibliography

G. Morgan (1986) *Images of Organization*. Newbury Park, CA: Sage, offers a superb overview of organizational theory that adopts a novel metaphorical approach to organize the literature. It is eminently readable and a classic resource. M. Pedler, J. Burgoyne and T. Boydell (1996) *The Learning Company* (2nd edn). London: McGraw-Hill, is a refreshing collection of ideas and techniques for stimulating management learning within an 'arena thesis' context and is a welcome practical alternative to Peter Senge's *The Fifth Discipline* (London, Random House, 1990). W.R. Scott (1995) *Institutions and Organizations*. Thousand Oaks, CA: Sage, provides a concise yet comprehensive overview of the institutionalist approach to organizational theory. It also includes a review of empirical work that has been done with this approach as well as a synthesis of the critique of the approach.

References

Argyris, C. and Schön, D.A. (1974) *Theory in Practice: Increasing Professional Effectiveness*. San Francisco: Jossey-Bass.

Baron, J.N., Dobbin, F.R. and Jennings, P.D. (1986) 'War and peace: the evolution of modern personnel administration in US industry', *American Journal of Sociology*, 92: 350–83.

Berger, P.L. and Luckmann, T. (1991) *The Social Construction of Reality*. Harmondsworth: Penguin.

Blantern, C. and Belcher, J. (1994) 'Participation in the learning company', in J.G. Burgogne, M. Pedlar and T. Boydell (eds), *Towards the Learning Company: Concepts and Practices*. Maidenhead: McGraw-Hill.

Bullock, A. and Stallybrass, O. (eds) (1977) *The Fontana Dictionary of Modern Thought*. London: Fontana.

Burgoyne, J.G. (1994) 'Stakeholder analysis', in C. Cassell and G. Symon (eds), *Qualitative Methods in Organizational and Occupational Psychology*. London: Sage. pp. 187–207.

Burgoyne, J.G. (1995) 'Learning from experience: from individual discovery to meta-dialogue via the evolution of transitional myths', *Personnel Review*, 24 (6): 62–73.

Burgoyne, J.G. and Stuart, R. (1977) 'Implicit learning theories as determinants of the effects of management development,' *Personnel Review*, 6 (2): 514.

Burrell, G. and Morgan, G. (1979) *Sociological Paradigms and Organizational Analysis*. London: Heinemann Educational Books.

Cyert, R.M. and March, J.G. (1963) *A Behavioural Theory of the Firm*. New York: Wiley.

Dalton, H. (1959) *Men Who Manage*. New York: Wiley.

DiMaggio, P.J. (1988) 'Interest and agency in institutional theory', in L.G. Zuker (ed.), *Institutional Patterns and Organizations*. Cambridge, MA: Ballinger. pp. 3–22.

DiMaggio, P.J. and Powell, W.W. (1991) 'The iron cage revisited: institutional isomorphism and collective rationality in organizational fields', *American Sociological Review*, 48: 147–60.

Foucault, M. (1980) *Power/Knowledge: Selected Interviews and Other Writings 1972–7* (edited by C. Gordon). London: Harvester Press.

Gill, J. and Whittle, S. (1993) 'Management by panacea: accounting for transience', *Journal of Management Studies*, 30 (2): 281–95.

Habermas, J. (1984/87) *Theory of Communicative Action* (volumes I and II). Cambridge: Polity Press.

Huczynski, A.A. (1993) 'Explaining the succession of management fads', *International Journal of Human Resource Management*, 4 (2): 443–63.

Jackson, B.G. (1996) 'Reengineering the sense of self: the manager and the management guru', *Journal of Management Studies*, 33 (5): 571–90.

Kakabadse, A. and Parker, C. (1984) 'The undiscovered dimension of management education: politics in organizations', in C. Cox and J. Beck (eds), *Management Development: Advances in Practice and Theory*. London: John Wiley. pp. 19–40.

Lawler, E.J. and Bacharach, S.B. (1983) 'Political alignments in organizations', in S.B. Bacharach (ed.), *Research in the Sociology of Organizations*. Greenwich, CT: JAI Press. pp. 83–108.

Meyer, J.W. and Rowan, B. (1983) 'Institutionalized organizations: formal structure as myth and ceremony', *American Journal of Sociology*, 83: 340–63.

Meyer, J.W., Scott, W.R. and Deal, T.F. (1983) 'Institutional and technical sources of organizational structure: explaining the structure of educational organizations', in J.W. Meyer and W.R. Scott (eds), *Organizational Environments: Ritual and Rationality*. Beverly Hills, CA: Sage. pp. 45–67.

Monahan, S.C., Meyer, J.W. and Scott, W.R. (1994) 'Employee training: the expansion of organizational citizenship', in W.R. Scott and J.W. Meyer (eds), *Institutional Environments and Organizations: Structural Complexity and Individualism*. Thousand Oaks, CA: Sage. pp. 255–71.

Morgan, G. (1986) *Images of Organization*. Newbury Park, CA: Sage.

Olshan, M.A., (1993) 'Standards-making organizations and the rationalization of American life', *The Sociological Quarterly*, 34: 319–35.

Pedler, M., Burgoyne, J.G. and Boydell, T. (1996) *The Learning Company* (2nd edn). Maidenhead: McGraw-Hill.

Pfeffer, J. (1981) 'Management as symbolic action: the creation and maintenance of organizational paradigms,' in L.L. Cummings and B.M. Staw (eds), *Research in Organizational Behaviour*. Greenwich, CT: JAI Press. pp. 1–52.

Pfeffer, J. and Salancik, G. (1978) *The External Control of Organizations: A Resource Dependence Perspective*. New York: Harper and Row.

Powell, W.W. and DiMaggio, P.J. (1991) *The New Institutionalism in Organizational Analysis*. Chicago: University of Chicago Press.

Prasad, P. and Prasad, A. (1994) 'The ideology of professionalism and work computerisation: an institutionalist study of technological change', *Human Relations*, 47 (12): 1433–58.

Scott, W.R. and Meyer, J.W. (1994) 'The rise of training programs in firms and agencies', in W.R. Scott and J.W. Meyer (eds), *Institutional Environments and Organizations: Structural Complexity and Individualism*. Thousand Oaks, CA: Sage. pp. 228–54.

Selznick, P. (1957) *Leadership in Administration*. New York: Harper and Row.

Silverman, D. (1970) *The Theory of Organizations*. London: Heinemann.

Suchman, M.C. (1995) 'Managing legitimacy: strategies and institutional approaches', *Academy of Management Review*, 20 (3): 571–610.

Townley, B. (1993) 'Foucault, power/knowledge and its relevance for human resource management', *Academy of Management Review*, 18 (3): 518–45.

Weber, M. (1947) *The Theory of Social and Economic Organization*. Glencoe, IL: Free Press.

Willmott, H. (1994) 'Management education: provocations to a debate', *Management Learning*, 25 (1): 105–36.

Zucker, L.G. (1987) 'Institutional theories of organization', *Annual Review of Sociology*, 13: 443–64.

4

Process Philosophy and Management Learning: Cultivating 'Foresight' in Management Education

Robert Chia

To philosophise . . . is to invert the habitual direction of the work of thought.

(Bergson, 1913a: 59)

Philosophy is not a mere collection of noble sentiments. . . . Philosophy is at once general and concrete, critical and appreciative of direct intuition. . . . In philosophy, the fact, the theory, the alternatives, and the ideal are weighted together. Its gifts are insight and foresight, and a sense of the worth of life.

(Whitehead, 1933: 121)

Contemporary Western modes of thought are circumscribed by two great and competing pre-Socratic cosmologies or 'world-views', which provided and continue to provide the most general conceptual categories for organizing thought and directing human effort. Heraclitus, a native of Ephesus in ancient Greece, emphasized the primacy of a changeable and emergent world while Parmenides, his successor, insisted upon the permanent and unchangeable nature of reality. The history of Western thought, ever since Plato, has, therefore, been little more than a continuing series of footnote attempts at synthesizing these two great but apparently irreconcilable intellectual traditions. One emphasizes reality as inclusively processual, the other privileging a homeostatic and atomistic conception of reality. The legacy of the tensions generated by these two competing systems of thought manifests itself in the current plurality of intellectual priorities and preoccupations within the various academic disciplines, including the fields of management and management learning. Within these latter fields of study, the controversial issues continue to revolve around the *ontological* assumptions about the nature of managerial realities, the *epistemological* status of management knowledge, the *intellectual* priorities of management research and theorizing, and the *pedagogical* imperatives of management education. A careful and systematic working through of these core theoretical issues, linking them to their rich intellectual traditions, is required in order to formulate a coherent and definitive account of *management learning* as a respectable academic discipline in its own right.

In this chapter I argue that the primary aim of management learning as a process-oriented theoretical enquiry is that of the systematic cultivation of what Whitehead (1933) called managerial *foresight*. Such foresight entails the unique capacity to grasp instinctively the relevant features of social currents and to elicit generalizations from particulars as well as 'for seeing the divergent illustration of generalities in diverse circumstances' (Whitehead, 1933: 120). The journey towards attaining this managerial foresight begins with the reflexive unpicking of the deeply entrenched and hence dominant organizing *codes* and academic *grammar* framing mainstream management theory and hence circumscribing the managerial imperatives arising therefrom. In so doing it reveals to us how such restrictive organizing frames collectively conspire to create an interlocking web of conceptual constraints which surreptitiously work to delimit what is thinkable in management theory and practice. The scope for managerial ingenuity is thereby, unnecessarily, curtailed.

This process of conceptual *de-ossification* gives rise to a deeper intuitive grasping of the essential interconnectedness characterizing the life of things. It is this consequent perceptive awareness which Whitehead (1933) recognized to be the crucial feature of the 'Business Mind of the Future'. Thus, a two-stage pedagogical process involving de-ossification followed by the subsequent intuitive acquisition of managerial foresight is what distinguishes the efforts of management learning as a unique form of process-inspired theoretical enquiry.

As an alternative to the predominantly recipe-driven orientation in management education, management learning privileges a strategy of ceaselessly destructuring the dominant *regimes of signification* populating contemporary discourse on management, and through this process, of sensitizing us to the necessarily arbitary and relativistic nature of symbolic knowledge.[1] This heightened awareness enables us to reach deeper into the more primordial forms of intuitive knowing we have always possessed. In this way a more enduring understanding of the fundamental nature of organizing, managing and learning can be systematically grasped.

The Organization of Management Knowledge

Management theories are academic products produced within the context of socially legitimized public institutions which are themselves already effects of primary ordering processes. Management theories are therefore, first and foremost, socially 'managed' bodies of knowledge claims whose very constitution serve to reinforce the dominant modes of ordering they purport to reveal. As Cooper and Fox (1989) observed, such management discourses are organized around the very programmes and protocols which constitute the process of organizational management. Both the management of organization and the organization of managerial discourse mirror each other, replicating and reinforcing the wider system of dominant values and prevalent symbolic systems characterizing a particular socio-historical epoch. This reciprocal relationship has not always been readily acknowledged, nor has its consequences for management theorizing and education been adequately explored.

What characterizes the academic approach itself, however, is the consistently rigorous adherence to a certain set of conventionally established textual codes governing the organization and presentation of ideas, information, observations and conjectures in such a way as to render them academically acceptable by the relevant community of scholars. The detailed instructional guides which established management journals frequently specify as requirements to potential contributors is one example of how such pre-coding of academic output is achieved and sustained in the production of management knowledge. They reflect the continued dominance of a *scientistic* mentality governing the organization and presentation of ideas and experiences.

The term 'scientism' has been used to describe the still overpowering belief that science constitutes, by far, the most valuable part of human learning and accomplishment. Scientistic thinking pervades academic theorizing and consequently shapes and influences all forms of knowledge considered acceptable by the academic community. Such an implicit regulation of the process of knowledge-creation applies equally to the discipline of management and organization as it does to the natural and social sciences. It is, therefore, by no means accidental that an age of science has also developed into an age of rationality, organization, control and management. Organized thought provides the impetus for organized action, and the dominance of *scientism* as a legitimized organizing code for regulating the admissability of assertions has provided the grammatical template, taxonomy of expressions and systems of representation for the development of contemporary management studies (including both the functional version and its supposedly more critical variants).

Through the establishment and control of this approved academic grammar, the manner in which knowledge is created and legitimized becomes self-reinforcing. Academic respectability is thereby maintained by an academic fraternity sanctioning and promoting this style of presentation and representation. Formal knowledge about management is, in turn, circumscribed by the organizing codes determining the *management of knowledge* itself. Such codes and ordering practices are, however, underpinned by relatively unexamined ontological and epistemological assumptions which work to render particular modes of thought thinkable while others are systematically marginalized. It is a critical examination of these philosophical assumptions and their consequences for management learning, and hence management action, that provides the theoretical focus for this chapter.

'Being' and 'Becoming' Ontologies

Contemporary Western theorizing is dominated by a mindset which tacitly presupposes the necessary existence of enduring spatio-temporal, and physical, forms of order governing the presentation of reality. Thus, the Newtonian description of matter unproblematically assumes an atomistic conception of reality in which clear-cut, definite things are deemed to occupy clear-cut, definite places in space and time. This apparently un-problematical assumption of the 'simple location' of matter, as Whitehead (1985: 61) persuasively argued, was what enabled Newtonian science to develop as it did. By postulating the prior existence of discrete and isolatable entities in space-time, it allowed Newton to formulate his now famous Laws of Motion. The associated concept of *causality* became, therefore, a handy conceptual tool for relinking these (initially assumed) isolated entities so that their characteristics could be adequately accounted for in a coherent system of explanation. Moreover, according to this Newtonian view, the state of 'rest' is considered normal while movement is regarded as a straightforward transition from one stable state to another. In this way, change, flux and transformation are construed as epiphenomena of basic Newtonian entities rather than as fundamentally constitutive of the latter. This *being* ontology is what provides the metaphysical basis for the organization of modern thought and the perpetration of a system of classificatory taxonomies, hierarchies and categories which, in turn, serve as the institutionalized vocabulary for representing our experiences of reality. A *representationalist* epistomology thus ensues in which formal knowledge is deemed to be that which is produced by the rigorous application of the system of classifications on our phenomenal experiences in order to arrive at an accurate description of reality. It is this paradigm of thought that has dominated the natural and social sciences in general and management studies in particular.

However, the contrary belief that 'all things flow' and are in a continuous process of *becoming* remains one of the most enduring, albeit vague, generalizations which the unsystematized and barely analysed intuition of humankind has produced. It appeared as one of the first propositions of pre-Socratic Greek philosophy in the form of the writings of Heraclitus. Since then it has occasionally resurfaced as in the work of Leibniz and more recently in the philosophical explorations of Henri Bergson (1913a, 1913b) and Alfred North Whitehead (1929, 1938). Whitehead, for one, insists that if we are to go back to that ultimate pristine experience unwarped by the sophistication of theory, the 'flux of things is one ultimate generalization around which we must weave our philosophical system' (Whitehead, 1929: 240). Likewise, Bergson maintained that 'It is movement that we must accustom ourselves to look upon as the simplest and clearest, immobility being only the extreme limit of the slowing down of movement, a limit reached only perhaps in thought and never realised in nature' (Bergson, 1913a: 44). It is this resurrecting of the primacy of movement and process over static entities and permanence, and its radical consequences for our understanding of the process of managing, which provides the pedagogical agenda for management learning as an essentially process-oriented form of theoretical enquiry. The significance of this, however, can only be fully appreciated by first undertaking a systematic excavation of the rich intellectual traditions surrounding these two competing systems of thought.

Heraclitean and Parmenidean Cosmologies

To the ancient Ionian question 'Is reality One or Many?', our commonsense experiences tells us that reality is multiple, heterogeneous and ever changing. For one thing, it is made up of opposites like hot and cold, wet and dry, light and darkness, all of which point us to accepting the changeable nature of the reality we apprehend. However, the evidence of our senses is always corrected by the 'God of Reason', for reason shows us that in changing there are none the less enduring aspects in our phenomenal experiences. For Heraclitus, reality is both One *and* Many – a singular unifying implicate reality with multiple explicate manifestations. Only wisdom achieved through critical reflection allows us to comprehend the One residing in the Many: 'To those who are awake the world-order is one, common to all; but the sleeping turn aside each into a world of his own' (Heraclitus 5.34, in Mansley Robinson, 1968: 95). Reality, for Heraclitus, is constantly changing and in the process of *becoming*, and it is this becoming process which unifies the apparently 'Many' disparate appearances. Heraclitean cosmology, therefore, provided one of the earliest comprehensive syntheses for reconciling experience and reason, appearance and reality.

The unanimity of this approach was shattered by Heraclitus' successor Parmenides, a native of Elea in southern Italy. The arguments Parmenides offered and the conclusions he reached were so utterly at odds with the Heraclitean viewpoint that it initiated a complete break with the whole intellectual tradition. Parmenides' response to the Ionian question was uncompromising. For him it is true that what is is One, and true that the 'God of Reason' is what tells us so. But for Parmenides, reason tells us more than this; it tells us that if what is is One then it *cannot* also be Many. There is in fact only one true world which is immediate, permanent and indestructible. Observed manifestations of change are not just apparent but misleading and false since the 'God of Reason' shows that what is one cannot also be many.

> One way remains to be spoken: the way how it is . . . [reality] must exist fully or not at all. Nor will the force of conviction ever allow anything over and above itself to arise out of what is not; wherefore Justice does not loosen her fetters so as to allow it to come into being or pass away, but hold it fast. . . . *Thus coming into being is extinguished, and destruction unknown.* (Parmenides 6.10, in Mansley Robinson, 1968: 113; emphasis added)

By elevating reason over the senses and permanence over change, Parmenidean thought sanctioned the primacy of a permanent, static and unchanging version of reality over a transient and processual one.

Such a Parmenidean inspired *being* ontology has encouraged a subject–predicate form of thought elevating 'nouns', 'states' and 'homeostasis' over 'verbs', 'relations' and 'homeorrhesis' in the academic vocabulary. In contemporary academic theorizing, widespread adherence to a modified Parmenidean world-order (what is commonly called Greek atomism) generates an intellectual attitude which treats entities, states and events as primary while process, relationships and interactions are regarded as epiphenomena of an essentially permanent and atomistic reality. This relegation of process and movement to a secondary status, and the elevation of static states generates clear tensions in academic theorizing, particularly within the human sciences. It leads to an overreliance on a logic of dualism. Advocates of this latter mode of understanding, however, discover almost immediately, that the is/is not, either/or structure of thought thereby generated is woefully inadequate for accounting for the dynamic and changing character of the real. It is this appreciation of the limitations of representationalist epistemology which has led to the recent resurgence in interest in process metaphysics and epistemology (see, for instance, Rescher, 1996).

Process Philosophy and Epistemology

Process philosophy begins with the fundamental assertion that the actual world is a 'process and that that process is the becoming of actual entities' (Whitehead, 1929: 26). In contrast to the dominant *being* world-order, a Heraclitean *becoming* ontology emphasizes a revised cosmology in which how things come to be defines what they are. Primacy, in this instance, is accorded to the changeable and processual nature of reality. Whitehead, in *Process and Reality*, makes this point succinctly:

> . . . how an entity *becomes* constitutes *what* that actual entity *is*; so that the two descriptions of an actual entity are not independent. Its 'being' is constituted by its 'becoming'. This is the principle of process. (1929: 28; original emphasis)

Whitehead points out that this philosophy of process 'seems to approximate more to some strains of Indian, or Chinese, thought, than to Western Asiatic or European thought. *One side makes process ultimate, the other side makes fact ultimate*' (1929: 6; emphasis added). On this view, relationships, process, transformation and the becoming of things are construed as fundamental aspects of reality. Through their interactions and self-transformations, these in turn generate the stabilized features of reality that we find so immediately necessary and familiar.

The use of an everyday mathematical example can help illustrate this principle of process and its relationship to outcomes much more clearly. Take the common mathematical expression 'twice-three is six'. This statement expresses adequately the principle of fusion sustaining the process of individuation. As Whitehead maintains:

> My contention is that the sentence contains a process and its issue. Of course, the issue of one process is part of the material for processes beyond itself. But in

respect to the abstraction 'twice-three is six', the phrase 'twice-three' indicates a form of fluent process and 'six' indicates a characterization of the completed fact. (1938: 125)

The statement 'twice-three is six' contains an unspecified principle of sustenance of character which is to be maintained during the process of fusion. Likewise, the existence of things is no more than the *actuality* of events experienced with the special characters connoted by the thing in question. Thus, if the same 'house-character' pervades a solid sequence of physical events visually observed, we say that the same house exists during the time of the sequence. What is observed is precisely the persistence of the character and solidity of the event sequence experienced (i.e., the absence of temporal gaps) in our perception. The thing called 'house' is no more than the enduring character in this historical sequence of events experienced. Likewise each individual social entity such as a person is not much more than an historic route of actual events coming together to form the relatively stabilized 'society of occasions' that thereby enables us to identify the individuality of the person concerned. For Whitehead (1929) each 'entity' is essentially a unit of experience and it is this process of experiencing which is our ultimate fact.

Process involves the continual building up and breaking down of actualized 'entities' through the assembling, dissembling and reassembling of past events into ever-newer entitative configurations in an interminable process of becoming. It involves change, reconfiguration and novel re-creation, always dismissing the old and replacing it by the new. Consider the following processual sequence of occasions as an illustration:

A feather, shall we say, is being painted in the hat of a person in a portrait. The picture of a woman without a hat has been abolished; instead there is something new – a woman with a feather. But the past is determined – it cannot be altered – and thus the new is affected and determined by it. The hat, in its featherless past, appeared on the canvas in a certain perspective, and the feather, when it is painted, is affected by this and appears on the canvas in the correct perspective. Further, one might say that the *character* of the past must be conformed with by the present. We will imagine that the hat belongs to the portrait of an Edwardian coster queen; in consequence, when it is painted in, the feather is an ostrich feather – not the sort of feather you would expect to see, for instance, on a Tyrolean trilby. . . . The character of the future is conformed with by the present. However exuberant the creative urge, the feather is not painted so large that it ends on the back of the canvas. It is as if it is already known that the picture is to appear in a frame of a certain size. (Jordan, 1968: 47; original emphasis)

Each novel advance into the future implicates the present and the past which both enables and constrains the possibilities for the future. In this manner, the past is immanent in the present which is its itself immanent in the future, so much so that each novel event embodies both what has gone past and what is to come.

It is easy enough to understand that the past is represented in the present, but how is it that the future may be implicated in the present? How can that which has not yet occurred be represented in the present? It seems rather obvious that the first review of a book on management learning published in the year 2020 does not now exist. It is less obvious that the first review of a book released last week does not now exist. If we bring attention to events closer at hand, it seems almost a falsehood to deny the existence of this sentence as a complete whole. As I wrote the words, 'If we bring attention . . .', the words 'sentence as a complete whole' lay in the future. But their sense had already been determined by the beginning of the sentence, and the future was rather compelled to follow the course initially set. Granted that there may be a number of variations, but the possibilities are always circumscribed. The future is stamped indelibly with the hallmark of the past and present, yet traces of such marks fade as more distant futures are considered.

Each such raw 'happening' or event forms the veritable slab of experience from, and of which, our material and social realities are made up. There is no enduring 'stuff' which events 'happen to'. There is nothing to be acted on which is itself not an activity. Process *is* the general character of everything and has no meaning apart from what happens. Thus, it is inappropriate to say 'There is the *process* of a portrait being painted'. Rather we can only point to the things which emerge from that process. As Jordan puts it succinctly: 'All *that happens is that things happen*' (1968; emphasis added). The universe is made up of an endless web of happenings – nothing more.

Process epistemology

An epistemology which makes process and emergence primary does not deny a role for entities, structure and substance. Rather it views structure and process as necessarily complementary to each other in a state of regenerative equilibrium or 'Creative Evolution' (Bergson, 1913b). As Cooper points out, the relationship between them is cyclic; it moves through 'the disintegration of structure – a temporary immersion in process – [to] the attainment of a new, more creative structure' (Cooper, 1976: 1000). In this manner there is an irrepressible urge to disapprove the adequacy of prevailing structures without necessarily having a prior conception of what should replace them. It is this evolutionary impulse which propels us into what Whitehead (1929) calls a 'creative advance into novelty'. Such an advance, rooted in the past and projected towards the future, is also what characterizes the kind of managerial foresight that Whitehead (1933) referred to in his discussion of the Business Mind of the Future. This aspect will be elaborated upon in a later section of the chapter.

Cooper (1976) identifies two crucial requirements for embracing an epistemology of process. First, he recommends that we adopt a Whiteheadian view of the individual and environment as mutually immanent in a unitary field of knowing. Thus, it is accepted that in an act of prehension the individuals involved are neither merely passive receivers nor dominant agents imposing their preconceived scheme of things on to that which they apprehend. Rather they feel themselves as significant nodes in a dynamic network of to-and-fro influences. For instance, if I am looking at a picture in an art gallery, it is the picture that is felt and which thereby constitutes the object of apprehension. The conventional understanding is that I am a passive receiver bombarded with light from the daubed canvas and the resultant effect is, say, an impression of the Rokeby Venus. This idea of passive receptivity, however, finds no place in an epistemology of process. Instead, the subject of this prehensive unification (myself, or what constitutes the historical route of previous prehensive unifications that make up 'me') is not a self-identical and completed entity standing there and waiting to be acted upon by the picture. Rather, 'I' myself *come into being* as a result of prehending the picture. The occasion of my prehension of the picture constitutes yet another actual happening in the ongoing constitution of my individuality. Likewise, the picture, before it was seen by me, is a different one now that I have encountered it. My 'gaze', within the context of it being displayed in an art gallery, has added to its realness as a socially constructed artefact and reinforced the status of that piece of work as an art piece. On my part, each occasion of prehension constitutes a novel advance of my being in a perpetual process of becoming other than what I am. It is this radically different style of thinking which characterizes a process-philosophical approach to the understanding of the human condition, and hence, ultimately, to our understanding of managing and learning.

Secondly, for Cooper (1976), following this epistemology of process, human knowing is 'ever open' and 'unfinished', always reaching out towards the horizon of the unknown. Representationalist epistemology, as I have tried to show, follows according to a linear model of 'knowledge-building' incrementally bringing us from the established known to the unknown. Thus, knowledge is deemed to be 'cumulative' and to increase according to the scope and variety of images people are able to acquire regarding a specific set of concrete circumstances. These are, themselves, necessarily wrought from the inadvertent *post-hoc* conceptual reorganization of past experience. According to this representationalist epistemology, images, therefore, precede action and serve to impose meaningful frames on to such intended actions. Paradoxically however, these imposed images, precisely because they are constituted a priori inhibit the possibilities for creative redefinitions of the meaning of actions which is necessary for the advance into novel forms of understanding and insight.

To suggest that human knowing is ever open, on the other hand, is to insist upon the necessity of 'pure' experimental action undirected by a governing image. It is this experiential imperative which underwrites an epistemology of process. As Cooper writes:

> In order to subvert the tyranny of the image, pure action, uncontaminated by a directing image, must be generated. The point of such 'action' is to create a cognitive vacuum which man [*sic*] must fill – since he so abhors a void – with images that break new ground. (1976: 1002)

Unmediated pure action becomes a means of revealing the latent and the unrealized in oneself and one's world. Through such pure action the invisible is rendered visible, the potential actualized and such actualized events assimilated into the becoming of one's individuality. 'Action painters' provide a useful illustration of this pedagogy of process. As Harold Rosenberg observes in his discussion of such experimental approaches:

> The painter no longer approaches his easel with an image in his mind; he went up to it with material in his hand to do something to that other piece of material in front of him. The image would be the result of this encounter. . . . In this mood there is no point to an act if you already know what it contains. . . . What matters always is the revelation contained in the act. . . . Art as action rests on the enormous assumption that the artist accepts as real only that which he [*sic*] is in the process of creating. (Rosenberg, quoted in Cooper, 1976: 1002)

It is this understanding of the experimental and creative novelty, characterizing much of living and managing, that has been inadvertently overlooked by a representationalist epistemology which, by its commitments to a static ontology, must necessarily assume a known-in-advance notion of knowledge and a correspondingly static and predetermined reality. An epistemology of process, on the other hand, attempts to chart the precarious emergence of every aspect of social life, including especially that which we call 'management' and 'learning'. Conceived thus, life becomes an interminable project of experimentation in which the ongoing *enactment* and *renactment* of social reality plays a central role in the individuals' attempt to recreate themselves through the processes of managing learning and learning to manage.

Managing here must now be understood, not in its narrower sense as a purely socio-economic activity, but as the ongoing accomplishment of modern living in the broadest sense we use when we say 'I managed to . . .'. It is in regard to this 'general economy' of management that the place of management learning as a reflective and critical form of inquiry can be more securely located. The idea that management has essentially to do with narrow performative concerns and that management knowledge is a 'commodity' that can be 'accumulated' and 'disseminated' accordingly, is predicated upon the assumptions of a *being* ontology and a *representationalist* epistemology. It generates a pedagogical preoccupation with 'transferring' knowledge rather than with the cultivation of insight and foresight. It is one which ignores the highly problematical and complex relationship between signs and their referents, between the linguistic products that we call 'management knowledge' and the phenomenal experiences of the practitioners of managing (our concrete lived experiences), and between the multitudinous acts of languaging and their 'outputs'. By so doing, it unwittingly helps perpetrate the intoxicating *regimes of signification* pervading contemporary management texts. A radically different view of knowing is required and with it the articulation of an alternative set of pedagogical strategies which resonate with the priorities of an epistemology of process.

The Primacy of Intuitive Knowing

In *An Introduction to Metaphysics*, Bergson (1913a) makes a crucial distinction between two types of knowing which he calls *intelligence* and *intuition*. Bergson insists that these are two profoundly different ways of knowing an experience. The first implies that:

> . . . we move round the object; the second that we enter into it. The first depends on the point of view at which we are placed and on the symbols by which we express ourselves. The second neither depends on a point of view nor relies on any symbol. The first kind of knowledge may be said to stop at the *relative*; the second . . . to attain the *absolute*. (Bergson, 1913a: 1; original emphasis)

For Bergson, intelligent (representationalist) knowing is always relative because it necessarily relies on a pre-established system of symbolic representations, so much so that we are, in this way, forever placed on the 'outside' of the object of our knowing. Representationalist knowing is a knowing *about*. It is a knowing which is *ab*stracted *out* forcibly from the initially undifferentiated totality of our brute experience. Such a reliance on systems of symbolic representation invariably produces an unending proliferation of alternative perspectives. Thus:

> In its eternally unsatisfied desire to embrace the object around which it is compelled to turn, analysis (i.e., intelligent knowing) multiplies without end the number of its points of view in order to complete its always incomplete representation, and ceaselessly varies its symbols that it may perfect the always imperfect translation. (ibid.: 7)

For Bergson, the crucial limitations of representationalist knowing are due to its incapacity to think in terms of movement and becoming. Representationalist analyses are predicated upon a static 'immobile' view of reality. They are not made to think *evolution* and *emergence* in the proper meaning of the words – that is 'pure' movement. They cannot possibly grasp the relational forces at the heart of the reality which necessarily overflows intelligent knowing. Yet this has not prevented the still widespread scientistic attempt to explain the phenomena of life in the same manner in which it appears to have been more successful with inorganic matter.

Intuitive knowing, on the other hand, entails the cultivating of a kind of 'intellectual sympathy' by which 'one places oneself within an object in order to coincide with what is unique in it and consequently inexpressible (i.e., through the system of conventionalized symbols)' (ibid.: 6). This empathetic quality is only achievable through the process of metaphysical inquiry in which ingrained habits of thought are inverted and the dominant systems of signification displaced. Only by insistently clearing away the cluttered-up legacy of signifying systems we have inherited from our forebears, particularly over the past three centuries or so, can we begin to reach nearer to the raw bruteness of our 'mobile' empirical experiences. This is not, however, to be confused with the 'false empiricism' associated with representationalist epistemology. Such a false empiricism is born of a 'confusion between the point of view of intuition and that of analysis.

Seeking for the original in the translation (i.e., the representation) where naturally it cannot be found, it denies the existence of the original on the grounds that it is not found in the translation' (ibid.: 27). On the other hand, 'a true empiricism is that which proposes to get as near to the original itself as possible, to search deeply into its life, and so, by a kind of *intellectual auscultation*, to feel the throbbing of its soul; and this true empiricism is the true metaphysics' (ibid.: 31; original emphasis). Instead of generating ever more perspectives, Bergson recommends that we reverse the direction of operation by which we habitually think. We can thus place ourselves *within* the moving, transforming reality and follow it 'in all its sinuosities' (ibid.: 59). In this way we can attain *absolute* knowledge through the philosophical method of *intuition*.

> What is relative is the symbolic knowledge [generated] by pre-existing concepts, which proceeds from the fixed to the moving, and not the intuitive knowledge which installs itself in that which is moving and adopts the very life of things. This intuition attains the absolute. (ibid.: 63; original emphasis)

The method of intuition involves the deliberate reversing of the habitual direction of our thinking processes and to thus insert ourselves into the mobile interior and feel the inexorable palpitation of the heart of reality. Only with such intuitive insights can a true managerial foresight be cultivated. This reversal of priorities in turn leads to an accentuation of *intuitive* knowing over intelligence and a pedagogy of experimental action over passive dissemination, a pedagogy in which a form of 'Negative Capability' is emphasized and the attainment of managerial foresight the desired outcome.

Negative Capability and Managerial Foresight

The first stage of management learning involves the cultivation of a resistance to the seductive appeal of the *regimes of signification* which make up what passes for formalized management knowledge. The pervasiveness of such *regimes of signification* are what accounts for the apparent plurality of perspectives on the practice of management. They only serve to deceive our senses, disorientate priorities, disable critical thought, and restrict vision in all spheres of managerial life. Conceptual resistance is better appreciated by what the poet John Keats calls 'Negative Capability'.

In a letter to his brothers written in December 1817, Keats identified a quality which he associated with those who had achieved much in life. He writes:

> And at once it struck me, what quality went to form a man of Achievement. . . . mean *Negative Capability*, that is when a man is capable of being in uncertainties, mysteries, doubts, without any irritable reaching after fact and reason. (Keats, letter of 21 December 1817)

Negative Capability involves the resisting of conceptual closure (of succumbing to the *regimes of signification*) when dealing with affairs of the world. It is an injunction for us to 'stay with the experience' and to wallow in the open-endedness and indeterminacy of that experience, soaking it up until we are saturated with it. Conceptual resistance thereby creates the necessary 'space' for the formulation of personal insights and from it the development of the form of managerial foresight that Whitehead (1933) spoke of.

In his illuminating discussion of the 'Business Mind of the Future', Whitehead (1933) identified the possession of 'foresight' as a crucial aspect of the successful business mentality in a world increasingly characterized by fluid and shifting business situations. For him, it is the cultivation of this mind of the future which defines the role of university business schools. Specifically, there are two aspects to this future business mentality. First, it is fundamental that there be a 'power of conforming to routine, of supervising routine, of constructing routine, and of understanding routine both as to its internal structure and as to its external purposes' (Whitehead, 1933: 119). Whitehead chides the sociological doctrines, in particular, for being oblivious to this fundamental sociological truth. For him 'it is the beginning of wisdom to understand that social life is founded upon routine. . . . Society requires stability, foresight itself presupposes stability, and stability is the product of routine' (ibid.: 111). Routine is the necessary 'god' of every social system.

However, such powers of conforming to the routine, while necessary, are not enough. What is required in addition for the successful business mind of the future is a 'philosophic power of understanding the complex flux of the varieties of human societies . . . [an] instinctive grasp of the relevant features of social currents . . . [and a] habit of transforming observations of qualitative change into quantitative estimates' (ibid.: 119). For Whitehead, it is this complementing of the powers of routine with the instinctive grasping of patterns of interconnectedness which together make up the special attribute of foresight. The latter, for Whitehead, is an 'unspecialized aptitude for eliciting generalizations from particulars and for seeing the divergent illustration of generalities in diverse circumstances' (ibid.: 120). The ability to perceive similarities in differences and differences in similarities is what allows a recasting and/or redefinition of the managerial situation at hand. It is this feature which constitutes what Whitehead terms management foresight. This is also precisely the pedagogical outcome sought through the process of management learning in management education. It is what allows the creative and intuitive aspects of our knowing to flourish and to enable us to conceive of radically new possibilities in situation-specific sets of management circumstances.

The cultivation of a determined resistance to dominant sign-systems and the inculcating of managerial foresight is what, therefore, underpins the aims of management learning as a process-driven form of inquiry. It has profound implications for the pedagogical priorities of the academic discipline.

Pedagogical Implications for Management Learning

Clearly, the implications of this 'process philosophy' for management learning is wide-ranging and requires careful and faithful elaboration. From this 'becoming' ontology formal *knowledge* needs to be reconceptualized as relatively arbitrarily stabilized configurations of perceptual relationships abstracted from and hence tenuously linked to an undifferentiated, fluxing and transforming *implicate* reality. There is, however, an alternative form of *knowing* which is not reducible to symbolic representation, but which nevertheless can be grasped. This, following Bergson, is *intuitive* knowing and it is a vital prerequisite for what Whitehead terms foresight. What this means is that management learning, as a critical and reflexive form of metaphysical inquiry, invites us to immerse ourselves in the *process* situations *as they emerge* and thereby to resist the premature stabilizing of our understanding until we reach a point of intellectual saturation where the experience itself 'speaks' directly to us. In this manner the 'intellectual sympathy' which Bergson referred to can be assiduously cultivated and the necessary foresight developed. This imperative to stay with the ambivalence and ambiguity of the not-yet-known constitutes the first pedagogical imperative for management learning.

A second pedagogical imperative of management learning is the insistence on recognizing that *how a situation emerges* crucially shapes its meaning, interpretation and social significance. This implies that the simple observation of outcome attributes, end-states, and the subsequent comparing and linking of such situations to generalized causal factors, as a model explanatory approach in management research, is self-defeating because it does not take into account the situation-specific sets of circumstances giving rise to a particular unique set of relational configuration which, in turn, make up the embedded significance of a particular state of affairs.

One very notorious example of this insensitivity to the genealogy of event-structuring has been the uncritical transposing of one set of evidently successful and/or desirable management practices on to another entirely different set of organizational circumstances. The archetypal example is the recent (but now much abated) wholesale importation of Japanese-styled management practices into Western organizations. However, there are many other less obvious examples that persist, including the still widespread assumption of the generalizability, usefulness and indeed desirability of what are clearly Western ideology-inspired theories of management and learning, for the wider global community, whether these contain neo-managerialist, neo-Marxist, neo-environmentalist, or neo-feminist overtones.

Essentially, the core question revolves around the extent to which situation-specific (contextual) knowledge is crucial in determining outcomes. With the constant need to readjust organizational priorities in response to shifting constellations of political and cultural sensitivities, technological developments and ideological imperatives, characteristic of a highly interconnected yet paradoxically highly fragmented globalized economy, it is becoming increasingly clear that the adoption of a pragmatic, reflexive and contingent approach to managing is more likely to be of any value in today's world.

There can be no recipe-type prescriptive managerial imperatives which can be unreflexively ingested and 'applied' accordingly. Rather, each managerial situation must be treated as 'loaded' with the historical traces of its becoming; with all the 'accidents, the minute deviations – or conversely, the complete reversals – the errors, the false appraisals, and the faulty calculations that gave birth to those things that continue to exist and have value' (Foucault, in Rabinow, 1984: 81). Each unique situation encountered must be appreciated to be carrying the *weight of its past* with it. Every situation one encounters is loaded with its history and carries with it a wide range of possiblilities in terms of future outcomes.

Thirdly, processual managing and learning entails the recogition that the way events *unfold* affects and is affected by the interaction between perceiver and perceived. Our understanding of a situation orients us towards particular types of response and the choice of a particular response, in turn, affects the shifting pattern of relationships. In this way our construction of what we understand shifts us nearer to embracing a particular version of reality, to which we then oftentimes unreflexively respond as if it had somehow been pre-determined.

One way of understanding how this process of reciprocal influencing works to become increasingly self-supporting and self-sealing in the becoming of things, is well illustrated by the evolutionary biologist Brian Goodwin's account of the emergence of what have come to be called the Amazonian rain forests in Brazil. Goodwin writes:

> As organisms change into different varieties and species with adaptation to particular habitats, the evolutionary scenario changes: the fitness landscape itself undergoes modification as species evolve and create new opportunities for survival. *Trees modify and enrich the soil by dropping their leaves and producing organic compost that retains water, so forest systems such as the Amazon developed on originally poor soil creating conditions for the stunning variety of species that has emerged in this vast ecosystem.* (1994: 157; emphasis added)

The imagery conjured up by this dynamic and ongoing process of reciprocal influencing and self-constituting provides a powerful metaphor for understanding the necessary toing-and-froing characteristic of the *unfolding* of events giving rise to a particular version of social reality. Instead of the dominant image of linear causal explications, this process of mutual influencing and self-constituting which takes place over a period of time to generate both the magnificent ecosystems such as the Amazonian rain forests, and the socio-political and economic systems which characterize much of the developed West, provides a more appropriate image for understanding the evolution of contemporary management realities. Indeed, it could even be argued that this is quintessentially how complex physical, biological and social systems emerge from basic patterns of relationships such as quarks, DNAs, or rudimentary verbal utterances, in the case of linguistic systems.

The term 'bootstrapping' (Capra, 1988: 52) has been used to denote this form of reciprocal influencing in which the idea of fundamental causal entities are denied and instead a claim is made that reality is always in a process of becoming and this becoming consists of an emergent dynamic web of interrelated events whose relative *densities* determine their apparent atomistic characteristics. No part of this relational web is more fundamental than others yet the totality of the system regulates and enhances itself, evolving in ever more creative ways whilst attempting to regulate and maintain the internal consistency of its relational structuring. It is the cultivating of this dynamic and unfolding orientation towards phenomenon which constitutes a key aspect of the pedogogical imperatives of managment learning.

Finally, management learning based upon a process epistemology empha-sizes the significance and importance of experimental action as a means of initiating the creative advance into novel understanding which Whitehead (1929) spoke of. The terms 'experiential learning' and 'action learning' have long been used to allude to the intuited value of direct engagement as a crucial aspect of learning. What has not, however, been adequately elabor-ated is a *metaphysics* of experiential learning which can withstand the criticisms of those committed to more conventionalized views of the learning process. In this regard, process philosophers like Bergson and Whitehead offer us a rigorously worked out cosmology which emphasizes an epistemology of process and which embraces this pedagogical imperative to place 'pure' action – acting *without a directing image* – at the centre of our pedagogical priorities. This emphasis on experimental action, as a means of surprising ourselves and thus of breaking new ground in our self-understanding, is what marks management learning as a reflexive and self-critical intellectual activity. It is also what makes possible the cultiva-tion of the necessary managerial foresight that is needed for dealing with the complex affairs of the postmodern world.

Conclusion

Management learning must be appreciated as necessarily a process-philosophical activity whose very *raison d'être* is the persistent questioning and destructuring of the symbolic forms of knowledge which inhabit contemporary management thought. In this sense it is a form of meta-learning which insists that while symbolic forms of knowledge are always relative because they are confined to talking *about* the object of their inquiry, the task of this meta-inquiry is precisely to go beyond such forms of knowledge and to grasp the brute impulsions at the heart of reality. This is made possible through the act of *intuition* by which we locate ourselves within the flux and transformation of reality in order to infuse into our very becoming and being, the mobility characterizing the inward life of things.

This embracing of the value and significance of intuitive knowledge is only possible if one commits oneself to a radically different cosmology from that circumscribing much of Western academic thought. Instead of subscribing to the still-dominant Parmenidean-inspired *being* ontology, it is the Heraclitean world-view of process, flux, change and transformation which provides the system of beliefs for an ontology of *becoming*. This, in turn, provides the epistemological platform for a theory of knowledge based upon the primacy of process and relations as the ultimate units of reality.

An epistemology of process accentuates four pedagogical priorities. First, it insists upon the necessity of *staying with an experience*, soaking it up until one becomes saturated with it. Secondly, it insists that every situation should be looked upon as *necessarily loaded with the weight of its past*. Its genealogy is contained within the very fabric of its articulation as an event or set of circumstances. Thirdly, it recognizes *mutual and reciprocal influencing* rather than linear causality as more appropriately characterizing how things, events, and end-states come to be what they are. Finally, it advocates the *necessity and desirability of pure unmediated experimental action* in order to ursurp the dominant symbolic order and to generate new insights into the human condition. These four pedagogical imperatives make up the key contributions that management learning, as a process-oriented metaphysical inquiry, can potentially offer to the efforts of management education in revitalizing society.

Note

1 The term 'regimes of signification' is used to allude to the dominant clusters of signs and symbols which significantly influence our thoughts and perceptions. For further explanation see Lash and Urry (1994).

Annotated Bibliography

For those who would like to familiarize themselves with the idea of process metaphysics and epistemology, I would recommend N. Rescher (1996) *Process Metaphysics: An Introduction to Process Philosophy*. New York: State University of New York Press. This gives a comprehensive and up-to-date summary of the various thinkers who have contributed to a metaphysics of process, as well as a succinct explanation of the key ideas and perspectives involved in this world-view. For a rigorous and thorough defence of the notion of 'intuition' as a method for apprehending reality, I would recommend H. Bergson (1913) *An Introduction to Metaphysics*. London: Macmillan. Finally, the idea of 'business foresight' was inspired by a recent reading of A.N. Whitehead's (1933) *Adventures of Ideas*. Harmondsworth: Penguin, in a chapter entitled 'Foresight' where he discusses the business mind of the future.

References

Bergson, H. (1913a) *An Introduction to Metaphysics*. London: Macmillan.
Bergson, H. (1913b) *Creative Evolution*. London: Macmillan.
Capra, F. (1988) *Uncommon Wisdom*. London: Century Hutchinson.
Cooper, R. (1976) 'The open field', *Human Relations*, 29 (11): 999–1017.

5

Groups, Groupwork and Beyond

Richard Boot and Michael Reynolds

No study of practice in management education and development could be complete without some account of the emergence of groupwork theory and practice. The origins of this development are diverse. The legendary research at Western Electric drew attention to the importance of groups in the workplace (Roethlisberger and Dickson, 1939) and in a very different setting, Bion's work in therapy groups with military casualties in the Second World War has given us arguably the most influential theory of group behaviour (Bion, 1961). Later still, the therapist and educator Carl Rogers (1969) transposed his earlier explorations of group training for counsellors into a more generally applied methodology.

In the 1950s, the movement in the USA to democratize organizations, or more particularly, their management practices, was supported by training and development based on groupwork. It was believed that a more participative, more humanized workplace was an improvement, both socially and in terms of profitability, on the hierarchical forms of organization which, until this period, were the norm. The body of practice, and to a lesser extent theory, which embodied these changing values became known as organizational development (OD).

Principal authors of OD, such as Chris Argyris (1964), Richard Beckhard (1969) and Warren Bennis (1966), advocated an approach to managing which valued teamwork, collaboration, an ethos of trust and more direct, open working relationships above the old order based on chain of command, bureaucratic control and hierarchical authority. At the core of this movement, theories of group dynamics were applied to the development of groups and teams, and managers from the larger organizations were schooled in groupwork as members and leaders. These methods, which included sensitivity training or T-Groups (Schein and Bennis, 1965) and 'team-building' activities (Blake and Mouton, 1969), were based on a predominantly experiential approach to learning and development.

Through these developments, it has become widespread practice for managers and management students to be offered learning opportunities based on groupwork of various kinds, ranging from role-play to action learning, from outdoor management exercises to business games and project teams. The older tradition of lecturing survives in educational institutions but outside them its use is mostly restricted to where the mass audience gathers to pay homage to the management guru. Even in the more traditional context of higher education, most postgraduate courses in management and business schools will supplement lectures and tutorials with work which is carried out and presented by groups.

It is unfortunate that development of understanding of the individual and social processes involved in group-based learning has not kept pace with the proliferation of practical applications available to teachers and trainers. So while the study of group dynamics from various perspectives (Tavistock, Lewinian, social psychological, etc.) is an accepted part of the organizational behaviour curriculum, the design and application of groupwork for educational purposes seems rarely to have been informed by group theory.

Management development has become especially prone to popularized models which are often much simplified versions of more complex ideas. What has been done to Kolb's (1984) original work on experiential learning theory and Tuckman's (1965) ideas on group development are familiar examples of this. Indeed, the influence of experiential learning theory has been particularly strong, and this, together with the attractiveness of educational methods which are more involving, and increasing dissatisfaction with more formal educational approaches, has encouraged the expansion of group-based activities referred to earlier.

The picture of groupwork in management education and development is therefore one of a mixture of educational methods and designed activities and a correspondingly wide range of both complex and simplistic theory used to explain group processes. Questions concerning the use of groups in education have been asked from different perspectives. Do they work? Are they dangerous? Do they support or undermine the values we would like to see in our organization? Do they give value for money? In addition, there has been disquiet among critical educators and more politicized professionals that the emphasis on openness, trust and self-disclosure in some versions of group-based training serves to obscure realities of power, difference and the conflicts of interest which characterize the workplace (see, e.g., Hollway, 1991).

In reviewing these aspects of groupwork, we shall explore its theory and practice in the context of management education and development, as well as the issues and debates associated with it. We shall go on to question the significance of the field as a whole and we shall end by considering the limitations of emphasizing the concept of the 'group' in management learning, and the opportunities which might be presented by an alternative focus.

Describing the Groupwork Field

In reviewing groupwork and its range of theories, practices and issues in the domain of management learning, we will not replicate existing and more detailed descriptions of the field. Suitable texts of this sort are included in the Annotated Bibliography at the end of the chapter. Instead, our approach will be to emphasize the way that the range of ideas in practice can be understood, and to some extent organized, in terms of the differences and similarities between them. In this way we hope to highlight some essential characteristics of groupwork, and in passing, introduce some examples of theory and practice.

In reflecting on our own practice as educators and writers, it seems to us that there are different kinds of question that can be asked about groupwork practice – questions that can provide a means of structuring a synopsis of the field as a whole:

- What ways are there of *differentiating between methods or approaches* used in managers' development? What are the differences between a role-play and a case study, or between Total Quality Management and the idea of the 'Learning Organization'?
- What other *ideas and principles* have become enshrined in groupwork practice? What are the 'taken-for-granteds', the unquestioned truths? Why, for example, has the idea of phases of group development become the most popular?
- How are we to interpret the *controversies and debates* within the field as a whole? For example, what are the tensions which are assumed to exist between academics who are characterized as studying groups, and practitioners who are seen as most likely to use them?

We will use these questions as the structure for what follows.

Differentiating between methods and approaches

The usual way of differentiating between group methods is to categorize them as, for example, 'structured' or 'unstructured'. There are problems with this. First, 'structure' is only one of a number of dimensions which could be applied, and it may not always be the most important one. Secondly, any attempt to categorize in this way takes no account of the interpretation of the method by whoever is using it, let alone ways its form may be influenced by those taking part. For example, the familiar assumption among management developers that games and simulations might be thought of as more structured than T-Groups does not allow for the different ways either method is applied in practice, nor is it clear about what 'structure' refers to specifically. And what of other ways in which a method in use might be characterized, such as its intended purpose, the degree of control offered to the participants, or the nature of the experience it is hoped will result from taking part?

Some years ago we developed a framework for describing different methods based on how experienced teachers and trainers distinguished between them (Boot and Reynolds, 1984). We identified a number of 'dimensions' which could be used to elaborate the distinctiveness of any educational method (at the time we were particularly interested in what were generally described as 'structured experiences'). The dimensions which emerged concerned aspects of tutors' *design intentions* (their aims, beliefs about learning and the educational process, the various decisions they would make in designing the activity, etc.) and their intentions or predictions as to the quality or *nature of the participant's experience* likely to result from the design (physical, emotional and intellectual involvement) and, more generally, whether the nature of learning could or should be predicted.

Our particular interest was in the degree of the trainer or tutor's control and participants' freedom of choice over the different elements of design decisions. As we wrote at that time:

> The distinction which it seems to us most important to make is between participation and control in the mechanics of the exercise (roles, rules and procedures) on the one hand and participation and control in the evolution and evaluation of knowledge which results in taking part in it (focus, material and framework). (Boot and Reynolds, 1983b: 46)

We called these two broad groups *structure* (the 'mechanics') and *scope* (evolution and evaluation of knowledge), and the dimensions of design and intended experience which each comprised provides the basis for differentiating among education and training methods. So taking one of the dimensions within scope, for example *material* (what will be examined in the process of learning), we can illustrate our approach.

Perhaps the most usual are those methods which are designed on the basis of *material drawn primarily from outside the group*. Familiar examples are seminars and course teams or 'syndicates', in which groups of participants draw on theories, research or case studies for discussion. A method which has become traditional within management education and development is action learning (Pedler, 1983, and Chapter 4 in this volume). Working in groups or 'sets', managers examine situations and problems drawn from their current work experience and this material, again primarily from outside the group, provides the basis of learning. They may work on individual projects chosen for this purpose.

In contrast there are methods in which learning is intended from the examination of *material generated within the group itself*, from participants' experiences and observations through activities designed for this purpose. In sensitivity training or T-Groups, and in 'working conferences' developed at the Tavistock Institute of Human Relations for studying group relations, the purpose is to present an opportunity for each participant to learn about groups through being in them. Learning is through examining the processes and behaviours generated as group members engage in the decisions and choices which constitute the life of their group as society in miniature.

Related to these methods are the many games and 'structured exercises', usually with more focused learning aims, such as communication, decision-making or leadership (see, e.g., Kolb et al., 1984). Here, too, the aim is to learn by reflecting on behaviours generated in carrying out the task prescribed for the group. Particularly elaborate examples of this approach are organizational simulations (Boot and Reynolds, 1985) and outdoor management development (Beeby and Rathborn, 1983). Finally, it could be said that a distinctive feature of methods such as business games and outdoor management development is that in their case *material is contrived.*

These clusterings were derived by thinking of a range of methods using groups and asking how they differed in terms of the choice of material. But different dimensions would have produced different clusters. So, for example, had dimensions of structure, such as rules or procedures, been chosen instead, different clusters would have emerged and T-Groups and outdoor management development, or seminars and syndicates, might not have been grouped together.

While we believe this approach to differentiating practice can provide a useful way of reviewing the field as a whole, its limitations must be remembered. There are important ways in which methods can vary, depending on who is involved and in what context. Equally, while we can speak of material being drawn primarily from within or from outside the group, this is itself a simplification. Participants in a seminar are also likely to make connections with their experience of work, and by the same token, members of an action learning set can learn from the way they work together.

At least we have provided a way of distinguishing among the range and variety of groupwork applications which may be used in the education of managers. Categorizations rarely do justice to variations in use. What makes more sense is to use dimensions such as these to characterize a *particular* design in the hands of particular tutors or trainers by asking such questions as:

- What is the intention behind this design?
- What kind of learning is hoped for?
- What material will be examined?
- How much direction or control will be exercised by the tutor over the different elements of the design?
- What kind of experience is hoped for?
- Are particular theoretical frameworks to be conveyed through the activity?

Ideas and principles

While there is much available which *could* be drawn on to inform the design, implementation and facilitation of learning groups of various kinds, it often seems as if theories of design are tacit. Either that, or there are ideas which have achieved the status of unquestioned 'truths', informing people's practice without apparently needing to be articulated, let alone challenged. So in practice, when teachers or trainers design group activities, run them, or talk about them after the event, what ideas about learning or about groups are they drawing on, if only by implication? What concepts do they use to explain why an activity did not turn out as they had hoped?

There are, of course, notable exceptions to this premise that theories informing design are often not explicit. The psychodynamic theories associated with the practice of working conferences at the Grubb Institute of

Behavioural Studies or the Tavistock Institute of Human Relations provide examples of a coherent set of principles which inform both the design of the conferences and the interpretation of what happens within them (e.g., Rice, 1971). In the domain of adult education, as in management development, theories of experiential learning – if in a much simplified form – often provide the basic framework for the design of training events and activities. David Kolb's (1984) influential adaptation of John Dewey's ideas of learning through reflection on experience can be seen in the 'activity–observation–discussion–application' model which is commonly used as the underlying structure for management development designs.

In reviewing the ideas and principles which inform the design of group-based learning, we shall illustrate examples of broad generic concepts and values which seem to have become *taken-for-granteds*, acquiring the status of fundamental truth. We will also describe a category of concepts which it could be argued are not only unquestioned but whose universal acceptance discourages exploration of alternatives. Their function seems to be *to obscure rather than illuminate* understanding.

Taken-for-granteds.   These are the ideas which have become widely accepted among professionals using group methods, as, for example, the notion that a group can be understood simply in terms of the different roles occupied by its members. There is, of course, a strong tradition for this in the study of group behaviour, especially the observation categories developed by Robert Bales (1950). The problem is that although the relative simplicity of this approach is appealing – and may account for the popularity of more recent derivatives – it does little to illuminate the complex social processes of which work groups or learning groups consist. What models of this kind may do is convey a false impression of having explained group processes while reinforcing the tendency for people to think of themselves in terms of 'I am a . . . (shaper, accommodater or whatever)'. This draws attention away from the other influences on their behaviour such as the organizational or social context.

Another example of a taken-for-granted in management learning is the idea of phases of group development, usually Tuckman's (1965) – often applied with a rigidity which does disservice to the original concept. The notion of phases of development is often associated with a further, more subtle assumption, which is that productivity is the ultimate criterion for measuring success. Similarly, the dependency–counterdependency–interdependency model is commonly used to explain the ways staff–participant relationships change during courses, and is valid in some situations. But its wide acceptance can result in its use as a spurious and patronizing means of avoiding staff responsibility, when participant resistance would be best understood in terms of what is wrong with the design rather than with students' mental states.

Value systems underlying methods can also go unquestioned. So, for example, 'working in the here and now' is a belief which pervades sensitivity training and other experiential approaches. The emphasis on the 'here and now' is the basis of experiential groups' distinctive capability as a learning method. But it is not without problems if applied slavishly as it can diminish the significance of history and context. It is, of course, possible to focus on 'here and now' material (the immediate detail of group members' behaviour and relationships) in ways which acknowledge its origins in social processes which exist beyond the boundaries of the group (Hudson, 1983). However, the application of the 'here and now' axiom is not always thought through to this extent.

The value attached to self-disclosure is another example of a practice which has become a feature of development work in management. Self-disclosure is embraced with as much enthusiasm by its proponents as it is condemned by those who distrust its function. Its use is most prevalent in personal development methods, whose origins are in the encounter group movement where disclosure of feelings, personal history, and even of problems in relationships, is thought, with good reason, to provide the basis for understanding self and others. But it is questionable in an organizational context where participants are in hierarchical relationship with each other, or in an educational setting with the backcloth of assessment (Hearn, 1983). Self-disclosure should not be used to promote cohesion among group and organization members by intruding into domains which should remain private.

Ideas that obscure. Some of the ideas in the theory and practice of groupwork which we have covered are not simply unquestioned. They appear to have an additional function of preventing alternative and presumably unwelcome sets of ideas from being considered. Experiential learning theory, for example, has had considerable influence on practice in both management development and adult education generally. Here is a system of ideas, an ideology which incorporates theoretical frameworks to explain the learning process, and a coherent set of values and beliefs about how people should learn. Personal growth or personal development are further examples of overarching idea systems which underpin the application of much groupwork in management learning, with origins in the 'person-centred' or 'learner-centred' ideologies of humanist educators such as Carl Rogers (1969), Malcolm Knowles (1975) and, more recently, Jack Mezirow (1991).

The significance of these idea systems is that, like movements or religions, they accumulate a core of teachings which become the point of reference for debating theoretical or operational differences. So that in questioning the detail of design, interpretation or evaluation of group-based experience, concepts of this magnitude are not only taken for granted, their principles can be invoked as the arbiter of what is truth and what is right, good or effective. So in the case of experiential learning theory, its essentially individualistic perspective pre-empts possibilities for a more contextualized, social or political point of view which would be more likely to 'foreground power and ideology' (Fairclough and Hardy, this volume). It must then be asked what interests are served by such an examination being pushed aside.

Controversies and debates

There are some aspects of groupwork in management learning which give this community of practice its particular character. These are the debates, divisions and mythologies associated with the field as a whole, as opposed to specific ideas and practices which have currency within it. For example, perhaps because of the constant need for learning to be applicable, there is a tendency to convert complex ideas about groups into simpler categorizations which can be used to describe and limit people in terms of their attributes, character and capabilities. As described earlier, the popularity of schemes which emphasize roles, the preoccupation with prediction and predictability and the value attached to measuring learning in terms of performance have all contributed to a perspective on groups which seems primarily directed towards the exploitation of people's potential, of reinforcing a perception of organizational members as 'resources'.

Yet at the same time, groupwork in the development of managers has had periods of idealism, with a vision of organizations as more fulfilling places in which to work and of working relationships as rewarding platforms for each individual's development. The prominence given to T-Groups and self-directed learning in the heyday of organizational development was an expression of this idealism. The combination of managerial and humanist values is a familiar paradox within management development and has attracted criticism from those who would accuse management educators of incorporating humanistic ideals in the service of exploitation.

A further feature of the field as a whole is the distinction often made between theorizers and practitioners – those who 'think' and those who 'do'. In groupwork this spurious division was accentuated by the anti-intellectualism of the 1960s and 1970s which formed part of a resistance to the domination of the social sciences by positivist-based research and teaching. Currently, the problem is reinforced by a number of factors: the pressure on academics to write in ways which are inaccessible to those not members of intellectual clubs; the division of journals between academics and practitioners; and the emphasis on performativity within organization-based management development.

Whatever the reason for the distinction, there is a tendency in groupwork for there to be two communities – those carrying out research into groups, and those who use groups as the basis of learning. So research findings are included in teaching in management schools, while management development professionals have done most to incorporate experiential methods of various kinds into practice. As a consequence, we have theoretical perspectives which lack grounding in practice, and practice which remains uninformed by relevant theory.

Making Sense of the Field

Our review of the ideas and practices of groupwork provides a platform for making sense of the field as a significant tradition within management learning. As before, our approach is based on the different kinds of question it is possible to ask. So, for example:

- How are we to interpret the different *perspectives on groups* which management educators bring to a discussion of the practice of groupwork? How do these different perspectives relate to each other?
- What is the *function and purpose of theory and practice*? Why are some concepts accepted and some well-established theories hardly heard of in management development? Is theory used to illuminate or to instruct people's thinking? Why are particular group-based methods favoured and others neglected? What interests are concealed in this selectivity?
- What happens if we *question the salience of 'group'* as the central concept? Why is this so taken for granted? What alternatives might be considered?

Perspectives on groups

The theoretical perspectives on groups and groupwork which inform thinking and practice in management education and development are largely drawn from various schools within psychology (whether social, psychodynamic or humanistic). Ideas about group behaviour have been selected and adapted in education (particularly by exponents of student-centred learning) and in management and organizational development. So, for example, contributions have been made to the understanding of the relationship of the individual in relation to the group (Sherif, 1936), of group dynamics (notably Kurt Lewin, 1963) and of relationships between groups (Higgin and Bridger, 1964). Other researchers (Wilfred Bion, 1961; Melanie Klein, 1959) have elaborated ideas about unconscious group processes which can usually be applied to both work and learning settings. Considerably fewer theories have been drawn from sociology or anthropology.

The lack of a sociological perspective in management learning generally has reinforced an underlying assumption of consensus in groupwork and especially in the practice of organizational development and its more recent derivatives. This perspective would add a dimension which is largely absent from theory and practice in managers' learning. There is a need for ideas to strengthen understanding of processes of power and control present in groups and in society. Group activities, however focused or prescribed, can reflect contextual processes of organizations, communities and society as a whole. Without the addition of a sociological perspective, an adequate examination of gender, culture, difference, or of processes of privilege and prejudice is less likely.

Our purpose here is not to provide a comprehensive account of theoretical influences in the domain of groupwork, but rather to point out how and why concepts are drawn on selectively. Ideas which have become accepted in management development are those which support a decontextualized notion of groups and groupwork. That is to say, prominence is given to ideas which avoid questions to do with social power or exploitation of difference – questions which would entail a critical examination of the interests represented in current social or organizational arrangements. Consequently, as a more sociological perspective would identify, hierarchy and control remain largely unexamined or inadequately examined, perpetuating an individualized version of work and learning.

Sadly, these different perspectives seem to provide a basis for drawing up battlelines rather than for engaging in dialogue. Traditionally, academic sociologists, untroubled by the practical realities of using groupwork for educational purposes, have been critical of the conflict-free assumptions of groupwork practice. Those using groupwork in management learning, on the other hand, for the most part base their work on impoverished conceptual foundations, thus sparing themselves the complication of ideas which might question the taken-for-granteds which underpin their work. It is more valuable, but in our experience less usual, to ground the design and practice of groupwork on a theoretical framework which draws on both the understandings offered by psychology and the critical perspective more usual within the sociological tradition.

The function and purpose of theory and practice

The function and purpose of theory.   Theories can, in the hands of different exponents, provide a stimulus to the development of individuals' understanding, or stifle sense-making through the imposition of 'received' wisdom. The embattled social science schools referred to in the previous section have one thing in common at least, that in criticizing each other's '-isms', whether psychologisms or sociologisms, each asserts its own authority. So what's the difference? The sociological perspective at least is more likely to contain within itself a tradition of critiquing the way systems of beliefs and meanings can be taken over by other, more dominant ones. But what would a non-imperialist application of theory look like?

In the previous section we referred to different dimensions of learning experience, distinguishing between *structure* (roles, rules and procedures) and *scope* (focus, material and framework). Any analysis of control must differentiate between these elements. So, for example, participants may have an opportunity to exercise individual choice in the structural elements of a group activity, but at the same time they may be subjected to unnegotiable frameworks of theory used by the facilitator in making sense of their experience of it. This distinction between controlling what people *do* and controlling what people *think* we have elaborated elsewhere (Boot and Reynolds, 1983a).

The alternative view is that the theory which matters is that which is developed *through dialogue* as students and teachers consider their own ideas as well as those in the public domain. This encourages generation of theory in response to a particular context, rather than the wooden application of recieved or 'fixed' concepts to a variable situation. From this perspective, theorizing enables individuals to make their own sense of things rather than have it created for them. It enables people to generate ideas from the particular in ways which help them learn about the world in general. It legitimates their own capabilities for wisdom and knowledge more than it reinforces the claims of professionals to be its arbiters. There is, therefore, a significant opportunity in participative groups for the creation of a living sense in learning, in that ideas from whatever source are not static, given or unchanging. On the contrary, they are the stimuli that foster each member's theorizing in and through the company of others. Participation in group learning should not be limited to methods that provide novel vehicles for the dissemination of 'accepted' truths. Questioning these truths should not be interpreted as some 'counterdependent' need to challenge authority. It is evidence of a dialogic relationship.

The function and purpose of practice. In the same way as it is possible to observe that theory in groupwork is used either to open up people's thinking or to constrain it, it is possible to interpret the practice of groupwork as indicative of significantly different agenda. The incorporation of groupwork in management education and development, often seems *instrumental* rather than as a support to learning for its own sake. For example, groups are often used as 'ice-breaking' devices in order to accelerate the process of participants getting to know each other, or for the *'motivational'* effects of being active and involved. Groups might even be used for administrative convenience.

Alternatively, the reasons for using group-based methods can be *pedagogical*, intended to provide opportunities for the kind of dialogue described earlier, through which people can learn from each other and develop their own ideas in the process. The reasons may also be *ideological*, if used in a Deweyan tradition, to learn in ways which reflect the belief that people should work and live together in a democratic environment. It could even be that emphasis on groupwork is an unconscious celebration of the group as the alternative to alienation and the threat of social fragmentation – an idea we develop in the next section.

In practice the intended functions are often combined, even though they may be unclear or unexpressed. The apparent or stated rationale may not even be the real one. For example, the reason given for using a group activity may be to increase interest in learning through more involving methods. Whereas in fact its adoption is adherence to current fashion in using educational methods from the experiential repertoire without thinking out why. Similarly, group methods can be used in management education and development to bring about cohesion and loyalty, rather than because the method is thought to be the best way to support learning. This is learning of a kind, but more as socialization into organizational values.

Questioning the concept

Throughout this chapter we have been conscious of the difficulty of raising questions about something which has been a pivotal part of our work as teachers and researchers. Our approach has been to emphasize tendencies, dilemmas and patterns in both theory and practice rather than to present a purely descriptive summary of the field. So we have pointed to the dimensions which can be used to make sense of the diversity among group-based approaches to learning and development, and the selectivity which is exercised when drawing on theory. We have also drawn attention to aspects of thinking and practice which have been granted the status of articles of faith within the domain of management learning, and have highlighted covert processes in groupwork such as the ways control is exercised.

It is through our own interest in the theory and practice of groupwork over many years that we find an examination of its taken-for-granteds of such interest. Nevertheless, disquiet accumulates on so often hearing spurious assumptions about groups recited with a reverence which is not justified by research findings nor expected by the original proponents of group theory. The importance given to the notion of 'the group' in everyday discourse is equally troubling, as when people seem undermined by the absence of members at meetings, feel unable to work if 'inquorate', or are unsettled by the prospect of supposedly weaker forms of membership such as part-timers or outworkers.

However, we are also conscious of how much of our lives are spent in working with or within teams, sets, groups, bands, committees, associations and households, and in helping others make sense of their experience of them. Our belief is that however valued these formulations and devices and the theories invested in them are, advances in thinking and practice can only start from a critique of what happens now and an examination of why that is. The previous sections of this chapter throw some major questions into relief. For example, why is the concept of 'group' so predominant? Are the assumptions associated with the concept of the group as likely to support continued development of creative ways in which people can work and learn together as other concepts, as for example, 'community' or 'network'?

There is much about the idea of the group to commend it. There is a large body of accumulated 'wisdom' which includes ideas about ideal size, predictable stages of development, useful roles and ideal combinations of role, leadership attributes and criteria, and a vast array of associated technologies for ensuring effective group performance. Groups are relatively straightforward to identify. You know who is 'in' and who is 'out', and superficially at least, the range of procedures and norms of behaviour to chose from are familiar to most of us, largely because of the attention given to these processes in the literature of social science, organizational behaviour and management development. Whether at work or in education, people often express a preference for small groups over larger or more dispersed formations because of the belief that 'you get more work done' in smaller groups, there is less time wasted, and generally speaking, they are the most comfortable arrangement for avoiding both the isolation of individual endeavour and the sheer frustration or terrifying anonymity of committees and crowds.

But our understanding of the psychodynamics of group life offers an alternative view of the reliance on groups. It may be an avoidance of the threatening, if more challenging, possibilities of less circumscribed formations. Is the attraction of the small group, and associated preoccupation with understanding its process, a response to the alternative spectres of social fragmentation and impending disorder? Ideas which are central to an understanding of how people work together are usually elaborated with reference to groups. By contrast, 'community' or 'network' offer less certainty, more ambiguity and there has been less written about them. The possibilities of size and complexities of structure mean that discerning where boundaries lie is not as straightforward as it is in a small group. Membership is therefore more difficult to work out, leadership is problematical and the sense of belonging not as sure.

By the same token it could be said that the distinct set of concepts which are associated with the idea of the group are not always supportive of the learning necessary to survive the uncertainties of the modern world. Perhaps more insight is to be gained by considering these core concepts – membership, boundaries, leadership and so on – in other contexts, particularly as this illuminates those aspects of the group which are as likely to stifle creativity as to stimulate it. As the saying goes, 'if you want to understand your own country, visit another one'.

In a group, membership tends to constrain independence because expectations and norms which govern behaviour are a condition of membership. This is not so pronounced in communities and networks. Similarly, communities are more likely to subsume assumptions of difference and diversity than groups are. They accommodate more paradoxical positions of value, belief and practice. Consequently, although in a community there is a higher risk of becoming unseen or lost, the price for membership is likely to be less. The emphasis in management learning on groups, however, obviates the need to understand processes like alienation, impotence and invisibility which unfortunately *are* all part of belonging to organizations, communities and societies.

Similarly, leadership is taken for granted as an essential element of any group. Indeed, it is arguable that the dominance of the group as a social arrangement is that it provides a ready vehicle for the more familiar versions of leadership. In networks, on the other hand, with greater ambiguities of continuity and membership, and with a more ephemeral and transient nature, the definition of appropriate leadership is more difficult. Paradoxically, this ambiguity may intensify the demand for leaders. But it is less clear how leaders emerge in networks or communities or how leadership should be exercised. What is the role of a leader in these conditions? How is leadership to take account of the essence of networks being expressed in their processes more than in their structure? We propose that the value of this kind of comparison is that it helps to question the assumptions about leadership and membership in the context of groups. Less introverted preoccupation with the behaviour of members, with norms, sanctions, guarding boundaries and worrying about ideal size, and more attention to understanding and managing the processes we have suggested these measures are intended to control, might enhance our understanding of learning groups and work groups.

Perhaps the point here is that living, learning and working with others is, more often than not, complex, uncertain and hard to predict. In contrast, a group can be seen as a way of limiting uncertainty, of creating a social entity which is more circumscribed and therefore more readily managed. Yet there is so much of social and organizational life that is denied by the simplification which this represents. While ensuring comfort of a kind, the bounded nature of groups precludes more creative alternatives. So, for example, while membership is a source of identity, the price of *group* membership is that individuality is relinquished in the interests of conformity.

Conclusion

We have ended with questions about the dominance of groupwork in management education and development in terms of what this signifies and what may be lost as a consequence. Our aim is not to jettison the concept of group but to change its status by recognizing how constraining on future possibilities the emphasis on it might prove. We acknowledge the central role played by groups in education and at work, but are conscious of the considerable taken-for-granteds and simplifications in both theory and practice. We suggest that groups are helpful in understanding organizations but limited when compared with the concept of 'community' or 'network'. These alternatives are more illustrative of the ambiguities encountered in organizations and wider society, less defined by assumptions of consensus, and less prone to simplistic explanations.

We would argue for caution in reinforcing the group at the expense of other forms and for an awareness of how this reinforcement is brought about through the content and method of education and training – even simple things like how we emphasize the concept of group in management learning practice by the way projects and tasks are constantly divided among 'syndicates', 'sets' and 'teams'. In the same way, groups in training and education are frequently presented with the ideal of internal collaboration and external competition. In contrast, concepts such as community or network contain the possibilities of collaboration and competition *co-existing* both internally and externally, and make them more appropriate for understanding organizations. The challenge is to continue to benefit from understanding and working in groups, but to be informed by ideas which have their origin in the exploration of community and network processes.

In privileging the group as 'figure' and the rest as 'ground', management educators limit understanding of alternatives and obscure their contribution.

Alternative arrangements are often judged by imposing the expectations derived from experiences in groups. This results in uncertainty and ambiguity being seen as bad rather than as neutral or good. Possibilities for creating new orders more appropriate to the demands of the current social and political milieu remain undiscovered – orders which, for example, support creativity though the process of working with rather than excluding, difference.

Annotated Bibliography

For detailed exposition of theories of group behaviour which have been hugely influential Bion (1961) and Rice (1971) present ideas which inform groupwork in the tradition of the Tavistock Institute, and Bradford et al. (1964) is a comprehensive account of the conceptual basis for the T-Group approach. Within this genre, Peter B. Smith's edited book, *Small Groups and Personal Change* (1980b), provides an account of the way groupwork has developed. The chapters by Peter Smith are particularly worth reading, as is his own book *Group Processes and Personal Change* (1980a). Jaques (1991) and Reynolds (1994) write about group theory and groupwork specifically in relation to educational practice, and Boot and Reynolds (1983b) examine related schools of thought in experiential learning more generally. In this last reference Annie Hudson's chapter 'The politics of experiential learning' introduces a much needed critical, in this case feminist, perspective on groupwork, and in the same vein, Wendy Hollway's *Work Psychology and Organizational Behaviour* (1991) presents an account of development work from the point of view of someone who, like Hudson, combines a critique of theory and practice with considerable professional experience of groupwork methods.

References

Argyris, Chris (1964) *Integrating the Individual and the Organization*. New York: Wiley.
Bales, Robert F. (1950) *Interaction Process Analysis: A Method for the Study of Small Groups*. Chicago: University of Chicago Press.
Beckhard, Richard (1969) *Organization Development*. Reading, MA: Addison-Wesley.
Beeby, J.M. and Rathborn, S. (1983) 'Development training – using the outdoors in management development', *Management Education and Development*, 14 (3): 170–81.
Bennis, Warren G. (1966) *Changing Organizations*. New York: McGraw-Hill.
Bion, Wilfred R. (1961) *Experiences in Groups*. London: Tavistock.
Blake, Robert R. and Mouton, Jane S. (1969) *Building a Dynamic Corporation through Grid Organization Development*. Reading, MA: Addison-Wesley.
Boot, Richard L. and Reynolds, Michael (1983a) 'Issues of control in simulations and games', *Simulation/Games for Learning*, 13 (1), Spring: 3–9.
Boot, Richard L. and Reynolds, Michael (eds) (1983b) *Learning and Experience in Formal Education*. Manchester Monographs. Manchester: Manchester University Press.
Boot, Richard L. and Reynolds, Michael (1984) 'Rethinking experience based events', in C. Cox and J. Beck (eds), *Management Development: Advances in Practice and Theory*. London: Wiley. pp. 207–22.
Boot, Richard L. and Reynolds, Michael (1985) 'Learning about organisation: an experiential method', *Journal of Further and Higher Education*, 9 (2), Summer: 14–23.
Bradford, Leland P., Gibb, Jack R. and Benne, Kenneth D. (1964) *T-Group Theory and Laboratory Method*. New York: Wiley.
Hearn, J. (1983) 'Issues of control in simulations and games: a reconsideration', *Simulation/Games for Learning*, 13 (3), Autumn: 120–5.
Higgin, Gurth and Bridger, Harold (1964) 'The psychodynamics of an intergroup experience'. *Tavistock Pamphlet* (No. 10). London: Tavistock.

Hollway, Wendy (1991) *Work Psychology and Organizational Behaviour*. London: Sage.

Hudson, Annie (1983) 'The politics of experiential learning', in Richard L. Boot and Michael Reynolds (eds), *Learning and Experience in Formal Education*. Manchester Monographs. Manchester: Manchester University Press. pp. 81–92.

Jaques, David (1991) *Learning in Groups*. London: Kogan Page.

Klein, Melanie (1959) 'Our adult world and its roots in infancy', *Human Relations*, 12: 291–303.

Knowles, Malcolm (1975) *Self-directed Learning: A Guide for Learners and Teachers*. Chicago: Association Press.

Kolb, David A. (1984) *Experiential Learning*. Englewood Cliffs, NJ: Prentice-Hall.

Kolb, David A., Rubin, Irwin M. and McIntyre, James M. (1984) *Organizational Psychology: An Experiential Approach to Organizational Behaviour*. Englewood Cliffs, NJ: Prentice-Hall.

Lewin, Kurt (1963) *Field Theory in Social Science*. New York: Harper and Row.

Mezirow, Jack (1991) *Transformative Dimensions of Adult Learning*. San Francisco: Jossey-Bass.

Pedler, Mike (1983) *Action Learning in Practice*. Aldershot: Gower.

Pedler, Mike and Boydell, Tom (1984) *Developing the Learning Community*. Aldershot: Gower.

Reynolds, Michael (1994) *Groupwork in Education and Training: Ideas in Practice*. London: Kogan Page.

Rice, A.K. (1971) *Learning for Leadership*. London: Tavistock.

Roethlisberger, F.J. and Dickson, W.J. (1939) *Management and the Worker*. Cambridge, MA: Harvard University Press.

Rogers, Carl R. (1969) *Freedom to Learn*. Columbus, OH: Charles E. Merrill.

Schein, Edgar H. and Bennis, Warren G. (1965) *Personal and Organizational Change through Group Methods*. New York: Wiley.

Sherif, Muzafer (1936) *The Psychology of Social Norms*. New York: Harper and Row.

Smith, Peter B. (1980a) *Group Processes and Personal Change*. London: Harper and Row.

Smith, Peter B. (1980b) *Small Groups and Personal Change*. London: Methuen.

Tuckman, Barry W. (1965) 'Developmental sequences in small groups', *Psychological Bulletin*, 54: 229–49.

PART II
BEING CRITICAL

In the previous section, authors used different approaches to make sense of management learning as a field of academic and professional endeavour. However, ways of making sense of education and development, as of any social process, differ considerably. The approach might be broadly descriptive, historical, or attempt to categorize ideas, methods and sites of practice which are to be found within the field as a whole. But as with the contributions in Part I, a critical approach will seek to make some kind of judgement or evaluation of theory and practice – to discriminate as well as describe.

What does it mean to work out of a critical perspective? The literature in management education contains different interpretations of what a critical approach entails, with correspondingly different implications for theory and practice. The concept of *critical thinking*, for example, usually implies thoughtful analysis and selection between available options. It can also denote careful examination and testing of assumptions and 'taken-for-granteds' which underlie these options, whether in educational or organizational contexts. *Critical reflection*, on the other hand, usually signifies an approach which involves clarification of the power relations implicated in educational or organizational practices, whether these are covert or explicit, and whether rooted in history or embedded in the immediate context. The contributions in this section are particularly of this type.

The Critical 'Turn' in Management Learning

In academic literature, at least, there has been growing interest in developing a more critical perspective within management education. Attention has been called to the need to introduce concepts into the content of managers' learning which encourage questioning of social, organizational and political processes (see, e.g., Alvesson and Willmott, 1992; Reed and Anthony, 1992). This represents a change from the previous tendency for management educators to align themselves with the dominant values of professional management, leaving more critical questions to be put by organizational sociologists from their distant vantage point in academia, or by environmentalists and other activists working within the community or the trade union movement.

Currently, educationalists and management educators who are adopting a more critical approach tend to draw on the ideas of the Frankfurt School – more especially the critical theory of Jürgen Habermas (1972). Habermas's concepts of dialogue, and of a more democratic society brought about by authentic, less distorted communication may strike a chord with management learning professionals who still base their work to some extent on humanist ideals. Habermas's ideas are perhaps more acceptable than the more confrontational position of Marxism, and more accessible than the specialized vocabulary of much postmodernist scholarship.

There are, of course, distinct versions of critical thought, and there are useful introductions to these both in the educational literature (Gibson, 1986) and in the domain of management learning (Cavanaugh and Prasad, 1996). But any approach that draws attention to power relations and to the realities of preferential interests served by education or management is likely to be sufficiently different from traditional practice that fine distinctions are of secondary importance. Feminist educationalists critical of the paternalism inherent in much radical pedagogy draw a similar conclusion (Luke and Gore, 1992) and stress the overarching kinship which should unite schools of thought within the critical perspective.

The relation of critique to practice, however, raises the uneasy association between the academic and professional realms. Management academics, originally admitted on sufferance to the more traditional universities, work the margins between management and academia, risking accusation of irrelevance by the first group and of selling out to more powerful sectional interests by the second. There are, nevertheless, reasons why a more critical approach could gain ground as managers are increasingly called on to address complex issues such as social discrimination and environmental damage, which do not lend themselves to formulized or purely technical solutions.

Yet given the nature of critical inquiry, is the intention to introduce it into the sphere of professional management realistic? Are the fundamentals of a critical approach compatible with an immediacy and relevance to current situations which managers, understandably, look for? To answer these questions, it is necessary to be clear as to the characteristics of a critical approach.

The critical perspective

From a critical perspective it is necessary to treat all generalizations about work and education as likely to indicate sectional interests. Neutrality, even if claimed, should not be assumed. Whether considering theory or practice, it is important to examine underlying assumptions, to reveal important 'taken-for-granteds' and to question claims for the obvious. As Gibson puts it: 'Critical Theory puts traditional notions of objectivity into question and is constantly alert to attempts to pass off sectional viewpoints as universal, natural, classless, timeless ones' (1986: 172). Sectional interests can easily be concealed by claims of 'common sense' or that they are generalizable, claims which should be questioned on principle.

From a similar perspective, Kemmis (1985), in applying the ideas of

Habermas, describes characteristics of critical reflection which seem applicable to management education. They can be summarized as follows:

- *It is concerned with questioning assumptions.* The fundamental task of critical reflection is to identify, question and, if necessary, change these taken-for-granteds. This involves making moral judgements, as well as practical or technical choices.
- *Its focus is social rather than individual.* Critical reflection acknowledges the essentially social, political and historical nature of experience, whether in the context of work or education. The socially situated nature of experience must therefore be taken into account for reflection on experience to have meaning.
- *It pays particular attention to the analysis of power relations.* Perhaps the most notable characteristic of critical reflection is the emphasis placed on questioning relations between power and knowledge and the way individuals' perspectives are inevitably influenced by their position in hierarchies of power.
- *It is concerned with emancipation.* Critical reflection is part of an ideology, a theoretical basis for social action and, above all, a set of beliefs as to how to bring about a more just society.

As with most interpretations of 'critical perspective', this description surfaces the tension for management learning professionals between the reasonable demand to provide workable solutions to managers' day-to-day problems and the need to stimulate more fundamental inquiry into the function and purposes of management, the values on which managing in different contexts is based, and to identify the points where sectional interests are in conflict.

Critical reflection will not find its place in management education if it is made difficult to comprehend, seems tangential to the daily struggle experienced by managers, or is unaware of, or unsympathetic to, their concerns and accomplishments. There is also a need for management educators to understand the possible consequences for individuals who adopt a more critical perspective, and the risks of disillusionment and marginalization which can accompany it. And there is a need to be alert to the tendency in management education and development for the *language* of critique to be accommodated or assimilated and its agenda neutralized.

The Chapters in this Section

In the opening chapter of this section, *Ian Cunningham* and *Graham Dawes* remind us of the value of questioning the doctrine and logic which pervades management learning, and of refusing to accept assumptions because they have become embedded in professional practice, however respected and longstanding, whether in educational institutions or development programmes in organizations. Management learning has a considerable repertoire of theories and practices – experiential learning or competencies, for example – which have come to comprise an unquestioned professional tradition. Cunningham and Dawes demonstrate that intelligent irreverence for this legacy is a potent basis for critique of theory and practice in any setting.

Decades ago, the social philosopher Herbert Marcuse, a forerunner of Habermas as a member of the Frankfurt School, proposed that changes in twentieth-century Western society, in particular the increasing affluence of the workforce, meant that it was less likely than Marx had supposed that social and political revolution would erupt from class struggle. It was more realistic, Marcuse believed, that significant social change would have its origins in minority movements and their resistance of inequality and discrimination on the basis of gender or race. In the management context this suggests an intriguing parallel. Even though the strongest tradition in management education has been based on unitary and consensus politics, feminisms have found a voice within the relatively affluent and privileged ranks of managers. The basis and distribution of power, and the gendered assumptions that maintain them, are being challenged, and the limitations these impose on the professional lives of both women and men are brought into the debate, as witnessed by the chapter by *Richard Boot* and *Morgan Tanton*.

The account of critical discourse analysis by *Norman Fairclough* and *Ginny Hardy* illustrates the subtle ways in which language constructs and maintains our assumptions about social relationships. Language can be used, in their terms, 'in order to hide certain aspects of power or to strengthen presuppositions or taken-for-granteds'. So embedded in everyday speech and writing are these processes that it requires a disciplined analysis of text to reveal them. Norman Fairclough and Ginny Hardy introduce critical discourse analysis and, in applying the approach, demonstrate how a systematic examination of management development texts can uncover the educational and management discourses which have been incorporated in the practices of management learning.

In the final chapter of Part II *Hugh Willmott*, who has made a significant contribution in advocating a critical perspective in writing on management and in the teaching of managers, elaborates the difference which inclusion of such critique should make. Elsewhere, he has advocated an incremental approach to incorporating a critical element into management learning, in preference to either purely negative critique or impracticable utopian proposals. In this spirit, his chapter develops the possibility that in action learning there already exists the educational means of combining immediacy to work problems with ways of making sense of them from a critical standpoint.

References

Alvesson, M. and Willmott, H. (1992) *Critical Management Studies*. London: Sage.
Cavanaugh, J. Michael and Prasad, Anshuman (1996) 'Critical theory and management

education: some strategies for the critical classroom', in Robert French and Christopher Grey (eds), *Rethinking Management Education*. London: Sage.

Gibson, R. (1986) *Critical Theory and Education*. London: Hodder and Stoughton.

Habermas, Jürgen (1972) *Knowledge and Human Interests*. London: Heinmann.

Kemmis, S. (1985) 'Action research and the politics of reflection', in D. Boud, R. Keogh and D. Walker (eds), *Reflection: Turning Experience into Learning*. London: Kogan Page. pp. 139–63.

Luke, Carmen and Gore, Jennifer (1992) (eds) *Feminisms and Critical Pedagogy*. New York: Routledge.

Reed, Michael and Anthony, Peter (1992) 'Professionalizing management and managing professionalization: British management in the 1980s', *Journal of Management Studies*, 29 (September): 591–613.

6

Problematic Premises, Presumptions, Presuppositions and Practices in Management Education and Training

Ian Cunningham and Graham Dawes

Organized management learning operates under various labels such as those of 'education', 'training', and 'development'. The focus of this chapter is management learning organized into time-bounded, structured courses or programmes. These may be long and qualification-based, as are MBAs, or short and topic-focused, like one-day workshops.

It is clear that such activities are different from other learning arenas used by managers. Our research (Dawes et al., 1996) indicates that most of what managers learn about managing does not come from such programmes. They learn most from their day-to-day work, from colleagues, from observing other managers, and from sundry life experiences (e.g., travel). Nonetheless, questions of how to help managers learn more – and more effectively – tend to be focused on organized programmes and, consequently, it is these which this chapter addresses.

Our contention is that most such programmes are based on unexamined, and problematic, assumptions. To go *beyond* what is currently offered in organized management learning we need to look *behind* it – hence the chapter focuses on these assumptions. This is not to take an absolutist stance that they are necessarily 'wrong' or 'untrue'. Our concern is that they are usually unexamined and thus lead to problems. Our approach will be to question some of the most significant of these assumptions. In doing so we will, in essence, be asking of those who design and provide such programmes what justification they have for what they assume. While we might indicate research which challenges a particular assumption (and therefore, in effect, justifies our questioning of it) the burden of justification must fall on those who stand on the positions we question.

We do not have the space here to go into possible solutions to the problems we pose: some directions are indicated in Cunningham (1994). Although we have mainly given examples based on practice in the UK, most of the assumptions we cover seem general in North America and Europe. The Asian scene is different and we have not examined that here.

The assumptions we have identified are divided into three categories:

those which seem common to all organized management learning whether it takes place in a university, an organization or a training establishment; those which apply mainly to the education world (as exemplified by the universities); and those which seem more in the domain of training, especially within organizations. We recognize that the distinction is blurred in many cases. Our challenge is aimed not at individual practitioners but at the 'culture of the field', using Hofstede's notion of culture as collective mental programming (Hofstede, 1980) or what some might call a paradigm (Burrell and Morgan, 1979).

General Problems of Organized Management Learning – in Any Context

No order of importance is implied in this listing. Nor does the amount of space given to a factor indicate its importance – some require more explanation than others. While we identify the problematic assumptions, we have not attempted a thorough analysis of the issues. Our question is: What is the justification for this assumption?

Assumption: Management exists as a subject or as a field of human activity – and it will continue to exist indefinitely

This assumption has its roots in a positivist epistemology (see other chapters in this volume) and the ahistorical nature of presumptions about management. It is assumed that what is done now under the name of 'management' exists in a de-historicized vacuum, yet there are plenty of signs to suggest that managers and the concept of management could cease to be of importance in the future. Some organizations have already deleted the term 'manager'. 'Management' is associated with a view of control, order and organization which these companies reject. The notion of the 'self managing organization' (Gimson and Dawes, 1996) or the 'intelligent organization' of Pinchot and Pinchot (1994) is different from the traditional hierarchy which assumes that there are the managers and the managed.

Could leadership become the dominant theme in the twenty-first century? Historically, it has been the more important activity. The case for leadership being distinctively different from management is well made by organizations such as the Center for Creative Leadership, as well as in numerous writings (e.g., Bennis, 1984). One reason why leadership is less favoured in organized courses (especially in universities) is that it is clear that learning leadership is tricky; and it includes domains such as the emotional (traditionally an uncomfortable arena for university academics – see Bain, 1996; Cunningham, 1994).

We are not saying that the concept or the practice of management will necessarily disappear. We are challenging the premise that the continued existence of management (as a necessary social process) is unproblematic – that it can be taken as a given in organizing management courses.

Assumption: Management is a context-free activity – there are things to learn which have universal validity

The research on national cultures by Hofstede (1980), Ratiu (1987) and Trompenaars (1993), among others, undermines this assumption. Their work is not matched by any comparable research giving a basis for the presumption of a wide range of universally valid theories and techniques. Nonetheless, almost all Anglo-American textbooks on management are written with the premise of such universals. Even within the same national culture, organizations have their own varying cultures. Consequently, standardized prescriptions within a national culture are of dubious validity.

At the national level in the UK, an example of this problem is the Management Charter Initiative (MCI) which assumes that all organizations are similar, the only significant difference being between levels of management. Thorpe and Holman's (1995) research shows that this is an unacceptable assumption. The MCI position stems from a bureaucratic, hierarchical model of management and assumes this culture for all organizations. Additionally, no account is taken of, for example, varying size, differences between public and private sectors and differences between international and purely UK companies. (See Cunningham, 1994, for a more extensive critique of the dangers of national lists of competencies.)

Universities make the same error in their standardized MBAs. Even where such courses are tailored to, say, the public sector, they still ignore crucial differences (e.g., accounting and financial management differences in various parts of the public sector, size differences, professional differences, etc.).

Hofstede (1985) also raises the important point that teaching/training methods themselves are likely to be culture specific. He uses his research to argue that cross-cultural teaching/learning situations are fraught with problems that often go unrecognized. With companies increasingly running programmes for managers from different countries, and business schools actively recruiting students from a range of countries, this problem has grown.

Assumption: What is taught equals what is learned

The assumption that what is taught equals what is learned underpins the idea of a syllabus, and of a timetabled design for a course. The premise is that knowledge and skill transfer is relatively unproblematic. These assumptions, and that what is taught *needs* to be learned, is inconsistent with the requirement of most universities for a 40 or 50 per cent pass-mark for masters degree. This allows the student to miss out on a large chunk of the syllabus and still easily get the degree. In addition, exams usually have a choice of questions. A choice of, say, three questions out of ten means you only need to learn 30 per cent of the syllabus (and then answer only to 40 or 50 per cent accuracy). This is not just theoretical; we know that it works.

In selection processes, the same 'what-is-taught-equals-what-is-learned' error leads selectors to assume that when various training courses appear on a CV the attendee has learned the content of those courses. In fact they may have been asleep at the back, or been in syndicates where others did all the work. Different people will take different learnings away from any experience, including a designed learning experience. The question can only be: What did this specific individual take from the experience?

Assumption: There is a self that learns – and learning is largely an individual activity

While it is assumed that there is a 'self' that learns, this self is not explored because many programmes are concerned with knowledge *about* management, that is, knowledge outside the self. However, the inclusion of any 'self-development' element raises the question: What is a 'self' that 'it' learns?

The idea of a self that accumulates knowledge and skills, and is able to apply them, is only one among many possible concepts of the self. In Tibetan Buddhist thought the self does not exist, and the practice of meditation is designed to reveal its absence. In a less exotic locale, our own eighteenth century, David Hume said much the same in *A Treatise of Human Nature* when he pointed out that he could never catch 'myself' at anytime without a perception, yet never could observe anything other than the perception.

Conventional Western ideas about the self assume individualism in social life. Cultures with different ideas foreground co-operation over individual interests (Hofstede, 1980). We view them as conformist cultures and deplore what we see as the inability of people to be real individuals. But is a 'real' individual a lone individual? The lines of John Donne ('No man is an Island, entire of it self [*sic*]; everyman is a piece of the Continent, a part of the main', etc.) are so (over)familiar that we tend to miss their resonance.

Is the individual the appropriate focus of organized management learning activity? Those advocating 'the learning organization' imply that it may not be. Whatever the intentions, approaches which harbour an implicit individualism exacerbate the self-centredness and 'wheeler-dealerism' which gives management a bad name. They also lead to a lessening of the amount of trust within organizations and cultures in general. Some of the effects of this are suggested in Fukuyama's (1995) claim that high-trust cultures have a significant economic advantage over low-trust cultures. Management learning initiatives which encourage individualistic stances, either through a totally individual focus or through developing competition between individuals, discourage awareness of the collective dimensions of organizational, as of social, life.

Assumption: Learning is all one thing – the verb 'to learn' covers only one process

Although the name of Gregory Bateson is well known, the import of his work, particularly his theory of learning, rarely influences the design of organized management learning (Bateson, 1973). He recognized that there were different types of learning. In his theory, Learning Zero is a mere reflex response. Learning One encompasses most of what is the focus of organized management learning. It is often conceived as being 'added on' to the person, or as if it can be accumulated ready for use, like charging a battery. The competenc(i)es orientation is an example. It is only with Learning Two that learning constitutes a change in individuals, and in how they think about what they are doing in their work and life. It involves a shift of assumptions after which both the person and their behaviour are different.

Being a different level of learning, Learning Two requires a different approach. It encompasses what is known as the 'hidden curriculum' in education, the unintended learning that comes about from the *form* of the learning experience. In our schools and universities, experts (the teachers and tutors) decide what students are to learn, how they are to learn it, and will judge whether or not they have done so. Thus are learners 'taught' (unintentionally) to depend on experts for their learning. While unnoticed by examinations, which test Learning One subject knowledge, this learning of dependency (Learning Two) is the more profound and pervasive learning. It is also the more difficult to change. Equally detrimental to the learner is the flip-side of dependency, the counterdependent and rebellious behaviour which can be triggered by the educational control system.

If we are serious about wanting participants to learn how to learn, both under their own steam and through drawing on others, and to be able to take charge of their lives, not only as managers but as people, then this must be considered in the design of learning experiences. While the content being learned may be in the Learning One domain, the *form* of the learning experience must produce useful learning at the Learning Two level. This would be to utilize the structure of the hidden curriculum to the participants' advantage.

Assumption: Learners are much the same and learn in similar ways

It is common to cover the Kolb learning cycle (Kolb and Fry, 1975), or some variant of it, on management programmes, yet the idea that people have different learning styles has little impact on programme design. Although open learning, for instance, allows learners to learn where they like and when they like, there is no more freedom over learning methods than on traditional courses. The recognition of individual differences gets a ritual nod as part of the content of management programmes but rarely gets applied to them.

*Assumption: Issues of the authority, control and power of staff
(trainers and tutors) over learners are unimportant*

Our experience suggests that many people are attracted (usually unconsciously) into teaching/training because they enjoy control over others. If it
is not the initial attraction, it grows into a valued part of the job because of
the culture of education and training. Obviously, there will be large
variations in the need for control among individuals; we are commenting on
the general teaching/training culture.

This control phenomenon is amplified in academic environments due to
the ability to give or withhold qualifications. Despite a rhetoric of learner-
centredness, the drift towards control has in most cases undermined radical
innovations in learning design.

Assumption: Means and ends can be separated

A common assertion is that education is about helping people to be more
autonomous, more able to operate in a democratic society, etc. Such
premises define the ends of education, yet the means used to achieve them
are the antithesis of the ends. Educational activity takes place in an
environment with little autonomy and/or democracy.

Similarly, most organizations want managers who can set goals and work
to achieve them. Yet training processes usually deny any opportunity for
managers to set their own learning goals or decide on how to achieve them.
The result of the means/ends split is that the ends are inadequately met.

*Assumption: The debate is between knowledge-based courses and
competency acquisition – 'there is no other show in town'*

The quote comes from an MCI official who was arguing that the only future
choices available for management education and training were between old-
fashioned knowledge-based courses or the MCI competency approach. The
corollary of this argument was 'if you're not with us, then you're against us
and for traditional taught courses'. This false polarity is a gross distortion of
the current scene but clearly suits certain political interests.

Mabey and Iles suggest that 'competency has been used as an attempt to
professionalize the previously ad hoc world of management training' (1994:
1). This indicates how the politics of the field are developing. Arguing
between professionalizing through competenc(i)es and professionalizing
through MBAs becomes a convenient battleground – and one which ignores
other positions.

Assumption: Courses really exist (design is not a metaphor)

Courses are presumed to have a life of their own – separate from their
designers – and can therefore be implemented by anyone. The syllabus is
assumed to dictate not just what is taught but how it is taught. The ultimate
extension of this is the open learning package (often in multi-media format

these days). However, the standard face-to-face delivered event is clearly very dependent on who is delivering it, and in what context.

In designing a chair, the chair stays a chair no matter who uses it. This is not the case with a course. It is not a concrete entity but an invented format. If we remember our basic English grammar lessons, a noun should signify a person, place or thing. A course is none of these. If we were to be strict about it, we would say that the noun should be replaced by a verb as we are describing a process not a thing.

This is not a trivial issue. We have been involved, with other colleagues, in designing two masters degrees – an MBA at Roffey Park Management Institute and an MSc in Managing Change at Sheffield Business School. These were Self-Managed Learning designs (as described in Cunningham, 1991). Those who have taken over the running of these courses interpret Self-Managed Learning in quite a different way from us. Hence the courses are no longer the same courses. However, as the title remains the same and the 'course' is assumed to be like a chair (i.e., unchanged by a changed owner), the customers probably think they are buying the same thing. (This does not imply that what we did is better than what others are now doing. There is no absolute way of defining 'better'. All we can say is that there is a significant difference.)

Assumption: Quality is best assured through control mechanisms

There has been a growing interest in using the concept of quality in trying to improve management courses. This has been most demonstrable in education, with the appearance of national bodies and internal university committees. However, organizations smitten with the TQM bug have also been active in this domain. The issue of concern here is how the notion of quality is addressed. The systems in place in most cases seem a long way from the Deming model, and have an emphasis on mechanistic controls and individualized blame systems (such as appraisals). The alternative view of quality is that it is a balance of dynamic and static processes (Pirsig, 1991). The control systems can be seen as part of what Pirsig describes as static – and he does not deny their value in tackling, for instance, the crooked operators.

Pirsig balances static quality with dynamic quality. The latter could be linked to areas such as continuous improvement and innovation. In this context, the role of staff is a crucial part of the dynamic domain. Our research (see Cunningham, 1984) indicates that the staff role is vital and that their capabilities are central to developing quality. However, the very problems that bedevil other training and educational activity undermine staff development. The problematic presumptions and presuppositions about management courses also, in the main, apply to courses for educators and trainers. We are in a vicious spiral with only a few institutions trying to break out of it.

Problems Specific to University-based Organized Management Learning

On the basis of the above general issues, we can note issues which seem more specifically to affect the university sector. Some of these also affect training activity, but we are postulating that the major impact is in the university sector.

Assumption: Third-person knowledge is all that is valued

Third-person knowledge is about the world 'out there', disconnected from me/us (first person) and from you (second person). At least, it is assumed that it can be. The role of the author of a research paper is presumed to be that of an objective observer, not an active creator of meaning. The case made by New Paradigm researchers (e.g., Reason, 1989; Reason and Rowan, 1981) seems to us a solid one. Their stance accommodates the wider first and second-person positions.

This leaves untouched the serious issue of whether management teachers have experienced the first-person position in management. Gibson (1984) indicates some important reasons why management tutors could need first-person knowledge. The most important reason may not be that the tutors can use that experience in class, but rather that individuals who have had significant management experience are likely to have absorbed the holistic sense of the role. They have experienced the heart and guts of managing as well as the head (rational) side. They may then be more able to integrate the first-, second- and third-person perspectives. Note here that we are saying: (a) that the third-person (detached knowledge) perspective has its place – it is not to be rejected; and (b) that the tutor 'may' be able to do this integration (experience, of itself, does not guarantee this).

A problem with third-person bias in business schools is that management research increasingly seems to be for the purpose of improving the research ratings of academics, with almost no sense of it being of use to managers (Jenkins and Gibbs, 1995). Being third-person knowledge, even when it is of relevance to managers, it can only be used for understanding and analysis. It is involved knowledge (first and second person) that is needed for decision-making and action, and universities seem less and less interested in engaging with the world of action (Gruneberg, 1995; Mullender, 1995).

Assumption: Reductionism and fragmentation into subjects is the only way to progress the teaching of management

As numerous writers (e.g., Burgoyne, 1991) have pointed out, the choice of subjects to be taught on, for instance, an MBA seems highly arbitrary. Subject disciplines are the primary basis for university structures and, in many cases, the syllabus is driven by which academic departments are available and can make a case for their involvement in MBA teaching. Subjects like statistics/quantitative methods become argued into the syllabus to give spurious rigour and credibility to MBAs (which are felt to be a less proper qualification for a university to offer). One business school dean asserted to us that 98 per cent of managers never use what they learn in quantitative methods courses. This is supported by our own research, yet in most MBAs it would be impossible to drop the subject.

A more serious challenge to subject teaching is made in the IMI Commission 2000 Report where they comment:

> Why is there a need for integrative learning? Because understanding reality, regardless of disciplines, is a complex and integrated process where many different levels of perception, knowledge, intuition and emotions interact to provide a coherent whole. To make this presumption central to management education involves a substantial challenge because much of past teaching and research has been oriented to analysis, accumulation of knowledge and diffusion of information in a fragmented manner. (1986: 8)

The report goes on to elaborate on the centrality of subjectivity, creativity and courage in management practice. Its authors see the subject-based model as undermining the need for managers to be visionary leaders, which requires them to be holistic thinkers and doers.

Assumption: Educational environments are good places in which to learn

This is accepted as an obvious truth by many. Libraries, access to academics and other features of the average university are taken as key to learning. In contrast, Raven's research (Raven, 1994, 1995) indicates that educational institutions may be the worst kind of learning environment. From Raven's research, and our own, we can list a few key requirements for a good learning environment (with a bracketed point about why universities may not meet that requirement):

- Opportunities to practise, to do the actual work involved. (At best universities offer such methods as case studies and computer simulations. These are not comparable to the kinds of practice that managers have to engage in. See Revans (1980) and Cunningham (1994) for elaboration of this point.)
- Emotional support. (Universities tend to ignore this except when distress is apparent – and then the person is sent to the counsellor. See Bramley, 1977.)
- Active engagement with the peer group, including sharing with others and informal joint activity on projects. (Universities often call this 'cheating' and punish people for it.)
- Chance to fail without punishment. (This has always been a problem for universities but has been made worse by continuous assessment methods. At least with end-of-course exams you could make mistakes in course work knowing that they would not count at the final exam.)
- Opportunity to ask questions of practitioners. (As universities do not usually have current practitioners on the faculty, this opportunity is only available through other means. Beard's (1992) research on MBA

students found that they wanted fewer lectures from faculty and more field visits and more visiting speakers.)

- Role models to draw from. This factor is a key benefit of real-work situations and is why such situations are more influential in managerial learning than universities. University academics provide:
  - detachment (when managerial work is the opposite);
  - analysis before action (when managerial work requires the integration of the two);
  - primarily auditory communication, as exemplified in writing (essays, articles, papers, books) and one-way oral communication (lectures) (when managerial work largely requires two-way oral communication and needs visual and kinaesthetic capability in addition to the auditory (see Bandler and Grinder, 1975). Beard (1992) found from his research on MBA students that one of their greatest criticisms of the MBA was the requirement to write a dissertation);
  - criticism – the ability to say what is wrong with something (when management requires the ability to innovate, to see if there is anything usable in something);
  - information from research and professional experts (when managers use multiple information channels, including the subjective feelings of those around them);
  - unilateral judgement of performance which excludes the views of learners, their peers, etc. (when managing requires complex multi-layered performance assessments as indicated by the increasing use of 360-degree feedback and related methodologies).

Assumption: Management qualifications signify management capability

The principle is that a qualification should signal to a selector that the individual has a particular capability which can be drawn upon. In the case of management qualifications, though, it only indicates knowledge *about* management. Unfortunately, it does not mean the person is *able to manage*. Much of the criticism of MBAs in recent years (e.g., Cunningham, 1994; Bain, 1996) recognizes that an MBA does not make someone a better manager.

In support of this contention, research at the University of Southern California indicates that performance on the Graduate Management Admission Test (GMAT) may be negatively correlated with management performance.[1] The Graduate Management Admission Council in the USA, which administers the GMAT, commented that the GMAT was designed to predict academic success (on the MBA) and not real-world management skill.

Assumption: Assessment must be through objective measurement

One of the arguments for unilateral assessment is that learners and their peers will be unable to be objective. The implication is that tutors, on the other hand, are able to 'divest themselves of the passions' and be Cartesian about the process. The extent to which they are, or are not, cannot be put to the test as they are not obliged to answer to the learner for their judgement; it happens behind closed doors and its workings usually never see the light of day.

Our own paper (Cunningham and Dawes, 1991) on this matter argued the case for inter-subjective assessments which involve the learners and others. This is closer to the growing use of 360-degree feedback in organizations. Whether you agree with such modes or not does not matter to our case here. We would reiterate that it is for those who claim unfettered objectivity to justify their assumptions on rational/empirical grounds and not, as at present, through the naked application of authority and power.

Assumption: Vertical grading is the only way to assess people

The notion of vertical grading is commonplace in education. Its most pernicious outcropping is in some schools where students are given form positions based on marks. But universities also do it through the degree grading system and the marking practices of academics. Horizontal grading requires the recognition of the multi-factor nature of management and the need to give feedback to people which reflects as much as possible the varying capabilities that each person has. Horizontal grading excludes crude notions of pass–fail or marking and requires a sophisticated exercise in assisting individuals to see the different strengths and weaknesses that they may have at any one time, and to recognize that strengths and weaknesses are also context-bound. A strength in one context may be a weakness in another and vice versa.

Some educational institutions have started to use records of achievement as a way of overcoming the crudity of vertical grading, but it is not apparent that this has had much impact yet on business schools.

Assumption: Politics in universities is relatively irrelevant to decision-making

Universities, like any social organization, are political systems. Yet the outcomes of political processes are presented to customers as the result of objective, rational decision-making. An example, repeated in a number of business schools, may suffice. The director of the MBA programme wants to change the balance of teaching, in response to the requests of his clients, and suggests to one professor that his area be cut back (in terms of class teaching time). The professor is an international name and indicates that this is unacceptable to him as it detracts from the status of his subject. He presents no academic or practical basis for his objection – only one of status (and, by implication, of power). The professor's view prevails and the programme remains unchanged. The balance of teaching time on the MBA is presented to clients as the result of rational analysis. The dishonesty of the face presented by the business school would be more acceptable if academics did not research other organizations exposing others' politics and power plays without accepting their own (Kakabadse, 1983).

Problems Specific to Organization-based Management Learning

While the general assumptions (discussed above) apply to this context, here we examine some which are *specific* to the organizational context. Again there is no implication that the balance of words written indicates the importance of any particular issue. Also, here we are still challenging assumptions on the basis of a case that needs to be addressed rather than an implication that we are promoting a truth. We merely want to open up for examination others' assumed 'truths'.

Assumption: Training is more practical than education

Trainers in many organizations assert, without providing evidence, that their courses are more practical (and, by implication, provide better pay-off) than those provided by the educational world. However, very few courses are subject to evaluation beyond 'volume-of-applause' criteria. Our own research has shown that the end-of-course 'happiness sheet' is still the most used method of evaluation. Yet when research is done thoroughly and looks at what people have learned from an event, the evidence is that immediate responses on the usefulness of a course are unreliable. Cooper and Bowles's (1977) study of T-Groups showed that initially many participants were unhappy with their experience, but months after could cite valuable changes in behaviour. Their work also showed that mythology is unreliable in judging courses. The common myth grew up that T-Groups were dangerous and harmed people. All the evidence points to the opposite. Yet, again in our own research, we found trainers basing their decisions on nothing better than mythology.

This conclusion is reflected in Burgoyne and Jackson (this volume) when they quote research by Monahan that training is taken on faith and when they use Meyer and Scott's analysis to argue that training has stayed locked in an educational model.

Assumption: The more management training the better

Before IBM experienced its major financial disasters it was lauded as an example of how a heavy investment in management training paid off. However, DeLamarter (1988) charges that IBM's success was based less on the nurturing of managerial talent than on driving competitors out of business by the abuse of its monopolistic power.

Beyond specific company cases, research going back to at least Fleishman's (1953) classic study showed that supervisors could learn to be more participative on a course but that the behaviour did not last. They reverted to the behaviour required by their bosses and the training had no demonstrable value. Argyris has provided one theoretical basis for this problem and has written at length on it over many years (see, e.g., Argyris and Schön, 1974) yet his work is daily ignored by most management trainers.

Assumption: Training needs analysis should be the basis for course design

The use of training needs analysis links back to the earlier point that the design metaphor can confuse people into believing a course is a real 'thing' with a life of its own. Training needs analysis is presumed to provide objective data upon which to base a design. However, our own research (Dawes et al., 1996) indicates that the generalizations that come out of a needs analysis provide a false certainty. Individual differences are quite large, but disappear in unidimensional analyses. And even if a majority say that they need, for example, 'better communication skills' what does that mean in practice?

Communication needs can be presentation skills, listening skills, interpersonal skills, writing skills, PR skills, etc. Even if a needs analysis pins it down to, say, presentation skills, managers will have different needs. Some will be good at preparing a presentation and poor at delivery, and others have the opposite problem. Both will manifest the same performance problem (poor presentations) but the reasons will be different and therefore so will the learning needs. But even if you pin it down to poor preparation, some will be poor at this because they are inveterate procrastinators, others because they are poor time managers, and so on. Problems in one area tend to loop into others and are not solvable through unidimensional, standardized training designs.

Assumption: Transfer of learning is relatively easy

Fleishman's (1953) study on the failures of transfer has already been quoted, so there is a clear and long-standing research basis for our concerns in this area. Casey (1980) has shown that even in areas such as action learning there are transfer problems of a significant nature. With the growing recognition of systemic factors (Senge, 1990) and the support for learning organizations, the reliance on sending individuals on courses and assuming that they will unproblematically make changes back in the workplace is under severe challenge.

Assumption: Training is developmental

Training departments have increasingly wanted to attach the word 'development' to their titles. Development is often seen as more up-market or of higher status than just training on its own. In the UK this was reflected in the Institution of Training Officers (ITO), renaming itself the Institute of Training and Development (ITD) before being taken over by the IPM (Institute of Personnel Management).

However, this attempted switch is not always successful. Training is often seen as a remedial function. Middle managers are sent on courses because in an appraisal interview they are identified as having particular weaknesses. They are only sent if they are no good at something. This places learning activity in a low-status position in the organization, and undermines a more developmental stance.

Assumption: Experiential learning is best

The value of experiential learning is taken as read in many training departments. The term has come to be applied quite widely, covering outdoor development, the accreditation of prior experiential learning (APEL), simulation exercises, and so on. While there are significant differences between all these modes, what is common is the emphasis on 'doing something active' as a basis for learning. Cunningham (1988) summarizes the problems with this stance. However, we will quote just two concerns here:

(a) Experience is always about the past. If we learn from the past that we cannot predict the future then that can be valuable (second order) learning (Bateson, 1973). If, however, our learning is solely first order, for example only knowledge and skills, then we may find that not only are these useless in the future, but that it is actually harmful to cling on to them and try to use them beyond their useful life.

(b) Much management learning is demonstrably not from experience. Managers learn from observing others, from reading, from being mentored, etc. Manager's who had planned to go to Bosnia to sell their products would have been happy to learn from the TV or the press the dangers of getting killed there without having to experience it at first hand in order to learn this. People going on to the shop floor for the first time will be delighted to be told not to put their hands in the way of equipment that could cut them off – and they will not be disappointed to be denied the experiential learning.

Conclusion

We have addressed a range of presumptions, premises and presuppositions about organized management learning. We find these problematic. We started by discussing some assumptions which we saw as generally applying in a wide range of situations. We then went on to consider the context of university-based programmes and we covered a number of common assumptions that are prevalent in this context. Lastly, we identified some assumptions that seem mostly to affect organizationally based programmes. In all cases we have wanted to present these usually unarticulated assumptions in order to raise important issues that affect how programmes are organized. The experience that learners have is fundamentally underpinned by the assumptions that drive professors, lecturers and trainers. We have articulated our concerns in a starkly negative manner in order to raise the challenge. Also, the assumptions in question are stated in bald terms. In few cases would anyone want to claim them as his/her own. And this is just the point, for these do not represent 'espoused theory' but 'theory in use'. Whatever the rhetoric, much organized management learning activity is underpinned by them.

There is not sufficient space to indicate the way we have addressed these problems ourselves. However, we are clear that they are all answerable to a greater or lesser extent. What we hope we have done is to challenge people to examine their own assumptions in order to progress the field of management learning. What concerns us is that we can get ourselves into real trouble if we try to progress on the basis of myth and fantasy.

Viewing this chapter, reflexively, as a site for assumptions, it may appear that we expect, through readers recognizing and re-thinking the assumptions underlying their practice, a 'great leap forward' in the field of management learning. Not quite. For that would be to assume that decisions are made solely on rational grounds. If that were so, there would be no difference between what is espoused and what is acted.

Note

1   The research was quoted in *Business Week*, 4 July 1994, and in the ASTD Management Development Report, Summer 1994, p. 4.

Annotated Bibliography

G. Bateson (1973) *Steps to an Ecology of Mind*. London: Paladin, is a collection of conceptually loaded papers which informs the perceptions and perspectives taken here, especially regarding learning and epistemology. I. Cunningham (1994) *The Wisdom of Strategic Learning*. Maidenhead: McGraw-Hill, presents solutions to many of the problems identified here, whereas G. Pinchot and E. Pinchot (1994) *The End of Bureaucracy and the Rise of the Intelligent Organization*. San Francisco: Berrett-Kohler, explores how the principle of self-managing can operate within large organizations. P. Reason and J. Rowan (eds) (1981) *Human Inquiry: A Sourcebook of New Paradigm Research*. Chichester: John Wiley, argues a particular view of knowledge (implicit in this chapter) and how it can inform research. P. Reason (ed.) (1989) *Human Inquiry in Practice*. London: Sage, concentrates on examples of application.

References

Argyris, C. and Schön, D. (1974) *Theory in Practice*. San Francisco: Jossey-Bass.
Bain, N. (1996) 'Management's vital component', in *Management Today*, March: 26.
Bandler, R. and Grinder, J. (1975) *The Structure of Magic* (vols 1 and 2). Palo Alto, CA: Science and Behavior Books.
Bateson, G. (1973) *Steps to an Ecology of Mind*. London: Paladin.
Beard, P.R.J. (1992) *The Reality behind the Myth: The MBA Experience*. London: Association of MBAs.
Bennis, W.G. (1984) *On Becoming a Leader*. Reading, MA: Addison-Wesley.
Bramley, W. (1977) *Personal Tutoring in Higher Education*. Guildford: Society for Research into Higher Education.
Burgoyne, J.G. (1991) 'Managing by learning', inaugural lecture, Lancaster University, Lancaster.

Burrell, G. and Morgan, G. (1979) *Sociological Paradigms and Organizational Analysis*. London: Heinemann.

Casey, D. (1980) 'Transfer of learning: there are two separate problems', in J. Beck and C. Cox (eds), *Advances in Management Education*. Chichester: J. Wiley.

Cooper, C.L. and Bowles, D. (1977) *Hurt or Helped*. London: HMSO.

Cunningham, I. (1984) *'Teaching styles in learner-centred management development programmes'*, PhD thesis, Lancaster University, Lancaster.

Cunningham, I. (1988) 'Learning to learn', in V. Hodgson, S. Mann and R. Snell. (eds), *Beyond Distance Teaching: Towards Open Learning*. Milton Keynes: Open University Press.

Cunningham, I. (1991) 'Self managed learning', in A. Mumford (ed.), *Handbook of Management Development* (3rd edn). Aldershot: Gower.

Cunningham, I. (1994) *The Wisdom of Strategic Learning*. Maidenhead: McGraw-Hill.

Cunningham, I. and Dawes, G. (1991) 'Management Qualifications: Is Objective Assessment Rigorous Enough?', paper presented to the Association for Management Education and Development/Ashridge Research Conference, Berkhamsted.

Dawes, G., Bennett, B., Cunningham, C. and Cunningham, I. (1996) *Learning and Development in Organizations*. St Albans: Strategic Developments.

DeLamarter, R.L. (1988) *Big Blue: IBM's Use and Abuse of Power*. London: Pan.

Fleishman, E.A. (1953) 'Leadership climate and human relations training', *Personnel Psychology*, 6: 205–22.

Fukuyama, Francis (1995) *Trust: The Social Virtues and the Creation of Prosperity*. London: Hamish Hamilton.

Gibson, M.D. (1984) 'Management experience and the management studies tutor', paper presented to the Sixth International Conference on Higher Education, Lancaster, 28–31 August.

Gimson, A. and Dawes, G. (1996) 'The self managing organization', *Croner HRM Professionals Briefing* (Issue 8), 5, 2–3 January.

Gruneberg, M. (1995) 'Publish and be paid', *Times Higher Education Supplement*, 15, 13 September.

Hofstede, G. (1980) *Culture's Consequences: International Differences in Work Values*. London: Sage.

Hofstede, G. (1985) 'Cultural differences in teaching and learning', paper presented to the Colloquium on Selected Issues in International Business, Honolulu, Hawaii, 10–11 August.

International Management Institute (1986) *Report of the Commission on the Year 2000*. Geneva: IMI. (IMI is now part of the Institute of Management Development (IMD).)

Jenkins, A. and Gibbs, G. (1995) 'Scandal of postgrad army', *Times Higher Education Supplement*, 15, 13 September.

Kakabadse, A.P. (1983) *The Politics of Management*. Aldershot: Gower.

Kolb, D.A. and Fry, R. (1975) 'Towards a theory of experiential learning', in C.L. Cooper (ed.), *Theories of Group Processes*. London: J. Wiley.

Mabey, C. and Iles, P. (eds) (1994) *Managing Learning*. London: Routledge.

Mullender, R. (1995) 'The virtues of silliness', *Times Higher Education Supplement*, 15, 13 September.

Pinchot, G. and Pinchot, E. (1994) *The End of Bureaucracy and the Rise of the Intelligent Organization*. San Francisco: Berrett-Kohler.

Pirsig, R.M. (1991) *Lila: An Inquiry into Morals*. London: Bantam.

Ratiu, I. (ed.) (1987) 'Multicultural Management Development', *Journal of Management Development*, Special Issue, 6 (3).

Raven, J. (1994) *Managing Education for Effective Schooling*. Oxford: Oxford Psychologists Press.

Raven, J. (1995) Address to Conference 'Beyond Competence to Capability and the Learning Society', Manchester, 21 November.

Reason, P. (ed.) (1989) *Human Inquiry in Practice*. London: Sage.

Reason, P. and Rowan, J. (eds) (1981) *Human Inquiry: A Sourcebook of New Paradigm Research*. Chichester: John Wiley.

Revans, R.W. (1980) *Action Learning: New Techniques for Management*. London: Blond and Briggs.

Senge, P.M. (1990) *The Fifth Discipline*. London: Random House.

Thorpe, R. and Holman, D. (1995) 'The Management Charter Initiative in higher education', *Capability*, 1 (1): 43–52.

Trompenaars, F. (1993) *Riding the Waves of Culture*. London: Economist Books.

7

The Gender Agenda: Passion, Perspective and Project

Richard Boot and Morgan Tanton

When a man and a woman are asked to write a chapter together on the subject of gender there is an implicit assumption that each has something different to offer. We, too, are aware of our differences. Although we both have strong feelings about the subject, the nature and origins of those feelings differ considerably, which is not surprising since our ways of viewing the subject, thinking about it, talking about it and experiencing it differ also. We decided, therefore, that these differences should be represented in the way we write about it. So, instead of attempting to find 'one middle way', we have written two halves of one chapter based on issues that we jointly feel are important to include. We are not implying that one half speaks for all women and the other speaks for all men. They are simply two views, one from a woman and one from a man. We share the belief, however, that despite separate passions and different perspectives, men and women can engage in a common project to change the nature of working relationships to the benefit of all. We also believe that management learning has an important part to play in this project. In a final section we address this issue together.

One Woman's View

Gender or women

When I was invited to write this chapter I was concerned that it was 'gender' and not 'women' that I had been asked to write into management learning. My concern was that my perspective would be constrained by another's, and this reinforced my experience of management – an institution constructed in others' terms – which constrains my style, creativity and passion. My integrity to the intentions of this chapter necessitated my asking why 'women' were important.

There are many reasons but I will initially restrict myself to three. First of all, there is the symbolic presence of the signifier 'women', for so long excluded from the organization.[1] Secondly, the voice of women needs to be represented within the 'politics of enunciation' (Braidotti, 1991) and not homogenized into an undifferentiated gendered mass because the women's

voices are still too rarely heard. Thirdly, as a site of location and positioning.

> . . . we are positioned through locations such as history, nation, gender, sexuality,
> class, 'race', age . . . [which] have influenced our access to locations such as those
> of education and employment. . . . All these locations and positionings impact
> upon whether we do research, consider ourselves to be researchers and the
> research we actually do. (Skeggs, 1995: 6–7)

Or whether we become managers, executives, members of the board or
secretaries. Language positions us, and although the gentle implications of
'gender' are less confrontational to many than they are to the feminist
'women', feminist texts are intended to challenge perspectives. So by explaining the necessity of including 'women' within the text, I simultaneously
make myself visible (a necessity for a feminist writer) and reveal the
patriarchal or phallocentric assumptions which might otherwise remain
hidden within 'gender'.

However, exploring 'gender' with a male colleague has given me the
opportunity to re-think my perspective, not only through discussions of the
content but also through the process of writing. This has allowed me to
'contest the limits and constraints currently at work' (Grosz, 1995: 23) not
only in the regulation of textual production and reception but also within the
practices of management. For example, I see that the constraint created by
'gender' – despite the well intentioned who use the term to include men as
well as women within the dilemma – is that the word simultaneously denies
women their presence. Men do not lose their place in organizations by being
homogenized into gender but an impression will be given that the issue of
'women' has become redundant, and in a stroke, women will have been
managed out of the organization. This sort of dilemma creates a stalemate
situation where neither men nor women have the right to speak nor the
'right' language and it takes a particular dedication by both to stay with the
seemingly irresolvable situation.

A power perspective

The experience of being 'managed out' may be the reason so many women
write on power, for sex is a power issue (see Firestone, 1971; Kanter, 1977;
Daly, 1979; McNay, 1992). I write from the position of a woman who
teaches in a university management school. Such an organization is traditionally and currently constituted almost totally without the study of feminist
knowledge. By feminist knowledge I mean that which is produced from
'female-embodied, situated subjects who are part of a specific, emergent,
conflictual history' (Skeggs, 1995: 7). This separatism leads many female
academics to an uncomfortable tension with a *feeling* that they do not
belong, yet *knowing* that they do belong. Calas and Smircich (1992) explain
this tension by describing 'doing knowledge' as part and parcel of the
reproduction of patriarchal conditions of power/knowledge.

Historically women were denied by being written out as Man created
himself at the centre of the universe, which necessitated the philosophical

creation of the devalued 'Other' (Hartsock, 1990: 160). Only through the difference between 'Other' and himself could Man be recognized. And in writing about the 'Colonizer' and the 'Colonized' (used by Hartsock as an allegory for the relations of gender) Memmi (1967) shows how the colonized ceased to be a subject of history and became the 'Other', characterized by three particular qualities: a lack or void; opaqueness; and an anonymity through their collectivity.

These stereotypical qualities of 'Other' will be familiar to women in organizations. It is often implied that they lack the valued qualities of logic and reason, that they are difficult to understand ('You never know what they think. Do they think?' (Memmi, 1967: 83)), and that they are not seen as individuals but as part of an anonymous group – 'women'. For this reason women's interests are usually, like the Women's Page of the newspaper, isolated, bound and tolerated, but not politically integrated into the organization.

The difficulty with the issue of power is that it is intangible and women's constructions of their experiences, through expressions of their feelings, often get written off within a system where emotion is not recognized as robust or rational [*sic*] enough to contemplate. One way to overcome this intangibility is to explore the implicit assumptions behind the often habitual and unquestioned practice of management learning, by posing the following question: How do the systems, the methods, the objectives and the rationalizations within your own practice – or your own organization – maintain power relations?

Systems within management development may simply be repetitions of those traditionally used. *Methods* of management education may reinforce one particular style of learning or model of management. *Objectives* which organizations pursue may simply be those which inadvertently maintain traditional values. And organizations are redolent with *rationalizations* which eliminate the need for questions about values and implicit assumptions.

This question is useful to explore because it incorporates a critique of the *past* (a heritage of systems, traditions, by-laws, etc. which we now assume are the right and only way to do things), the *present*, (what methods are we using now?), as well as our intentions for the *future* (is the goal of the organization to have equal numbers of women and men on the board?). The focus on rationalizations creates a whole from the parts and critiques the *context* which allows us to keep repeating old power systems. For example, if we take one area, Recruitment and Selection, and begin by looking at the systems currently used, we see that the practices have evolved from a heritage which assumed leadership as the territory of the landed gentry who knew instinctively from birth how to manage their estates, and later it was assumed that this quality enabled them to manage industry: '. . . success in management depends upon personal qualities, an ability to handle people and situations – on something that is inherent in men "born" to be leaders in industry' (Urwick and Brech, 1957: 123).

Although statements like the one cited above (from the original in 1913) would now be publicly criticized, there is a way in which such values still seem insidiously to linger through not only the marketing posters for management schools (with the one glamorized, bespectacled woman amidst the many suited men) but also in more explicit statements. For example, McCarrey (1994) stated that some North American researchers were imply-ing that the dramatic drop in proportion of women in positions of seniority in organizations in the UK, the USA and Canada indicated that women could not cope with pressure 'at the top'. But by asking 'what recruitment systems are we using?', we may discover that there is something in the heritage of systems which reflects the 1913 values to the detriment of women.

For example, if Jane Austen presented herself for an executive position before a recruitment panel who did not have the benefit of hindsight, the panel would assume from her demure style of dress that she was 'dependent, passive, non-competitive, illogical, less competent, less objective' – the terms that most men use to describe women (Broverman et al., 1975). Then take the character of Mr Darcy in *Pride and Prejudice*. He is a landowner and, hence, a 'manager'. He could be described as self-assertive, separate, controlled, clear, rational, analytic, discriminating, active, reaching out, thrusting, independent, in control of his external world and questing out-ward, all of which terms have been taken from Judi Marshall's (1995) archetypes of male values ascribed generally to men. Yet look at Jane Austen herself, the creator of this stereotypical traditional heroic figure. It would be equally possible, from what we know of the author from her letters and other works, to assume that she was similarly self-assertive, separate, controlled, clear, rational, analytic, discriminating, active, reaching out, thrusting, independent, in control of her external world and questing outward. A woman cannot easily meet the expectations of any recruitment panel because the systems we use are predicated upon the image of a traditional manager. She cannot establish herself in the mould of a manager to those who have a 'mind-set of a potential Mr Darcy' without either being labelled negatively as unnatural and deviant, and therefore troublesome (as were possibly the two women who did not respond compliantly to the Hawthorne researchers and who were therefore dropped from the famous study which then left those who remained, the compliant ones, to become the stereotypes for working women (Roethlisberger and Dickson, 1939)), or positively and exceptional. Unfortunately, the ex-prime minister, Mrs Thatcher, has become the stereotype for exceptional women that is now harnessed by many to warn recruitment panels of the dangers afoot if they select exceptional women. This is an uncomfortable comparison for many but it makes the point.

The loss, for organizations and for women as managers, is that many women do not place themselves before the recruitment panel because they are not able to see themselves as (senior) managers because of the vestigial expectations of characteristics of the ideal landed gentleman/manager from the past. Some of these characteristics are inherent within the language of the recruitment function, although they are fraught with assumptions and confusion. Terms like leadership, authority, personal strength and charisma permeate job descriptions, although their interpretation depends on the culture.

For example, the quality of leadership, which is often listed as a required characteristic for a key management position (without any discussion of its meaning), is often referenced back as an attribute of Caesar. But pose against Caesar another Roman, Antoninus, described as '. . . one of the best princes that ever mounted a throne . . . [whose] thoughts and energies were dedicated to the happiness of his people' (*Smaller Classical Dictionary*, 1937: 50), and there is a chasm of misunderstanding. Antoninus's obscurity derives from the fact that his reign was 'almost a blank caused by the suspension for a time of war, violence and crime' (ibid.). His leadership was so successful that he kept his people away from war and pursued instead their happiness. If we determine quality of leadership by warrior-like success and no battles are fought, then leadership cannot be recognized. It is the taken-for-granted assumptions emanating from a male heritage of landed gentry and warriorship which still form the background of systems of recruitment and selection practices in organizations.

The methods we currently use are often dependent on this implicit system, which is starkly demonstrated by the following example. A few years ago a woman whom I did not previously know telephoned to tell me of her experience as a member of an interview panel for a senior position in her organization – 'I just had to tell someone, I am so angry'. The committee (comprising all men but herself) agreed that the one woman candidate was significantly ahead of the male candidates but they decided not to appoint her 'since they had never had a woman in that role before'. Unfortunately, they did not stop to question their traditional rationalizations and assumptions.

But this would necessitate a re-evaluation of objectives. Do we want more women (and hence fewer men) on the board? And if we look critically at the objectives of 'gender' programmes, we might argue against the assumption that 'Women in Management' programmes are for women participants. If the 'real' objective was to improve the gender balance, probably the best participants would be those men who have not yet considered the issues of working with women. Equally useful programmes for women would be those dedicated to understanding 'Men in Management', but these are almost unknown. So the two kinds of dedicated programme stay compartmentalized – the majority of which imply there is no gender issue and the very few 'women only' short courses are often run by a few very dedicated women.

The nature of difference or blurring the boundaries

In recent years postmodernists have pointed out that whether managers are men or women is irrelevant since all of us are subjected to policies and practices which create us. This means that there is no intrinsic self, no individual, only the subjected self, created by the systems and structures. Many women have rejected this approach, critically asking, 'Why is it that just at the moment when so many of us who have been silenced begin to demand the right to name ourselves, to act as subjects rather than objects of history, that just then the concept of subjecthood becomes problematic?' (Hartsock, 1990: 163).

But postmodernism does not deny the marginals' voice. The recognition that their marginal positions result from the policies subjected upon them gives an 'unidentified' voice to speak from, which overcomes the stigma of writing as marginalized women or a person of colour. This is important because, largely, only women hear women's voices and only blacks hear blacks' voices. Overlooking such marginally constructed subjects and instead observing the policies and practices – those conventions to which we are differently subjected – opens up a dialogue across the 'borders' (Giroux, 1992) of management stereotypes.

Stereotypical differences between the sexes have been emphasized in the past, but there is now a move to blur the boundaries. Yet, the transition seems slow, and I wonder if a ritual is needed to facilitate the process, for example an era celebrating Women in Management:

THE NATURE OF DIFFERENCE	⇒	CELEBRATION OF WOMEN IN MANAGEMENT	⇒	BLURRING THE BOUNDARIES
Moving from the past		to the present		and into the future

The celebration might explore some of the advantages that women have brought into management. For example, the distinctiveness and difference that women – as a stereotypical body of workers – originally brought to management was a challenge to the assumption that there was only one style of management, that based on a stereotype of traditional male qualities and values which were as injurious or limiting to men as they were to women. The arch stereotype of women's management style opened up an appreciation that there were multiple ways and styles of managing.

It could be argued that women in management have begun to make the organization a more tolerable place in which to pass one's working hours – there are better facilities and more humane conditions, better communication and co-ordination, better personnel departments, more criticality, more understanding, more attention to detail, more rigour, more tolerance, more openness, more responsibility. . . . The list could be endless.

Managing sexuality

In making a move to blur the boundaries there is support – again from postmodernists – who critique our constructed power/knowledge as based on binary opposites. We are taught to assume a polar position. One is either mad or sane, sick or well, right or wrong, and hence male or female. But just as there is a range of alternatives between these polarities, the science of genetics shows that maleness and femaleness are not distinct categories of difference – there is a range of characteristics both visible and hidden.

And yet despite this rational argument, I find myself confronted by my emotional response to sexuality which is difficult and which I would prefer to avoid. Like so many issues which make the subject of women in management difficult to address, it arouses feelings. Amanda Sinclair (1995) pulled no punches and starkly named the issue 'Sex and Management'. I do not want to get caught up in the winge of 'It's not fair' for women in management. Nor do I want to have to face uncomfortable issues like the time I discovered a man on a crowded London bus putting his hand up my skirt – 'I am imagining it. Ignore it and it may go away'. 'Sexuality' – and I find myself withdrawing. Ultimately, gender issues turn on this primitive issue which is most usually ignored except in private. But once the issue is acknowledged it is possible to articulate some of the dynamics. For example, during my research in European business schools I observed that the presence of women took one of three forms – debasement, denial and dialogue.

- Debasement: In the formality of the all-male courses (not designated as such but constructed as such) women were only present as fantasy figures, referred to by tutors as 'leather-clad blondes riding motor bikes', as jokes over the bar or through the presence of a roly poly kissogram brought in for the director of the course on the final evening. During the night, as the only woman in the building, I was continually harassed by men knocking on my door.
- Denial: During courses which had only one or two women on them, the women held themselves in a way which seemed to attempt to deny their difference. They held their bodies straight and still, using few hand or arm movements, they used few facial expressions, and some even said they felt the same as their male colleagues. They said there was no difference and yet when the lectures finished and the drinks before the final dinner began, they had changed from their dark suits into soft floral dresses, drawing attention to themselves as women by flirtatious behaviour.
- Dialogue: In courses where there were approximately equal numbers of women and men the issues of women's interests were raised quickly and easily and dialogue of gender interests followed, often including men who initially had said there was no issue for them.

Facing the issue of sexuality is a practical necessity for men and women working together, and by not denying sexuality, but acknowledging it and respecting the differences, it may be possible to develop new values, and allow flexibility and creativity into the workplace. Acknowledging such differences would then open the way to an acceptance of and respect for other differences. The passions and perspectives of men and women *are* different, but together they share a common project.

One Man's View

Masculinity and feminism

As a man writing this I acknowledge from the outset that my own understanding, not only of gender but also of organizational dynamics, particularly power dynamics, has been enriched by feminist theorizing. I am also aware that not all men would make the same claim. Men's responses to 'feminism' seem to range between two extremes. One is founded on a denial of the diversity of feminist philosophies. By responding 'You're not one of those feminists, are you?' to any woman who attempts to draw attention to inequity or inequality in organizational life, it implicitly evokes the gross bra-burning, dungaree-wearing, man-hating caricature still prevalent not only in the tabloid press and public bar but also in many an office. Placing women in such a double-bind is one way of policing their activities.

The other extreme is ultimately, I believe, just as negative in its effect. It is founded on men's rejection of their own masculinity. It is as if they have heard the charge that masculinity is by its nature oppressive to women and, not wishing to collude with such oppression, they have decided their only option is to plead guilty and give up masculinity. Unfortunately, this not only means turning their back on a distinctive source of energy, but more worryingly it feeds other men's fear that women's aim is to deprive them of their potency. Within this inadequately thought-out response to feminism lie the seeds of a 'men's rights' backlash. Thus Roger Witcombe, chairman of the so-called UK Men's Movement, is quoted as saying 'Our problem is not a crisis of masculinity, but that the anti-male ethos of feminism has infiltrated the law courts and popular culture. . . . Things have got out of control. We need to be more aggressive in taking on feminism and standing up for our rights as men' (Cohen, 1996: 30). I believe a more positive alternative to either of these responses must involve reworking current conceptions of masculinity and its role in organizations.

The practices of power

Looking more closely at discussions of power relations between men and women I am struck by how frequently I encounter the terms 'patriarchy' and 'patriarchal values' used to argue that organizations are ruled by men. Remy (1990), however, suggests that by using these terms to refer to male rule in general an important distinction is being obscured between rule by the fathers (patriarchy) and rule by the brother(hood)s (fratriarchy). Patriarchy is based upon the idea of the authority of the elders – the 'wise old men' in society – and is concerned with maintaining a moral order, albeit a paternalistic one. Fratriarchy, on the other hand, is altogether more insidious in that it is concerned with furthering the self-interest of the association of men itself. It is maintained by means other than and in addition to those of hierarchy. Thus in two separate organizations I have worked in recently it was thought that for individuals to progress to more senior positions they had to fulfil certain personal criteria in addition to competence. In one they had to be 'clubbable' (as in suitable for membership of a gentleman's club) and in the other they needed to be fluent in 'blokespeak'. More perversely, in a third organization, consisting primarily of highly qualified scientists who provided technical services to client organizations, I was told that women were given much less of a hard time in their presentation rehearsals than men, even though it was acknowledged that this probably left them less well prepared to face the client. The significance of the distinction between patriarchy and fratriarchy is that while under the former the interests of women might not be understood, under the latter they would be actively ignored. This would imply that quite different strategies would be required for tackling each.

There are plenty of examples in the literature of the ways in which power differentials in organizations can be signalled and reinforced at the interpersonal level. For example, those who regard themselves as more powerful tend to talk more in meetings and are more likely to interrupt; they are more likely to address others by their first name than be addressed so themselves; they are less likely to disclose personal information about themselves; and they are more likely to 'invade the personal space' of others by, for example, standing too close, making more eye contact or physically touching. The complication is that these behaviours seem to be generally true not only of men in relation to women, but also of superiors in relation to subordinates of either sex. The question is, are these processes a function of gender or of hierarchy? Could it be that these are one and the same thing? Again the implied strategy is likely to differ according to the answer. For some the strategy must concentrate on getting greater numbers of women to the top of today's organizations, for others it must concentrate on creating new forms of organization altogether.

This does, however, highlight one of the recurrent tensions in this chapter. Men are not all powerful in every situation and women are not always powerless. And, despite being predominantly male constructions, modern organizations do not function unequivocally to the advantage of all men. More men are troubled by what is assumed to be the masculine nature of organizations than is usually acknowledged. Many, if not most, are simply surviving. But, as long as they keep their misgivings to themselves in order that they continue to survive, they not only perpetuate but they reinforce the public world of organizations from which they so often seek refuge in private. The difference, then, between men's experience of organizational life and women's is less straightforward than some would have us believe.

Organizing, managing and difference

I know that, for me, working with men feels different from working with women. But to what extent am I responding to some essential biological difference (sex) and to what extent am I, and they, simply responding to how, in our society, men and women are assumed/believed/expected to differ (gender)? Unfortunately sex and gender are so intertwined – each mediated through the other – that this simple question has no correspondingly simple answer. As White says, 'We are born either female or male. Gender begins when someone notices what sex you are and makes something of it. You can be sure they will, because sex is loaded with significance' (1989: 17). Men are not born masculine and women are not born feminine. Masculinity is the instruction on how to be a 'proper man' in our society and femininity is the instruction on how to be a 'proper woman'. By implication, then, individual men and women have a degree of choice in the extent to which they conform to these instructions. The trouble is that we are encouraged to believe that they are the rules of nature so it is hard for many of us to recognize the choice, let alone feel free to exercise it.

With regard to masculinity, Kimmel (1990) suggests that there are four basic rules in our society: (a) no sissy stuff: avoid all behaviours that even remotely suggest the feminine; (b) be a big wheel: success and status confer masculinity; (c) be a sturdy oak: reliability and dependability are defined as emotional distance and affective distance; and (d) give 'em hell: exude an aura of manly aggression, go for it, take risks. He also suggests that the effects of adhering to these rules show up in the disproportionate rate among men of stress-related diseases, of incidents of violent accidents of all types and of mental illness. You might think that if these are the costs, it would be in all men's interests to change. The snag is, however, that for so long the stereotype of a 'good manager' has coincided with the hard-nosed stereotype of masculinity – logical, competitive, assertive, ambitious, etc. Perhaps more significantly, it has been at odds with the soft-hearted stereotype of femininity – intuitive, collaborative, accepting, caring, etc. I say stereotype of a good manager but the evidence is less than thoroughly supportive of the stereotype. So, for example, research such as that carried out by the Center for Creative Leadership (Morrison et al., 1992) is used to argue that there is no difference between the way men and women manage (which usually means that women have adequately conformed to the masculine stereotype). On the other hand, Rosener (1990) argues from her research that there is a new generation of women managers who are succeeding in these times of rapid change by approaching their leadership role in a manner conforming more to the feminine stereotype. Loden (1985) too has argued that organizations, now more than ever, require 'feminine leadership' which, given their experience, women are particularly well equipped for. And Powell, following his review of the research, concludes emphatically that 'the stereotype that men make better managers is simply not true' (1993: 175) and 'it makes no more sense for us to believe that better managers are masculine' (ibid.: 180).

So where does this get us? Is research also telling us men that for the sake of organizational success we must reject masculinity in favour of femininity? I think not. The case is being made for more balanced organizational leadership. After all, if you are unbalanced standing on one leg, you probably will not become more balanced by moving on to the other. But why is it so difficult to get both feet on the ground? This may in part be because for so long men's identity as men has been inextricably bound up with employment. 'Who are you?' usually means 'What's your job?'. 'Strip me of my job and you strip me of my identity. Make my job less masculine and you make me less masculine.' This, however, is to treat it as if it were purely an issue at the level of the individual. But it is not. As I have explored elsewhere (Boot, 1994) these stereotypes have become institutionalized in, and therefore are reinforced by, the structures and processes of our organizations and business schools. Thus organizations are typified by hierarchy, control, division and competition, both internally and externally. And learning, as represented by the curriculum of most business schools, is typified by an emphasis on quantification, analysis, objectivity and the study of separate subject 'disciplines'. I referred to this as the 'white male heritage' and suggested that organizations based on the 'feminine principle' would be typified by networks, empowerment, connection and co-operation, and learning would be typified by an emphasis on quality, intuition, subjectivity and holism. I am not alone in using the masculine/feminine metaphor to differentiate between organizations (see, e.g., Marshall, 1994) and I have found it a useful way of highlighting approaches to organizing which offer an alternative to those which predominate at the moment. I am not sure, however, that stereotyping organizations as masculine or feminine does not lead to an unnecessary polarization which, given what I was saying earlier, causes many men in particular to become concerned about what they might have to give up in order to bring about change, rather than to consider how they too might benefit from the change. It may also help to perpetuate the myth of two different kinds of managerial work – men's work and women's work – with men responsible for providing direction and formulating strategy and women responsible for maintaining and supporting the organization in its pursuit of that strategic direction.

Sexuality at work

There is another aspect of the difference between women and men which until recently had received virtually no attention in the literature on management and organizations – that is, sexuality. Sexuality, however, is also inextricably entangled with power, so perhaps it is not surprising that it has been the increasing attention paid to the processes of sexual harassment at work which seems to have made it legitimate to study the wider implications of sexuality in organizations. Despite this attention, there is still a lot of ambiguity about what actually constitutes sexual harassment. An individual's own definition, therefore, plays an important part in determining what sexually oriented behaviour he or she sees as acceptable to initiate or respond to. This may range from regular sexual jokes, through unwanted touching, to forcible sexual aggression. And according to Powell 'men consistently see less harassment than women do and are more likely than women to see the women as contributing to their own harassment, either

by provoking it or not properly handling "normal" sexual attention'
(1993: 126). We are frequently blind to those things which work to our
advantage.

Harassment, then, represents unwanted and unwelcome sexual attention.
But what of mutual sexual attraction and the sharing of welcome attention?
Given the amount of time many spend at work in the presence of others, the
workplace is an obvious place for meeting new partners. Where proximity is
accompanied by the performance of similar tasks and the pursuit of common
work goals, the likelihood of a relationship developing is increased. This is
particularly so when the job is typified by periods of intensive demand,
during which individuals are expected to spend long hours co-working or
travelling extensively together. The shared excitement of such conditions
can interact with the excitement of sexual attraction. There are dangers,
however, in assuming that the power dimension so obvious in harassment is
absent in these relationships. After all, what one person sees as an act of
commitment another can see as a short-term fling. Consider this in conjunc-
tion with the fact that such relationships are most frequently between people
of unequal status in the organizational hierarchy, typically a higher status
man and a lower status woman, and the potential for exploitation becomes
clear. Although there may be no problems in the relationship itself, there still
may be in the reactions of others who fear that they themselves will be
disadvantaged in either task or career terms as a result of the 'special'
relationship. It is not surprising, therefore, that Cockburn states that:

> . . . the asymmetry of power between men and women renders sexuality itself a
> factor in women's subordination. This is not to say that women themselves do not
> want to be sexual and to live and work in a sexualized environment. Most would
> ideally wish to do so. But the gender relations in which we are embedded ensure
> that we can seldom do so on terms that do not disadvantage us. (1990: 83)

Of course the excitement produced by mutual attraction and that certain
'sexual chemistry' between two people can often find its expression in a
creative working relationship which does not involve physical intimacy.
This does not, however, stop employers or colleagues from assuming it does.
What I have said so far has implicitly referred to relationships between
people of opposite sex, but most of it could also apply to relationships
between people of the same sex, although in most organizations reactions
are likely to be even more complicated.

Tackling the gender agenda

The equal opportunities policies proudly proclaimed by so many organizations represent an attempt to tackle the inequalities of power which seem to
permeate the whole gender agenda. But how successful have these policies
been in practice? Needless to say, the answer to that question is 'it depends'.
I referred earlier to the difference between strategies to improve the lot of
women in organizations as they are at the moment and strategies to
transform the nature of organizations. The former tend to have a shorter time

scale and to focus on the technicalities of various personnel procedures and practices – recruitment, selection, remuneration, promotion, etc. Transformation is a longer-term agenda and implies not only changing the structure of organizations, but also rethinking their very purposes and the attitudes and values which underpin them. It requires a process of fundamental resocialization which cannot be confined within the boundaries of any given organization. Some would see the former as a necessary step on the road to the latter. Others, however, see it as yet another tactic in the process of sanitizing and containing the forces for change. It is no good men treating women *as if* they are equal. They have to believe they *are* equal. It is not sufficient to clean up your act and adopt 'politically correct' language. If you don't mean it, it doesn't work. Legge (1987) even maintains that what success there has been is illusory. Using her analysis of women in personnel management, she claims that women can 'reach the top' of an occupation that is regarded as neither central nor strategic but once that occupation becomes recognized as more powerful, then 'women, if not elbowed out, are politely pushed aside, often with their own unconscious collusion' (Legge, 1987: 34). She goes on to suggest that even framing the problem of women's careers in these terms is to see them from a male perspective and to subject them to male values. Given all this, it is, perhaps, not surprising that Cockburn concludes that 'it is those who espouse the long agenda that have been most disappointed to date' (1990: 74). She suggests, in effect, that many have given up on it.

Paradoxically, I believe there may be a way forward by addressing the meaning of 'career' for men. It is undoubtedly true in our society that women's career expectations (as opposed to aspirations) are more constrained than men's. On the other hand, I suspect that men generally experience themselves as having less choice as to whether to work or not. Of course we work – we are men. Our jobs are who we are. Even in families where both partners are employed many men find it difficult not to think of themselves as the primary bread-winner. We are brought up to believe this is our role in life. Conversely, although many men would prefer to spend more time at home with their children, they are never made to feel guilty about not being there in the same way as women are. Women are 'working mothers' – men are fathers in their 'private lives'. The transformation agenda then goes beyond ending discriminatory practices at work. It entails men in particular rethinking the relationship between career and identity, public life and private life, work and home. This will require them to examine what Seidler refers to as the 'tension between what men grow up to want for themselves, for example, to do well at work, to be successful, to achieve, and their feelings for what matters most to them in their lives (1990: 226). It seems to me that this is an essential prerequisite to establishing modes of organizing that work to the benefit of all. I am sure that many men would welcome the opportunity to take on such a project, but I am less sure how many organizations (or the powerful men within them who have a vested interest in maintaining the *status quo*) would wish to support them in doing so. To date, tackling gender dynamics at work has been seen primarily as a women's project. Sympathetic men have offered their help but have been unable to 'own' it. The transformation agenda offers the prospect of a common project which can engage the energies of men and women alike. The challenge to those of us working in management learning is to find ways of giving it life.

The Common Project

As a woman and a man we have each viewed the subject of gender from a different position. Each position inevitably allows some things to be seen while leaving others obscured. What is clear to both of us, however, is that there is a need for change and that change must involve men and women together. If only we could formulate some neat prescription for how to set about that change . . . but we cannot. Instead, we are aware of the tensions and dilemmas that confront all who wish to embark on such a project.

Is it about making things better in the world of organizations as they are or is it about changing that world? In either case it is not clear where best to focus the energy for change. To date it seems to have proved far easier to change personnel procedures than individual attitudes. But the gender dynamics that we have been exploring are deeply rooted in most organizational cultures and it is attitudes which shape and reinforce those cultures, not least the attitudes of those who currently hold power. The prospect becomes even more daunting as we consider that these attitudes have their origin outside the boundaries of organization. So in three simple steps we have moved from changing individuals to changing personnel procedures and changing organizational cultures to changing society. No wonder it frequently feels such a hopeless task. But this too may be a question of perspective or, more appropriately, time scale. To focus on smaller, shorter-term changes does not have to mean giving up on the larger project. It is a matter of of sowing seeds and accepting that they will not come into maturity for many seasons. The metaphor is more one of forestry than market gardening. From this perspective it is possible to take heart from the seeds that were sown by others some time ago and are still growing. After all, 20 years ago it would not have been thought essential to include a chapter like this in a book of this nature.

It was never our intention to end this chapter with a 'therefore what you need to do is . . .' section. Our hope is that what we have written so far will help those committed to change to generate their own agenda for action. There are, however, a number of general issues we would like to highlight. First, learning the business of being a manager is not only done, or even primarily done, in formal management development contexts. The process of learning managing is often wrapped up in the process of managing itself. This implies that management developers need not only to attend to the gender processes contained within their own practice, but also to highlight the way management learning is channelled by the existing organizational structures and practices. Secondly, there are many people, particularly men in positions of power, who regard themselves as having a vested interest in maintaining the *status quo*. To influence them it will be necessary to go beyond critique of the way things are at present. But there are dangers in trying to construct a good 'business case'. To do so may simply be colluding with things as they are. Imagination is required to create alternatives that genuinely appeal to men and women alike. It is our belief that this can only be achieved through true dialogue between the sexes. Dialogue is not about choosing sides, nor is it about finding a compromise. It is about producing a synthesis which cannot be predicted.

The common project, then, may need to begin with men and women in the management learning profession talking and listening to each other, engaging with each other's passions, attempting not only to understand but also to accept each other's perspective. We do not pretend that this will be an easy task. Indeed, we have been reminded of some of the difficulties while writing this chapter together. But this does not mean that it can never be a source of energy and fun. Fortunately, we have also been reminded of that.

Note

1   The term 'signifier' orginating from linguistics where it indicates the material aspect of a word as different and distinct from the mental or conceptual aspect of the word. (For fuller explanation, see Sturrock, John (ed.) (1984) *Structuralism and Since.* Oxford: Oxford University Press. pp. 6–7.)

Annotated Bibliography

Diane Elam (1994) *Feminism and Deconstruction.* London: Routledge, is a book for those who like to be challenged by ideas. It is a fun book if you want to explore some of the more problemetic conceptual aspects of feminism. J. Hearn and D. Morgan (eds) (1990) *Men, Masculinities and Social Theories.* London: Unwin Hyman, is a useful book in that it represents a range of different perspectives on the study of men, emphasizing in particular the importance of understanding 'masculinities' in the plural. A very easy to read book which confronts subject matter that has largely been neglected or avoided elsewhere in academic writing is J. Hearn and W. Parkin (1987) *Sex at Work: The Power and Paradox of Organization Sexuality.* Brighton: Wheatsheaf Books. We would suggest Judi Marshall (1984) *Women Managers: Travellers in Male World.* Chichester: Wiley, because it is the one, more than any other, which women have said is the most useful. It is very readable and accessible and clearly sets out the issues. Judi's writing is also tight and rigorous, and demonstrates the best sort of academic writing – that which is intended to be of value to others! G.N. Powell (1993) *Women and Men in Management* (2nd edn). Newbury Park, CA: Sage, is rather dry and short on British material, but is a well-organized and thorough overview of much of the theory and research relating to women and men at work. Shjulamit Reinharz (1992) *Feminist Methods in Social Research*, Oxford: Oxford Unversity Press, is probably of more use to those who are interested in research. It is suggested here because it also demonstrates the issues with which feminists deal. Education, and therefore research, are important aspects of the feminist discourse. Morgan Tanton (ed.) (1994) *Women in Management: A Developing Presence.* London: Routledge, is included because it was the result of an international conference on women in management learning which was held in 1992 on the day that Opportunity 2000 was launched. It is a guide to some of the issues for anyone starting to explore the topic.

References

Boot, R. (1994) 'Management learning and the white male heritage', in M. Tanton (ed.), *Women in Management: A Developing Presence*. London: Routledge. pp. 162–71.
Braidotti, Rosi (1991) *Patterns of Dissonance*. Cambridge: Polity Press.
Broverman, I.K., Vogel, R., Broverman, D.M., Clarkson, F.E. and Rosenkrantz, P.S. (1975) 'Sex-role stereotypes: a current appraisal', in M.T. Schuch Mednick, S.S. Tangri, and L.W. Hoffman (eds), *Women and Achievement: Social and Motivational Analyses*. New York: Hemisphere Publishing. pp. 32–47.
Calas, M. and Smircich, L. (1990) 'Rewriting gender into organizational theorizing: directions from feminist perspective', in M.I. Reed and M.E. Hughes (eds), *Re-Thinking Organization: New Directions in Organizational Research and Analysis*. London: Sage. pp. 227–53.
Cockburn, C. (1990) 'Men's power in organizations: "equal opportunities" intervenes', in J. Hearn and D. Morgan (eds), *Men, Masculinities and Social Theories*. London: Unwin Hyman. pp. 72–89.
Cohen, David 'It's a Guy Thing', *Guardian Weekend*, 4 May. pp. 26–30.
Daly, Mary (1979) *Gyn/Ecology: The Metaethics of Radical Feminism*. London: The Women's Press.
Dworkin, Andrea (1981) *Pornography: Men Possessing Women*. London: The Women's Press.
Firestone, Shulamith (1971) *The Dialectic of Sex: The Case for Feminist Revolution*. London: Jonathon Cape.
Giroux, H. (1992) *Border Crossings: Cultural Workers and the Politics of Education*. New York: Routledge.
Grosz, Elizabeth (1995) *Space, Time and Perversion*. London: Routledge.
Hartsock, Linda (1990) 'Foucault on power: a theory for women?', in Linda J. Nicholson (ed.), *Feminism/Postmodernism*. London: Routledge. pp. 157–75.
Kanter, Rosabeth Moss (1977) *Men and Women of the Corporation*. New York: Basic Books.
Kimmel, Michael (1990) 'After fifteen years: the impact of the sociology of masculinity on the masculinity of sociology', in J. Hearn and D. Morgan (eds), *Men, Masculinities and Social Theories*. London: Unwin Hyman. pp. 93–109.
Legge, K. (1987) 'Women in personnel management: uphill climb or downhill slide?', in A. Spencer and D. Podmore (eds), *In a Man's World: Essays on Women in Male Dominated Professions*. London: Tavistock. pp. 33–60.
Loden, M. (1985) *Feminine Leadership or How to Succeed in Business Without Being One of the Boys*. New York: Times Books.
Marshall, Judi (1994) 'Re-visioning organizations by developing female values', in R. Boot, J. Lawrence and J. Morris (eds), *Managing the Unknown by Creating New Futures*. Maidenhead: McGraw-Hill. pp. 165–83.
Marshall, Judi (1995) *Women Managers Moving On*. London: Routledge.
McCarrey, M. (1994) 'Women on the Move', *Financial Times* 6 May, 14.
McNay, Lois (1992) *Foucault and Feminism*. Cambridge: Polity Press.
Memmi, A. (1967) *The Colonizer and the Colonized*. Boston MA: Beacon Press.
Morrison, A.M., White, R.P. and Van Velsor, V. (1992) *Breaking the Glass Ceiling: Can Women Reach the Top of America's Largest Corporations?* Reading, MA: Addison-Wesley.
Powell, G.N. (1993) *Women and Men in Management* (2nd edn). Newbury Park, CA: Sage.
Remy, John (1990) 'Patriarchy and fratriarchy as forms of androcracy', in J. Hearn and D. Morgan (eds), *Men, Masculinities and Social Theories*. London: Unwin Hyman. pp. 43–54.

Roethlisberger, F.J. and Dickson, W.J. (1939) *Management and the Worker*. Cambridge, MA: Harvard University Press.

Rosener, J.B. (1990) 'Ways women lead', *Harvard Business Review*, 68: 6.

Seidler, V.J. (1990) 'Men, feminism and power', in J. Hearn and D. Morgan (eds), *Men, Masculinities and Social Theories*. London: Unwin Hyman.

Sinclair, Amanda (1995) 'Sex and the MBA', *Organization*, 2 (2): 295–317.

Skeggs, Beverley (ed.) (1995) *Feminist Cultural Theory – Process and Production*. Manchester: Manchester University Press.

Smaller Classical Dictionary (1937). London: J.M. Dent.

Tanton M. (1994). 'Developing authenticity', *Women in Management Review*, 7: 20–6.

Tanton, M. (1994) *Women in Management: A Developing Presence*. London: Routedge.

Urwick, L.K. and Brech, E.F.L. (1957) *The Making of Scientific Management* (vol. 2). London: Pitman Publishing.

White, Alistair (1989) *Poles Apart? The Experience of Gender*. London: J.M. Dent.

8

Management Learning as Discourse

Norman Fairclough and Ginny Hardy

The purpose of this chapter is twofold. We wish first to argue that the study of management learning can be significantly enhanced by the discourse analysis of its language – of the various spoken and written language texts which constitute management learning. We shall advocate more specifically the use in teaching, research and the practice of managing, of one particular method of discourse analysis which is known as critical discourse analysis (Fairclough, 1992a, 1995). Our second purpose is to introduce readers to the application of this method to management learning texts by working through an example – a comparison of two publicity brochures produced by the same outdoor training organization, one of which is aimed at the general public, the other at the world of management and organizational development.

The first section of the chapter discusses critical discourse analysis as a perspective in social science research generally and the study of management learning in particular, and the second section sketches out an analytic framework. The third section discusses management learning as an 'order of discourse' or 'field of discourse', focusing upon its diverse language practices, their complex interrelationships and their shifting configurations. We argue that it is essential to frame analysis of particular language practices within such a holistic account of the order of discourse. In the fourth section, we illustrate the critical analysis of management learning discourse through an analysis of the outdoor training example. The concepts and terminology introduced in the second section will become more familiar through this worked example. The chapter concludes with suggestions about how readers might themselves take this approach further, including annotated references to relevant publications.

Critical Discourse Analysis in Social Science and Management Learning

Critical discourse analysis (henceforth CDA) is actually a family of approaches which have developed from within Linguistics. We shall focus on the version of it referred to above. CDA attempts to bring together recent social, theoretical insights into language and traditions in Linguistics of close textual analysis. CDA challenges mainstream Linguistics for failing to develop an adequately social account of language. It develops theories of language and ways of analysing language which, so to speak, 'operation-alize' – put in a practically usable form – insights of social theory, including the key insight that language is constitutive of society and culture – that is, that language texts construct knowledge, beliefs, social relations and social identities in particular and varying ways.

The socioculturally constitutive nature of language entails that social relations of power and ideological processes have a centrally linguistic character, and most practitioners of CDA see their work as 'critical' in the sense that they foreground power and ideology. Referring to the use of language as 'discourse' entails seeing language use in this way as a mode of social practice which is socially shaped but also socially shaping. CDA has also stressed that this sort of theorization of language reflects an historical development in human societies which has progressively enhanced the role of language in the business of social life, including the workplace, and in processes of social and cultural change. The 'linguistic turn' which has taken place in social theory, and has given analysis of language and discourse such a central place in social analysis, corresponds to a 'linguistic turn' which has taken place in social life.

But CDA also challenges theorists of language and discourse in the social sciences. Analysis of discourse in the social sciences is often extremely vague and often manages to avoid saying anything concrete at all about language texts. This is true, for instance, of Foucault's influential writing on discourse (see Fairclough, 1992a for discussion). Where particular texts are analysed, it is very often only their content that is discussed. CDA argues that discourse analysis is always strengthened – helped to make whatever case is being made more forcibly – by analysis of what we can call the 'texture' of texts (Fairclough, 1992b). The texture of a text is the particular way it is put together – its particular weave, to use another metaphor – its particular formal and structural properties. Close reference to texture allows the analyst to show how social and cultural processes, which are often described in rather general terms, are concretized in the detailed behaviours of people's lives. It also foregrounds the often contradictory, ambivalent and even messy nature of what people actually do in ways which are easily lost sight of in general statements about discourse and discourses. CDA thus has a particular contribution to make as one method among others in social and cultural analysis.

The analysis of management learning would seem to be a particularly fruitful area of application for CDA. Management learning can be seen to be about interventions to shape and reshape the identities of managers. It involves the generation, projection and circulation of diverse constructions of the managerial self, the processes of management, the organization and so forth. But these constructions are generated and transmitted in discourse, the variety of types of spoken and written language text – advertisements, textbooks, practitioner journals, training events and materials, etc. Language use – discourse – is clearly central to the whole process of management learning. And so in particular are questions about the construction, through discourse, of forms of workplace identity, social relations in work, and the nature of workplace organizations and processes. Analysis of how the practices and texts of management development articulate together shifting configurations of discourses and genres in order to bring off this constitutive work would seem to be a significant contribution both to the academic study of management learning and to reflective practitioners who wish to be more aware of those aspects of their professional life generally taken for granted.

A Framework for Critical Discourse Analysis

The version of CDA we shall work with here sees the discourse analysis of a particular discursive event – a particular social occasion of spoken or written language use – as a combination of three different forms of analysis: analysis of *text*; analysis of *discourse practice*; and analysis of *sociocultural practice*. This is represented diagramatically in Figure 8.1. Throughout this section, we give brief examples but the bulk of our illustration of this approach comes in the fourth section.

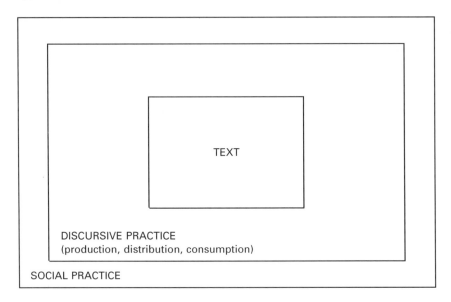

Figure 8.1 *Three-dimensional conception of discourse (reprinted from Fairclough, 1992a: 73)*

Discourse practice

Let us begin with analysis of discourse practice, because this is the hinge which links the other two – or to put it differently, discourse practice mediates the link between text and sociocultural practice. By discourse practice we mean, in general terms, processes of text production, distribution and consumption – the way people put texts together, the way texts are socially distributed and circulated, and the way people interpret and more generally use (consume) texts. We focus here, though, on one aspect of discourse practice affecting production and consumption: how do people draw upon the available cultural resources for discourse – the available models of different types of text – in producing and consuming the particular text under analysis? We can call these 'cultural resources' discourses and genres. A *discourse* is a particular way of constructing or constituting some area of social practice, and there are usually alternative – and often competing – discourses available. For example, there are various discourses which construct the social practice of managing in various ways, for instance a Taylorist or scientific management discourse of management or a human relations discourse of management (Hollway, 1991). A *genre* is a way of using language associated with some particular form of social activity. For instance, we can talk about the genre of interview or the genre of advertising, or of a textbook such as this one.

It is useful to analyse how these cultural resources, discourses and genres are structured in particular areas of social life, and the concept of 'order of discourse' is used for this. An *order of discourse* is the set of discourses and genres associated with some domain of social life, for example the order of discourse of management learning, the order of discourse of the contemporary workplace or the order of discourse of a university department (as these examples show, orders of discourse can be identified at different levels of generality). In describing an order of discourse, the emphasis is upon relations between discourses and genres – how closed or permeable the boundaries between them are, for instance, whether or not they are freely combined in texts – and on the dynamism of the system, shifts in those relationships and boundaries. Texts often draw upon orders of discourse in complex ways, crossing boundaries not only between different genres and discourses but also between different orders of discourse. For example, many contemporary advertising texts mix scientific and technical discourse with informal conversational discourse.

Textual analysis

We use the term 'intertextual analysis' for the process of identifying all the genres and discourses that are drawn upon in producing or consuming a text, and the particular ways they are combined together. Intertextual analysis is on the boundary between analysis of discourse practice and textual analysis. It shows how combinations of genres and discourses are materialized in the texture of the text. Textual analysis is also linguistic analysis – analysis of linguistic features of a text, that is the particular properties of its language which makes a text different from other texts. It is helpful to classify linguistic features according to function. According to the 'systemic' linguistic theory of Halliday (1985), any part of a text will be simultaneously doing three things: it will be representing and constructing reality; it will be projecting and negotiating social relationships and social identities; and it will be setting up links with other parts of the text and with the context so that the whole is a text rather than just a jumble of sentences. These are respectively the *ideational, interpersonal* and *textual* functions of language in texts. Many different sorts of linguistic features at various levels may be of interest in text analysis (see Fairclough, 1992a, for some detail). Here we shall just identify a few possibilities.

Ideational function. In connection with the ideational function, we are interested in our experience of reality and how we represent this. One aspect of reality is what is happening around us and how we talk or write about this. One feature which is often worth attending to, then, is the *type of process* and associated participants that predominate in a text. Is it, for instance, an 'actional process' with agents (e.g., 'the time will come when management trainers throw away their flip charts' is an actional process – throw away – with management trainers as agent), or a 'mental process' such as processes of cognition (e.g., 'we *believe* education is vital'), or a 'relational process' of being (e.g., 'education is overwhelmingly important') or possession (e.g., 'the competency movement has two compelling schools of thought').

Another feature of ideational function is *nominalization* – to what extent are processes nominalized, that is to say turned into nouns in a text? An example would be 'organization'. This is used as a noun but is a nominalization of the process of organizing. Such a nominalization can then be talked about in different ways. We can talk of 'the organization needs' or 'has decided' or 'effective organizations' or 'organizational learning'. What gets lost when a process is nominalized are tense, modality and also a sense of the associated participants (see above) in the process. Who is organizing? What are they organizing? And in particular, who is being organized? Heavily nominalized texts are typically scientific, technical or technicist (where an area outside science or technology mimics them linguistically). Features such as the consistent use of particular processes, passive sentences with no agent, and a preponderance of nominalizations can have ideological significance, that is these features may be being used in order to hide certain aspects of power or to strengthen presuppositions or taken-for-granteds (see Fairclough, 1989, for more detail).

Interpersonal function. In connection with the interpersonal function, a question to ask is about grammatical *mood* – whether a text predominantly uses declarative sentences (typically statements), or questions, or commands, and how it mixes the different moods together if it uses a range. Another important feature is *modality*, including the different degrees of commitment to or affinity with propositions that text producers show in their texts (compare the categorical assertion 'that *demands* an increasingly team-centred approach', with the more weakly modalized assertion 'that *may demand* an increasingly team-centred approach'). Another feature worth attending to with respect to the interpersonal function is the *choice of pronouns* in a text: some texts directly address their readers (using *you* extensively) whereas others do not; some texts identify their producers (as *I* or *we*) whereas others do not. These are just a few among many possible analytical foci.

Textual function. When focusing on the *textual* function of language, some of the relevant features are the ways in which sentences are joined together: for example, by connective words such as 'and' and 'but'; by repetition of words or phrases; by reference to things elsewhere in the text; and in the higher level structuring of the text – its overall shape or pattern.

Sociocultural practice

So far we have looked at two elements of this framework of analysis, discursive practice and textual analysis. The final aspect is sociocultural practice. Analysis of sociocultural practice is a summary heading for various types of social and cultural analysis of the discursive event, at different levels of generality: the immediate situational context; the wider institutional context of the event; and the widest cultural and social context within which the event is framed. The aim of critical discourse analysis is to show how discourse practice and its associated language texts are a part of, constituted by but also themselves constituting, social and cultural structures, relations and processes which can be described at any of these levels.

The final part of the analysis is in fact a synthesis: an account of the discursive event which tries to link detailed features of the text with characteristics and tendencies in the sociocultural practice within which they are embedded, via the mediation of discourse practice. What this means is that (a) the particular nature of the discourse practice – whether, for instance, it reproduces conventional boundaries within and between orders of discourse, or transgresses such boundaries in mixing orders of discourses, discourses and genres – depends upon properties of the sociocultural practice it is part of – whether, for instance, there is a scenario of social and cultural stability or (as so often now) of rapid social and cultural change; and (b) these properties of discourse practice are realized in features of texts – for instance, a discourse practice which heavily mixes orders of discourse will be realized in texts which are heterogeneous in their texture and their meanings (e.g., in their modality – see below for this).

Management Learning as an 'Order of Discourse'

As we noted in the second section, an order of discourse is the set of conventions that a particular discursive event can typically draw on and we can think of these conventions as the discourses and genres associated with a particular domain of social life. So what can be said about the order of discourse of the domain of management learning? What are the conventions, the discourses and genres associated with the social domain of management learning?

For our purposes, and in line with others in this book, we take management learning to mean that area of social life concerned with managers' formal or informal learning. This would include all of the people, practices, activities and structures which come together around the focus of management learning – training or development departments in organizations and business schools, courses and training programmes, conferences, meetings, journal articles, professional networks, and so on. This, then, is the domain of management learning.

One way of thinking about an order of discourse in a given domain is as the total collection of discursive events in that domain. So here we are interested in particular activities which take place within management learning. And given the nature of our domain and the significance of language in management learning practice, the activities or events will be primarily discursive in nature. (A different social domain, such as professional football or trawling, might consist of many social practices which were not predominantly discursive in nature.) The type of discursive event we might see within management learning includes the assessment interview, an experiential event, the establishment and maintenance of a professional network, a managerial competency course. Associated with each discursive event is a particular set of conventions, or discourses and genres, and it is this totality of discursive events and associated discourses and genres which, together with the relationships between them, make up the order of discourse for this domain.

The genres that might be drawn on include the lecture, business seminar, 'guru' textbook, in-house magazine or business article. Associated with genres are particular textual structures and participant roles (Kress, 1985). So, for example, a traditional business school lecture will have a particular kind of generic structure associated with it – one person at the front of a lecture theatre talking for most of the given time, an opening, the main body of the talk usually with OHTs or slides, ending usually with some time for questions, a large number of listeners taking notes and occasionally asking questions. This particular discursive activity positions participants as lecturer or student.

Sometimes it might not be quite as clear-cut as this. A similar classroom-based event for managers might draw on a mixture of genres – business seminar, lecture, experiential activity, informal conversation. The 'teacher' in this case may be positioned as a combination of trainer, facilitator or appraiser, depending on the activity, while the 'learners' may also be positioned as clients or customers. We would still expect to find certain structures (textual or otherwise) associated with a social activity such as this.

You could perhaps argue that the 'training session' has become a genre in its own right and one that would be recognized by trainers and developers throughout the field. Yates and Orlikowski (1992) have looked in-depth at the genres of an area related to management learning – organizational communication – including the ways in which such genres (the memo, letters, meetings) change over time and through the introduction of new media. An example they give is of the impact of electronic mail on the memo genre.

The discourses that form management learning include, but are not simply, management discourses. Barley and Kunda (1992) have argued that in the USA five major managerial discourses have dominated since the 1870s: industrial betterment, scientific management, human relations, systems rationalization and organizational culture/quality. They identified different concepts (features, ideas and rationales) pertinent to each. So, for example, the organizational culture discourse of management they see as being characterized by an emphasis (at the content level) on shared values and beliefs, teamwork, quality, flexibility and service. These are the sorts of ideas and terms we might expect to find within texts drawing on this discourse. Willmott (this volume) refers to a study by Watson which identifies an 'upbeat "empowerment, skills and growth discourse"' and 'the more downbeat "control, jobs and costs discourse"'.

Questions that could be asked at this level include what constitutes the order of discourse of management learning? Who defines it? Who constitutes it in one way rather than another? What issues are marginalized or excluded? Journals such as *Management Learning* and books such as this one are part of a process of defining and constituting management learning. Are we as authors part of a process which is seeking to include a 'critical' discourse within the order of discourse of management learning? Do radical or critical discourses, which might threaten or challenge the *status quo* of management practice, become transformed, modified or appropriated? Is management learning a complex order of discourse where discourses compete or evolve, or is it stable and homogeneous?

In one way management learning has always been complex by virtue of its position between the world (and order of discourse) of management and business, and that of education and learning. Tensions exist between discourses of management which emphasize efficiency or people as resources, and those discourses of education and learning which emphasize personal development or emancipation. Particular discourses of management, such as human relations or organizational culture, could be seen as the outcome of some of these tensions – the generation of new discourses which attempt to resolve the tensions or live with them in different ways. Interestingly, it is within management learning, its order of discourse and practice, that a site for such tension exists. It is there where particular discourses are passed on, where managers are trained or developed in particular ways, where ideas are developed or modified and put to work.

Critical Discourse Analysis of Management Learning Discourse: An Example

For this section we carried out a detailed comparative analysis of two specific texts. Each text is a brochure produced by the same organization, advertising outdoor training and development courses. Neither the emphasis on outdoor education, nor the chosen organization, was significant in selecting the texts. Other training materials or brochures would have been equally suitable. What was significant was that there were two brochures, both produced by the same organization, both advertising similar, though not the same, courses, one of which (Text 1 on team-building) was aimed at the management development or organizational development world, whereas the other (Text 2) was aimed at 'adults over the age of 25'. The introductory first inside page of each brochure is reproduced below. By comparing the two texts (we concentrate on the extracts reproduced) we can begin to explore management learning discourses and how they differ from other discourses and the ways in which these texts construct the idea of managers and 'others'. Using the CDA framework, we look in turn at discourse practice, textual analysis and sociocultural practice (see the second section above).

Discourse practice

Both texts are promotional, advertising brochures aimed at persuading people to use the services of Outward Bound and attend its courses. In some ways, the two texts are similar – in layout, style, the use of colour and photographs, all of which suggest the genre of commodity advertising. However, when we look more closely at the texts, there are significant differences.

Text 1 is generically complex. While there are aspects of the genre of commodity advertising (see above), there are also features of the text which do not fit in with this genre – for instance, its complex clauses and sentences. These are more suggestive of exposition associated with academic management texts or guru management texts – assertive, expert, formal (more about how this is 'realized' textually later). Text 2 draws more explicitly on the genre of commodity advertising (short, simple sentences, addressing the customer directly, informal, chatty style) and particularly adventure holiday advertising. Text 2 also draws on a narrative genre – we are presented with a story.

What, then, are the discourses drawn upon in these texts? Text 1 draws on a rationalist discourse of management (scientific management or systems) with a hint of organizational culture or human relations discourse in places – the individual can 'develop his or her unique abilities to the full'. Text 2, by contrast, is dominated by a consumerist discourse of individual choice.

The discourses and genres drawn upon by these two texts are positioning the reader and writer in different ways. In Text 1, the consumer of the text,

---

TEXT 1	TEXT 2
The corporate environment is changing faster and more dramatically than at any period in recent history.	It's a familiar story.
	Every year you decide to opt for a 'different' kind of holiday. Something new. Something stimulating. Something exciting. But the chances are, you usually end up with just another variation on the standard mix of sun, sea and sand.
To keep pace, managers and staff at all levels, will also have to change. In order to change they have to learn – and the best and simplest way to learn is by experience not by rote, example or simply by commitment.	
That's the view taken by leading management authorities. It is certainly that taken by Outward Bound. In short, the need for all organisations to anticipate, keep pace with and manage change is vital.	The truth is that, no matter where you go, most holidays these days are a lot more routine – and often a lot less inspiring and refreshing than they might be.
	So why not take a chance on something *really* different? An enjoyable challenge? A rich, rewarding adventure that's out of the ordinary, out of the crowd and out of doors.
That demands an increasingly team-centred approach. One in which each individual is provided with the power, skill and opportunity to develop his or her unique abilities to the full and to contribute those skills in the most effective manner possible.	Why not go Outward Bound this year?

(*Sources:* The texts are taken from *Building Powerful Work Teams* (Text 1) and *The Experience of a Lifetime* (Text 2), both brochures produced by the Outward Bound Trust, Chestnut Field, Regent Place, Rugby CV21 2PJ)

---

the reader (who could be a corporate client purchasing services for others or an individual manager or management developer) is positioned as inexpert, a person needing to be told/convinced/explained to, in contrast with the producer's expert knower/instructor role. In Text 2, the reader is addressed directly as an individual and is positioned as customer or consumer of the product but also as subject hero of the narrative. The producer is more opaque.

What are the ways in which these discourses and genres are realized through the texts?

Textual analysis

We shall focus on the three aspects of textual analysis introduced earlier –
ideational, interpersonal and textual. Each text or part of text is analysed
clause by clause in terms of all aspects of textual, ideational and interpersonal functions.

Ideational function

- *Processes and associated participants.* Both texts use a number of
  relational processes (e.g., 'the truth is that' or 'it's a familiar story').
  These are not processes which tell us about what is happening, what
  someone or something is doing, saying or thinking, but ones which tell
  us what something or someone *is* or *has*. In Text 1, the participants in
  processes are either the course itself (the product), or references to it, or
  nominalizations (see below). In Text 2, as well as the product, 'you' is
  the most common participant.
- *Nominalization.* A further difference in the two texts is in the use of
  nominalizations. These have the appearance and function of nouns but
  are actually, or were originally, processes which have been transformed
  into nouns. Text 1 uses a lot of nominalization whereas as Text 2 has
  only one or two examples. So, in Text 1 we have:

  - the corporate environment
  - the need for all organisations to anticipate, keep pace with and
    manage change
  - team-centred approach
  - personal effectiveness
  - corporate priorities

  When nominalization occurs certain things get lost. So, for example,
  'personal effectiveness' has lost the sense of what person or people are
  being talked about, in what way they are or were effective, who says so,
  and so on. Nominalization is a feature of many professional discourses
  and can be seen as reinforcing shared taken-for-granteds and adding to
  the authority of the writer through its aura of technicality and because
  nominalization is less easily challenged than unnominalized processes. It
  will certainly be recognized as a familiar feature within management
  learning.

Interpersonal function

- *Mood and modality.* The mood of both texts is predominantly declarative. Both texts use statements more than any other form and these are
  categorical statements with no modal markers, the most authoritative
  form. They are not 'softened' in any way by the use of words such as
  'possibly' or 'I think', but are of the form:

  In order to change they have to learn . . .
  That demands an increasingly team-centred approach.

Declaratives such as these and strong modal forms are ways in which relationships of expert/novice or teller/told between writer and reader are realized textually. The use of such categorically assertive declaratives is a common feature of management texts. In addition, this textual form is a way of presenting ideas and beliefs as facts, with an expectation of agreement or shared taken-for-granteds between writer and reader. In Text 2 only, the declaratives occur with a number of questions:

> So why not take a chance on something *really* different?
> An enjoyable challenge?

Questions are a common feature of advertising discourse, with the reader being put more into the role of client/customer with a choice.

- *Pronouns.* Perhaps the most striking difference between the texts is the widespread use of 'you' in Text 2 and its absence from Text 1. In both texts, the organization itself features in many clauses as subject and theme, which is not unusual given the role of the brochure in advertising the organization and its services. By placing itself in theme and subject positions an emphasis is kept on the product, the organization. Other subjects and themes in Text 1 include 'the corporate environment' (and other nominalizations – see above), 'our clients', 'this work', 'the results'. In Text 2, however, 'you' functions as the subject and theme in most clauses: 'Every year you decide' and 'you usually end up with'. In addition, 'you' also functions as agent in many of these clauses, representing active processes.

In Text 2, then, there is a much clearer picture of who the reader is, of who the potential customer is. This customer is addressed less formally (the use of *I* or *you* in the subject position is more common in spoken language than written) and is appealed to in a different way, a much more engaged way. Where claims made in Text 1 are supported, they are supported by logic and rationality and by appeal to externalized authority, for example:

> That's the view taken by leading management authorities.

In contrast, in Text 2 the appeal is emotive and authority is internalized:

> But why take our word for it.
> Don't just read the brochure, come and find out for yourself.

Textual function. Given the fact that both brochures were produced by, or for, the same organization and that both were advertising similar courses, we were surprised to find a lack of overlap in the vocabulary of the two texts. Below are listed words and expressions which appear in one text but not the other.

Text 1	**Text 2**
work teams	memorable outdoor experience
corporate environment	challenge your limitations
organizations	fun
change	inspirational
team-centred	pleasurable
effective	excitement and adventure
development	respond to a challenge
personal effectiveness	enjoy taking a fresh look at yourself
participating organizations	
value for money	
sensibly priced	
goals	
quantifiable results	

So, very similar activities are presented in very different ways, each drawing on vocabularies associated with very different discourses.

Both extracts have the same logical structure:

Block one   Assertion (which the reader is expected to agree with)
Block two   Justification/argument
Block three   Conclusion/resolution of problem (Outward Bound).

In Text 1 the mode is argumentation. We are presented with a clearly developed argument which builds to its climax. In Text 2 we are offered a narrative, a story into which we can insert ourselves as character.

Another of the textual features is the kind of connection made between sentences. Again, the two examples are strikingly different. Text 1 uses a lot of repetition of words. So we have:

The corporate environment is *changing* . . .
. . . managers and staff . . . will also have to *change.*
In order to *change* they have to *learn* . . .
. . . the best and simplest way to *learn* . . .

There is an echoing of words which fit the problem/solution structure of the argument, in which clauses give the solution to the problem of the previous clause. In Text 2, however, repetition only occurs in rhetorical parallelism:

Something new. Something stimulating. Something exciting.

This structure is typical of commodity advertising. Coherence in Text 2 is achieved mainly by the use of the narrative structure.

Finally a brief comment about the photographs used in each brochure. Photographs in Text 1 are of groups of people, many outdoor shots but some indoors accompanied by flip charts and seminar rooms. Text 2 photographs include a few group shots, but mainly individuals or twos with no indoor shots and no flip charts.

Sociocultural practice

All of the features above are potentially normative, reinforcing a particular view of managers, management training and development that already exists – seminar rooms and flip charts, professional language and nominalizations, use of 'strong' declaratives and the emphasis on external authority – setting up, among other things, strong messages about what it means to be a manager. Clearly, texts may not 'work' in this straightforward way; readers may be cynical, disinterested or actively resistant.

The 'corporate environment', the world of managers, is changing dramatically. The day-to-day experience of managing is one of change, fragmentation, uncertainty and constant decision-making, often on the basis of insufficient evidence. No wonder then that the texts of management learning display a confidence and certainty in the face of such uncertainty. Such texts surely help construct, or at least reinforce, desired managerial identity – that of competence, an ability to act, to get things done, to achieve results against the odds – as well as that of management learning, for it is within management learning that such people are trained, developed or constructed

Critical Discourse Analysis and Management Learning Professionals

In this section we look first at the ways in which CDA could be used by management learning professionals and then at how to begin applying CDA in practice. As we said in the first section, CDA is based on the view that language not only reflects our social world but also constructs it. Language has a central role in social life, and so the management learning professionals who want to look critically at their own practice must look at language. And, as we have argued, CDA allows language to be looked at in a more focused way than much of the vague discussion of discourse in social science.

Many management learning professionals will be very aware of language already, particularly aspects of vocabulary such as 'human resources' for 'people', and terms like 'downsizing' and 'outsourcing', or the accepted language of equal opportunities (see examples below). Focusing on aspects of language as a way of highlighting taken-for-granted features is not dissimilar to the work that might be carried out by internal or external process consultants or by a good facilitator to a group or team. Using CDA provides a framework which supports a *systematic* examination of practice – in reading books or promotional material, or facilitating groups of course participants as well as in research. As we have said earlier, this can both bring to attention factors otherwise missed and allow us to demonstrate or give evidence for our views and arguments, to ourselves and others.

CDA can also be used to support ongoing changes in discourse practice. One area within organizations where attention is paid to language is equal opportunities. Managers responsible for the implementation of training and development to support equal opportunities might feel that the desired changes were not happening. By focusing critically on language use they might see a discrepancy between the intended message of various policy documents and training materials and the actual message embodied in the structure of the texts. So the intended message may see employees or potential employees from disadvantaged groups in very positive and active ways. However, analysis of texts could reveal them as actually constructed in a passive role, as objects of clauses rather than subjects, for example: 'Ways have to be found to accommodate disabled employees on the premises' or 'the most commonly voiced concerns are about means of escape in the case of fire for disabled people'. Such examples could be indirectly reinforcing a stereotypical image inspite of the opposite intention. Changing language alone cannot change social practice, but it can support wider processes of change.

More broadly, CDA, while emphasizing the power of language to constitute our social world and to impose constraints on our place within it, also provides the mechanisms for understanding such constructions and constraints so that practitioners can resist or challenge them.

Having analysed texts such as those in the previous section and begun to examine the ways in which identity is constituted, we might ask the questions: 'Is this construction of my social identity as a manager one with which I agree? Am I happy with the effect of such discourses in relation to myself, my colleagues, my employees and, given my position in society, the social world generally?' If I answer yes, then I might use CDA to help me to do this work more effectively, to make my actual message match my intended message. Discourse analysis can be and is used (exploited?) within the worlds of advertising and marketing in this way. If I answer no, what would I want to be different? What function and identity do I want for myself, for managers, for management development, and how can I change what I do in order to achieve that? How can I use language to constitute a different reality, one more in keeping with my values and beliefs?

Finally, then, how to get started on such analyses? The complete body of texts produced in management learning – course materials, advertising brochures, journal articles, training needs analyses, the content of courses themselves – can all be thought of as the domain of management learning and therefore as potential source material for analysis. What is included within the domain, and what is not, is itself an interesting and significant question. Only someone who is a cultural insider, someone who is a member of that domain and who is familiar with the associated texts and social activities is in a position to explore this fully. There is no attempt at objectivity here. We are interested in understanding social practice from within, although an outsider can be helpful in asking naive or culturally ignorant questions which can challenge aspects that insiders take for granted.

The first problem is that of choosing texts for analysis from this huge amount of material. What we choose depends on our particular interest and focus. So, for example, our analysis of outdoor training brochures might be part of a wider study focusing on the outdoor management development from a discursive perspective. We might look at a video of an actual course, carry out interviews with course members, trainers or client organizations, or examine course materials and handouts as well as the promotional material itself. As researchers we might be interested in whether and in what way, managers' identities are socially constructed. Can management learning be thought of as being concerned predominantly with the construction of managerial identity? We might examine job adverts, CVs, individual interviews, as well as all of the material described above.

In applying the framework of CDA in research, in management education, or in ordinary practice, there are various questions we can use for guidance.[1] For instance:

- *Discourse practice:* What genres are being drawn upon? What discourses? Is there a complex mixture of genres and discourses, or is the text relatively simple? Is the mixture conventional, or innovative?
- *Text:* How is the mixture of genres and discourses realized in the language? Specifically:
  - what sort of vocabularies and metaphors are used?
  - what sort of processes are used?
  - is there much nominalization?
  - what mood (declarative, interrogative, imperative) is the main one used?
  - what modality features does the text have?
  - how are the sentences of the text linked together?
- *Sociocultural practice:* What social and cultural features of management learning, of work, and of the social context of work, are the features of the discourse a part of?

Summary

In this chapter, we have introduced readers to the approach of critical discourse analysis and shown how it might be used to enhance understanding of the world of management learning and of management learning practice. Management learning seems to us to present a particularly rich area of study. It is an important site for the development of managerial identity and, as we have argued in this chapter, is a site of tensions and competing discourses. Further study could help to show the impact such discourses have on management learning practice. In what way are those of us working in this field constrained or enabled by existing discourses? In what way do we contribute to their maintenance or transformation?

Note

1   For more detailed sets of guidance questions, see Chapter 8 of Fairclough (1992a) or Chapters 5 and 6 of Fairclough (1989).

Annotated Bibliography

The texts mentioned here can be divided into those that focus on critical discourse analysis (CDA), or particular aspects of it, and related areas of language theory and those which focus on management learning or related subject areas but not from a CDA perspective. Beginning with the former, Fairclough (1989, 1995) provide a general and thorough introduction to the ideas of critical language study and to the application of CDA as a method. Fairclough (1989) includes many examples and a framework of questions with which to approach a study of your own texts. For a more in-depth and theoretical account of CDA, see Fairclough (1992a). Jay Lemke (1995) gives another excellent introduction and overview. Gunter Kress (1985) focuses on discourses and genres and their relationship to wider sociocultural practice. He uses many examples of texts, including some from education. One text which bridges both CDA and management learning is that by Hodge, Kress and Jones (1979) who have analysed interviews with middle managers. Wendy Hollway, as well as providing an historical account of the rise of human relations discourses of management in the UK and USA (Hollway, 1991), also writes a very interesting and accessible account of the idea of subject positioning within discourses using sexuality as her example (Hollway, 1992).

References

Barley, S.R. and Kunda, G. (1992) 'Design and devotion: surges of rational and normative ideologies of control in managerial discourse', *Administrative Science Quarterly*, 37: 363–99.

Fairclough, Norman (1989) *Language and Power*. London: Longman.

Fairclough, Norman (1992a) *Discourse and Social Change*. Cambridge: Polity Press.

Fairclough, Norman (1992b) *Critical Language Awareness*. London: Longman.

Fairclough, Norman (1995) *Critical Discourse Analysis: The Critical Study of Language*. London: Longman.

Halliday, Michael (1985) *An Introduction to Functional Grammar*. London: Edward Arnold.

Hodge, B., Kress, G. and Jones, G. (1979) 'The ideology of middle management', in R. Fowler, B. Hodge, G. Kress and T. Trew (eds), *Language and Control*. London: Routledge and Kegan Paul. pp. 81–93.

Hollway, Wendy (1991) *Work Psychology and Organizational Behaviour: Managing the Individual at Work*. London: Sage.

Hollway, Wendy (1992) 'Gender difference and the productivity of subjectivity', in H. Crowly and S. Himmelweit (eds), *Knowing Women*. Cambridge: Polity Press. pp. 240–74.

Kress, Gunter (1985) *Linguistic Processes in Sociocultural Practice*. Oxford: Oxford University Press.

Lemke, Jay L. (1995) *Textual Politics – Discourse and Social Dynamics*. London: Taylor and Francis.

Yates, J. and Orlikowski, W.J. (1992) 'Genres of organizational communication: an approach to studying communication and media', *Academy of Management Review*, 17 (2): 299–326.

9

Critical Management Learning

Hugh Willmott

This chapter applies critical thinking to the process of learning about the theory and practice of management. To date, critical thinking about management has challenged established ideas about management (Alvesson and Willmott, 1992a). Much less attention has been paid to the question of how critical understandings of management might be made more accessible and meaningful to students and practitioners. Yet, if the contribution of critical thinking is to extend beyond the confines of academics and research students, it is necessary to consider the relevance of such thinking for the process of management learning.

Diverse meanings are attributed to the terms 'management', 'learning' and 'critical thinking'. What these terms mean depends upon the framework of interpretation favoured by different commentators (Willmott, 1984; Reed, 1989). I begin therefore by indicating how these terms are being used in this chapter. I then apply critical thinking to explore the nature of managerial work and the process of learning about it. Before proceeding further, though, it is worth noting that while angled towards management within the private sector, public-sector organizations and utilities that remain publicly owned (at the time of writing) are being subjected to discourses and disciplines derived from the private sector; and, indeed, many public-sector organizations are increasingly obliged to compete with the private sector in order to raise revenues in an effort to compensate for the progressive reduction of public funding for established activities. Many of the tensions and dilemmas experienced by managers in the private sector are present in the public sector; and, indeed, they are often intensified precisely because, historically, the goods and services provided by the public-sector organizations have not been commodified or subjected to 'market testing' (see, e.g., Willmott, 1995b).

Conceptualizing Management, Learning and Critical Thinking

'*Management*' has both a general and a more specific, historical meaning. The universal meaning arises from our comparatively open relationship to the world: in every society, human beings are continuously involved in reflexively accomplishing our everyday lives. The term 'managing' is often used to describe this activity. For example, I might ask a friend whether she had 'managed' to see a mutual acquaintance, or whether a colleague had 'managed' to convene a meeting. The historically specific meaning of 'managing' and 'management', which supplies its usage to describe mundane, everyday organizing, is chiefly associated with the governance of work organizations and, more specifically, with particular practices and (usually) hierarchical positions deemed necessary for their effective operation.

Much confusion arises from a tendency to conflate these meanings. Necessity and inevitability – the universal aspects of management – are frequently attributed to its historical manifestation within a *social division* of labour. This division of labour is not itself universal or inevitable. Rather, it owes its existence to political processes through which managerial work is defined and ascribed to a privileged social group, a group deemed to possess the expertise and ethos relevant for husbanding privately owned assets (see Bendix, 1966).

'*Learning*' refers to the acquisition of ways of relating to the world. It includes the development of our relations with others, through which a (precarious) sense of identity and autonomy is constructed. In learning to become separate, purposive beings, it is easy to overlook the interdependence of human action and, not least, the interdependencies within contemporary work organizations that exist despite the foundation of these organizations upon social divisions of ownership, gender and/or control. In the context of work organizations, learning is directed at developing more effective means of controlling the interdependence (e.g., by redesigning jobs to secure increases in collective employee productivity). Or learning addresses and seeks to transform the social divisions of ownership and control that motivate, but also subvert and frustrate, efforts to achieve given objectives (e.g., increased productivity). The first, conservative form of learning assumes the necessity and/or inevitability of established objectives and associated structures of ownership and control (e.g., patriarchy). The second, critical form of learning, which is often an unintended consequence of conservative learning, questions their necessity as it diagnoses these structures as a source of unnecessary waste and suffering.

'*Critical thinking*' involves a process of reflection upon the adequacy and value of conventional wisdom and methods of learning. For example, a version of critical thinking has been used to challenge established management discourses and practices in which the necessity and efficiency of 'bureaucratic' systems and procedures is assumed (Barley and Kunda, 1993; Jacques, 1996). What, today, is characterized pejoratively as 'bureaucratic' and 'inflexible' was once revered as 'rational' and 'scientific'. What is now distinguished and exalted as 'organic' could, in time, be identified as excessively chaotic, pressured and insecure. More 'flexible', 'organic' approaches, it is claimed, can reap the benefits of increased employee involvement, empowerment and commitment by facilitating continuous learning, and thereby achieving more rapid adaptations to changing circumstances. However, critical thinking extends beyond a narrow, instrumental assessment of the efficacy of a particular technique. As I shall attempt to demonstrate in this chapter, 'critical thinking' can challenge the credibility of established forms of 'management' and 'learning'.

Scare quotes have been repeatedly used in the previous paragraphs. Their use is intended to highlight the constructed, contextual and disputed nature of the diverse meanings that are attributed to these concepts. 'Management', for example, can be understood *inter alia* as an economic resource, as a group of people possessing distinctive competences or as a system of power and authority in which people pursue different individuals and collective strategies (Child, 1977). Etymologically, the term 'management' is derived from the Italian *maneggiare*, 'to handle a horse'. Though seemingly obscure, this semantic root is instructive in its portrayal of the social divisiveness of management as a contradictory process – a process in which a person simultaneously takes responsibility for and seeks to control a valuable, yet wilful and potentially resistant, resource. Likewise, what is meant by 'critical thinking' and 'learning' varies with the frame of reference invoked and the context of their use – a context which, arguably, is not simply disclosed but is actually constituted through the meanings that are ascribed to such terms. Concepts do *not* describe or reflect aspects of reality that exist 'out there' in the world. Rather, they are inscriptions or sounds that invoke connotative meanings, and, through a process of learning, communicate and/ or establish particular understandings that may be more or less widely shared. The meaning of concepts is not given any more than the practices which they purport to reflect and serve to reproduce.

In the following discussion, there is a concern to acknowledge and explore the diversity of ways of applying critical thinking to understand and change management practice. These range from thinking that questions and refines alternative means of achieving given ends to a broader conception of critical thinking that interrogates the rationality of ends and, relatedly, the value-neutrality of a managerial focus upon the refinement of means (see Alvesson and Willmott, 1992b). The latter, radical and wide-ranging application of critical thinking engages in a more extensive consideration of the intellectual coherence, moral defensibility and historical sustainability of management theories and practices.

Towards a Critical Understanding of Management[1]

Received wisdom assures us that, as a consequence of processes of modernization, organizations are now managed on a more rational basis. Scientific thinking, this wisdom contends, has swept away much of the irrationality surrounding traditional methods of organizing work. The specialist expertise of managers has been developed and honed to ensure the efficient and effective fulfilment of the needs of organizations and society. 'Professional management', it is claimed, provides the key to the good society:

> Our society has in this century become a society of organizations. Organizations depend on managers, are built by managers, directed and held together by managers and made to perform by managers. Once an organization grows beyond

a very small size, it needs managers who practise professional management. This means management grounded in a discipline and informed by the objective needs of the organization and of its people, rather than management based upon ownership or political appointment. (Drucker, 1977: 32–3)

Such views assume that integrating 'the needs' of the organization with 'the needs' of its employees is a matter of replacing amateurs with expert managers. The objectives of management are portrayed as objectively given; the division between managers and managed is presented as 'natural' or functionally necessary for achieving these objectives; and the efficacy of the techniques for securing the give objectives is assumed to be un-problematical.

Post-rational management theory

The coherence of this rationalist understanding of managerial work has been contested on a number of counts. Limitations upon human information gathering and processing have been stressed (March and Simon, 1958). It has also been argued that decision-making, in respect of 'the objective needs of the organization', is invariably guided and restricted by managers' particular allegiances, preoccupations and hunches (e.g., Pettigrew, 1973). The hunches, proven recipes and 'biases' of managers, and not just their limited capacity to process information or commercial pressures to reach closure, lead managers to depart from the rationalist logic of classical management theory. Decision-making, Child concludes, 'is an essentially political process in which constraints and opportunities are *functions of the power exercised by decision-makers in the light of ideological values*' (1972: 16; my emphasis).

Such analysis has been guided by a concern to make the practice of management more perfectly managerial by enabling managers to appreciate the role of values in shaping their perceptions, and/or appreciate the nature and significance of organizational politics (see, e.g., Pfeffer, 1981; Kotter, 1982). Or, as Pettigrew has expressed this view in respect of developing more effective means of achieving business strategies:

. . . changing business strategies has to involve a process of ideological and political change that eventually releases a new concept of strategy that is culturally acceptable within a newly appreciated context. . . . In the broadest sense, this means, prescriptively, that step one in a change process should be to improve and build upon any natural processes of change by tackling questions such as how existing processes can be speeded up, how the conditions that determine people's interpretations of situations can be altered, and how contexts can be mobilized toward legitimate problems and solutions along the way to move the organization additively [*sic*] in a different strategic direction. (Pettigrew, 1985: 314 and 316)

In post-rational accounts of management, attention is focused upon the ideological and political dimensions of organizing as a means of *smoothing* processes of top-down change. Established priorities and values are assumed to be legitimate. Social science is prized as a technology for identifying and honing political and propagandistic skills, and not for its capacity to stimulate a debate on the legitimacy of current priorities (and prescriptions). In this respect, post-rational management theory provides academic legitimation for the prescriptions of contemporary gurus (e.g., Peters and Waterman, 1982; Hammer and Champy, 1993) who commend the use of 'soft' methods of management control and advocate the replacement of functional 'silos' with process-based forms of organization (see Willmott, 1993, 1995a). Precious little consideration is given to the merits, or rationality, of the 'ends' of management. Post-rational thinking finds nothing problematical, ethically or ecologically, in the application of whatever means are claimed to be most effective in securing established ends. It simply extends the refinement of means to encompass the political skills deemed effective for the management of 'people's interpretations of situations' (Pettigrew, 1985: 316). It does not promote critical reflection upon the historical formation of management practice and theory within divisive contradictory structures of economic organization.

Beyond managerial ideology

Embracing a technocratic ideology in which management theory and practice is evaluated primarily on the basis of its contribution to the refinement of means is not without risks and costs: the logic of technocracy 'demands' that managerial work is itself subjected to the same rationalizing processes that it visits upon others (Fletcher, 1973; Willmott, forthcoming). The application of powerful information technologies in the name of progress and efficiency currently threatens to automate or abolish the work of many supervisors and managers. As Anthony has observed, managers

> are more likely to be the unwitting victims of reorganization (more and more frequently); transferred, retrained or dismissed at the behest of organizational plans drawn up by distant consultants; regarded as human resources, shuffled and distributed by specialists in management development and planning. (1977: 310)

The contemporary enthusiasm for employee involvement and corporate culture programmes promotes an 'internalization' of supervisory responsibilities among multi-skilled, 'self-disciplined' operatives, and thus undermines the status and employment of supervisory staff and middle management. When steeped in and disciplined by technocratic ideology, these managers are ill-prepared to make (critical) sense of, let alone resist, the contradictory operation of valued 'logics' that simultaneously pose a threat to their employment and suggest the relevance of critical thinking for making sense of such developments.

The contradiction at the heart of managerial work is that managers are sellers of labour whose value is ultimately assessed, in the context of capitalist enterprise, in terms of their capacity to demonstrate their contribution to profitability. Legally and structurally, they are positioned as agents of the owners of corporate assets. But, as the sellers of labour, they have an investment in their continued employment, their occupational identity and their career prospects (Willmott, forthcoming). The principal asset or 'property' of most managers is their labour power that takes the form of particular, potentially redundant, forms of expertise. As sellers of expertise, they are compelled to negotiate a payment for this property within the labour market. Mindful of their future employment and career prospects, managers are not necessarily willing to assimilate and implement rational or 'post-rational' principles of work organization, especially if these are perceived to devalue the worth of their expertise, though they may well pay eloquent lip service to them. In practice, principles and logics of organization are interpreted and enacted in relation to perceived opportunities for securing or advancing a mêlée of identity-securing concerns and values – such as the expansion of a specialist area, speedy promotion, the chance of more challenging work, the continuation of a quiet life, etc.

As employees, albeit comparatively privileged ones, managers experience the pressures as well as the rewards associated with the controls to which they are subjected (e.g., budgets, appraisals, targets). Currently, differences of status and entitlement between middle managers and other employees are being eroded in an effort to boost profitability and responsiveness to market volatility by reducing managerial overheads (Ezzamel et al., 1995). Much managerial work is becoming intensified and/or rendered insecure as hierarchies are flattened and 'middle management' is squeezed. Career paths are becoming more uncertain as the comparative safety of specialist, functional 'chimneys' is being eroded by moves to so-called team-working. Of course, some managers are beneficiaries, in the short term at least, as they make rapid, 'fast-track' progress up (shortened) corporate hierarchies. For them, the experience of being treated as commodities, to be 'shuffled and redistributed' (Anthony, 1977: 310) if not dismissed, is considerably attenuated, or somewhat compensated, by increases in salary, status and other benefits (share options, for example). But, equally, many other managers are becoming the victims (in terms of stress and insecurity), and not just the perpetrators, of control systems that they design, operate and police.

An illustration: practising management at ZTC Ryland

I have argued that managerial work is a medium and outcome of the contradictory forces that play upon it. I now illustrate and support this claim by drawing upon Watson's (1994a) study of 'ZTC Ryland' (a pseudonym). I have chosen this study not only because it is one of the best ethnographies of managerial work, but also because it allows me to clarify my understanding of management in relation to Watson's rich and sophisticated but, I will argue, ultimately limited account of managerial work.

Watson (1994a, 1994b) focuses upon the presence of *two rival discourses* which, he argues, competed for the attention and allegiance of ZTC managers. First, there was an up-beat *'empowerment, skills and growth discourse'*. Most forcefully articulated by a number of senior managers, this came into conflict with, and was contradicted by, an alternative, more downbeat *'control, jobs and costs discourse'*. Managers at ZTC were obliged to rehearse, and wanted to believe in, up-beat ideas about empowerment and growth. However, their everyday experiences and anxieties about an uncertain (employment) future led many of them to interpret their situation in terms of increased controls and pressures for cost-cutting. In turn, these pressures kindled a desire to be in (secure) *jobs* rather than to be identified as possessors of (transferable) *skills*.

Watson notes how managers at ZTC were heard 'confusingly and confusedly switching back and forth' (1994a: 114) between elements of these discourses. These tensions and confusions were brought into sharpest relief during bouts of redundancy. Talk of empowerment and growth then came into direct conflict with 'a policy of tight cost control and the maintenance of profit levels over the short term' (Watson, 1994b: S83). The tension was plainly articulated by a manufacturing manager:

> How the hell can you preach this flexibility, this personal and business development at the same time as you are getting rid? As some one said to me yesterday, an operator, 'Why am I in here now doing the best I can getting this product out when tomorrow morning you can give me a brown envelope?' I had no answer. (ibid.)

Watson accounts for these tensions in terms of a particular, self-defeating *view* of managerial work, most strongly ascribed to those occupying the most senior positions, in which ZTC managers were conceived as 'the rational planners and unemotional builders of organizational systems' (Watson, 1994a: 179). Such a view, Watson contends, created a dysfunctional social distance between managers and what they managed as it set them 'above and apart from the action of which they need to be a part' (ibid.). As a consequence, Watson argues, many managers ended up knowing less about 'the core work of the organization' and so were obliged to manage 'an impression of knowing it all' (ibid.: 179–80). In turn, Watson understands this contradiction to be productive of 'bouts of bad temper and screaming frustration'; and, more damagingly for the company, to result in managers resorting to managing-at-a-distance through structures, systems, initiatives and fads that become ends in themselves rather than means of 'sharing ideas and developing solutions to shared problems and agreed tasks' (ibid.: 180).

So, Watson diagnoses the tensions at ZTC as a product of senior managers' assuming an erroneous *view*. It was this view, on Watson's account, that led them to promote and hype an 'empowerment, skills and growth' discourse that flew in the face of 'the action' from which they had become distanced as it operated simultaneously to extend and legitimize this distance. In contrast, I interpret the tensions and the views associated with them as expressive of the contradictory forces that structure the very organization of managerial work, which is not to deny that diverse conflicts and inconsistencies are likely to be encountered in every kind of human organization. Watson understands management to be basically 'concerned with "shaping" the activities of the work organization as a whole to bring about its *long-term survival*' (ibid.: 38; my emphasis). I would say that top management, in particular, frequently seek to present their role in this way as a means of gaining public legitimacy and inducing the co-operation and effort of employees, middle managers included. But, *in practice*, managers in capitalist enterprises like ZTC are under relentless and intensifying pressure to organize the work of others in ways that at least minimally satisfy shareholder priorities. At least one eye is kept on share price movement. Profitability, not survival *per se*, is the critical issue; and the contradictions which structure managerial work derive from the pressures to induce productive effort from labour – through the empowerment discourse, for example – including other managers, while simultaneously exercising the option or the veiled threat to dispose of their labour – for example, through the control discourse. Much of the time, this tension is experienced in comparatively 'attenuated' or low-profile form, and its manifestation is routinely attributed to the attitude of 'bolshy', 'troublemaking' or 'politically motivated' *individuals* who are deemed to lack the requisite discipline or ambition, rather than to broader, structural contradictions. However, occasionally, as when a wave of redundancies occurs, it becomes more apparent that it is not so much long-term survival as short-term profitability that precipitates the loss of jobs.

In an ideal world, perhaps managers would or at least 'should see their primary role as contributing towards the overall performance of the organization as a whole' (ibid.: 39). But in the lived world of 'ZTC Ryland', as Watson's own findings indicate, such a view is profoundly ideological in the sense that it impedes rather than promotes critical reflection upon, and learning about, contradictions which lie at the heart of capitalist enterprise. It implies that pursuit of 'the overall performance of the organization' can be accomplished independently of the *social relations* of production that simultaneously exert pressures upon employees to 'pull together' and 'perform' as they operate to divide managers and employees by setting the former 'above and apart from the action' (ibid.: 179). This 'setting apart', as Watson describes it, cannot be adequately explained purely in terms of managers subscribing to an erroneous or dysfunctional *view* of management, even if the excesses of such a view, such as multiple dining facilities, can be rationalized in the name of the equalization of employee benefits. It is necessary instead to consider the material and ideological conditions that give rise to the elevation of the view ascribed by Watson to senior managers and the associated reluctance to subject it to critical examination.

Contra orthodox management theory, I have argued that managers are not neutral technicians. And *contra* post-rational management theory, I have argued that managers are more than skilful fixers of organizational politics and culture. As Watson's study of ZTC shows, managers routinely struggle with conflicting loyalties and moralities; but he attributes the existence of conflicting loyalties of management to an erroneous view of their work rather than to the structure of social relations that lends it plausibility. Largely absent from management textbooks is a way of making sense of the mundane features of managerial work described by Watson (1994a). In the absence of such thinking, managers can easily become hardened, find rationalizations for their actions or simply become bewildered and overwhelmed by the scale and complexity of the dilemmas that they encounter. The task of *critical action learning* is to present and command an alternative to the seeming neutrality and authority of orthodox management theory as a means of opening up and facilitating a transformation of management practice. But, in doing so, attention must be paid to the *embodied character of practice*, and not just to the deficiencies or irrationalities of established – rational and post-rational – management theory.

Towards a Critical Understanding of Management Learning

An obvious place to begin is with learners' experiences and problems, and then to explore different perspectives for making sense of their experiences and for addressing their problems (Grey et al., 1996). Such an approach is broadly congruent with the pedagogic philosophy developed within action learning (Revans, 1982).

McLaughlin and Thorpe (1993) differentiate action learning from traditional management education along the lines summarized in Table 9.1.[2]

Traditional management education invites students and practitioners to acquire knowledge of relevant facts and techniques that, in principle, are of universal relevance. The world is assumed to have the status of an exterior, independent object which can be known about. By acquiring a body of knowledge, the student or practitioner becomes an expert who can better use, manipulate and control human and material resources. *Action learning*, in contrast, emphasizes the contiguity of learners and their knowledge of the world. It is critical of the narrowness of traditional management education

Table 9.1   *Traditional and action learning approaches to management education (adapted from McLaughlin and Thorpe, 1993)*

	Traditional management education	Action learning
World view	The world is an exterior 'object' to be learned about.	The world is a contiguous 'subject' to act upon and change.
	Self-development is unimportant.	Self-development is very important.
	Some notion of correct management practice, established by research, defines the (formal) curriculum.	Content and/or delivery of learning is defined by the organization and/or the learners.
Modus operandi	Mananagers should learn theories or models derived from research.	Learners should be facilitated by a tutor to solve problems.
	Experts decide on what should be learnt, when and how much.	Experts are viewed with caution.
	Models, concepts, ideas are provided to offer tools for future thinking and action.	Models, concepts, ideas are developed in response to current problems.

which, put at its simplest, may enable students and practitioners to acquire more knowledge, in the form of abstract theory, but does not equip them to learn from their experience or to advance their capacity to deal with, and learn from, the specifics of particular problems. From an action learning standpoint, knowledge is always more or less embodied in the lived experience of the students or the practitioners; knowledge is effectively useless unless they have the capability to appreciate its relevance for a particular situation and to apply it, which generally involves the engagement of others, and that is why self-development is central to the philosophy of action learning. The role and contribution of experts is viewed with some caution as the value of knowledge is appraised primarily in relation to its practical relevance for tackling live problems rather than the universal, abstract value ascribed to it by authorities.

To the extent that action learning engages with the struggles of individual students and practitioners, it may also open up an appreciation of, and sensitivity towards, 'darker' aspects of organizational life that are generally acknowledged, or at least coded, within traditional management education. As McLaughlin and Thorpe observe:

> At the level of their own experience, managers undertaking Action Learning programmes can come to know themselves and their organization much better. *In particular, they can become aware of the primacy of politics, both macro and micro, and the influence of power on decision making and non-decision making, not to mention the 'mobilization of bias'.* (1993: 25; my emphasis)

As the references to 'the primacy of politics' and 'the "mobilization of bias"' imply, there is a link to be made here between the embodied insights generated by action learning and the theoretical contributions of diverse traditions of critical analysis (see Alvesson and Willmott, 1996). In different ways, each offers a means of penetrating conventional idealized representations of management and managers, and thereby brings to light some of the tensions and disjunctions within managerial work. However, as Vince (1996) has recently commented, action learning offers comparatively little in the way of *theory* that *actively encourages* or guides 'working with the *emotional and power dynamics* in learning processes' (1996: 119; my emphasis).

As Vince indicates, the denial or marginalization of emotions within action learning sets is closely associated with the *politics* of learning; and, I would add, with the gendered constitution of managerial work as a medium of masculine identity formation and confirmation. Learning is inhibited or distorted when people in organizations, or in learning groups, are 'positioned unequally, in and by organizations and groups as a consequence of social constructions of their identity' (Vince, 1996: 124). Learning experiences are invariably mediated by social relations of power between teachers/ facilitators and the members of learning sets. However, in action learning, there is 'the pervasive humanist myth' (ibid.: 127) of egalitarianism between set members – a myth which operates to deny the realities and truth-effects of power, including the notion that the formal equality of set members is not significantly distorted and compromised by substantive differences in their respective identities, in terms of gender, ethnicity, age, corporate status, and so forth.

Vince (1996) makes repeated reference to 'socially constructed power differences' but there is no analysis or consideration of how these differences are constructed or become 'truths' within particular contexts. It was precisely such lacunae in the theory and practice of managerial work, including management education, that the discussion of management in the previous section was intended to redress. There it was suggested that the critical study of management must go beyond simply identifying power differences or noting that these have been constructed. In addition, it must address the legitimacy of these differences and explore the potential for changes that can challenge practices and ideologies through which established exploitation, oppression and subjection become institutionalized. For example, critical thinking draws attention to the likely connection between social relations of power (e.g., capitalism, patriarchy) and an inclination to banish emotion from work organization (Fineman, 1993) – not least because the latter, expressed as frustration, anger, resentment and so on, can provide a engaged basis for resisting established structures and patterns of interaction.

In common with action learning, critical action learning seeks to address the immediate, practical problems of living and working as a student or practitioner of management. And to this extent, its concerns resonate with a number of action learning's criticisms of traditional management education. However, action learning abstracts processes of individual self-development from the institutional media of personal and social transformation. By locating both problems and solutions in individuals, action learning fails to appreciate how the problem-solving capabilities of individuals are conditioned – enabled but also constrained – by their development and embeddedness within structures of social relations. Some key differences between conventional and critical action learning are summarized in Table 9.2.

When applied to management education, critical action learning combines the pedagogic philosophy of action learning with critical traditions in an effort to better understand and transform the contradictory forces that play upon organizational work. In broad outline, the process of critical action involves the following moments which I illustrate *in italics* by referring to Watson's (1994a, 1994b) study of managers at ZTC Ryland (see earlier section):

1 An experience of tension (e.g., anxiety or doubt) or the identification of contradiction (e.g., success *and* unhappiness).

   . . . at ZTC, the tension between the two rival discourses – of 'empowerment, skills and growth' and 'control, jobs and costs'.

2 The interpretation of tension/contradiction as avoidable, such as the diagnosis of this tension as a social and political phenomenon rather than a 'given' or a natural occurrence.

Table 9.2   *An alternative approach to management education using a framework adapted from McLaughlin and Thorpe (1993)*

	Conventional action learning	Critical action learning
World view	The world is a contiguous 'subject' to act upon and change.	The world is a contiguous psycho-political field of action and change.
	Self-development is very important.	Self-development and social development are interdependent.
	Content and/or delivery of learning is defined by the organization and/or the learners.	Content and/or delivery of learning is guided by critical social theory and reflection upon experiences derived from its practical application.
Modus operandi	Learners should be facilitated by a tutor to solve problems.	Learners are potentially receptive to, and can be facilitated by, the concerns of other groups, in addition to individual tutors, when identifying and addressing problems.
	Experts are viewed with caution.	Received wisdom, including that of experts, is subject to criticial scrutiny through a fusion of reflection and insights drawn from critical social theory.
	Models, concepts, ideas are developed in response to current problems.	Models, concepts and ideas are developed through an interplay of reflection upon practice and an application of ideas drawn from critical traditions.

The belief that basic elements of the tensions between the two discourses were the product of the contradictory demands of capitalist enterprises which require labour to be at once committed and dispensable, dependable and disposable.

3   Analysis of the tensions/contradictions, including the conditions that are understood to produce them.

An analysis that does not attribute the tensions between the discourse to be the view held by (senior) management; but, rather, understands this view itself to be conditioned by the positioning of (senior) managers within capitalist relations of production.

4   Recurrent efforts to resolve tensions/contradictions through struggles to change their conditions of existence. This includes strengthening the capacity to identify, analyse and address tensions/contradictions.

Recurrent efforts to mobilize the energy associated with the experience of contradiction to expose their existence and challenge their inevitability. Not only does this reveal the self-defeating consequences of adopting a view that sets managers 'above and apart from the action of which they need to be a part' (Watson, 1994a: 179); it also appreciates how this view is tendential within a social division of labour founded upon structural inequalities of wealth and control.

5   An experience of new tensions and/or the identification of contradictions arising from the process of struggle. Go to 2.

Addressing reactions and resistance to efforts to change the theory and practice of management.

Contradictory principles and practices of work organization repeatedly disrupt established conventions and prescriptions. In turn, instability and crisis present recurrent opportunities for questioning received wisdoms and transforming established practices. Critical action learning explores how the comparatively abstract ideas of critical theory can be mobilized and applied in the process of understanding and changing interpersonal and institutional practices. By combining a pedagogy that focuses upon management as a lived experience with theory that debunks conventional wisdom, managers can be enabled to develop 'habits of critical thinking . . . that prepare them for responsible citizenship and personally and socially rewarding lives and careers' (Porter et al., 1989: 71). And, in this way, it may be possible to advance forms of learning that are guided less by a compulsion to pre-serve the irrationalities and inequities of a decomposing *status quo* than by an interest in personal and social renewal.

For those concerned to translate the insights of critical management studies into new kinds of management education and learning, the challenge is to move from intellectual critiques whose audience is principally fellow academics to encompass a broader constituency of students and practitioners in a debate about management theory and practice that can contribute to its transformation (Willmott, 1994). An important precondition of this debate is a discrediting of the representation of *management* as a politically neutral, progressive technology (see also Grey and Mitev, 1995). As Watson notes of his study of ZTC Ryland:

> managerial work involves having to cope with a lot more than the list of tasks we see in typical management textbooks. These individuals are struggling to manage their lives, their identities, their value-based conceptions of the 'sort of people they are' as well as their formal managerial responsibilities. (Watson, 1994b: S85)

Ethnographic studies, such as Dalton's (1959) and Watson's (1994b), invariably indicate that managing is a multi-faceted process that is not reducible to the images presented in textbooks or captured by their 'formal managerial responsibilities'. In turn, this suggests that management educators have a 'way in' to managers' working lives through facets that are unacknowledged by, and indeed stand in a relation of some tension with, conventional textbook and guru cookbook representations of management. But, of course, transforming the practice of managing will require more than an intellectual re-orientation on the part of management educators. Management academics may be tempted to collude in maintaining a distance between ourselves and practitioners, either because we are disdainful about the business of managing and/or because we find it difficult and insecurity-inducing to find a way of communicating with a wider audience about management or with managers 'without becoming absorbed in the managerialist values from which they wish to keep a critical distance' (Burgoyne, 1995: 95). For many of us, developing the will to confront orthodoxy and dogma may also require a change of heart in which managers are no longer positioned as an (unenlightened or hostile) other.

Summary and Conclusion

In this chapter, I have sought to conceptualize and illustrate how critical thinking can be applied to learning about the theory and practice of management. Initially, attention was paid to the nature of, and connections between, 'management', 'learning' and 'critical thinking'. Importance was attached to the openness of human nature, the interdependence of social relationships and the role of power in structuring and legitimizing those relationships as a backdrop for exploring alternative accounts of managerial work and conceptions of management learning. The understanding of managerial work as a manifestation of contradictory pressures encountered within modern, capitalist work organizations was then illustrated by reference to Watson's indepth study of ZTC Ryland. This provided a way of illustrating the shortcomings identified in 'rational' and 'post-rational' accounts of management, and to argue for a critical approach which, for example, interprets the key importance ascribed by Watson to erroneous views of management held by senior ZTC managers to their positioning within a contradictory structure of production relations. This understanding of the structural organization of managerial practices and ideologies was then applied to the activity of management learning where a comparison was made between traditional management education, action learning and critical action learning. It was argued that the latter builds upon the philosophy of action learning but in a way that is attentive to the role of power in learning processes, both within organizations and within learning sets. The play of contradictory pressures upon managers and their work was identified as potentially facilitating, and not just inhibiting, progressive changes in the theory and practice of management.

Embodied reflection upon problems experienced in everyday practice, which *in principle* is facilitated by action learning, is of crucial importance if the possibilities of personal and social transformation, anticipated by critical theory, are to be fulfilled. In the absence of critical self-reflection, the tendency is for action learning to individualize and psychologize the diagnosis of problems in a way that disregards their embeddedness in the structural media of power relations. Likewise, unless there is a commitment to work with the insights of critical theory, they may do little more than fuel cynicism or guilt (Fay, 1987). The challenge for *critical management learning*, then, is to counter the partiality and obfuscation of 'rational' and 'post-rational' accounts of, and prescriptions for, managerial work; and, moreover, to envision and advance the development of discourses and practices that can facilitate the transformation of 'management' from a divisive technology of social control into a collective means of emancipation.

Notes

I would like to thank Michael Reynolds for his comments and suggestions on previous drafts of this chapter.

1 The following paragraphs are adapted from Alvesson and Willmott (1996).
2 The following paragraphs have been revised from Willmott (1994).

Annotated Bibliography

The following provide overviews of the field in addition to making distinctive contributions to a critical perspective on management: Peter Anthony (1986) *The Foundations of Management*. London: Tavistock; Michael Reed (1989) *The Sociology of Management*. Brighton: Harvester; and Mats Alvesson and Hugh Willmott (1996) *Making Sense of Management: A Critical Introduction*. London: Sage. Books which illuminate diverse issues in management education and indicate the relevance of critical thinking for its development include: Robert Locke (1989) *Management and Higher Education since 1940*. Cambridge: Cambridge University Press; Robert French and Christopher Grey (1996) *Rethinking Management Education*. London: Sage; and 1996 Lars Engwall and Emmert Gunnarsson (eds) (1994) *Management Studies in an Academic Context*. Uppsala University of Uppsala Press. A number of other books can be recommended to anyone who is interested in pursuing ideas which resonate with concerns explored in this chapter: Paulo Freire (1972) *Pedagogy of the Oppressed*. Harmondsworth: Penguin; Henri Giroux (1983) *Theory and Resistance in Education*. London: Heinemann; and David Knights and Hugh Willmott (forthcoming) *Living with Management: Power, Insecurity and Identity in Contemporary Organizations*. London: Sage.

References

Alvesson, M. and Willmott, H.C. (1992a) *Critical Management Studies*. London: Sage.
Alvesson, M. and Willmott, H.C. (1992b) 'On the idea of emancipating in management and organization studies', *Academy of Management Review*, 17 (3): 432–64.
Alvesson, M. and Willmott, H.C. (1996) *Making Sense of Management: A Critical Introduction*. London: Sage.
Anthony, P. (1977) *The Ideology of Work*: London: Tavistock.
Barley, S.R. and Kunda, G. (1993) 'Design and devotion: surges of rational and normative ideologies of control in managerial discourse', *Administrative Science Quarterly*, 37 (2): 363–99.
Bendix, R. (1966) *Work and Authority in Industry*. New York: Wiley.
Burgoyne, J. (1995) 'The case for an optimistic constructivist and applied approach to management education: a response to Grey and Mitev', *Management Education*, 26 (1): 91–102.
Child, J. (1972) 'Organizational structure, environment and performance: the role of strategic choice', *Sociology*, 6 (1): 1–22.
Child, J. (1977) 'Management', in S.R. Parker, R.K. Brown, J. Child and M.A. Smith (eds), *The Sociology of Management*. London: George Allen and Unwin. pp. 113–26.
Dalton, M. (1959) *Men Who Manage*. New York: Wiley.

Drucker, P. (1977) *Management*. London: Pan.

Ezzamel, M., Green, C., Lilley, S. and Willmott, H.C. (1995) *Changing Managers and Managing Change*. London: Chartered Institute of Management Accountants.

Fay, B. (1987) *Critical Social Science*. Ithaca, NY: Cornell University Press.

Fineman, S. (ed.) (1993) *Emotion in Organizations*. London: Sage.

Fletcher, C. (1973) 'The end of management?', in J. Child (ed.), *Man and Organisation*. London: Allen and Unwin. pp. 135–57.

Grey, C. and Mitey, N. (1995) 'Management education: a polemic', *Management Learning*, 26 (1): 73–90.

Grey, C., Knights, D. and Willmott, H.C. (1996) 'Is a critical pedagogy of management possible?', in R. French and C. Grey (eds), *Rethinking Management Education*. London: Sage. pp. 94–110.

Hammer, M. and Champy, J. (1993) *Reengineering the Corporation: A Manifesto for Business Revolution*. London: Nicholas Brealey.

Jacques, R. (1996) *Manufacturing the Employee: Management Knowledge from the 19th to 21st Centuries*. London: Sage.

Kotter, J.P. (1982) *The General Managers*. New York: Free Press.

March, J.G. and Simon, H.A. (1958) *Organizations*. New York: Wiley.

McLaughlin, H. and Thorpe, R. (1993) 'Action learning – a paradigm in emergence: the problems facing a challenge to traditional management education and development', *British Journal of Management*, 4 (1): 19–27.

Peters, T.J. and Waterman, R.H. (1982) *In Search of Excellence: Lessons from America's Best-Run Companies*. New York: Harper and Row.

Pettigrew, A. (1973) *The Politics of Organizational Decision-Making*. London: Tavistock.

Pettigrew, A. (1985) 'Examining change in the long-term context of culture and politics', in J.M. Pennings (ed.), *Organizational Strategy and Change or Strategic Decision-Making in Complex Organizations*. San Francisco: Jossey-Bass. pp. 269–314.

Pfeffer, J. (1981) *Power in Organizations*. London: Pitman Publishing.

Porter, J.L., Muller, H.J. and Rehder, R.R. (1989) 'The making of managers: an American perspective', *Journal of General Management*, 14 (4): 62–76.

Reed, M. (1989) *The Sociology of Management*. Brighton: Harvester.

Revans, R. (ed.) (1982) *The Origins and Growth of Action Learning*. Bromley: Chartwell-Bratt.

Vince, R. (1996) 'Experiential management education as the practice of change', in R. French and C. Grey (eds), *Rethinking Management Education*. London: Sage.

Watson, T. (1994a) *In Search of Management: Culture, Chaos and Control in Managerial Work*. London: Routledge.

Watson, T. (1994b) 'Managing, crafting and research: words, skill and imagination in shaping management research', *British Journal of Management*, 5 (Special Issue): S77–S87.

Willmott, H.C. (1984) 'Images and ideals of managerial work', *Journal of Management Studies*, 21 (3): 349–68.

Willmott, H.C. (1993) 'Strength is ignorance: slavery is freedom: managing culture in modern organizations', *Journal of Management Studies*, 30 (4): 515–52.

Willmott, H.C. (1994) 'Management education: provocations to a debate', *Management Learning*, 25 (1): 105–36.

Willmott, H.C. (1995a) 'The odd couple: reengineering business processes, managing human resources', *New Technology, Work and Employment*, 10 (2): 89–98.

Willmott, H.C. (1995b) 'Managing the academics: commodification and control in the development of university education in the UK', *Human Relations*, 48 (9): 993–1028.

Willmott, H.C. (forthcoming) 'Rethinking management and managerial work: capitalism, control and subjectivity', *Human Relations*.

PART III
VALUES AND PURPOSES

Any analysis of the field of management learning, whether purely descriptive or from a critical perspective, will inevitably surface the different value systems which have influenced, sometimes implicitly, the development of theory and practice. But how do values and purposes become part of the management learning debate? Explicit concern with values and beliefs seems to sit more comfortably in the context of the church, home or community. Consideration of values in work seems more peripheral, and likely to be subjugated to preoccupations with 'the goals of the enterprise' unless it is thought possible to harness them to that end.

Examples of where questions of values become more central might be when consultants turn down invitations to work with industries they regard as damaging to the community or the environment, when course participants refuse to comply with a training method they see as encouraging an unreasonable intrusion into their personal lives or private thoughts, or when training managers resist a research programme they do not believe will either value or respect the ideas and experience of employees who are asked to take part.

More difficult to identify – as part of the shadow-world of taken-for-granteds discussed in the previous section – are misgivings about the social consequences of particular organizational designs or procedures – the emergence of the human relations movement in management is an example of this, as is its subsequent critique. In these areas of enquiry and debate, in the workplace or the training department and management programme, values and moral and 'professional' standards are entwined with definitions of ideology and ethics. Whether concerned with professional standards in working with students, participants, clients or paymasters, expectations of consistency between espoused values and those evidenced by practice, or with struggles for an emancipatory platform within work and education, we are in the realm of values and purposes which, until recently, have not played as central a part in management as they have within education, health, law or social work.

Within management learning, some themes seem perennial and reflect the differences between instrumental and emancipatory purposes, or more generally still, expressions of the tension between humanism and materialism. The choice of methods and structures within organized work or educational practice illustrate these dilemmas. The case for and against participative management, whether or not to base educational programmes on measurable objectives or competencies, the use of psychometrics, or the development of experiential methods, raises not just questions of efficacy of means but also questions of value. Are particular choices appropriate or in some sense 'right' in terms of their personal and social consequences? And questioning practice within management learning raises deeper questions still as to the perspective from which these issues should be considered. This is itself a matter of values and not only of logic.

Re-visiting the Humanist Project within Management Learning

A familiar example of where questions of value are implicated is in the argument as to whether individual needs can be met while satisfying organizational requirements. Since the demise of more extreme forms of hierarchy and authoritarian approaches to gaining compliance, the concept of individual–organizational congruence has offered hope to liberals seeking ways in which organizational goals might be achieved and employees gain self-fulfilment in the process. This keeps alive the romantic vision of prosperity without inequality, of wealth without exploitation.

Alternatively, the proposal that personal needs and organizational purposes can be integrated is seen by some as part of a sophisticated manipulation through which loyalty to senior management objectives is ensured. This critique is particularly levelled at training methods which promote an illusion of consensus, fostering a belief that differences can be happily resolved in appealing to 'superordinate goals' which serve everyone's interests. This ideology provided the foundation of the early human relations movement, which Hollway describes as 'a well-aimed but only partly successful attempt to enlist the cooperation of workers in the goals of the company without changing its structures or technology' (1991: 76).

More recently, but inheriting the same value system, quality of work–life programmes, job enrichment and quality circles draw on the ideas of self-fulfilment and 'empowerment', but it is doubtful whether any of these approaches materially affect the distribution of power in organizations or differences in power between hierarchically arranged groups. More recent appeals to organizational congruence can be seen in the appropriation of the concept of 'culture' as the means of developing a homogeneity of values within an organization. Yet as Hollway points out, applications in practice of concepts such as 'culture.' do not spontaneously emerge; they are shaped and controlled from the top. Even models of organization which claim a more pluralistic arrangement are usually based on the assumption that conflicts of interest will either be voluntarily resolved in deference to overarching objectives, or be 'managed' – that is to say, be brought under control – so as to ensure unity of purpose.

> Management is thus focussed on balancing and coordinating the interests of organizational members so that they can work together within the constraints set by the organization's formal goals, which really reflect the interests of shareholders and others with ultimate control over the fate of the organization. (Morgan, 1986: 190)

In one way or another these dilemmas of value and purpose find their way into the ideas developed by writers in management learning, including the contributions to this volume. Perhaps the question to be asked at this point is what is the significance of the persistent preoccupation with values and purposes which this illustrates? In the postmodern era, drawing attention to values, let alone standing firm on particular sets of values, may seem anachronistic. Does this book represent a reluctance to let go of the ethos of the 1960s, during which management education and development were shaped? Might it herald a return to the human relations agenda, albeit from a more critical perspective?

As the authority of 'grand narratives' of humanism and Marxism have been weakened, and various (and sometimes competing) disciplines develop their own systems of authority within the social sciences, there still seems to be a need to establish values, principles and morality which looks further than the expedience of day-to-day performativity. The desire to search for a deeper meaning in work, education and relationships within each of these domains persists, as does the importance attached to upholding principles of justice in the lives of men and women. The warning is commonly made that technocratic rationalization has pushed aside considerations of ethics, values and questions of social responsibility, that professional practice in education, law, government and health has been taken over by the instrumentality which characterizes science, technology and commerce, that liberal ideals for education have been supplanted with a preoccupation with training, skills and competencies. Yet there is a tradition within management education and development that is not taken account of by such pessimism, as the contributors to this section illustrate.

It could be asked as to whether ideas developed either from a traditional humanist or a more critical perspective ever find their expression in action? We submit that theory should generate practice as well as debate, and that critical theory should generate critical practice, or praxis – a useful term because it marks the difference between problem-solving within an un-changed context and action which is intended to bring about contextual change (to structures or goals) because the theory it is based on has paid attention to social and political as well as technical processes. Critical theory is not a substitute for action, aiming 'both to understand the world *and* to change it' (Burrell and Morgan, 1979: 294). Indeed, it should be said that if theory does not lead to significant change, it has not been critical in the sense it is used throughout this book.

In supporting the case for values and purposes to be at the core of management learning debate, however, it is important that they should permeate theory and practice and not be compartmentalized into specialist departments or obscure locations on library shelves. This goal is not easily achieved, especially for example in the English culture where the tendency to divide people between those who do and those who think is quite deep-rooted. To be preferred is the arrangement proposed by Cunningham:

It is possible to argue that rather than seeing ethics as an interesting option in the business school curriculum, we need to start managerial learning on a base of examining issues of morality, ethics, values and social responsibility. The decision of what is right and good for a manager to learn must start from rightness and goodness being treated as moral questions. (1994: 111)

The Chapters in this Section

The point about questions of value permeating ideas in practice is illustrated by *Robin Snell*'s argument for the study of business ethics to be an integral part of the education of managers. His chapter also bears out the point of this introduction, that critical theory should be manifested in practice – in this case educational practice – and underlines a belief in the capability of management education to influence managers' professional work. Robin Snell's account also supports drawing on the traditions of experiential learning to bring this about, integrating the methodology of humanist education with a postmodern critical agenda.

Vivien Hodgson and Monica Lee both confront the values implicit in training and development practice and, taken together, illustrate how workers in management learning can use both personal and social perspectives on values and purposes to reflect critically on practice. *Monica Lee* is concerned with the motives which influence educators' work and confronts the questions raised earlier as to whether training and development is as much in the interests of enabling individuals as it is in ensuring their commitment to organizational requirements, whether they are compatible with individuals' needs as *they* experience them, or not. *Vivien Hodgson* addresses a dilemma which has arisen with the increased use of computer technology in learning, which is whether it enables or undermines the possibility of more egalitarian relationships in work or in education. Computer-assisted learning might seem an essentially isolating experience, but the use of contemporary 'groupware' is thought by some educationalists to enable people to communicate and study together through more democratic relationships. This contrasts with the more familiar view that computer applications are depersonalizing. Like the other chapters in this section, Vivien Hodgson's chapter supports the belief that the quality of human endeavour can be enhanced by learning and scholarship and that technology can be designed to enrich both.

Research in management presents an interesting dilemma in that it exemplifies perhaps more than any other activity, the potential for conflict between academic tradition and managerial activity. *Judi Marshall* and *Peter Reason* and their colleagues have developed an approach to research which acknowledges the importance of taking account of the totality of day-to-day experience both as managers and researchers. They describe the programme which they designed to help researchers work out a perspective on knowledge and understanding which explores the ways in which both are socially constructed, while refining a research methodology which is rigorous in its attempt to make sense of events and of personal and collective experience of them. In this, the authors clearly demonstrate how deeply held values can be expressed in professional action.

References

Burrell, Gibson and Morgan, Gareth (1979) *Sociological Paradigms and Organizational Analysis*. London: Heinemann Educational Books.
Cunningham, Ian (1994) *The Wisdom of Strategic Learning*. London: McGraw-Hill.
Hollway, Wendy (1991) *Work Psychology and Organizational Behaviour*. London: Sage.
Morgan, Gareth (1986) *Images of Organization*. London: Sage.

10

Management Learning Perspectives on Business Ethics

Robin Snell

Business Ethics Defined

Some commentators regard ethics and morality as synonymous terms, since they stem from the same word taken from the Greek *ethos* and Latin *mores* respectively, meaning 'custom'. Accordingly, Trevino and Nelson define business ethics as 'behaviour that is consistent with the principles, norms and standards of business that have been agreed on by society' (1995: 14).

Such pragmatic definitions have two major shortcomings. First, in emphasizing conformity to custom and practice, they neglect rapidly changing contexts where moral standards for a modern business community are underdetermined, as in the developing economies of China or Central and Eastern Europe. Secondly, genuinely open studies of ethics must entail rigorous questioning of all practices and establishments. De George therefore places business ethics within the broader field of philosophical ethics:

> Ethics studies morality. . . . [I]t can be defined as the systematic attempt to make sense of our individual and social experience, in such a way as to determine the rules that ought to govern human conduct, the values worth pursuing, and the character traits deserving development in life. The attempt is systematic and therefore goes beyond what reflective people do in daily life. (1995: 19)

Business ethics is therefore a critical and norm-creating subject. Typical writings are not 'anti-business', but criticize ethically minimalist approaches based on self-interest, bare legal compliance, and microeconomic logic, ignoring the moral claims of wider stakeholder groups. Fairness, honesty, integrity, respect for employees' human rights, environmental protection, product safety, and corporate social responsibility are examined as core business principles. The intangibility of such principles, and the complexities of their application, means that business ethics does not deliver final answers or proofs, but rather provokes lively debate.

Even in free-market 'Meccas' such as Hong Kong, governments regulate business through legal frameworks and occasionally move or intervene directly. The ethics of government–business relationships are therefore important. If there are webs of special favours and secret donations, and the public finds this out, the tide of outrage can be overwhelming, as recently observed in Japan, South Korea and Italy, where leading politicians and businesspeople have been implicated and humiliated. Electorates have been rather less concerned than business ethicists about bribery and extortion in international business, so that the recent Pergau Dam scandal did little damage to the governments concerned (Britain and Malaysia). The deal involved linking the award of defence contracts with the provision of foreign aid for an environmentally suspect development project.

Scope of this Chapter

In studying business ethics from the perspective of management learning, this chapter will focus on selected *process issues* related to the learning of business ethics. How did business ethics become part of the business and management curriculum? What are its educational goals? What teaching strategies are employed? What is the impact of business ethics education? What is the hidden curriculum of business ethics, acquired through socialization in educational and business institutions? How might business organizations be made more virtuous? How might apparent cultural differences in business ethics standards and practices be resolved?

This chapter does not examine the *content* of business ethics. There are more than 100 business ethics textbooks, and at least four established journals (*Journal of Business Ethics, Business and Professional Ethics, Business Ethics Quarterly, Business Ethics: A European Review*). These cover the substantive debates (e.g., deontology versus utilitarianism, cultural relativism versus universalism, the ethicality of particular practices and arrangements) that I omit. I assume that there are fundamental moral standards common to all humanity, regardless of circumstantial or cultural pressure, and that corrupt systems and cultures may be improved through exposure, principled dissent, public debate and education. Thus I am biased towards deontology, universalism and development.

Modern Social Movements

For 200 years there have been two competing modern Western narratives about the conduct and organization of business. The dominant one still is *systematic modernism*. Expounded in such late eighteenth-century texts as Adam Smith's *Wealth of Nations*, it promises wealth and the elimination of social problems through efficiency and technical progress. Much has been achieved (Fox, 1990), so systematic modernism continues to attract top businesspeople, politicians, scientists and economic commentators, who disseminate it authoritatively.

The alternative narrative is *critical modernism*, a diverse set of radical alternatives based on the need for progress which increases dignity and spiritual integrity at work. Besides the nineteenth-century works of Karl Marx, which are a robust reference point, there have been countless other authors with varying perspectives, such as William Morris and Erich

Fromm, whose common concern has been that industry organized on hierarchical principles and designed to serve narrow vested interests, produces stress, alienation, exploitation and misery.

Marx's logic was an initial inspiration for the former Soviet Union, but was soon submerged under Stalin's war-communism, a form of systematic modernism. In the West during the 1930s, 1940s and 1950s, official ideologies about the nature of the Soviet Union (friend or foe) varied to suit military interests, but the narratives of critical modernism themselves were either downplayed or denounced as evil. Thus it was that at the time of the Cold War of the 1950s, 1960s and 1970s, systematic modernism ruled on both sides of the Iron Curtain.

From the 1960s, there have been strong undercurrents of protest in the USA and elsewhere. De George notes:

> . . . the emergence of a counterculture, the divisive Vietnam War, the growth of ecological, pollution, and nuclear and toxic waste problems, and protests against the so-called military-industrial complex . . . and the growing strength of the consumer movement. Business came under attack for harming society in a myriad of ways. Business schools responded by instituting social issues courses. (1995: 17)

The protests had little immediate effect on business – major cultural transformations entail a shift in the balance and nature of discourse in society (Latour, 1987, 1988; Boje, 1994) which takes decades to come about. Instead, systematic modernism became aggressively individualistic in the West in the 1980s, with tax cuts for the wealthy, the abolition of foreign exchange controls and the privatization of the former public sector. Business leaders responded greedily, and there were many reports of corporate misgovernance, junk bonds, hostile takeovers and asset stripping.

These scandals resulted in more disenchantment. Middle managers learned from experience to became cynical about organizational life. A majority faced ethical dilemmas at work (Toffler 1986; Waters et al., 1986; Derry, 1991). While managers did not particularly want to talk about their moral dilemmas to others (Bird and Waters, 1989), they wanted, but did not get, moral example from their leaders. Cold business logic drove the big players to find the cheapest labour regardless of national borders, to get new markets, and to locate technology wherever it was most convenient for these new markets. Senior USA managers may have worried about breaching the Foreign Corrupt Practices Act of 1977 (which covered dealings with high officials only), but otherwise could turn a blind eye to different standards of safety, working conditions and contractual probity. 'Irregular' requests at the end of tortuous, time-consuming and high-stakes negotiations disturbed their conscience but how could they refuse?

The protest continued. Business ethics teaching burgeoned in the 1980s, spreading to most business schools in the USA (Schoenfelt et al., 1991) and in Canada (Singh, 1989). Harvard Business School received a large donation to develop its business ethics teaching (Tomko, 1987). Something similar, but smaller, happened in the UK and the rest of Europe, marked by the setting up of the European Business Ethics Network in 1987. Growth in teaching was paralleled by the adoption of corporate codes of ethics by more than 90 per cent of large USA companies and by around 50 per cent of top European firms (Weaver, 1993). Social responsibility became a selling point for companies such as the Body Shop, with the charismatic Anita Roddick (Roddick, 1991), a figurehead for environmental protection, fair trading, animal rights, and the intellectual property rights of indigenous peoples.

Until the slowdown of Western economies at the end of the 1980s, systematic modernists could readily dismiss the protest as chic-guilt. In the 1990s, however, there has been increasing moral outrage among the Western middle classes. At a time of expanding global business, many middle managers and professionals face redundancy and uncertainty as jobs have been exported. There is also acute anxiety about ecology: the greenhouse effect, holes in the ozone layer, nuclear accidents and the dumping of toxic waste.

Business Ethics Narratives

De George (1995) claims that business ethics is now a social movement. Critical modernism is still the 'underdog', but competes with systematic modernism for the moral agenda in business schools. Dialogue between the two narratives may at last be in prospect. Table 10.1 summarizes their differing emphases.

Systematic modernism is the apologetic voice of business leaders and beleaguered politicians, saddled with legitimation problems. Jackall (1988)

Table 10.1   *Competing modern narratives on business ethics*

Issue	Typical systematic modern narrative	Typical critical modern narrative
Corruption: bribery and extortion	Bad because it dents local or national pride, deters inward investment, and is a sign of backwardness.	Bad because it is inherently unfair, disadvantaging the politically and economically weak.
Protection of the environment	Our sons and daughters will suffer or perish unless we adopt proper controls.	Indigenous peoples, rare animal species and future citizens are entitled to a habitable environment.
Inflated executive salaries	One should set up systems of corporate governance overseen by non-executive directors to safeguard minority shareholders' interests.	One should campaign for wider social justice, including action to help the poor and reduce unemployment.
The function of codes of ethics	They are tools for inspiring the confidence of customers and investors, and a means of controlling staff.	They are a starting point only. People should be encouraged to develop their own personal moral code.
Preferred Kohlberg stages	Conventional reasoning: preserving stability, the rule of law and order and social respectability.	Postconventional reasoning: concern for social welfare, justice and universal ethical principles.

condemns it as platitudinous and empty. Critical modernism has become popular among business academics from all disciplines, some of whom have taken offence to pressure from right-wing governments to apply free-market principles to course provision and research funding. Sociologists and philosophers have been spurred into taking apart the assumptions and dysfunctions of 'enterprise culture'.

Among businesspeople, a new systematic modern stance on business ethics has evolved. This is typified by recent developments in Hong Kong, where the old conundrum of whether business ethics is an oxymoron has been replaced by a heavy consensus (in public) on the side of the angels. Reports of increased corruption and fraud in cross-border trade with China, and within Hong Kong itself, have worried financial analysts, who are concerned about the future Special Administrative Zone's competitive edge. At a conference for chief executives on 4 May 1994 (ICAC, 1994), Governor Chris Patten lamented that only 20 companies (out of the 487 domestic listed ones) had corporate codes of conduct, and urged their formal adoption. By 2 May 1995, nearly 1,000 companies and trade associations had done so (ICAC, 1995). Patten had offered them no financial or legal inducements; this explosion of active interest reflects some concern among the business community about corruption. Few want Hong Kong to go back to the *modus operandi* of the 1970s, where 'oiling the wheels' was endemic.

In the USA, codes of ethics serve corporate self-interest more directly. Federal Sentencing Guidelines enacted in 1991 allow companies to claim reduced fines if they could show that they had taken steps to dissuade employees from breaking the law (De George, 1995: 18).

Current Teaching

Business ethics teaching has spread beyond the West, with classes run in South Korea, Singapore, Indonesia, Japan and the Philippines (James S. Kemper Foundation, 1993). Wherever it is done, the standard teaching approach is:

> [To] include some ethical theory and an appreciation of its applications to business and management situations. Normally it also provides an understanding of relevant organizational, business and management theory with reference to the ethical issues raised. To this can be added . . . the stakeholder model as a basis for analysis, and theories of moral learning and development. (Maclagan, 1992: 325)

Such teaching, with its heavy theoretical, factual and analytical emphasis, may have little impact. Herndon (1996), reviewing evaluation studies of business ethics teaching, found evidence of short-term improvement in students' moral judgement in some studies, but not in others. He found no evidence of long-term improvement. Without even considering actual conduct, the results have been disappointing.

Is this because business ethics is still immature, a morass of incommensurate paradigms, no good for helping people make sense of complex contemporary moral conflicts (MacIntyre, 1988)? Given the strength of the business ethics movement, this reason is unconvincing. Four alternative reasons may be given, to do with the process, context and culture of undergraduate teaching. First, the facilitators may not properly focus or contextualize the material. Thus Herndon (1996) advocates the teaching of a systematic decision-making model (see Ferrell et al., 1989), tailored to specific types of problem situation and business discipline. Secondly, if students are not in a position to put the teachings into immediate practice, the problems discussed remain abstract and rarefied. That may encourage surface-level approaches to learning based on rote-memorization and replication, rather than deep-level, personal meaning-derivation approaches (Marton and Saljo, 1976). Thirdly, Weber and Green (1991) point out that adults aged between 18 and 21 have not fully developed in terms of moral maturity (this point is developed in the following section on socio-moral development). The majority may not be ready to appreciate the depth and power of ethical principles which have exercised the minds of professional philosophers. Fourthly, formal business ethics teaching may be over-shadowed by a 'hidden curriculum' which implies that ethics is a token subject of little relevance to real business. Thus Foglia reports on a survey of undergraduate students at Wharton:

> Numerous students claimed that they were taught to be unethical in some of their business courses. One student complained that there was minimal emphasis on social welfare, and repeated jokes and admonitions regarding how to make the most money. Others said they were taught 'creative accounting', to collude but not get caught, that they are hired for their skills but not their ethics, and that reputation and being fair is less important than attaining a strategic benefit. Hopefully these students misinterpreted what their professors were trying to say, but it is much easier for such misinterpretations if ethics are never mentioned in the course. When ethical considerations are ignored and business advantage is emphasized, it is easy for students to interpret the off the cuff, sarcastic and/or humorous comments as signals that business people stop at nothing to make a profit. (1993: 10)

> Wharton students agreed on the stereotype of the greedy, socially irresponsible Whartonite. One student argued that Wharton students must be indoctrinated to have no ethics. Some students were shocked by hearing classmates argue that an individual 'should leave their own ethics at the door and adopt company ethics', in that 'the only thing Milken did wrong was get caught'. The infamous effects of peer pressure, in conjunction with the assumption that these are the people who will make up the business community into which the students hope to become integrated, foster the feeling that unethical attitudes are the standard for them to meet. (ibid.: 11)

In 1991 the Wharton School set up a programme to integrate business ethics into its undergraduate business curriculum, introducing ethics through a number of courses, rather than concentrating it all into a single business ethics course. Foglia (1993) found that students were generally in favour of the programme, but many courses were unaffected and the residue of a previous era persisted.

Table 10.2 *The Kohlberg model of moral judgement*

Level*	Stage	Orientation	Moral motives	Definition of 'right'	Social perspective
PME	ZERO	Impulsive amorality	None	Right is what I want, right now, even if it harms others	None
	ONE	Obedience and punishment-avoidance.	Irrational dread of punishment; fear of those in positions of authority.	Rules and authority are to be obeyed rigidly, to the letter, in order to avoid punishment or physical damage.	One is preoccupied with self-preservation, obsessed with what those in charge seem to want, and fearful of the immediate physical consequences of obedience or dissent. What will happen to me, if . . . ?
PRCM	TWO	Means to personal pleasure and reward; trade and exchange when needed.	Personal gain and reward. Working out whether to risk punishment in pursuit of gain.	One must serve one's own needs; making deals with other people if necessary.	One is aware that others have their own vested interests, too. Willing to cooperate and seek goodwill by 'knock for knock' or 'give and take' bargaining. What will I gain (and risk), if . . . ?
	THREE	Interpersonal expectations, approval and conformity.	Avoiding disapproval by others, which would lead to guilt or shame.	One should be good to others and not hurt their feelings. One must trust and be loyal to partners. Live up to others' expectations.	One considers relationships with other close individuals. Willing to 'put oneself in their shoes'. Shared feelings, agreements and expectations become more important than narrow individual interests. What will they think, if . . . ?
CM	FOUR	Maintaining law and order; maintaining the social system.	Fulfilling one's formal duties, thus avoiding official dishonour.	One must perform one's duty to society, uphold law and order, and contribute to social institutions.	One feels obliged to occupy roles and follow or enforce rules laid down by the system as a whole, rather than meeting interpersonal demands. What am I required to do . . . ?

FIVE	Justice and welfare; prior rights and social contracts, as defined in reasonable debate.	Striving to be reasonable, consistent and purposeful in pursuit of principles that are good for the community.	For the betterment of society as a whole, basic rights and values must be upheld even if existing institutions do not protect them.	One concerns oneself with the 'greater good': what would be in the best interests of society and consistent with the basic rights and needs of its members, regardless of existing laws and institutions. What should the law be, in order to . . .?
POCM				
SIX	Universal principles of justice and welfare.	Firmly applying well worked-out principles, which one is confident to debate openly and non-defensively with all-comers.	Following universally generalizable principles: e.g., never excluding or exempting any group or individual from a right or moral duty (including me even in special circumstances).	One holds firmly, with no exception, to the basic human premise of respect for other persons because they are ends in themselves, not mere tools to meet others' purposes. What are the principles against which societies and their aims should be judged? How can I apply these in my daily life?
SEVEN	The cosmos as an integral whole: oneness.	Being at one with the cosmos, respecting and preserving its wider harmonies and paradoxes.	Right extends beyond what is immediately useful or interesting to humanity, e.g., respecting the needs of beings and systems which may currently pose a threat to humanity.	One is concerned for the integrity of all systems and entities making up the universe, not simply for people alone or for the systems which immediately sustain them. What is the natural law governing all systems and interrelations between systems?

Key: PME = premoral existence PRCM = preconventional morality CM = conventional morality POCM = postconventional morality
Source: Model adapted from Kohlberg, 1981: 121–2, 128 and 409–12, and from Kohlberg and Ryncarz, 1990: 193–5

Social-moral Development

No account of business ethics education is complete without Kohlberg's stages model of moral reasoning development. The model is fully explained elsewhere (Kohlberg, 1981, 1984). It holds that after an initial stage (zero) of impulsive amorality, people develop through up to seven stages of progressively robust and wider-encompassing ethical reasoning. The final formulation of the model appears in Kohlberg and Ryncarz (1990) and is paraphrased in Table 10.2

Stages one and two are *preconventional*. People at that level of moral development place no intrinsic value on social norms and conventions. They operate purely out of self-interest and expediency, namely 'I will lose this deal if I offend these people now'. Faced with ethical problems, their typical preoccupations are 'What's in it for me? Why should I bother? Who's in charge (and therefore may punish or reward me)? What's in it for them?'. They may engage in Machiavellian politicking, dressing up self-serving proposals in the language of common goals and aspirations.

Beyond stage two is the level of *conventional* morality, where people come to value conformity for its own sake. Those at stage three focus on parochial moral norms, living up to the expectations of close friends, family and associates. Those who have reached stage four become preoccupied with professional integrity and pursuing corporate goals in accordance with systems of laws, procedures and standards laid down by formal authority.

Morality at stage five and beyond is *postconventional*. People reaching this level realize that rules or conventions are invalid unless based on a concern for justice and welfare. They may campaign for laws which better serve these ends, or may simply lead by altruism and moral example. They value due process in moral decision-making for its own sake, namely 'I disagree with you entirely, but I will defend your right to argue your viewpoint persuasively to others'.

Moral development is a life-long process, but fewer than 20 per cent of adults reach stage five (Hersh et al., 1979) and virtually no one attains stage six (Colby et al., 1983: 60). Kohlberg's definitions of postconventional morality have been criticized as too narrow, excluding values associated with caring (Gilligan, 1982). My reading of the definitions of postconventional morality is that, *pace* Gilligan, they include mercy, compassion and empathy (for all people, not just for my inner circle).

The model has given rise to debate about the goals of business ethics education. Some authors (e.g., Penn, 1985; Snell, 1993; Kjonstad and Willmott, 1995) propose that educators should aim to foster postconventional ethical reasoning. Others (Fraedrich et al., 1994) caution against encouraging postconventional reasoning because that may lead to the questioning of authority relationships in organizations, producing dissent and disharmony, and jeopardizing their efficient functioning. The differing positions in this debate represent critical modern versus systematic modern stances. Both 'camps' would want to draw learners away from preconventional morality. In doing so, educators need to take account of where the learners are. According to the model, stages cannot be skipped: moral development takes place by becoming fascinated by, and drawn into, the next stage along. Teaching stage four to the stage two learner is futile; it will appear too abstract or vague (Weber and Green, 1991).

Penn (1985) reports success in fostering postconventional reasoning through a one-semester MBA elective class on business ethics at St Edwards University in Texas. The 19 students had an average age of 35. Most were assessed at Kohlberg's stage four before the course began; seven moved to stage five by the end of the course. Penn regularly referred to the Kohlberg model during class discussions of cases in international business ethics. He sought consensus by adopting Kohlberg and Elfenbein's (1975) ideal role-taking method, paraphrased below (from Penn, 1985: 79):

1 Imagine yourself in the position of each party in a situation and consider all the moral claims that they might wish to make.
2 Next, imagine you are under a 'veil of ignorance' regarding which party you would be. From that objective position, which claims would you uphold and which would you disqualify?
3 Proceed to a moral judgement based on the claims upheld in step two.

Whole-person, Lifespan Approaches

What else may be done? Callahan (1980) set out the following goals of business ethics teaching:

● stimulating the moral imagination;
● recognizing ethical issues;
● eliciting a sense of moral obligation;
● developing analytical skills;
● tolerating and reducing disagreement and ambiguity.

Elaborate frameworks, such as the template curriculum offered by Snell (1993: 183–4), imply that business ethics should teach more than intellectual development (analytical rigour, creative problem-solving) alone. Heart and spirit (affective and conative domains) may be engaged. Social skills such as assertiveness and empathy may be practised. To Callahan's list may be added micro-political sensitivity and the avoidance of game playing and manipulation (Snell and Binsted, 1981; Baddeley and James, 1987), and the skill of building, delivering and defending an ethical case. Principled whistleblowers and ethical advocates risk being misconstrued as egotistic troublemakers by the powers-that-be (Vinten, 1992). Those who have reached the stage of principled morality (stage five) may need to learn how to 'package' their arguments for a less ethically attuned audience.

Maclagan and Snell (1992) argue that business ethics teaching and learning is best treated as a lifespan process. Students in their early years, up to and including undergraduate level, may get most from being taught programmes emphasizing cognitive understanding, aided by case studies. Some of these cases may be headline-grabbing corporate-level and big-player scandals, to emphasize the topicality and public relations value of business ethics. Other cases may be mundane 'kitchen-sink' stories developed from middle managers' ethical dilemmas (Mathison, 1988; Snell, 1991, 1993, 1995; Maclagan, 1992; Maclagan and Snell, 1992; Snell and Maclagan, 1992), offering an indication of what may lie ahead for aspiring managers, thus aiding learning transfer. Post-experience education may usefully draw on action learning (Revans, 1979), counselling, role-play and other experiential approaches to develop personal and interpersonal skills, such as maintaining objectivity under stress and assertiveness.

The success of such developmental approaches depends on the tutors' willingness to model ethics-seeking approaches in their own work, and to be open to the questioning of their own authority and expertise. In addressing affective domains of learning, such teaching may offend standard conventions about academic teaching. This requires sensitivity in handling colleagues' objections, and good management of relationships. Staff who teach business ethics will lose credibility if they are authoritarian in curriculum management and Machiavellian in office politics.

Moral Ethos and Formal Responsibility

It may be unrealistic to expect moral education on its own to change organizational behaviour. Snell (1996) found that managers did not consistently resolve their own moral dilemmas in accordance with their highest stage. Why not? Fraedrich, Thorpe and Ferrell (1994) and Trevino (1992) have argued that ethical reasoning is governed more by the immediate business context than the individual's character. One aspect of this context is an organization's *moral ethos* (Jackall, 1988), a hidden moral curriculum which comprises the spoken and unspoken norms, prohibitions, social pressures and incentives, and typical operating principles into which members are socialized.

Some authors have identified moral ethos stages matching the Kohlberg model (Higgins and Gordon, 1985; Petrick and Wagley, 1992; Snell, 1993). One body of opinion is that the typical moral ethos emphasizes lower stages, does not foster moral development, and may even render higher-stage ethical reasoning difficult or impossible (Jackall, 1988; Schwartz, 1990). Schlegelmilch and Houston (1990) have a different emphasis, claiming that a moral ethos which encourages open and principled discussion (stage five) may advance members' ethical reasoning. Research by the author (Snell et al., 1996; Snell et al., 1997) in six companies in Hong Kong sought, but did not provide, empirical support for this view. In two companies ('Beauty' and 'Lucky'), both of which had international reputations for good business ethics, postconventional values were more prominent in the moral ethos than in the other four companies, but that was not reflected in the way the managers thought about their own ethical problems. In all six companies, managers used conventional-level reasoning almost exclusively for their real dilemmas.

It is possible that another aspect of the organizational context, a manager's formal positional authority and responsibility, may limit the stage-level of ethical reasoning that is at his/her disposal. At Beauty and Lucky, moral responsibility may have been screened out before decisions reached the managers' desks. They trusted their superiors to take good care of the bigger picture.

Most organizations still operate on the 'pyramid principle' of decision-making according to seniority status. Principled middle managers may currently exert greater moral influence as consumers than they do as managers. The influence of the Green movement was felt in the recent change of heart (in June 1995) by Shell over the dumping at sea of a North Sea Oil Platform, prompted by consumer boycotts in Germany.

Just Communities

If the balance of power is to change, so that moral energy comes from within rather than being thrust upon organizations from outside, then industrial democracy, derailed in the 1970s, may need to come back on to the organizational learning agenda. Drawing on Kohlberg's 'just community' approach to education (see Higgins, 1991), Trevino and McCabe have suggested that business schools should model a democratic way of organizing for ethical decision-making:

> Borrowing from a 'town' meeting model (Power et al., 1989) a representative council consisting of equal numbers of students, administration, faculty and support staff could meet weekly in open meetings to discuss and make decisions about substantive issues of concern to the community. Relevant discussion topics would include the development of school rules and norms, school governance issues, the honour code itself, and making sanction decisions about honour code violations. Students must be equal participants and decision makers along with other community members. (Trevino and McCabe, 1994: 412)

Does this Western-based, critical modernist aspiration for moral discourse go far enough?

Postmodern Discourse

Why not have democratic curriculum and course management? The learning community approach (Pedler, 1981) models a direct, anarchic form of democracy. Participants engage in collaborative enquiry and jointly develop knowledge, and skills. A learning community thus rewrites the scripts of modern education which have hitherto assumed that education entails experts passing their knowledge down to novices, or (more recently) that clients purchase tailor-made solutions. Everyone is a potential facilitator and curriculum manager and, in a programme focused on ethics, is also accountable to principles of autonomy, pluralism, altruism, empathy and justice (Snell, 1993: 214).

Postmodern learning communities promise a suitable moral ethos, along with sufficient authority and responsibility, for moral development to take place. To survive, they themselves need to be located in an institution which approves of the following features (after Snell, 1993: 219):

- Students get selected for their ability to tolerate differences and lack of imposed structure, for their sense of vocation, and for their appreciation of collaborative learning relationships.
- Open curricula are adopted which do not specify in detail what must be covered and tested.
- Credit (i.e., allocation of marks) is based not on mastery of the cognitive domain alone, but also allocated, on a peer-review basis, according to demonstrated self-insight, relevant personal qualities and interpersonal skills.

In addition, any formal teaching process audits within the institution would need to make due allowance for the inherently unprogrammable nature of collective self-management.

Such enlightened institutions would promise genuinely postmodern discourse (Boje, 1994) on business ethics, and allow great diversity of views and voices. Under such conditions, debates would not polarize between opposing 'camps'. Codes of ethics, rights or duties would be regarded as evolving tools for debate and self-inquiry, designed to help people to create their own insights and learn from their own moral dilemmas.

Looking East

Modern educational institutions are some way away from this state of affairs. This may reflect a pervasive global impasse. At present the West dominates discussions of global business ethics. The West, metaphorically speaking, is the teacher setting the agenda, laying down the content and marking the students.

In a recent survey of perceptions among the Western business community of corruption in Asian locations conducted at the University of Goettingen (Anonymous, 1995), three stood out above the others as having relatively high standards of business ethics: Hong Kong, Singapore and Japan. In Hong Kong, colonial modernism has given rise to the excellent Independent Commission Against Corruption (McDonald, 1994). Singapore has imposed strict Confucian discipline through the rule of law. In Japan, the Institute of Moralogy has been influential, and obvious national chagrin about corruption at the highest levels appears to have reassured outsiders about business integrity.

Elsewhere in the emerging economies of Asia, corruption is rampant. Hofstede (1995) reports that scores on the University of Goettingen 'corruption index' correlate with the amount of power distance in the country or territory concerned – the extent to which the less powerful organizational members expect and accept that power is distributed unequally (see Hofstede, 1980, for definitions). Absolute power corrupts absolutely. He also reports that power distance is negatively correlated with per capita GNP, suggesting that economic development may help bring about cultural change. Asian crusades against corruption may be battles of systematic modernism against the premodern 'yoke of custom'.

The growth of postmodern ethics depends on widening the terms of international debate. If Western domination of international business ethics is to cease, it is important that developed economies, such as Japan, Singapore and Hong Kong, be encouraged to engage in open internal debates about business ethics. It is to be hoped that they develop fresh critical modern concepts of their own, possibly grounded in rediscovered pre-modern cultural traditions (that of spiritual harmony with the environment, for example), as the basis for renewed challenges to the West.

Annotated Bibliography

(Compiled by Robin Snell and Anthony Wai-kei Cheng, who works at the Vocational Training Council, Hong Kong. Review comments represent his views and not those of his employer.) Founded in 1972, The Business Roundtable advises on corporate ethics. Its *Corporate Ethics: A Prime Business Asset. A Report on Policy and Practice in Company Conduct* (New York, 1988) includes 10 case studies of how codes of ethics have been developed and used to guide and regulate conduct. The values of participative, as opposed to authoritarian, management, are espoused. P. Singer (ed.) (1991) *A Companion to Ethics*. Oxford: Blackwell, is a grand volume of 47 chapters, clarifying contending traditions (e.g., Buddhist, Classical Chinese, Islamic and various Western strands), and their contemporary application. The editor likens ethics to a complex jig-saw puzzle, that is philosophers have laid out nearly all the pieces and offer a fuzzy outline of the whole picture. He argues, rather unconvincingly, that the theories will eventually converge. M.G. Velasquez (1992) *Business Ethics: Concepts and Cases* (3rd edn). Englewood Cliffs, NJ: Prentice-Hall, demolishes the standard objections to business ethics, and inspires soul-searching by his comprehensive, argumentative approach. In discussing complex court cases involving multinationals, he subjects CEO level decisions to robust criticism from multiple perspectives, none of which, he argues, should be taken as the sole standard of ethics. G.J. Williams (1992) *Ethics in Modern Management*. New York: Quorum Books, provides a clear, practical explanation and critique of some basic moral theories: Thomistic natural law (reason-based principles of absolute right and wrong) comes off by far the best in the author's discussions of performance appraisal and other human resource issues, and forms the basis of his guidelines for whistle-blowers and for boards of directors. J.W. Weiss (1994) *Business Ethics: A Managerial, Stakeholder Approach*. Belmont, CA: Wadsworth, explains the steps entailed in stakeholder analysis and urges companies to perform social audits. While his framework aims to serve all parties, it may be open to abuse by those concerned with narrow vested interests.

References

Anonymous (1995) 'Hard graft in Asia', *The Economist*, 27 May: 71.
Baddeley, S. and James, K. (1987) 'Owl, fox, donkey and sheep: political skills for managers', *Management Education and Development*, 18 (1): 3–19.

Bird, F.B. and Waters, J.A. (1989) 'The moral muteness of managers', *California Management Review*, 32 (1): 73–88.

Boje, D.M. (1994) 'Organizational storytelling: the struggles of pre-modern, modern and postmodern organizational learning discourses', *Management Learning*, 25 (3): 433–61.

Callahan, D. (1980) 'Goals in the teaching of ethics', in D. Callahan and S. Bok (eds), *Ethics Teaching in Higher Education*. New York: Plenum Press. pp. 61–80.

Colby, A., Kohlberg, L., Gibbs, J. and Lieberman, M. (1983) 'A longitudinal study of moral development', *Monographs of the Society for Research in Child Development*, Series 200, 48 (1, 2): 1–107.

De George, R.T. (1995) *Business Ethics* (4th edn). Englewood Cliffs, NJ: Prentice-Hall.

Derry, R. (1991) 'Moral reasoning in work-related conflicts', in W.C. Frederick and L.E. Preston (eds), *Business Ethics: Research Issues and Empirical Studies*. Greenwich, CT: JAI Press. pp. 25–49.

Ferrell, O.C., Gresham, L.G. and Fraedrich, J. (1989) 'A synthesis of ethical decision models for marketing', *Journal of Macromarketing*, 9 (Autumn): 55–64.

Foglia, W.D. (1993) 'Integrating ethics into the Wharton undergraduate curriculum', Report, Wharton School, University of Pennsylvania, Philadelphia.

Fox, S. (1990) 'Strategic HRM: postmodern conditioning for the corporate culture', *Management Education and Development*, 21 (3): 192–206.

Fraedrich, J., Thorpe, D.M. and Ferrell, O.C. (1994) 'Assessing the application of cognitive moral development theory to business ethics', *Journal of Business Ethics*, 13 (10): 829–38.

Gilligan, C. (1982) *In a Different Voice: Psychological Theory and Women's Development*, Cambridge, MA: Harvard University Press.

Hersh, R.H., Paolitto, D.P. and Reimer, J. (1979) *Promoting Moral Growth: From Piaget to Kohlberg* (2nd edn). New York: Longman.

Herndon, N.C. (1996) 'A new context for ethics education objectives in a college of business: ethical decision-making models', *Journal of Business Ethics*, 15 (5): 501–10.

Higgins, A. (1991) 'The just community approach to moral education: evaluation of the idea and recent findings', in W.M. Kurtines and J.L. Gewirtz (eds), *Handbook of Moral Behaviour and Development: Application* (vol. 3). Hillsdale, NJ: Erlbaum. pp. 111–41.

Higgins, A. and Gordon, F. (1985) 'Work climate and socio-moral development in two worker-owner companies', in M.W. Berkovitz and F. Oser (eds), *Moral Education: Theory and Application*. Hillsdale, NJ: Erlbaum. pp. 241–68.

Hofstede, G. (1980) *Culture's Consequences: International Differences in Work Values*. London: Sage.

Hofstede, G. (1995) Seminars as Visiting Professor, City University of Hong Kong, October/ November.

Independent Commission Against Corruption (1994) Conference on Business Ethics, 4 May. Convention Centre, Hong Kong.

Independent Commission Against Corruption (1995) Conference on the opening of the Business Ethics Resource Centre, 2 May. Convention Centre, Hong Kong.

Jackall, R. (1988) *Moral Mazes: The World of Corporate Managers*. New York: Oxford University Press.

James S. Kemper Foundation (1993) 'Bringing a global perspective to teaching business ethics', Report, Wharton School, University of Pennsylvania, Philadelphia, March.

Kjonstad, B. and Willmott, H. (1995) 'Business ethics: restrictive or empowering?', *Journal of Business Ethics*, 14 (6): 445–64.

Kohlberg, L. (1981) *Essays on Moral Development, Volume One: The Philosophy of Moral Development*. San Francisco: Harper and Row.

Kohlberg, L. (1984) *Essays in Moral Development, Volume Two: The Psychology of Moral Development*. New York: Harper and Row.

Kohlberg, L. and Elfenbein, D. (1975) 'The development of moral judgements concerning capital punishment', *American Journal of Orthopsychiatry*, 45 (4): 617–37.

Kohlberg, L. and Ryncarz, R.A. (1990) 'Beyond justice reasoning: moral development and consideration of a seventh stage', in C.N. Alexander and E.J. Langer (eds), *Higher Stages of Human Development*. Oxford: Oxford University Press. pp. 191–207.

Latour, B. (1987) *Science in Action: How to Follow Scientists and Engineers through Society*. Cambridge, MA: Harvard University Press.

Latour, B. (1988) *The Pasteurization of France*. Cambridge, MA: Harvard University Press.

MacIntyre, A.C. (1988) *Whose Justice? Which Rationality?* London: Duckworth.

Maclagan, P. (1992) 'Management development and business ethics: a view from the UK', *Journal of Business Ethics*, 11 (4): 321–8.

Maclagan, P. and Snell, R. (1992) 'Some implications for management development of research into managers' moral dilemmas', *British Journal of Management*, 3 (3): 157–68.

Marton, F. and Saljo, R. (1976) 'On qualitative differences in learning: outcome and process', *British Journal of Educational Psychology*, 46 (1): 4–11.

Mathison, D.L. (1988) 'Business ethics cases and decision models: a call for relevancy in the classroom', *Journal of Business Ethics*, 7 (10): 777–82.

McDonald, G.M. (1994) 'Value modification strategies on a national scale: the activities of the Independent Commission Against Corruption in Honk Kong', in W.M. Hoffman, J.B. Kamm, R.E. Frederick and E.S. Petry (eds), *Emerging Global Business Ethics*. Westport, CT: Quorum Books. pp. 14–35.

Pedler, M. (1981) 'Developing the learning community', in M. Pedler and T. Boydell (eds), *Management Self Development: Concepts and Practices*. Aldershot: Gower. pp. 68–84.

Penn, W.Y. (1985), 'Kohlberg and business ethics', in P. Werhane and K. D'Andrade (eds), *Profit and Responsibility: Issues in Business and Professional Ethics*. New York: Edwin Mellen Press.

Petrick, J.A. and Wagley, R.A. (1992) 'Enhancing the responsible management of organizations', *Journal of Management Development*, 11 (4): 57–72.

Power, F.C., Higgins, A. and Kohlberg, L. (1989) *Lawrence Kohlberg's Approach to Moral Education*. New York: Columbia University Press.

Revans, R.W. (1979) 'The nature of action learning', *Management Education and Development*, 10 (1): 3–23.

Roddick, A. (1991) *Body and Soul*. London: Vermillion.

Schlegelmilch, B.B. and Houston, J.E. (1990) 'Corporate codes of ethics', *Management Decision*, 28 (7): 38–43.

Schoenfelt, L.F., McDonald, D.M. and Youngblood, S.A. (1991), 'The teaching of business ethics: a survey of AACSB member schools', *Journal of Business Ethics*, 10 (3): 211–19.

Schwartz, H. (1990) *Narcissistic Process and Corporate Decay*. New York: New York University Press.

Singh, J.B. (1989) 'The teaching of ethics in Canadian schools of management and administrative studies', *Journal of Business Ethics*, 8 (1): 51–6.

Snell, R.S. (1991) 'The context for managerial dilemmas: moral quicksands and webs of deceit?', *Management Research News*, 14 (7/8/9): 61–5.

Snell, R.S. (1993) *Developing Skills for Ethical Management*. London: Chapman and Hall.

Snell, R.S. (1995) 'Does lower-stage ethical reasoning emerge in more familiar contexts?', *Journal of Business Ethics*, 14 (12): 959–76.

Snell, R.S. (1996) 'Complementing Kohlberg: mapping the ethical reasoning used by managers for their own dilemma cases', *Human Relations*, 49 (1): 23–49.

Snell, R.S. and Binsted, D.S. (1981) 'The tutor–learner interaction in management development, part 2: games tutors play – how covert tutor manoeuvres affect management learning', *Personnel Review*, 10 (4): 3–13.

Snell, R.S. and Maclagan, P.W. (1992) 'Towards a diagnostic instrument to facilitate managers' moral development'. Conference Proceedings, *Business Ethics: Contributing to Business Success*, Sheffield Business School, Sheffield, April 1992. pp. 229–42.

Snell, R.S., Chak, A. M.-K. and Taylor, K.F. (1996) 'The impact of moral ethos on how ethical dilemmas are experienced and resolved in six Hong Kong organizations', *Management Research News*, 19 (9): 71–90.

Snell, R.S., Taylor, K.F. and Chak, A. M.-K. (1997) 'Ethical dilemmas and ethical reasoning: a study in Hong Kong', *Human Resource Management Journal*, 7 (3).

Toffler, B.L. (1986) *Tough Choices: Managers Talk Ethics*. New York: Wiley.

Tomko, J. (1987) 'Newsletter from the Harvard Business School', *Multinational Business*, Autumn: 62–4.

Trevino, L.K. (1992) 'Moral reasoning and business ethics: implications for research, education, and management', *Journal of Business Ethics*, 11 (5/6): 445–59.

Trevino, L.K. and McCabe, D. (1994) 'Meta-learning about business ethics: building honorable business school communities', *Journal of Business Ethics*, 13 (6): 405–16.

Trevino, L.K. and Nelson, K.A. (1995) *Managing Business Ethics: Straight Talk about How to Do It Right*. New York: Wiley.

Vinten, G. (1992) 'Whistle blowing: corporate help or hindrance?', *Management Decision*, 30 (1): 44–8.

Waters, J.A., Bird, F. and Chant, P.D. (1986) 'Everyday moral issues experienced by managers', *Journal of Business Ethics*, 5 (5): 373–84.

Weaver, G.R. (1993) 'Corporate codes of ethics: purpose, process and content issues', *Business and Society*, 32 (1): 44–58.

Weber, J. and Green, S. (1991) 'Principled moral reasoning: is it a viable approach to promote ethical integrity?', *Journal of Business Ethics*, 10 (5): 325–33.

11

The Developmental Approach: A Critical Reconsideration

Monica Lee

This chapter explores some of the dilemmas associated with 'development', and, in essence, poses questions. What do we mean by development and what are the implications of this for those who are involved in it? What are the 'costs' of development and what are the motives of those who promote it? Definitions can over-structure or constrain the debate, such that they illuminate some features at the expense of others. However, despite my concerns about categorization, many of the questions asked here hinge around our understanding of the word 'development'. I start this chapter, therefore, by proposing four different views of 'development'. I suggest that each of these is associated with a different underlying value base and thus carries different implications for the role and practice of the 'developer'. I then outline some of the dilemmas and ethical implications that are associated with this analysis, and conclude by offering a holistic interpretation of development.

Defining the Area

As evident in the rest of this book there are a range of accounts of management learning, and many different perspectives from which it is viewed. All, however, include notions of change, movement or difference over time. However, when I talk about 'transformation' am I really indicating the processes to which someone else might apply the word 'change'? When I read a book about development, is the author coming from a value base that I can identify with? And so on. I shall use, and expand upon, these concepts later in this chapter, but first, what do they have to do with the arena of management learning? We talk about managing our work loads or ourselves (normally as a process of establishing and working towards self-determined 'goals'), and also about management as an interactive and goal-driven process involving self and others. Management learning, therefore, appears to encompass all aspects of individual and organizational learning in which people are collectively engaged (if only by collusion) and (supposedly) working towards a joint output. This broad-band definition of management learning assumes that 'management' is a relatively simple concept and that discussion around the processes of 'learning' can apply equally to individuals and organizations.

When we talk of organizations 'learning' or groups 'transforming' we take a leap in what we mean by the word 'identity'. This leap in meaning becomes more acceptable if we consider the nature of the individual (the 'I' or 'me') in the paragraphs above. I do not have a fixed view of myself. I know my actions and thoughts change with my circumstances, and that I am no longer the same person that I was as a young child. Despite my enduring sense of self I have learnt and, at times, transformed. I do not really have a single identity, yet I talk about myself as if I do. Despite being aware of the flexibility of my own identity I am also quite capable of ascribing unitary identities to others, especially those I do not know very well. As an 'outsider' I can describe them and give them a coherence that I am not able to give to myself. Similarly, as an outsider I can describe the parameters and 'feel' of an organization or group – treating it as a single entity. As I get to know it better, become a member, an insider, then I find it harder to capture its unique identifying features.

I suggest, therefore, that it is as legitimate (or as problematic) to talk of a 'group' having an identity as it is to talk of our own identity, and thus as appropriate to talk of a 'group' learning as to talk of our own learning. I am not suggesting that individual and group learning can necessarily be described in the same way, but that it is as sensible to adopt an individual approach as it is to adopt a collective focus. As will be seen in the following discussion, however, the different views of 'development' that I propose are also coupled to different views of 'identity' and of 'management'.

So What is Development?

A brief glance at the promotional literature gives me several different meanings of 'development'. The first meaning can be seen in literature that uses 'development' in a stage-like, largely pre-determined, or historically rooted way – it presents development as a process of *maturation*, for example, 'Child development', 'The lifespan development of individuals', or 'Gender development'. Each of these approaches 'development' as if it were an inevitability. It can be described by the authors because of their wide understanding of how a large number of similar 'categories' have gone along the same path, and thus the authors can, with some certainty, predict that all will follow that path.

The second interpretation of 'development' classes it as a *shaping* process, and examples of this include programme titles such as 'Developing people skills', 'Developing a learning organization', or 'Team development toolkit'. The descriptions are illuminating: 'develop positive attitudes and communication skills to build the most successful relationships'; 'develop the benefits of empowerment in your organization'; 'a range of tools appropriate for developing teams at every stage . . . significantly improve team performance'; 'blueprint for effective group development'; and '[the development function] offers ways of establishing policies and practices that are in line with corporate objectives'. As used here, 'development' assumes that there is something lacking, some weakness or gap, that can be added to or filled by the use of the appropriate tools or blueprints. It also assumes that things will stay in the same (impoverished) state without active intervention. It is important to notice the evaluative nature of this interpretation. The initial state is 'bad', while the developed state is 'good'.

This is in contrast to the third way in which development is used – as a *voyage* of exploration in which there is no end-point, no clear path, and thus no guide. There are fewer examples of this use of the word in the promotional literature, yet this is often the way in which we mean it as we talk of our own 'development' – we talk of ourselves as being actively engaged in a process in which we become something different and new, something that we have no prior conception of.

The fourth way of seeing development views it as *emergent*. The process has no pre-defined goals, and 'development' arises out of the mess of life. Reference to this interpretation of development can be found in the management literature, but more often in terms of visionary ways of working together than in practical and implementable descriptions of how this might happen or than in examples of it already happening. I suggest that this is because we are effectively talking here about societal transformation – the messy ways by which societal aspiration becomes transformed into societal 'reality'. The individual is contextualized within a web of influences, and 'development' occurs through mutual negotiation of the boundaries of these influences.

These four main ways of understanding the word 'development' can be seen in Figure 11.1. I suggest that much of the confusion around such a simple word exists because each of the four interpretations is associated with a distinct value-base and view of 'life'. I shall therefore examine what these might be.

Development as maturation

In this approach 'development' and 'management' are described as if they follow inevitable cycles – they react predictably to predictable forces in the external environment. The 'system', be it an individual, a group or an organization, is embodied. It is seen as being a coherent unitary force with clearly defined boundaries – the organization is discussed as if it were a single living element. The structures and existence of organizations develop along routes that are well understood through expert analysis. Groups go through inevitable stages of development. Group roles can be labelled (and the labelling can take precedence over the individual). Individuals react predictably, as subservient to, or colluding with, their appropriate position in the developmental unfolding. Concepts such as empowerment and change-

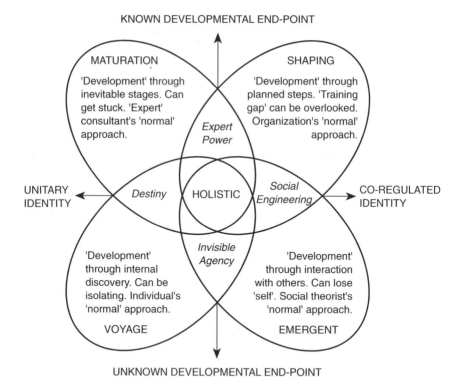

KNOWN DEVELOPMENTAL END-POINT

MATURATION

'Development' through inevitable stages. Can get stuck. 'Expert' consultant's 'normal' approach.

Expert Power

SHAPING

'Development' through planned steps. 'Training gap' can be overlooked. Organization's 'normal' approach.

UNITARY IDENTITY

Destiny   HOLISTIC   *Social Engineering*

CO-REGULATED IDENTITY

Invisible Agency

'Development' through internal discovery. Can be isolating. Individual's 'normal' approach.

VOYAGE

'Development' through interaction with others. Can lose 'self'. Social theorist's 'normal' approach.

EMERGENT

UNKNOWN DEVELOPMENTAL END-POINT

Figure 11.1 *Approaches to development*

agency are irrelevant – how can one be empowered when the notion of development has no place for unpredictable events or freedom of individual choice? The notion of change agency is meaningless if one adopts a perspective of social determinism.

The role of the developers is to understand the parameters of the inevitable unfolding that will occur, and to facilitate or enhance this inevitability as best they can. When playing this role we have the sureness of the (relatively) uninvolved expert. We are confident about our knowledge of the 'stages' of individual, group, or organizational development. We know at which stage the processes are, and have some certainty about what will happen next. We know roughly what the necessary factors might be to shift the organization from one stage to the next, and we try to ensure that these are in place, and thus that the organization does not get 'stuck'. We are not inextricably tied to the 'development' of the entity, as we know that it is likely to occur regardless of our intervention, but we do have some interest – we know that by intervening we can help facilitate that development. We sell our services as 'expert consultant' to those who wish to have deeper understanding of the changes they are going through, an easier transition period, and reassurance from the 'expert' that all will be well.

Development as shaping

Within this interpretation of development, 'management' is a complex phenomenon. In the previous interpretation, development was seen as an inevitable unfolding, and thus the 'developmental' force was the process itself, and it was the process that defined the end-point. Here, development is still seen to have known end-points, but these are defined by someone or something external to the process of development. The organization is stratified and 'senior' management define the end-point for 'junior' management. The wishes of the corporate hierarchy create the developmental force. This approach assumes that the 'training gap' can be appropriately identified and thus filled in. Individuals (their aspirations and their values, as well as their skills) are malleable units that can be moulded to suit the wider system. 'Empowerment' and 'individual agency' can be part of the developmental agenda, but not in their own right – they are acceptable developmental end-points only if ratified by senior management. This, of course, has implications for concepts such as 'empowerment'. Organizations might wish their employees to become 'empowered', but only within limited terms. 'Empowerment' becomes a tool to enhance performance and decision-making, but the term is unlikely to encompass the questioning of senior management or the emergence of the *agent provocateur*.

The developer is the process expert who can not only clearly help senior management identify an enhanced future, but can also apply the tools necessary to ensure that such a future is achieved. As developers, we sell a 'better' (and otherwise unobtainable) view of the future (to individuals, groups and organizations) and the blueprint to get there. Those that are being 'developed' are encouraged/moulded to meet the end criteria, regardless of whether such criteria are enhanced skills, positive attitudes or the achievement of corporate objectives.

Development as a voyage

The notion of development as a voyage into one's 'self' came to the fore in the 1960s. It was largely inward-looking and carried the understanding that one developed as one discovered more about oneself. This interpretation of development assumes that there are no known end-points to the development – it is a life-long journey upon uncharted internal routes. The only limitation is the extent to which one is able to look into one's self. One way of looking at this is to suggest that individuals construe their own frames of reference and place their view of self within this, such that each of us construct our own version of 'reality' in which our 'identity' is part of that construct. The concept of a 'frame of reference' implies that this frame has a coherent structure and that we are motivated to make sense of the world in a logical manner.

Development as a voyage is therefore an active process in which individuals are continually reanalysing their role in the emergence of the processes they are part of, and in doing so also confronting their own ideas, unsurfaced assumptions, biases and fears, while maintaining a core of ethicality and strong self-concept (Adler, 1974). Such development is often painful. It involves stepping outside the 'known', and cannot therefore be planned for. How can one 'know' what the result of the 'unknown' will be? It is therefore a process forced upon individuals by changing circumstance, through which individuals find that their frame of reference is no longer adequate to represent existence (as the individuals understand it), entailing a need for deconstruction and recomposition. As a colleague wrote to me recently, 'seeing a skeletal Indian woman attempting to suckle a starving child sitting in mud brought on rather more of a personal crisis than my Vice Chancellor's exhortations on research findings'. 'Development' involves a transformative shift in approach that enables critical observation and evaluation of the experience, such that the learners are able to distance themselves from it rather than 'replay' it – experiencing becomes a way of restoring meaning to life (Vasilyuk, 1984).

In so far as 'management' is an interactive and goal-driven activity, there is little room for 'management' or 'organizations' within this interpretation of development. Here, development is for the individual and occurs through the reflective activities of the individual. The external world might be a mirror that aids such activity, events in the external world might catalyse such activity, and the individual might seek help from the external world to facilitate such activity, but it is the individuals who are the sole owners and clear driving force behind the process. The individuals might well become more 'empowered' through this process, but such empowerment would be within their own terms, and might have little regard for organizational objectives.

The role of the developer within this scenario is one of helping others to help themselves (see, e.g., Rogers, 1951, 1959). The developer works with the individuals in attempting to understand their frame of reference – listening and questioning, challenging and confronting, supporting and enabling. The developer brings 'expert' skills that help the individuals to recognize their self-imposed bounds and widen their horizons, but does so without calling upon the 'power' of expertise that describes a particular path and end-point as 'best' for the individuals concerned. The individuals cannot say 'I will transform into this sort of person' because the knowing of where they will end up implies that they are already on the journey. They can only say 'I want to be different' and thereby open themselves to possibilities. No one else can map out the route for the individuals as no one else has their unique understanding of themselves within their world.

Development as emergent

At times one has to turn to the outside world, and in doing so, one can realize that people are unique individuals with their own versions of 'reality'. My 'individuality' is situated within a web of other people's interpretations of their own individuality and of 'me'. My 'self' becomes interpreted as a postmodernist construction, in which my frames of reference are fluid interpretations and emerge through implicit or explicit negotiation with others. My 'self-hood' is a function of the wider social system (be it a family grouping, a small or medium-sized enterprise, a large bureaucracy, or a nation – or parts of each) and as that system transforms so do 'I'. Therefore the interpretation of development as emergent also adopts a transformative perspective, and many of the points made in the previous section can be re-presented as relevant to the 'social system' as well as to the 'individual'.

This approach encompasses individuals' unique perceptions of themselves within a social reality which is 'continuously socially (re)constructed' (Checkland, 1994: 33), in which 'individuals dynamically alter their actions with respect to the ongoing and anticipated actions of their partners' (Fogel, 1993: 34), and in which they negotiate a form of communication and meaning specific and new to the group and relatively un-accessible or un-describable to those who were not part of the process (Lee, 1994). Together, whether actively or through collusion, the individuals develop a way of working such that the individuals feel a sense of belonging (Soyland (1994) suggests that this is through myths, metaphors and rhetoric). Thus the surfacing of assumptions between members is part of the organizational development process (Senge, 1990).

Emergent development of the group-as-organization is no different from development of any social system. It is messy, confusing, complex and emergent. It cannot be driven by any single sub-section (be it senior management or the shop-floor). Discussion about top-down versus bottom-up change is irrelevant, as the words themselves imply some sort of structure to the change. This approach is, of course, in direct conflict with traditional ideas and structures of 'management' that assume that, at the least, senior management have responsibility and power to establish the strategy and the tasks (goals or outputs) of the organization. As with individual development, the norms of an organization might shift to accommodate the wider picture, and the organization might transform if that wider picture forces a dis-junctive. Indeed, Romanelli and Tushman (1994) offer empirical support for rapid, discontinuous transformation in organizations being driven by major environmental changes.

The role of developers is also confused. They might act as the 'con-sultants', bringing in different understanding and widening the group's frames of reference, they might catalyse 'development' by confronting the group's version of reality with alternative views of reality, or they might act as a facilitative 'interpreters', translating different viewpoints within the organization and thereby easing the negotiation of boundaries. To some extent, however, these roles would be played by each member of the organization. Thus the developers hold no 'unique' or special status. Developers are as similar and as different as each other member is, and although they (perhaps) have less vested interest in political machinations (and thus might be able to view circumstances more objectively), they are as directly involved in the life of the organization as any of the individuals they are supporting in co-development.

Dilemmas of 'Development'

Each of the views of development outlined above carries with it different interpretations of the nature of management and organizations, and of individual existence and the role of the developer. If we adopt a goal-driven or bounded approach (maturation or shaping), we also adopt the assumption that existence is predictable. We place importance in 'expertise' and we believe that individuals and organizations are, or can be, moulded towards predetermined ends. Adopting a less bounded approach (voyage or emergent) implies unpredictability, a diminished focus upon expertise and a belief in self-determinism for individuals and organizations as collectives. In a bounded approach the developers take the role of expert social engineers, while in a less bounded approach the developers are more like self-deprecating facilitators and co-workers. A bounded approach reinforces the *status quo* and supports traditional views of stratified organizations and concurrence with the objectives of the organization (as defined by senior management), while a less bounded approach supports anarchy and deviance, and questions the existence of organizations as we know them.

When talking of our *own* development we normally address it as if it is a voyage. When senior managers talk of organizational development they normally talk of it as if it were shaping. When social theorists talk of development they normally adopt a maturational or emergent perspective (depending upon their theoretical bent). When 'expert' developers talk of development they normally talk of it as if it were maturational or shaped, while 'facilitative' developers normally adopt an emergent or voyage interpretation. Senior management normally prefers clear outcomes associated with status-awarding expertise. It is a rare organization that seriously wants to pay for facilitation that cannot define its objectives clearly, cannot prove its cost-effectiveness, and is likely to promote dissension.

Obviously, the situation is much more complex than this, and I am sure that each of the groups that I have labelled so cavalierly would wish to quibble with the broad-brush picture that I have painted of them. The point I want to make, however, is that 'development' is often presented (erroneously) as a unitary concept – as some process that moves individuals and organizations forwards in an enabling and liberating way, something in which we all believe and to which we all agree. The connotations of the word 'development' frequently remain those that were associated with the self-development movement of the 1960s: empowerment and transformation. The recent focus upon the need to maintain competitive advantage in an increasingly complex, unpredictable and multicultural environment has led to 'development' being seen as a 'good' thing to apply to organizations and societies. The connotations remain, yet, as illustrated by the promotional literature, the values underlying the practice of development differ considerably. The rhetoric is clear – develop or die – yet the lack of clarity in the understanding of 'development' leads to organizations, individuals and developers adopting different perspectives (and ideologies) upon that which is apparently simple and straightforward. Individuals and organizations do not necessarily know what they are buying in to, and developers (who hold some responsibility for the ideology they are consciously or subconsciously transmitting) are presented with ethical dilemmas. In the remainder of this chapter I shall explore some aspects of these ethical dilemmas.

Playing with the Power of 'Expertise'

The first of these dilemmas is associated with the use and abuse of the power of the 'expert', and is linked (in particular) to the shaping and maturational approaches to development. Both of these approaches assume that there is an end-point to development that can be assessed, measured or evaluated, that individuals or the organization can be 'rated' according to how far they have developed – and, therefore, can also be judged to be 'failing'. Professions, qualification structures and 'expertise' are built around such assumptions. They are part of our lives and we seek the power that we can obtain by evidencing that we have leapt the hurdles, have developed and are thus part of an exclusive club (Lee, 1991). Our society is built upon this, but it is not without problems. When we define a particular set of standards to judge by, we are also defining an 'acceptable' way of being, and are anticipating the future in that likeness. If we adopt a maturational view, then we say that the future will be like this because there is no way of avoiding it. If we adopt a shaping view, then we actively seek to create the future. In either case, however, the developer is seen as the expert who can predict the future and steer the individual or organization towards it.

The developers are successful in so far as they are able to remain infallible. What organization would employ someone who said: 'Well, actually the world is chaotic and I don't really know what will happen. We could try this. It will cost quite a bit, and will upset the workforce, but people will probably be different by the end of it – though I couldn't tell you how.' There is a tremendous temptation for the developers to provide the quick answers, to adapt tortured theory into slick categorizations and easy models, to pretend that life is understandable and controllable. What if the models and answers do not mirror 'life'? What if the developers are fallible? How far will they go to protect the power of their expertise? What are the implications for providers? MBA programmes, for example, are often believed to confer 'expertise' to the participants through offering a recipe for success, such that some MBA's have the reputation for providing 'Models, Balls and Answers'. However, does the MBA really stand for 'Move Before Armageddon' (go in, take the money, make a mess, and leave quickly)?

There is no easy answer to this. We cannot inspire individual and organizational commitment if people do not trust us and our expertise. Our role is often to clarify and simplify – if managers had the time and expertise to explore dense theory, they would be their own developers. Perhaps it is an issue of responsibility – to do the best we can within our own circumstances.

The Manipulative Role of Development as Social Engineering

The role of the developers as agents of organizational change is most obvious in the shaping and emergent interpretations. This role anticipates the future (changing to what?). I have suggested elsewhere (Lee, 1996) that these two interpretations are slanted towards different organizational futures. In supporting shaped development, the developers are also supporting (through their actions, if not their beliefs) a short-term, goal-driven, competitive society in which individuals are fitted for externally defined roles, while, in supporting emergent development, developers are encouraging a more ethically aware but less profitable situation in which individuals are less than the sum of the parts. In either case, however, through their actions and inactions, the developers as change agents inevitably influence the situation. Willingly or not, the developers act as missionaries for their particular view of life. They reify and reinforce their preferred cultural message. They attempt to manage heresy on the part of the recipients (whatever form that might take) and compromise on dilemmas caused by culture clash (Lee, 1995b). The role of the developers as change agents, therefore, is inevitably one that contains some elements of social engineering. In other words, the individual's development of 'self' is (whatever the rhetoric) sacrificed upon the altar of conversion to group conformity, marking a shift from 'control-by repression' to 'control-by-seduction' (Reed, 1992), 'encouraging' commitment to the organization and working with peoples' attitudes and values such that they become corporate acolytes (Hopfl, 1992).

You might, by now, have thrown up your hands in horror. For many developers (including myself) their reason for working is to help others help themselves, to empower and to enable. For such people manipulation and social engineering are generally considered to be 'bad' things. Here am I stating that we have no choice. If we act as *agents of change* (whether deliberately 'shaping' others, or by attempting to co-create the emergent future), then we engage in manipulation and social engineering whether we wish to or not. If we deny this, then we also deny any responsibility we might have for our actions. We become unthinking tools of the situation we find ourselves in; we unwittingly collude with and reinforce that situation. It is more honest to acknowledge this role openly and explore what the implications of it might be for all stakeholders. We might, for example, choose to act in a way that reinforces the *status quo*. We then do so, however, in the knowledge that we have tried to consider the ethical dilemmas we face, and with some confidence that we can justify the stance we take – both to ourselves and to others.

Managers (as individuals) can obviously develop, as can the collectivity, but it is only when we assume that development is a form of social engineering that we can (as much of the literature does) legitimately talk of management development. This sort of wording assumes that development is generally applicable, identifiable and measurable, and feeds into the sort of course brochures that implicitly promise that by the end of the course all participants will be empowered, magnificent 'new' people. There are many good reasons for developers to support the *status quo*. Financial support normally follows 'expertise', clarity of objectives, the delineation of an attractive future and the promise of deliverable means of getting there. There are few people who can honestly say that they have never been in a situation in which they have had to compromise their guiding principles in order to satisfy their short-term needs. This, however, is a cynical approach.

Less cynically, and more realistically, developers as agents of change do the job they do because they believe in working towards a particular future. In practice, they actively believe in the work they are doing. They might, themselves, be corporate acolytes who passionately believe in the corporate message that they transmit. They actively choose to adopt a goal-driven approach in their activities. They are not 'forcing' the recipients of their activities to accept their message. Instead, they are clarifying the boundaries sufficiently to enable recipients to make their own informed decisions about whether they wish to agree with the message or leave the organization. Through clarity, the developers empower the recipients by enabling them to bear some of the responsibility for the choices they makes.

The Invisibility of Agency

The third dilemma, that of the invisible agent, is almost the opposite of 'expert power' and is most pertinent to the interpretations of development as emergent or as a voyage. In both of these interpretations there is no known developmental end-point. Thus the developers act either as co-creators of the development or facilitative supporters to those undergoing the development. As co-creators the developers have no unique or different status to the other co-creators, and as facilitative supporters, assertion of the developers' uniqueness might well hinder the development process. In either case, if the developers were to impose a particular 'developmental' route, then they are also preventing development (as interpreted here). Emergent development would no longer be co-created and the individuals within 'development as a voyage' would either have to adopt the framework of the developers (and thus become a clone of them) or continue in a non-committed and thus fundamentally non-transformative way. Clearly, the developers do have expertise and use it to influence the processes of development, but it follows from this that the developers are most successful in their role when they become so invisible that the 'recipients' perceive themselves to be the agents of their own development, and thus fail to appreciate the role that the developers have played.

The problem is that developers, along with the rest of humanity, have egos and occasionally like to feel that their expertise is recognized. In addition, how can someone who is invisible, whose expertise is not recognized, and whose way of working rejects the idea of influencing others through 'expert' power, obtain work? No one is likely to pay hard cash for the unknown and invisible. Similarly, how can one promote a 'developmental' course that has no clear end-goals? We could say that 'by the end of the course you will probably have changed', but individuals and organizations will want to know by how much and into what? By becoming invisible the developers might stick to their principles, at the expense of becoming unemployable.

The Subversive Role of Development as Destiny

This dilemma is mostly associated with the interpretation of development as a voyage, or as maturation. Developers who are essentially socially deterministic (believing that the future is necessarily predicated on the past) will also believe (fundamentally) that despite the stories individuals tell themselves, they cannot really influence the future or effect change. There is little need to look to the future, therefore, other than to foretell what is going to happen. Similarly, to developers who are fundamentally individualistic and see development as a voyage, the changing nature of wider society is little more than a back-drop to their concerns for the individual. In both cases, development can be seen as a journey towards destiny. There is a clear inevitability about the maturational process, and a similar (if less pronounced) inevitability about a voyage into one's 'self' in which the individuals become their own hero and victim (Lee, 1995c).

As described above, both the 'maturational' and 'voyage' interpretations of development involve a sense of destiny – the organization or the individuals moving towards fulfilling their innate 'potential'. The developers are people who help them along the journey. There is no problem so long as the destiny of individuals and organizations follow the same paths. I suggest elsewhere (Lee, 1995a), however, that individual development is, at least in part, dependent upon questioning and opposing the norms (or frameworks) of others and of the group, and thus occurs in opposition. If development of 'self' occurs (even partially) through a process of opposition, then the role of the developers is that of supporting the individuals along a journey that is inevitably subversive to the organization. If the organization supports individual development, then the organization is encouraging its members to challenge and reject elements of the organization's frame of reference. In other words, it is funding the creation of a subversive and potentially divisive force.

By encouraging the individuals to work towards their developmental potential, are the developers not just creating dissatisfaction, lack of commitment and alienation on the part of the individuals? What is the personal cost of learning to accept a wider repertoire of ways of being? How often does creative tension become soul-destroying conflict? Additional complexity is added to this account when we acknowledge that whatever 'theoretical' interpretation of development we adopt, in practice we are working along-side individuals. Our actions and inactions will influence those around us and, regardless of our intentions, those around us are taking their own voyages. We could turn round and say that, through clarity, the developers empower the recipients by enabling them to bear some of the responsibility for the choices they make, or that in choosing to engage with the develop-mental process the recipients also choose to bear the responsibility and personal costs that might arise from goal-free exploration. To what extent, however, is this a rather neat way of passing the responsibility for pain and upheaval on to those who have little choice in whether to accept it?

Summary: Holistic Development – Responsibility for Self within Diversity

I have outlined four different approaches to development, and four dilemmas associated with the intersections of these approaches, yet I do not really believe that 'life' is separable in this way. My experience of development is that at any one time all or several of these approaches or dilemmas might be in play, and the others would be round the corner to pounce on me unawares. I talk glibly about people making choices and taking responsibility for themselves, but it is extremely hard to make informed decisions when 'development' has a range of meanings that are situation-specific and slide around according to the value-base of the people using the word at the time and according to the power that such people have to impose their preferred value-base. Who decides the appropriateness of a particular developmental approach? The individuals at the expense of the organization? The organiza-tion at the expense of the individuals? What role do the professional bodies play? At present they appear to be moving towards the delineation of required competencies for recognition. Yet that threatens inertia, fails to accept the challenge of exploring alternative ways of working, and poten-tially hinders the ability to benefit from advances in the field. How are the conflicting needs of the stakeholders reconciled? What is the role of the developers as stakeholders?

The human resource development (HRD) Pathway Unit at Lancaster University offers a pathway of qualifications in Strategic Human Resource Development that attempts to straddle the boundaries between different approaches to development, and between the needs of the different stake-holders – and there appears to be no easy way of achieving this. These dilemmas face us in design, promotion and practice. They are an integral and unsettling part of the provision. At times they feel like a challenge, a reflection of 'real' life, an image of creative tension. At other times I think with fondness of Marshall and Stewart's (1981) contented middle managers. Throughout, I wonder about my own motivation. I believe in the value of this approach. I promote it and try to work within it. To what extent am I on a crusade, trying to engineer a microcosm of society into my holistic vision?

In essence, I am suggesting that it is almost impossible to avoid multiple and differing interpretations of 'development'. They are brought to the developmental experience as the legitimate clothing of the different stake-holders and are rooted in differing views about self, identity, society, management and organizations. They are an inevitable (and potentially very valuable) part of the developmental process. This value, however, can often go as unacknowledged, or even be seen as painful, conflictual, destructive – and therefore to be avoided. Perhaps the most honest way through it is to attempt to explore and progressively clarify and negotiate the boundaries such that all participants are able to make informed choices. I suggest that this includes 'soul searching' on the part of all participants (including the developers), and is likely to involve 'frank and honest' exchange of what might be socially less acceptable admissions – for example, like saying 'I am a manipulator'.

Perhaps development is best seen as a process by which developers (whether the individuals themselves or those who promote development) critically evaluate the norms with which they collude and choose their own paths through them, and that this notion contains elements of Drucker's 'responsible society' (1993). This suggestion is in accordance with my preferred approach – the emergent interpretation of development. The problem with the emergent view, however, is that regardless of the outcome of the development process I am not sure that the activities involved can be conducted in an informed way without exploring their associated bound-aries. If we are to be responsible developers, then we must, in the first place, be able to contextualize our individual value-bases, and those of our provision. However, the extent to which one is able to stand outside one's value-base is arguable. Developers cannot easily be both an equal part of the process (as in the emergent approach) while at the same time standing outside themselves as a necessary part of reflecting upon and critically evaluating what they are doing.

This leaves me with some questions. Do we, as developers and providers, have some responsibility to develop ourselves and others along the lines that we, personally, believe in? Or can we call all change 'development', regardless of whether it is painful for the individuals, destructive of the organization, or socially irresponsible? What right do we have to influence others towards our chosen route? And in doing so, are we actually prevent-ing development (as defined above)? Do we not have some responsibility for the social costs meted out to those who, through a developmental process, are no longer happy with their previous situation (be it organizational or their personal relationships)? Or do we argue that development only occurs to those who are ready for it? Are we but catalysts? Is development the universally beneficial process it is portrayed to be?

Annotated Bibliography

If you are interested in exploring these ideas further I would suggest taking a look at Carl Rogers' (1951, 1959) work for an insight into helping others help themselves, and Fogel's (1993) book for ideas about how individuals and societies develop in a co-regulated manner through social interaction. You might also wish to read Stewart and McGoldrick (1996) for recent thoughts on Human Resource Development, and Lee, Letiche, Crawshaw and Thomas (1996) for a multi-perspective view of the role of change agents in the 'new' Europe. Finally, if you wish to explore different approaches to envisioning the future, I would suggest, for a start, Senge (1990) and Mc Whinney (1992).

References

Adler, Peter S. (1974) 'Beyond cultural identity: reflections on cultural and multicultural man', *Topics in Culture Learning*. Honolulu: East–West Culture Learning Institute. pp. 23–40.

Checkland, Peter (1994) 'Conventional wisdom and conventional ignorance', *Organization*, 1 (1): 29–34.

Drucker, P.F. (1993) *Post-Capitalist Society*. New York: HarperCollins.

Fogel, Alan (1993) *Developing Through Relationships: Origins of Communication, Self and Culture*. Hemel Hempstead: Harvester Wheatsheaf.

Hopfl, Heather (1992) 'The making of the corporate acolyte: some thoughts on charismatic leadership and the reality of organisational commitment', *Journal of Management Studies*, 29: 24–33.

Lee, Monica M. (1991) 'Playing the guru', *Management Learning*. 22: 302–9.

Lee, Monica M. (1994) 'The isolated manager: walking the boundaries of the micro-culture', in O. Westall (ed.), *Proceedings of the British Academy of Management Conference*. Lancaster, September. pp. 111–28.

Lee, Monica M. (1995a) 'The opposing self: the truth is there is no truth', paper presented to Standing Conference on Organizational Symbolism, Turku, Finland, July.

Lee, Monica M. (1995b) 'Working with freedom of choice in Central Europe,' *Management Learning,* 26 (2): 215–30.

Lee, Monica M. (1995c) 'Gender and future realities', paper presented to Aesthetics in Organizations Conference, Bolton, March.

Lee, Monica M. (1996) 'Competency and the "new" manager in Central Europe', in Monica M. Lee, Hugo Letiche, Robert Crawshaw and Michael Thomas (eds), *Management Education in the New Europe*. London: Routledge. pp. 101–16.

Lee, Monica M., Letiche, Hugo, Crawshaw, Robert and Thomas, Michael (eds) (1996) *Management Education in the New Europe*. London: Routledge.

Marshall, Judi and Stewart, Rosemary (1981), 'Managers' job perceptions, part 2: opportunities for and attitudes to choice', *Journal of Management Studies*, 18: 263–75.

McWhinney, Will (1992) *Paths of Change*. Newbury Park, CA: Sage.

Reed, Michael I. (1992) *The Sociology of Organizations: Themes, Perspectives and Prospects*. London: Sage.

Rogers, Carl R. (1951) *Client Centred Therapy*. Boston, MA: Houghton Mifflin.

Rogers, Carl R. (1959) 'A theory of therapy, personality, and interpersonal relationships as developed in the client-centred framework', in S. Koch (ed.), *Psychology: A Study of a Science* (Vol. 3). New York: McGraw-Hill.

Romanelli, Elaine and Tushman, Michael L. (1994) 'Organisational transformation as punctuated equilibrium: an empirical test', *Academy of Management Journal*, 37: 1141–66.

Senge, Peter (1990) *The Fifth Discipline*. New York: Doubleday.

Soyland, A. John (1994) *Psychology as Metaphor*. London: Sage.

Stewart, Jim and McGoldrick, Jim (eds) (1996) *Human Resource Development: Perspectives, Strategies and Practice*. London: Pitman Publishing.

Vasilyuk, Fyodor (1984) *The Psychology of Experiencing: The Resolution of Life's Critical Situations* (English translation, 1991). Hemel Hempstead: Harvester Wheatsheaf.

12

New Technology and Learning: Accepting the Challenge

Vivien Hodgson

New information and communications technology (ICT) is increasingly becoming part of our everyday lives and is certainly now a major aspect of organizational life. As in all major areas of human activity, much has been claimed for the contribution ICT can or will have upon educational practice. In this chapter I would like to take a somewhat eclectic look at some of these claims as they relate to the characteristic features of new information and communications technology, and as they link with prevalent ideas about the way people learn, the management of learning, and the function of education. In particular I will examine how information and communications technology changes our capacity to represent and communicate information and, ultimately, construct knowledge. I will explore the impact this might have upon education and learning, and mention some of the concerns that have been raised about the effects of technology on the learning process. I will then go on to present an argument which suggests that as technology is of our own making and a material extension of our own processes, the way we come to adopt it in our educational practice is very much our own choice. Its potential and power as an educational tool provide a tremendous opportunity to extend our capacity for understanding and for learning. However, as in all educational endeavours, the ultimate impact upon learning will depend on the educational intentions and beliefs underpinning the decision to use technology. To this extent I will be looking at technology from the point of view of its ability and potentential to support dialogue in learning and critical reflection, both of which are assumed as key processes in management learning.

One of the most significant characteristics of information and communications technology is the capacity it gives to store, edit and retrieve information in an ever-increasing variety of ways and forms over unlimited spans of time and space. Because of this capacity it is possible to design sophisticated multimedia educational software which allows learners to access and interact with information in ways that were not previously possible. The same capacity allows learners to interact with others, be they other learners, teachers, mentors or whoever, and over whatever distance or time. Most importantly, however, whether it is in the form of multimedia programmes or computer-mediated communications systems, new technology, quin-tessentially, provides us with an entirely new cultural apparatus for both representation and memory.

It is this feature of information and communications technology which arguably makes it so significant from an education and learning perspective. Representation and memory are, in fact, key processes in education and the changes which new technology gives to both our capacities and our methods of representation and memorizing will inevitably impact upon education and training at all levels. In view of this, it is necessary that anyone responsible for education, in whatever capacity, needs to be aware of the potential of the new information and communication technologies to change the way we think about education and what we do in the name of education.

While it is not possible, or ever will be, to predict the precise nature of the impact that new technology will have upon approaches and thinking about education, we can nevertheless identify some of the potential concerns and issues that need to be considered, in addition to some of the new and exciting possibilities that could emerge. We can examine the potential consequences of using technology to create and support learning environ-ments which no longer require the physical or indeed visible presence of the actors involved.

I will be looking at the possible impact of working in such environments for contributing, or not, to the processes of personal development and critical reflection, as well as the potential for supporting other ways of working and learning than those currently practised in traditional educational environ-ments. Throughout the discussion, it is the intention to look at technology from a clearly educational perspective and to raise questions and issues pertinent to the use of technology for educational purposes, thinking and practice.

Representation and Memory in Education

First, however, it is necessary to elaborate upon the claim that representation and memory are key processes in education and learning. As Diana Laurillard (1993) explains in her book on the effective use of educational technology, the nature of academic knowledge is second-order knowledge, that is to say, knowledge of descriptions of the world rather tham knowledge of the world. She comments further that because of its second-order character, academic knowledge relies on symbolic representation which requires interpretation and, therefore, suggests that: 'Teaching is essentially a rhetorical activity, seeking to persuade students to change the way they experience the world. It has to create the environment that will enable students to learn the descriptions of the world devised by others' (Laurillard, 1993: 28).

It is precisely because education is concerned (although not exclusively) with second-order knowledge that it is important to recognize that the way information is recorded, transferred and communicated (memorized) is itself an important dimension of the educational process. Lyotard (1991) has written about the effect that technology has upon this dimension. He would claim that until now descriptions of the world devised by others are rooted in an ethnocultural apparatus for memorizing information. That is to say that the mechanism or processes whereby information has been recorded, transferred, and communicated have been tightly bound to an historical and geographical context.

This is perhaps no more dramatically illustrated than in the way accounts of conflicts between peoples and nations have been recorded and communicated in the past. Key events are 'remembered' differently by different communities depending upon where they are located geographically. The same event will have a different history and a different meaning depending on the geographical and historical location of the given community 'remembering' the event. As a consequence, the view of the event which is recorded and memorized in one location is different from the view of the event held by another community in a geographically distant location. Furthermore, information of this kind, which is tightly bound to an historical and geographical context, shapes and influences attitudes and values held by each person within that context or location.

The Impact of Technology on Representation and Memory

With the advent of telematics (all those technologies which allow us to communicate electronically over a distance, including, for example, the telephone and television) and in particular of new communications technology, which increases the speed, capacity and scale of communication over distance – computer conferences, the Internet and satellite broadcasting, for example – the situation becomes fundamentally different. Previously, events and information that were communicated and transferred were inextricably bound to the global site and its culture, within which the event occurred. According to Lyotard, they were in effect rooted in an ethnocultural apparatus for memorizing information.

Education, of course, has been recognized for some considerable time as a process through which culture is transmitted and the cultural function of education is frequently addressed in the radical educational literature (see, e.g., Freire, 1972; Giroux, 1992). Dewey (1944) captured the issue succinctly over 40 years ago when he told us that the main distinction is whether education is a 'function of society' or whether 'society is a function of education'. Or to put it more in the terminology of such liberal educators as Freire, whether it is regulative (and oppressive) or transformative (and liberative).

The important point here, however, is the potential impact that new information and communication technology will or could have upon the cultural dimension of education, as a consequence of moving from an ethnocultural apparatus for memorizing information to a telegraphic apparatus which is no longer rooted in local culture but diffused across the surface of the globe (Lyotard, 1991: 63). Basically, until now the processes of education have for the most part, although not exclusively, worked with second-order knowledge which is both represented and memorized within a local context or situation. New technologies, on the other hand, stand to change all of this. Being diffused across the global surface rather than rooted in the local context, cultural models are presented which 'provide a remarkable means of overcoming the obstacles traditional culture opposes to the recording, transfer and communication of information' (ibid.).

What Lyotard appears to be suggesting is that, because of the character and nature of ICT, what information is selected and how it is recorded will no longer be inevitably constrained by traditional attitudes and beliefs associated with a given location and culture, but will be open to other approaches and alternative attitudes. However, as we are already seeing with the increased use of the Internet, much of what is recorded and communicated is not always seen as a positive feature of technology from an educational point of view. In fact, Lyotard himself has pointed out that: 'It scarcely seems that this generalised accessibility offered by this new cultural good is strictly speaking a progress. The penetration of techno-scientific apparatus into the culture field in no way signifies an increase in knowledge, sensibility, tolerance and liberty' (ibid.: 84). On the contrary, using again the Internet as an example, there are many examples of extreme political groups as well as other groups considered to be unacceptable for social, criminal or whatever reason that utilize the Internet to support their work and communication. More than probably any other medium, the Internet allows such groups to communicate in their own telegraphic communities without interference from state or national bodies and without fear of recrimination from those who find their beliefs and attitudes unacceptable.

Lyotard, in his comments, is referring, as much as anything, to the increasingly incessant exposure to globally generated media products and programmes. From an educational perspective the concerns that have arisen about such exposure and the information conveyed or contained in technology-based environments appears to be directly related to the consequence of separating such information from traditional culture and all that traditional culture represents. It confronts issues that for many are at the very heart of the educational process. For example, 10 years ago Larsen made the following comment about the use of new technology for educational purposes:

> We should now transcend the pioneer era of the use of new information technology in education, and direct our attention towards how these new powerful tools are interfaced with human activities like discussion, explanation and personal understanding. This is not just a simple question of good software or courseware, but of realising that education is a matter of human development that must never be reduced to mere instruction. (Larsen, 1986: 335)

A number of authors have commented upon the consequences of the increased use of technology-based learning environments. For example, Russell (1994) points out that within hypermedia/multimedia environments it is difficult to identify the source of knowledge as it is generally unattributed, and that the usual 'handles' – such as the author – used for the determination of underpinning values, are not available. Russell believes that the potential non-ideologically controlled management of exposure to different values via technology is dangerous without the opportunity to investigate issues relating to values, ethics and morality. He concludes that:

> What is clear, however, is that the characteristics of the technology have contributed to problems in the teaching of values to students. Such problems might be tackled by an understanding that there is a basis for concern, and an acceptance that teachers, software designers and corporations have significant responsibility for the shaping of the ways in which students will view the world. (Russell, 1994: 171)

Chandler (1990), writing about the potential of computer simulations to redefine experience so that human relations become peripheral rather than central, comments: 'In a human community interpretations are multifarious, so no one interpretation can be absolute; meaning is negotiated through human discourse. When we detach the knowers from the known we divorce knowledge from community, from history, from wisdom' (1990: 166). Chandler to some degree captures the nub of the concern when he speaks about detaching knowers from the known and divorcing knowledge from the community, from history from wisdom. What is significant about his comments is the implicit assumption that such a movement will lead to a loss of wisdom.

The Status and Relationship of Technology in Learning

For both Russell and Chandler not only is the cultural significance of education clearly assumed, but it is also threatened by the advent of technological learning environments. Such comments are quite transparently rooted in an humanistic view of empowerment of the individual through the processes of education in preparation to participate in an egalitarian democratic society. While such concerns are clearly important and should be raised, there are other beliefs about the use of ICT for educational purposes which are equally relevant but frequently ignored. For example, whether technology is a tool which is separate and distinct from ourselves or whether technology is us and we are it, so that any discussion of technology which assumes that it is something that is distinct and separate from ourselves is inappropriate.

Haroway, for example, makes the point: 'The machine is not an it to be animated, worshipped, and dominated. The machine is us, our processes, an aspect of our embodiment. We can be responsible for machines: they do not dominate or threaten us. We are responsible for boundaries; we are they' (1991: 180). Lyotard himself points out that technologies, with their electronically generated data-processing capacities, are 'material extensions of our capacity to memorise' and claims that 'technologies show in their own way that there is no break between matter and mind' (Lyotard, 1991: 43).

So although technology, as we have already seen, provides us with a new cultural apparatus for representing and memorizing, technology itself should not be seen as something which is either separate or different from that which is us. If we take such a view and, arguably, it is not possible to take any other, then we need to look again at the consequences of the new cultural apparatus that technology offers, not as something which is separate and different from human experience, but as a new dimension to it which will have an impact upon the processes of education which occur in society.

As we have already seen, one of the critical issues for some appears to be that those who are responsible for the development of technology, and in particular technologically supported learning environments (software designers and programme producers, for example), are no longer only those whom society has appointed to carry out the specific responsibilities and tasks assigned to educators and/or trainers. It is the consequent assumed lack of ability to control the selection, transmission and dissemination of information that is not rooted within a particular, localized, view of the world and coming from an 'acceptable' source of expertise is the real issue which is apparently being identified by authors such as Russell who, it will be recalled, sees the responsibility for the issue needing to be acknowledged and accepted by teachers, software designers and corporations alike.

However, the problem is perhaps not as great or as difficult as Russell and others might lead us to believe and is, possibly, more of an issue of how to adapt our educational thinking and approaches to these new learning environments. If we take as an example the importance and significance given to dialogue in educational theory and consider the position of such thinking within technology-supported learning environments, we find that there is no contradiction but rather a belief in opportunities to develop further the potential and importance of dialogue in learning.

Dialogue in Learning

The importance of dialogue in the learning process is a well-established facet of much educational thinking. Diana Laurillard comments, for example, that there appears to be 'no escape from the need for dialogue' (1993: 85) and asserts that from current understandings of the experience of learning, mere telling is insufficient. Within adult learning there is, particularly within the liberal tradition, an equal emphasis on the importance of dialogue. Here, however, the emphasis is no longer on a dialogue which encourages students to change the way they experience (and understand) the world, but rather dialogue which encourages individuals to be critically reflective about their world and their position in it. This was initially proposed by such people as Freire (1972), who believed dialogue in learning to be necessary if education was to 'liberate' rather than 'oppress'.

Increasingly, within the adult education literature, there has grown an important emphasis towards critical reflection and analysis. As Brookfield explains: 'In a body of recent work in our field, the development of critical thinking and critical reflection have been proposed by a number of writers as organising concepts to inform adult education practice' (1993: 64). As explained by Giroux, critical or liberal education has come to operate on two basic assumptions: 'One, there is a need for a language of critique, a questioning of presuppositions . . . the second assumption of radical education is a language of possibility. It goes beyond critique to elaborate a positive language of human empowerment' (Giroux, 1992: 10). In his writing, Giroux signals the importance of having both a language to examine experience, which, as he comments, never simply speaks for itself, and a language that will enable people to think and act critically. For Giroux and his associates, such a language is necessary to achieve democracy, which, from their perspective, is the aim or purpose of critical education.

The important question is then whether the intention of education is to enable learners to understand descriptions of the world devised by others, or to encourage individuals to be critically reflective about their world and their position in it. Or whether it is both of these things, in which case dialogue can be seen as a fundamental element of the teaching and learning process. Consequently, to assume that dialogue is no longer required in a techno-logically supported learning environment clearly conflicts with both experi-ence and well-established beliefs about learning and the process of learning. Yet the concerns identified earlier about the increased use of new informa-tion and communications technology for educational purposes appear to be based on an assumption that the opportunities for dialogue will not be present within technology-based learning environments. This is neither an inevitable nor – from an educational perspective – desirable consequence of such environments.

Technological Environments in Support of Dialogue

A number of examples of technology-supported learning environments can be found where the importance of dialogue is clearly assumed. However, the context, nature and the medium of dialogue that takes place within telematic learning environments can mean that it has very different characteristics from dialogue which takes place in most conventional educational settings between individuals who are situated within the same context and physical location. This does not, however, necessarily mean that the dialogue is, educationally speaking, qualitatively inferior and unable to facilitate the processes of understanding, reflection and interpretation. On the contrary, it is possible to design technology-based learning environments that actively encourage critical reflection as a direct result of some of the inherent characteristics of the environment. For example, as discussed by David McConnell in this volume, the learning conversations which take place in computer-mediated conferences within a postgraduate programme, where the educational philosophy is to encourage critical reflection, are found by many students and tutors to be positively facilitated by the medium because it allows a different tempo and rhythm from that of face-to-face dialogue.

The characteristic feature of computer conferences to store and consequently retain a permanent record of discussion gives individuals an opportunity to study the comments of others before making their own response, without fear of interruption or the need to talk over others. It allows them more time to consider how they want to formulate their response and, of particular interest, it allows them to study their own responses in the same way that they are able to study the responses of others. These are all features of dialogue which take place in computer conferences not normally applicable to the traditional educational medium and are experienced by those involved as contributing to the processes of self-awareness and critical reflection.

Other technology-supported environments can similarly be designed to support positively the processes of self-awareness and critical reflection. For example, Paul Topham (1990) developed an interactive video programme which was designed to support self-development. Topham incorporated into the design of the programme the principles of Rogerian psychology. He achieved this by designing an interactive video computer programme which asked the learner to identity and describe a current professional, social or personal problem. The programme then recorded the learner on camera while he or she described his or her particular problem and then, by repeatedly playing back to the learner his or her own descriptions and analysis of that problem, the programme allowed the learner to engage in a conversation with him or herself. Topham found that as a result of this process how the problem was perceived, and the relationship that the individual had with the problem, changed, and in the majority of cases the individual came to regard the problem as more manageable and showed more willingness to accept responsibility for it.

In the above examples the nature of the educational dialogue that takes place is demonstrably different from conventional face-to-face learning. Nevertheless, in both cases those involved believed that the technology used increased rather than decreased the potential for critical self-reflection and personal development which, as I have already discussed, is considered to be one of the most important reasons for ensuring that dialogue is part of the educational process. In both instances, however, this was as a result of conscious and intentional dimensions of the educational design. The reasons for using the technology were first and foremost educational. It is when technology is viewed from this perspective that its potential becomes so much more interesting.

'Telegraphic' Culture and Learning

I referred earlier to whether or not the 'delocalized' and 'detemporalized' nature of telegraphic culture identified by Lyotard, within which technology-based learning environments exist, can be seen as a positive or negative characteristic from an educational perspective. While we saw that to work and communicate in electronic environments with their distributed tele-graphic culture might remove the usual obstacles found in traditional earthbound cultures in the way information is recorded, transferred and communicated, I also commented that this was not necessarily a positive thing. Some of the ensuing comments and discussion tended to present arguments which on balance support the view that telegraphic culture has the potential to be amoral and unethical without some kind of control. However, I argued that this does not have to be the case if we retain processes in technology-supported learning environments that are considered important from an educational point of view, such as ongoing and participative dialogue.

Indeed, it is also possible to take a perspective which considers what telegraphic culture will add to the educational process rather than maintain or even take away from it. Take, for example, groups who feel marginalized and oppressed by traditional culture. As Yuval-Davies (1994) explains in her article 'Women, ethnicity and empowerment', one of the main difficulties with traditional cultures has been the persistence of inequalities within them. She suggests that policies which encourage their continuation has led to the construction of cultures as if they were 'static, ahistoric and in their "essence" mutually exclusive from other cultures' (Yuval-Davies, 1994: 185). The problem with this, she explains, is that it perpetuates the status of, in this case, women within state and society. Telegraphic cultures, on the other hand, in which, as Lyotard explains, 'States are not the agencies in control' (1991: 51) and in which 'specific modes of tele-graphy, writing at a distance, removes the close contexts of which rooted cultures are woven' (1991: 50), do offer an environment which is able to support other kinds of dialogue and in which, as sought by Yuval-Davies herself, 'the dialogue rather than the fixity of location becomes the basis of empowered knowl-edge' (1994: 192).

It is probably correct to say that, until now, technology-supported en-vironments have not been viewed as particularly conducive from a gender perspective. Elizabeth Gerver (1986) has, among others, commented, for example, on the predominately male values and attitudes reflected in most computer applications and computer games. The dominence of men over women in the use of the Internet is well documented and there have been a number of studies which identify some of the difficulties women apparently experience within existing electronic learning environments (see, e.g., Kramarae and Taylor, 1993; Hardy et al., 1994). As a consequence, there is a danger that, as in traditional cultures, telegraphic-based culture will increasingly be inhabited and dominated by the same values and ideology despite the opportunities and potential that telegraphic environments offer for new kinds of learning experience and knowledge development. Hope-fully, this will not be the case, and educationalists and, perhaps more importantly, learners will accept and take up both the challenge and opportunities offered by information and communications technology.

If we do not take up these opportunities, the future will mirror the past and the promise which is on offer within telegraphic culture and technology-based learning environments will be haunted by the images and voices that should be left behind in the rapidly disappearing era to which they belong and within which they are rooted. Only with time, however, will we know whether we have had the foresight, imagination and creativity to accept the full potential and challenge that information and communications technology offers for learning, including, if we allow it, management learning.

However, before this can happen, learners, tutors and trainers must examine their attitudes towards their roles and their responsibilities in the learning process. If learners and tutors alike are going to avail themselves of the full potential and opportunities offered by technology to support learning, they must first be provided with the necessary hardware and skills to know how to use and find what they want from technology-supported learning environments; they must not feel dependent upon those 'who know' how to work the technology or those who design the educational software or even the learning environment itself. It is all too easy to put the learner into the dependent role, overawed by the power and authority of technology and, implicitly, of those who manage it. As explained earlier, technology is an aspect of ourselves and our processes, which means not just some people but all of us. We can all, in the right circumstances with the right kind of support, use technology for extending experience and understanding of the world in which we live and act.

Annotated Bibliography

Although written before the extraordinary and exceptional expansion of the Internet and associated technological developments, Diana Laurillard's (1993) *Rethinking University Teaching: A Framework for the Effective Use of Educational Technology.* London: Routledge, is none the less a very pertinent examination of the use of technology for educational purposes. Although primarily concerned with university level education, the approach taken is relevant to other educational contexts, not least because it is written from the perspective of the learner's experience of learning. J.E. Lyotard (1991) *The Inhuman: Reflections on Time.* Cambridge: Polity Press, is a collection of essays in which Lyotard examines questions of the inhuman and time, and looks in particular at the impact that the exponential growth of sciences and technology has had upon the issue. Of most relevance to the issues discussed in this chapter is 'Time today' which looks in depth at how information technology has replaced and consequently changed the traditional ethnocultural apparatuses of memorizing that were tightly bound to the historical and geographical context in which they operated. Also relevant is the essay entitled 'Logus and teaching, or telegraphy', where Lyotard claims that computer-mediated 'writing at a distance' removes the close contexts of which rooted cultures are woven and prevents states being the agencies in control. In C. Mantovani (1994) 'Is computer-mediated communications intrinsically apt to enhance democracy in organizations', *Human Relations*, 47 (1): 45–62, the author challenges some of the claims that have been made for the impact of technology and computer-mediated communication, in particular on social and organizational processes. His article points out that what happens to the networked organization using e-mail depends more on the culture, on the social actors' goals, and on local circumstance than on technology *per se*, and is a salutary reminder of the powerfulness and pervasiveness of social patterns which will not be changed by technology alone. N. Yuval-Davies (1994) 'Women, ethnicity and empowerment', in K.K. Bhavnani and A. Phoenix (eds), *Shifting Identities Shifting Racisms: A Feminism and Psychology Reader*. London: Sage, is of particular relevance in that it describes an alternative approach to dialogue 'where dialogue rather than fixity of location becomes the basis of empowered knowledge'. Yuval-Davies claims the approach is based on 'tranversalism' rather than the more usual 'universalism'.

References

Brookfield, S. (1993) 'Breaking the code: engaging practitioners in critical analysis of adult educational literature', *Studies in the Education of Adults*, 25 (1): 64–91.

Chandler, D. (1990) 'The educational ideology of the computer', *British Journal of Educational Technology*, 21 (3): 165–74.

Dewey, J. (1944) *Democracy and Education*. New York: Free Press.

Freire, P. (1972) *Pedagogy of the Oppressed*. London: Penguin.

Gerver, E. (1986) 'The under-representation of women in computing', *Open Learning*, 1 (2): 28–32.

Giroux, H. (1992) *Border Crossings: Cultural Workers and the Politics of Education*. London: Routledge.

Hardy, V., Hodgson, V. and McConnell, D. (1994) 'Computer conferencing a new medium for investigating issues in gender and learning', *Higher Education*, 28: 403–18.

Haroway, D.J. (1991) *Simians, Cyborgs and Women: The Reinvention of Nature*. London: Free Association Books.

Kramarae, C. and Taylor, H.J. (1993) 'Women and men on electronic networks: a conversation or a monologue', in H.J. Taylor, C. Kramarae and M. Ebben (eds), *Women, Information Technology and Scholarship*. Illinois: University of Illinois, Center for Advanced Study.

Larsen, S. (1986) 'Information can be transmitted but knowledge must be induced', *P.L.E.T.*, 23 (1): 56–61.

Laurillard, D. (1993) *Rethinking University Teaching: A Framework for the Effective Use of Educational Technology*. London: Routledge.

Lyotard, J.F. (1991) *The Inhuman: Reflections on Time*. Cambridge: Polity Press.

Russell, G. (1994) 'Valuing values: reflections on a social value paradigm of educational computing', *British Journal of Educational Technology*, 25 (3): 164–71.

Topham, P. (1990) 'Humanistic computing in the management learning field', unpublished PhD thesis, Lancaster University, Lancaster.

Yuval-Davies, N. (1994) 'Women, ethnicity and empowerment', in K.K. Bhavnani and A. Phoenix (eds), *Shifting Identities Shifting Racisms: A Feminism and Psychology Reader*. London: Sage. pp. 179–97.

13

Collaborative and Self-reflective Forms of Inquiry in Management Research

Judi Marshall and Peter Reason

Creating Knowledge in and for Action

Many managers seeking learning find their way on to some form of postgraduate research programme. In this chapter we explore forms of research which are collaborative, self-reflective and action-oriented. These seem particularly likely to be useful to people wanting to develop knowledge in the service of more effective individual and organizational action. They have been influential in the management learning field under titles such as 'new paradigm research' and 'action research'. They are founded on significantly different principles from mainstream traditional social science research and have gained much legitimacy and acceptance since the early 1980s. But they may still be seen as bold and challenging by many people.

This chapter is written as a selective, retrospective story told from our experience of working with ideas about and practices of research in the School of Management at Bath University. We have chosen this form because it is in the community we share with our postgraduate students that we have developed our own approaches and experimented with those of other people in this field. Also, we see developing inquiry as a continuing process in which ideas and practice are explored alongside each other, and are lived and tested among colleagues willing to support and challenge each other. Developing our educational approaches to working with postgraduate students has been a significant strand in this story. These 'students' are mainly mid-life people who register for part-time research degrees to explore issues which have strong professional and personal significance for them. Each one brings expertise, ideas and values to the research community that contribute and move our practice and thinking on.

As we tell this story we shall pause to explicate key features of the research approaches we are reviewing, to refer to key writings which have influenced us, and to note current challenges. But we do not want to freeze any exposition in time as if it is definitive. These are formulations in continual process. They are valuable to work with, but the issues they address – such as what is valid knowing – have to be engaged with anew and as an exercise in self-creation for any aspiring researcher. So, we feel that we are continually moving on, repeatedly replenished and tested out in mutually educative, alive encounters. It is important to state that this is not always easy or comfortable. We have recently advised prospective students that working as we do 'will involve struggles as well as harmonious engagement' and 'will sometimes be delightful and sometimes uncomfortable or painful'. We note with interest that new generations of students seem to enter where we are; we do not have substantially to recap history for them. We take a tentative sense of validation from this, as if our development is in tune with some trends in a more widely evident, and growing, interest in action research approaches.

We do not intend this chapter to become self-congratulatory. We are pleased with much we have done and do. *And* this is not a perfect picture: there have been difficult, stuck or conflictual times; we have not been able to work well or fruitfully with everyone who has registered with us; and we have sometimes judged ourselves less than competent, or the situation impossible. We continue to learn – we hope.

This story charts key features chosen retrospectively. It is a reconstruction told for the purposes of showing how ideas and practices have been used and developed within a community. We have structured the account into three phases, reflecting shifts in significant issues addressed, educational forms used and staff involved.

Phase 1: Initiating the Postgraduate Research Group

Together with our then colleague, Adrian McLean, we formed our first 'Postgraduate Research Group' in about 1980. We suggested this to the postgraduate students whom we were then singly or jointly supervising to provide a forum for exploring exciting ideas and research methods, and for discussing people's projects in supportive rather than adversarial ways. We wanted to move towards creating a community of inquiry in which all, including staff, were partners in the learning process. We each brought our research interests of the time into the group. Adrian was interested in organizational cultures, change and ethnography. Peter was just completing editing *Human Inquiry* with John Rowan (Reason and Rowan, 1981), and especially offered the research form of co-operative inquiry. Judi was developing notions of research as personal process, researching women in management and engaging with feminisms, themes illustrated in *Women Managers: Travellers in a Male World* (Marshall, 1984).

This group was 'open' in the sense that people joined when they registered with us to do research degrees and left when either they graduated or decided to stop for some other reason. This format could be intimidating for newcomers, some of whom reported staying silent for many months, overwhelmed and resentful as other people used long words or appeared confident. Our meetings were day-long, monthly. In them we discussed literature we had all read and experimented with research methods such as co-operative inquiry, storytelling and psychodrama. Also we often discussed or worked with people's research studies in some depth, but mostly these were supported through additional supervision sessions with staff members.

In its very early days the group was quite an uncomfortable, not very trusting place to be. People were unsure of its value, and seemed hesitant, confined. After a while these tensions seemed to reduce, although we cannot now remember whether there were any agreed reasons for them or for their reduction. One related initiative was introducing regular process reviews into our meetings to give space for group dynamic and interpersonal issues to be addressed. (These reviews often slipped off busy agendas, however, as we noted with a jokiness which only occasionally seemed defensive.)

There is another theme here which we realize has been very significant. It is about our development as persons and as educators. This has been facilitated through disciplines such as psycho-therapy and co-counselling, and through our developing friendship and colleagueship, which has enabled us to work together robustly and flexibly, with openness and challenge. Major aspects of this are: our capacity to hold a space for people to work in-depth with their inquiries; our differences, offering people choice; and how we have learnt to take our authority where appropriate. In the early days of the Postgraduate Research Group we still had much to learn about these issues.

In this phase of development there were-six main emphases:

- legitimating post-positivist inquiry;
- working with different forms of knowing;
- recognizing research as often personal and political process;
- developing practices of co-operative inquiry;
- working with other emerging research methodologies; and
- developing congruent practices of research supervision.

We shall look in turn at these strands (taking the story ahead where appropriate to avoid later overlap).

Legitimating post-positivist inquiry

We realized early on that we were not just advocating qualitative instead of quantitative research, a move which was at the time portrayed in many quarters as suspect and risky enough, but advocating a shift of paradigm, a different way of knowing and being. Peter, with others, had established this ground in *Human Inquiry* (Reason and Rowan, 1981) and it was being reinforced from other sources. Over the years since the early 1980s we have seen a significant shift from inquirers initially needing to justify their research approach through a well-reasoned rejection of traditional social science assumptions to a much less apologetic and more assertive stance. People are now more likely to claim and define their place within an array of post-positivist approaches which are each developing distinctive flavours and grounds for their own legitimacy.

Early on, though, it was helpful to have clear articulations of the wider trends in knowledge-making. For example, Lincoln and Guba (1985), with whom we established a friendly working relationship, were especially clear in articulating five axioms of an emerging naturalistic paradigm and contrasting these with a positivist paradigm. Their naturalist axioms were that:

- realities are multiple, constructed and holistic (rather than reality being single, tangible and fragmentable);
- knower and known are interactive and inseparable (rather than independent, a dualism);
- hypotheses are time- and context-bound (rather than time- and context-free generalizations);
- all entities are in a state of mutual simultaneous shaping (rather than there being real, single, identifiable causes); and
- inquiry is value-bound (rather than value-free). (Lincoln and Guba, 1985: 37)

Other sources were charting the challenges to scientific rationalism generally, for example Capra (1982) in *The Turning Point*, Berman (1981) in *The Reenchantment of the World*, Gregory Bateson (1972) in *Steps to an Ecology of Mind* and Skolimowski's early work which led to the recent publication of *The Participatory Mind* (1995). These, and similar sources, provided valuable reading materials and ideas.

It is interesting to remember how challenging and difficult some of this material seemed at the time, particularly when we tried to explore what it might mean in practice for our thinking and acting. We especially remember, very early in the group's life, reading a report entitled *The Emergent Paradigm: Changing Patterns of Thought and Belief*, produced by SRI International (Schwartz and Ogilvy, 1979). It documented a survey of a wide range of academic disciplines such as biology, mathematics, physics and psychology, and claimed to find evidence of an emerging paradigm shift with common characteristics. The movement charted was *from a dominant paradigm* which favoured explanations which were simple, hierarchic, mechanical, determinate, linearly causal, based on assembly and objective *towards an emergent paradigm* which saw explanations as needing to be complex, heterarchic, indeterminate, mutually causal, concerned with morphogenesis and acknowledging perspective.

That first time, members of the group were excited and intellectually stimulated, but found the ideas hard to encompass. What if the world really were to change in the ways described? Would it really be possible to think like that? Our heads ached. We went to lunch bemused. Reading the report again some years later, with a new group of students, was strange, almost a non-event. The ideas seemed acceptable, quite easy to incorporate.

Working with different forms of knowing

From these early times we have always been working with what we would call an 'extended epistemology'. This builds on the ideas of John Heron that knowing takes multiple forms and is at least propositional, experiential, practical (Heron, 1981) and presentational (Heron, 1992). Thus:

- *Propositional knowledge* is knowing about. It is the realm of ideas, concepts. It is expressed in words and can be readily debated. This is the main form of knowing recognized in traditional academic discourse, but it is essentially limited. Theoretical knowledge can be held separately and discordantly from practice.
- *Practical knowing* is knowing how to, we enact it. This form of knowing is embodied.
- *Experiential knowing* is knowledge by encounter. It is the pre-verbal ground from which other knowledges arise, it incorporates emotional knowing.
- *Presentational knowledge* is patterned in our perceptions before we catch these with our conceptual, categorizing intellect. It is analogic, a matter of form, often only tacitly apprehended (unless appropriate attention is paid). Presentational knowledge can be expressed in images, dreams and narrative.

We have kept in contact with John Heron over the years, for example inviting him to be a keynote speaker at one of our conferences.

Propositional knowledge is given primacy in most academic communities and is the focus of research attention and practice. We hold, however, that these four territories of knowing (at least) are all important, and should all be worked with. Their congruence or incongruence is also important. But primarily knowing is discovered in and for action. Also issues of presentational knowing become important when people want to write from their research. Traditional modes of academic writing are often inappropriate because they reshape and distort what has been discovered by forcing it into incompatible form (see below).

In discussions in the Postgraduate Research Group people would move between forms of knowing, exploring also congruities and incongruities. If a person talked about key intellectual ideas in their study, they might be challenged if their presentation seemed to lack engagement (was this propositional knowing without experiential relevance and testing?), or if they seemed engaged in unreflective action, they might be challenged to incorporate the rigour of the propositional.

We also believe that the knowings generated in research are emergent, unfolding. Many cannot be adequately anticipated at the outset. Simply stated hypotheses and grand research plans are therefore usually inappropriate. More often people will work through several research cycles, in which the understandings and puzzles from one cycle become the questions and curiosities for the next. Often the cycles involve regular movements between action and reflection (Rowan, 1981). We would therefore expect people to take research steps awarely and choicefully, and to review periodically what their purposes are. Changing purposes and understandings can be (must be) incorporated into the research design rather than having to be denied or obscured. These ways of proceeding, keeping close to the ground of one's various forms of knowing, seem very different from the linear, large-scale trajectories of most traditional research studies. To many people it is a relief to find that they do not have to take an abstracted, disconnected route.

Recognizing research as often personal and political process

From our own work and that of many students we came to recognize how much research seemed to emerge from and address a person's life process, rather than being a purely intellectual, objective matter (Marshall, 1992).

> All good research is *for me, for us* and *for them*: it speaks to three audiences, and contributes to each of these three areas of knowing. It is *for them* to the extent that it produces some kind of generalizable ideas and outcomes. . . . It is *for us* to the extent that it responds to concerns of our praxis, is relevant and timely. . . . It is *for me* to the extent that the process and outcomes respond directly to the individual researcher's being-in-the-world. (Reason and Marshall, 1987: 112; original emphasis)

In these statements we were trying to right an imbalance in much academic study, which fails to recognize a vital source of the energy which underpins research.

And later we came to emphasize how much research is also political, as people address issues of power and social positioning, often encountered through their own experience, and seek to change aspects of their social worlds. Recently, for example, we have drawn on the exciting and challenging work of the black feminist scholar bell hooks (e.g., 1989) who warns against over-emphasizing personal insight relative to political action in academic development. Much research on gender and race is clearly political in these ways. But any inquiry affirming non-mainstream approaches – for example, using collaborative action research in a Health Service setting – is likely to have this quality (and so to prove disturbing to someone).

Developing practices of co-operative inquiry

This was a time of working especially actively with the principles and practices of co-operative inquiry, which we see as research *with* and *for* people rather than *on* people.

> In traditional research, the roles of researcher and subject are mutually exclusive. The researcher only contributes the thinking that goes into the project, and the subject only contributes the action to be studied. . . . In co-operative inquiry these mutually exclusive roles are replaced by a co-operative relationship based on reciprocal initiative and control, so that all those involved work together as co-researchers and as co-subjects. (Reason and Heron, 1995: 125)

As co-researchers people participate in the thinking that goes into the research – framing the questions to be explored, agreeing on the methods to be employed and together making sense of their experiences. As co-subjects they participate in the action being studied. The co-researchers engage in cycles of action and reflection: in the action phases they experiment with new forms of practice; in the reflection stages they review their experiences critically, learn from them and develop theoretical perspectives which inform their work in the next action phase. The initiating researcher(s) engages with others to establish the co-operative inquiry group, through which people learn to (re)claim their capacities for knowledge creation and so to transform their work and lives. (See also, Heron, 1996.)

Collaboration, more generally, can thus be seen as both an epistemological and political imperative. It enhances the knowledges produced and sits within an emancipatory vision of inquiry. Collaborative practice demands, in addition, an integration of authentic, vulnerable authority with respect for individual autonomy and choice. It is not an easy formula to apply, but requires much skilled attention.

Some people were attracted to register with us because of Peter's role in co-editing the book *Human Inquiry* and his association with the co-operative inquiry model. Many wanted to adopt co-operative inquiry forms in their research. In the group as a whole we conducted some trial inquiries – for example in one we looked at processes of interpersonal feedback – reviewing the methods and learning more about issues of applying them. Based on these and more recent experiences, it has become increasingly apparent that as people try to adopt any ideal model of research a tension arises between following advocated procedures precisely (which can degenerate into being over-controlling), and allowing the research to find its own emergent form (which can degenerate into lack of systematic rigour). We now articulate and debate this tension overtly with students, hoping to prompt aware and continuing choice in their approach.

Peter edited a collection of case examples as *Human Inquiry in Action* (Reason, 1988). Introductory chapters made more explicit some of the issues and choices in applying co-operative inquiry principles and models to research practice. These were greatly informed by our work in the Postgraduate Research Group.

Working with other emerging research methodologies

During this phase we experimented with other emerging research methodologies such as storytelling (Reason and Hawkins, 1988), psycho-drama (Hawkins, 1988), sub-personalities exercises, and various approaches to working with qualitative data. As always, 'students' of the time contributed greatly to these initiatives, bringing expertise and ideas, and developing approaches with us. The chapter by Reason and Hawkins (1988) includes a key framework generated at this time through a collaborative reflective exercise (p. 84). The framework juxtaposed explanation and expression as alternative modes of working with qualitative data in sense-making, especially affirming the values of the latter as an alternative route.

This was a time of much circle-dancing in the Group and at the conferences we ran (see below), an expertise brought strongly by one member. There were other aspects of the format of our meetings which seemed to us to encourage participation, such as the importance of meeting in a circle (see Reason, 1988, for a fuller account of how the group operated). We note with interest that our meetings now seem more conventional in format, to which we should perhaps be attending.

Developing congruent practices of research supervision

During this phase we developed a process model of research supervision which honoured the personal, political and process natures of research (Marshall and Reason, 1993).

> Given our view that research is not an impersonal, external and solely intellectual endeavour, but rather a complex personal and social process, we approach supervision intending to pay attention to a wide range of themes or 'strands of concern'. We see our role as helping bring into the foreground, to make *figural* in a gestalt sense . . . those themes which currently require attention and to help the student work with them. In order to achieve this we are always scanning internally and externally for clues about issues behind those being discussed, incongruities, aspects of the research which are currently being neglected, and so on. We generally surface our ideas and intuitions as suggestions or possibilities, for the student and us to consider. (ibid.: 118)

During this phase also we initiated the bi-annual *Emerging Approaches to Inquiry* conference series (the first was in 1986). We wanted to disseminate what we were doing, invite people to share in explorations and make contacts with like-minded people. The themes and visiting speakers chosen for these conferences reflect current interests within our research community. Through them we have developed and maintained contacts with people in the UK and other parts of the world, especially the Department of Management Learning at Lancaster University and the Social Ecology Group at the University of Western Sydney at Hawkesbury, Australia.

Phase 2: Recruiting a New Postgraduate Research Group: Hints of Some Core Curriculum

Moving on to the next phase of postgraduate community history will seem neater in retrospect than it was at the time. Certain things did change, although their timing may not have happened simultaneously. Adrian left to become a consultant. Then, for various personal and professional reasons, we did not register any postgraduate students for a year, despite some eager, talented applications. We renewed our commitment to such work by recruiting a 'New Postgraduate Research Group', a fresh cohort of 12 people. (This ran in parallel to the 'Old' Postgraduate Research Group until 1996, when the latter came to the end of its life.)

By this stage we had largely dropped the 'New Paradigm Research' label. We adopted various descriptions of our work – such as 'experiential', 'self-reflective' and 'collaborative' – to reflect its different facets and our different individual approaches. For example, Judi was developing critical feminist analyses of issues such as career theory; also her work had strong self-reflective strands. Peter was still highly committed to co-operative inquiry, but now saw it as one method within a family of collaborative approaches to action research (Reason, 1994).

The core themes of this phase were:

- feeling we had something to teach;
- emphasizing the primacy of the practical;
- respecting diversity in inquiry;
- extending approaches to self-reflective practice; and
- maintaining permeable boundaries while holding a distinctive space.

Having something to teach

In establishing this group we realized that after some 10 years of this sort of work, we had perspectives to offer as well as wanting to engage in a community of inquiry with students. The new challenge was both to take our authority as teachers and to remain student-centred. We departed from our previous ways of operating by devising a more formal programme to cover, fortnightly for the first year, wanting to pass on our enthusiasms and to expose everyone to some of the core ideas and models of practice by then available in the field.

During this phase we felt less need to justify or defend our choices of research approach. A whole variety of new forms of inquiry were gaining currency, and we were achieving a reputation for our particular approaches. Developing our practice further seemed far more important than being defensive about it. Our 'core curriculum' for that group's first year included the six emphases outlined above (p. 228). We also worked actively with Torbert's (1991) notion of action inquiry (see below) and explored feminist work, especially for its insights into the power and politics of knowledge-making.

Another key element was some of the work of Gregory Bateson (Bateson, 1972; well explicated in Berman, 1981). It is impossible to do this justice here. We would, however, consider a systemic world-view as appropriate in much of our work. We also find Bateson's notion of levels of learning valuable. Learning III involves realizing that the frameworks through which we see and construe life are constructions, and that none can be proved inherently 'true'. Thus ways of punctuating events, unexamined premises and 'character' as previously enacted become open to question and change. For us, good research – and the development of management competence – involves aspiring to this kind of self-reflexivity. (While we find these ideas appealing, we realize that they too are a frame rather than a statement about reality.)

To pursue the various themes above, readings, presentations and exercises were offered to the group with the intention of generating engaged discussion and experimentation rather than of creating notions of orthodoxy. But this group experience was at times difficult, and even in retrospect we have no clear understanding of why that was. Certainly the chemistry of membership brought tensions, and we were not able to manage the group as effectively as we wished. What we take from this experience is that extended time needs to be devoted to developing a group as a community and also that discussions of individuals' research best take place in smaller forums where trust can be built, and anxiety and competition (which we believe are rife in groups aspiring to postgraduate degrees) minimized.

Emphasizing the primacy of the practical

Through reading and meetings with others, we realized that we seemed to have a strong practice orientation. This links back, of course, to notions of an extended epistemology. We had lots of research examples and experiences (our own and those of our students) to complement our philosophical approaches to research. This phase saw a strengthening sense that this was and is our contribution. It is a stance we choose to take in an academic world which still seems to over-emphasize intellectual knowing and is insufficiently concerned about quality action. Our commitment comes partly from seeing what people can do in their lives and organizations by pursuing enquiry in the alive senses of that term. We are therefore committed to education for the whole person and for professional practice, to developing knowledge in, through and for action. Theory and ideas *are* also very important to us.

Respecting diversity in inquiry

As members of the group each created their own research projects our growing sense of inquiry as diverse was heightened. As Reinharz (1979) concluded, each person has to become their own kind of social scientist. Methods cannot be copied, they must be creatively developed with subtle attention to suit particular individual and organizational contexts. Often the apparent problems which initially seem likely to undermine quality research are the very characteristics which, if addressed head-on, give methodological creativity and appropriate form.

As a community we were, then, becoming more likely to challenge potential orthodoxies, such as people feeling they should use co-operative inquiry, and to advocate variety as possible, necessary. But within this diversity we were strongly maintaining a collaborative intent.

Extending approaches for self-reflective practice

Research is always from a perspective, in the pursuit of some purpose. All those involved in an inquiry project need to engage in practices which will develop increasing awareness of how their perspectives shape their understanding and action. We have used the term *critical subjectivity* (Reason, 1994) to describe this kind of self-reflective attention to the ground on which one is standing. It cannot, of course, ever be complete, 'clear'. We are not implying 'unbiased' perception. The most important point is that any understanding is always provisional, open to further inquiry. We talk often of needing to 'hold any truth lightly', respecting both its potential to interest, excite or generate action and the impossibility of it ever being 'true'.

Over the years we have explored various ways of developing qualities of attention and self-reflectiveness. At one conference, for example, we invited a Tai Chi teacher to lead a stream of exercises which we thought would help people to notice more about their personal patterns, and then invited them to consider how they brought these to their research and sense-making. To illustrate: one exercise is called 'sticking'. One person closes their eyes and rests one palm on the top of their partner's hand. The latter is invited to move their hand and the person who is 'sticking' must follow, keeping as gently contacted as possible. It is remarkable how revealing such a simple exercise can be. It often, for example, reflects back patterns around control, risk-taking and uncertainty-management.

We have found the model of action inquiry, as developed by Torbert (1991; Fisher and Torbert, 1995), very helpful as a particularly elegant and demanding mapping of awareness possibilities. He suggests that an action system (person or community) requires knowledge about four 'territories' of human experience: their purposes (through intuitive or spiritual knowledge of what goals are worth pursuing); their strategies (as choices made through intellectual or cognitive knowledge of possibilities); their behavioural choices (involving practical knowledge of skill); and knowledge of the consequences of their behaviours in the outside world (an extended epistemology again). The active, self-challenging, scanning of these various frames of knowing provides a rubric of attentional inquiry. Some students use a self-reflexive research process such as action inquiry to explore their own professional practice when more overtly collaborative forms of research would be inappropriate to their research question or dangerous in their professional setting. We have met and worked with Bill Torbert in various settings.

Maintaining permeable boundaries while holding a distinctive space

As the story so far may indicate, developments and ideas from elsewhere enter our community and then are actively experimented with. And we also have a sense of our distinctiveness. So while we may draw on Torbert's work, for example, *we think* we use his ideas differently from the way that he does. We think some of the qualities of our distinctiveness are that we acknowledge and hold lightly the influences of humanistic psychology, augmenting these with modifications and developments such as attention to feminist work, to political issues in research and, tentatively, to a vision of the inquiry process as a spiritual quest for meaning in an uncertain world. We strongly emphasize the necessary rigour of individual and collective inquiry as personal and interpersonal endeavours. We especially emphasize the importance of emotional, interpersonal and process competencies in inquiry.

Our approach is partly revealed in our uses of and reservations about postmodernist sources. During this phase of the community's life we became increasingly aware of postmodernist writing, and its apparently growing popularity in management theorizing. Our approach to participatory knowing is, we believe, postmodern in several senses, but it is importantly different from deconstructionist postmodern perspectives. While we share with the latter the view that all knowledge is relative and socially constructed through processes of power, we consider deconstructive perspectives typically maintain the fundamental sense of separation incorporated in modernist notions about reality. They could almost be called *ultramodern* for they deny any validity of experience, including the experience of being embodied in the natural world. The problem of radical relativism disappears once participation is acknowledged as a component in all experience and all knowledge. Participatory knowing seeks to be grounded in radical experiential encounter with a co-created world, and so may provide a foundation from which coherent meaning and action can develop (Reason, 1994; Heron, 1996).

Phase 3: Formalizing the Postgraduate Programme in Action Research in Professional Practice

In 1994 we established the Centre for Action Research in Professional Practice, partly to formalize our work in a new postgraduate research degree. We joined forces in this venture with our colleague David Sims and with Jack Whitehead from the School of Education. They had been working together on action research programmes, and Jack had a long history of working with teachers to help them develop living educational theories. We chose 'action research' as an encompassing and politically neutral term, although we have some problems with the way it has been used and abused since Lewin first coined it in the 1940s. We wished to emphasize that we were drawing on a range of action-oriented methodologies, including educational action research, participatory action research, and feminist inquiry, as well as on co-operative inquiry and action inquiry. Similarly, we chose the term 'professional', despite the possible connotations of restrictive professionalism, because we wanted to engage with people from a wide range of settings who wished critically to examine their practice.

In designing our programme, we started from the premise that our students, as mature professionals wishing to reflect on their practice, were already action researchers in important ways, and that we needed to respect their self-directing abilities as adult learners. We needed to find a creative balance between this, our own authority to teach and share our experience, and the need to deliver a programme that was efficient in teaching resources. We designed our programme in three phases: Diploma, Masters and Doctoral. The Diploma stage is not a 'lower' level of activity, but an intensive initial engagement in researching which provides the base for later work and tests the fit between participant and programme. It involves a series of two-day workshops in which we introduce the theory and practice of collaborative forms of action research. During this phase we move down a gradient from being relatively authoritative shapers of activities towards shared responsibility with students. The Diploma phase involves cycles of action and reflection from the very beginning: between workshops students engage in self-chosen mini inquiries. They plan and review these in small staff-facilitated groups. Some participants start with clear research agendas and pursue these from the outset. Others are much more tentative, knowing, for example, that they need to reflect at length on their recent experiences before engaging in further experimental action.

At the end of the Diploma stage students write papers reviewing their learning, addressing general issues we have specified. They are also invited to state their own criteria of quality. They present this work to a group of staff and students, and it and future directions are discussed in detail. This is an important transition which we aim to manage as a learning opportunity. It focuses attention on the students' progress, and requires them to write early in their studies. Students may then either transfer to the Masters phase, decide to leave the programme with a Diploma or, in rare cases, be asked to leave by staff if we do not think they are likely to be successful in their aspirations. People who transfer on then proceed with their inquiries and either complete at Masters level or engage in a similar formal transfer process to move to the Doctoral phase.

In addition to the theoretical and methodological concerns discussed above, in this new phase we have especially been focusing or re-focusing on:

- representation;
- questions of validity and quality; and
- the balance between different forms of knowing.

Representation

Denzin and Lincoln (1995) identify the 'crisis of representation' as one of the key moments in the development of qualitative research. As research and writing become more reflexive, moving beyond traditional canons of objectivism, questions arise concerning the authority of the writer to represent experience, and the form that such representation may take. These questions encourage us to pay even more attention to presentational knowing in our extended epistemology. First, representation involves the place of presentational knowing as the often unacknowledged bridge between experiential knowing and propositional knowing; it is the pre-linguistic warrant both for ideas and theories *and* for action in the world. Secondly, presentational knowing is an important aspect of *speaking out* to the world, since it addresses how we find appropriate forms in which to represent our knowing. These are especially challenging issues for those wishing to portray their inquiries in concordant ways while also paying attention to traditional academic canons.

In our teaching, these issues are partly addressed in the workshop we call 'Accounting for ourselves', in which we raise these questions in an attempt to deconstruct traditional notions of academic language and offer students a range of alternatives. We encourage students to experiment with forms of representation and writing, both to portray their experience to themselves and to find creative ways to speak to wider audiences. In research work, Judi Marshall's book *Women Managers Moving On* (1995) is an exploration of representational form as well as an account of senior women managers. The text weaves between stories written in multiple voices and reflections which invite readers to engage in their own sense-making as they read rather than take the writer's sense-making for granted.

Questions of quality and validity

Throughout our work we have pondered the nature of high-quality research in a participative paradigm: issues of validity were addressed in *Human Inquiry* (1981) and *Human Inquiry in Action* (1988), and most of our students have engaged in extended discussions of quality issues in their theses. In 1995 Peter and Yvonna Lincoln initiated an international conference 'Quality in Human Inquiry', with participants from major schools of participative work (Reason and Lincoln, 1996). This conference emphasized that quality within a collaborative and action-oriented paradigm concerns the nature of *practice*: if knowledge is derived in and for action with people, then the test of quality lies not in any abstract characteristics, but in its ability to guide effective and ethical action. One test for this when presented with an action-research thesis is to explore the questions: 'Has this inquiry helped to develop the quality of aware action among those involved?'; 'Is there evidence of improved action-inquiry capacities?' This does not mean that we are not interested in questions of creative theory or rigorous evidence; it means that these are seen as accompanying and often in the service of effective practice. We also believe strongly that quality or validity is not guaranteed by method (as in orthodox research) but should be sought in the aware and self-reflective consciousness of inquirers.

The balance between different forms of knowing

These reflections on validity lead us to ask ourselves about the balance of experiential, presentational, propositional and practical knowing as represented in a student's eventual thesis. Is it acceptable for a PhD thesis to include profound experiential knowing yet minimal theory? Can presentational knowing, say in the form of a novel, be a research thesis? Our students' work often raises these issues, and we attempt to frame them as questions for creative exploration. When recently discussing the final draft of a particularly unusual PhD thesis (Treseder, 1995), we wondered out loud if it included a sufficiently wide-ranging exploration of literature. After a pause for self-recollection, our student told us forcibly, 'There is a lot of theory in this, and you will find it integrated throughout the text. But more importantly, what I have written here is known through my body, my imagination and my practice. The quality of my work is in its integration with my whole being, not simply in academic theory.' We accepted her argument, as did the external examiner.

Conclusion

Thus has our practice developed through our own cycles of action and reflection. In some ways we would claim that our practice has developed from uncertain beginnings towards greater maturity. We are now much more comfortable with our authority as teachers and exponents of selective approaches to inquiry, and we find it less difficult to hold our authority *and* acknowledge the agency of our students. We believe we have developed a programme design which creatively balances pre-arranged structure with emergent form.

At the same time, some issues go round and round, re-appearing regularly to confront us, albeit in new forms. There are in the end no firm answers to the dilemmas of working in a learning community. In a post-modern world there are no permanent criteria of quality work. We continually ask ourselves how to balance the various components of our programme to give due attention to experience, to theory, to practice. We worry from time to time that we have settled comfortably into a fixed frame, and are fooling ourselves in claiming we see through our frames. We struggle in our relationships as staff with our diverse interests and emphases. And so on. This is the stuff of a living-learning community of inquiry.

Summary

In this chapter we have reviewed some of the core characteristics of self-reflective, action-oriented and collaborative forms of management inquiry. We have especially emphasized the necessary interweaving of different forms of knowing; the value of cycling between reflection and action in order to develop good quality theory and advanced management practice; the significance of acknowledging and working with personal and political aspects of inquiry; and the importance of developing appropriate disciplines of self-reflectiveness. We have reviewed the influences of a range of potential methodologies such as action inquiry, co-operative inquiry, story-telling and feminist research. We have discussed how we have worked with these ideas and potential practices in our research community – and therefore illustrated our view that research is best supported by working alongside other people, alongside friends willing to act as enemies, and as friends. These practices have included developing a process model of postgraduate supervision; balancing our authority as staff members with student-centred approaches; and working on our own development as professionals and persons. We have located our work as being in the broad fields of post-positivist and action research, showing how we relate to some other approaches and claiming our own distinctiveness, for example in emphasizing the primacy of the practical, maintaining an ethic of diversity and enjoying finding appropriate forms for representing research outcomes. During the chapter we have illustrated our concerns with issues of quality – in the practices of research and research facilitation. We think it is wholly appropriate – essential even – that our practice is in the field of management. The approaches to inquiry we advocate greatly enhance the potential for research to be grounded in 'real world' concerns and issues, for theory to be applicable in practice, and for management researchers to become more aware, skilled and effective practitioners as a central, rather than auxiliary, outcome of their research.

Annotated Bibliography

J. Marshall (1995) *Women Managers Moving On*. London: International Thomson Publishing Europe, is a self-reflective account of sense-making and an exploration in representation. J. Marshall and P. Reason (1994) 'Adult learning in collaborative action research: reflections on the supervision process', *Studies in Continuing Education, Research and Scholarship in Adult Education*, 15 (2): 117–32, gives a process account of research supervision and identifies potential themes and issues facing practitioner postgraduate students. P. Reason (1994) 'Co-operative inquiry, participatory action research and action inquiry: three approaches to participative inquiry', in Norman K. Denzin and Yvonna Sessions Lincoln (eds), *Handbook of Qualitative Research*. Thousand Oaks, CA: Sage. pp. 324–39, outlines three participative research approaches and discusses their contributions and limitations. The book includes a good bibliography on these methods. P. Reason (1994) *Participation in Human Inquiry*. London: Sage. Four theoretical chapters exploring the nature of participation in research, followed by six examples of participative forms of inquiry

References

Bateson, G. (1972) *Steps to an Ecology of Mind*. San Francisco: Chandler.
Berman, M. (1981) *The Reenchantment of the World*. Ithaca, NY: Cornell University Press.
Capra, F. (1982) *The Turning Point*. London: Wildwood House.
Denzin, N. and Lincoln, Y.S. (eds) (1995) *Handbook of Qualitative Research*. Thousand Oaks, CA: Sage.
Fisher, D. and Torbert, W.R. (1995) *Personal and Organizational Transformations: The True Challenge of Continual Quality Improvement*. London: McGraw-Hill.
Hawkins, P. (1988) 'A phenomenological psychodrama workshop', in P. Reason (ed.), *Human Inquiry in Action*. London: Sage. pp. 60–78.
Heron, J. (1981) 'Philosophical basis for a new paradigm', in P. Reason and J. Rowan (eds), *Human Inquiry: A Sourcebook of New Paradigm Research*. Chichester: Wiley.
Heron, J. (1992) *Feeling and Personhood: Psychology in Another Key*. London: Sage.
Heron, J. (1996) *Co-operative Inquiry: Research into the Human Condition*. London: Sage.
hooks, b. (1989) *Talking Back*. Boston, MA: South End Press.
Lincoln, Y.S. and Guba, E.G. (1985) *Naturalistic Inquiry*. Beverly Hills, CA: Sage.
Marshall, J. (1984) *Women Managers: Travellers in a Male World*. Chichester: Wiley.
Marshall, J. (1992) 'Researching women in management as a way of life', *Management Education and Development*, 23 (3): 281–9.
Marshall, J. (1995) *Women Managers Moving On*. London: International Thomson Publishing Europe.

Marshall, J. and McLean, A. (1988) 'Reflection in action: exploring organizational culture', in P. Reason (ed.), *Human Inquiry in Action*. London: Sage. pp. 199–220.

Marshall, J. and Reason, P. (1993) 'Adult learning in collaborative action research: reflections on the supervision process', *Studies in Continuing Education, Research and Scholarship in Adult Education*, 15 (2): 117–32.

Reason, P. (ed.) (1988) *Human Inquiry in Action*. London: Sage.

Reason, P. (1994) 'Co-operative inquiry, participatory action research and action inquiry: three approaches to participative inquiry', in Norman K. Denzin and Yvonna Sessions Lincoln (eds), *Handbook of Qualitative Research*. Thousand Oaks, CA: Sage. pp. 324–39.

Reason, P. and Hawkins, P. (1988) 'Storytelling as inquiry', in P. Reason (ed.), *Human Inquiry in Action*. London: Sage. pp. 79–101.

Reason, P. and Heron, J. (1995) 'Co-operative inquiry', in R. Harre, J. Smith, and L. Van Langenhove (eds), *Rethinking Methods in Psychology*. London: Sage. pp. 122–42.

Reason, P. and Lincoln, Y.S. (1996) 'Quality in human inquiry', *Qualitative Inquiry*, 2 (1) (Special Issue).

Reason, P. and Marshall, J. (1987) 'Research as personal process', in D. Boud and V. Griffin (eds), *Appreciating Adult Learning*. London: Kogan Page. pp. 112–26.

Reason, P. and Rowan J. (eds) (1981) *Human Inquiry: A Sourcebook of New Paradigm Research* Chichester: John Wiley.

Reinharz, S. (1979) *On Becoming a Social Scientist*. San Francisco: Jossey Bass.

Rowan, J. (1981) 'A dialectical paradigm for research', in P. Reason and J. Rowan (eds), *Human Inquiry: A Sourcebook of New Paradigm Research*. Chichester: Wiley. pp. 93–112.

Schwartz, P. and Ogilvy, J. (1979) *The Emergent Paradigm: Changing Patterns of Thought and Belief*. Analytical Report No. 7, Values and Lifestyles Program, SRI International, Menlo Park, California.

Skolimowski, H. (1995) *The Participatory Mind*. London: Arkana.

Torbert, W.R. (1991) *The Power of Balance: Transforming Self, Society, and Scientific Inquiry*. Newbury Park, CA: Sage.

Treseder, J. (1995) 'Bridging incommensurable paradigms: a training consultant recovering the wholeness of being', unpublished PhD thesis, University of Bath, Bath.

PART IV
DEVELOPMENTS IN DESIGN

While conceptual and technical developments accumulate, accompanied by shifting concerns for social and environmental issues and re-evaluations of previously powerful and competing world-views – positivism, Marxism humanism and so forth – it remains to be seen whether significantly changed practice will result. It would be disappointing if new ideas were to be rebottled in old containers, the traditional range of management learning practice continuing with no signs of being influenced by recent thinking and research.

Changes in management learning practice have originated from different sources and reflect a balance of different influences. The accumulation of studies of managers' work, for example Kotter (1982), Mintzberg (1973) and Stewart (1976), have found their way into the curriculum for both postgraduate and postexperience programmes. In educational methodology, experiential learning theory has had considerable influence on management development and increasingly on management education. Other developments have proved more contentious, as for example the growth of the competencies industry – as much in the interests of control as in explicating the complexities of management effectiveness.

The questions raised about new developments, therefore, are in terms of both their origins and also their function. Why are particular changes in either content or method in management learning adopted and others ignored or actively discouraged? Why do some methods simply fade away? Do these choices reflect advances in research, dissatisfaction with current practice, or are they indications of fashion or of political imperatives? Are new developments simply modifications which leave principles and politics unaffected, or do they carry within them the potential for significantly changing professional practice and even for influencing the wider social context?

More of the Same?

Some notable examples from the last 50 years illustrate the earlier point that there have been different origins of developments in management learning and by different routes. Motivational theory, for example, might be said to have evolved through models of organizational climate, ideology and culture before providing the basis of current ideas about the 'learning organization'. Another quite different innovation, which can be seen as having evolved from pre-existing ideas in practice, is 'outdoor management development' (OMD), a particularly popular method in the UK and Ireland (Krouwel and Goodwill, 1994). OMD, with its emphasis on reflecting on the process and outcome of practical activities, is a natural successor to earlier applications of experiential learning theory such as simulations, games and other activities used for individual and team development.

But while some developments appear as a logical extension of existing theory and practice, or adaptations to take advantage of new technology, others have apparently arrived 'out of the blue'. So, for example, the advent of the sensitivity group ('T-Group') in 1946 seems a much clearer break with traditional educational method. The T-Group method – a way of understanding group behaviour experientially – grew out of sessions which Kurt Lewin held with his researchers in order to make sense of their observations of groups taking part in a conference for community workers. Conference delegates invited themselves to these research sessions and their additional views added considerably to the analysis of the groups' dynamics. This episode led Lewin to believe that a new and powerful method of understanding behaviour in groups had been discovered – apparently quite by chance (Smith, 1980).

Without diminishing the element of serendipity in discoveries of this nature, an understanding of how developments in education or training come about should not discount the influence of historical or contextual factors. While the T-Group method was apparently discovered by chance, it is also true that similar developments were taking place around that time, most notably in the USA in work of Carl Rogers, who was using groupwork for the training psychologists in counselling, and in Wilfred Bion's work with therapeutic groups in the UK. It seems reasonable to suppose therefore that even the sudden appearance of the T-Group was in some way due to resonance with changes in ideas about learning which were emerging at that time, and more profoundly, to increasing preoccupation among the middle classes in post-war America and Europe with understanding and improving the quality of social relationships. In the same way action learning can be seen both as a logical development of experience-based methods and as a direct response to managers' demands to be able to base learning in their current work experience.

A criticism which is often levelled at 'new' ideas and methods in management learning, by both educators and managers, is that change is more style than substance, disguising recycled or repackaged material. This raises the question as to whether developments which are presented as building on advances in research or theory, or as responses to shifts in social values or beliefs, actually only reflect changes in fashion or in the current market for management development solutions.

As well as questions about why theory and methods appear, there are questions about why they decline. Even that is more complicated than it appears. Using T-Groups as an example, are they used a good deal less than they used to be because the alternative model of authority, on which the method was based, and its insistence of critically questioning assumptions of authority of any kind, posed an unacceptable disturbance to established hierarchy? Or, more optimistically, could it be said that elements of the T-

Group approach have been incorporated into a wider range of methods still used in management development – and to a lesser extent in management education – in various forms of personal and team development methods? The T-Group has undoubtedly contributed to the current emphasis placed on understanding and working with the social processes involved in working in groups and teams.

A more recent example is the dramatic growth of interest in the concept of the learning organization and its application. Although the concept of an organizational learning process has a long pedigree in the academic literature, it is a fairly recent development in the world of practice (Senge, 1990; Pedler et al., 1991). The concept can be seen as new in its emphasis on collective rather than individual learning, and as a useful reaction to the possibly regressive practices of total quality management and business process re-engineering. However, it may fall into the trap of recycling the old, as represented by systems theory and some of the underlying assumptions of humanistic organization development which resurface in some of the more participative aspects of organizational learning thinking.

On the positive side, there are signs that the debate surrounding the learning organization is to some degree critically aware of some of these problems, and there are reasons to hope that the idea will evolve to be more genuinely innovative as the result of it being worked with as an area of critically reflective practice (see, e.g., Coopey, 1995; and Easterby-Smith, 1997).

In summary, it is clear that the origins of changes in management learning practice are varied, as are the reasons for them and the form the change can take. There can be developments in the content or focus of an educational programme, in the methods used, and more fundamentally, in the intended purpose. The stimulus for development may come from research, from changes in social awareness, from demands for education to be more immediate in its relevance to managers' experience and problems, from excursions into unfamiliar disciplines or philosophies, or in response to changes in legislation or pressure groups, as well as in fashion and style, or as a reflection of someone's idea of an exploitable product. New theory and practice may even reflect a belief that education and development can contribute towards greater equality in work and in the community.

The Chapters in this Section

Action learning has undoubtedly proved one of the most successful approaches in support of managers' development in both in-house and academic contexts. In his reconsideration of action learning, *Mike Pedler* considers criticisms of the approach in the light of alternative interpretations of it. He developes one of these in particular – action learning as social construction – as the possible basis of a more creative and collective process of 'action and learning'. Mike Pedler's account – as Hugh Willmott's chapter in an earlier section – demonstrates that there is value in foregrounding the assumptions and rationale which underlie educational method if it is to provide a vehicle for the development of reflective, and especially critically reflective, practitioners, whether in organizational or educational settings.

Two developments which are prominent in management and management education alike are the growth of international involvement, which is the focus of *Anna Lorbiecki*'s chapter, and recent advances in communications technology available to management educators, which *David McConnell* describes. Both authors draw on research in illustrating the educational and social issues which need to be addressed if management education is to keep up with and benefit from these changes. Both chapters exemplify how developments in research, and in the social and cultural context within which managers work, generate a pressing need for parallel developments in management learning theory and practice.

The final chapters in this section are examples of proposals for revising educational method to include ways of thinking about managers' learning which question traditional assumptions. In the first, *Victoria Marsick* and *Karen Watkins* draw on their previous research which has stimulated considerable rethinking of the priorities within management education and development. Their emphasis is on how much learning is derived from day-to-day experience of work and working relationships. The informal, unplanned and unlooked-for events in managers' lives contribute hugely to their professional development, as well as any which might result from planned educational programmes. The challenge which Victoria Marsick and Karen Watkins take up is how those of us working in management learning can use this awareness to redefine our roles in support of managers' development.

In the last chapter in this section, *Michael Reynolds* proposes the basis for a design which responds to the call for a more critical focus in management education, but in particular considers the implications for educational design of acknowledging that learning is as likely to result from the methods used as from the content they are designed to convey. This account reflects some of the themes of earlier chapters in this volume, in particular complementing the one by Hugh Willmott.

References

Coopey, J. (1995) 'The learning organization, power, politics and ideology', *Management Learning*, 26 (2): 193–214.

Easterby-Smith, M. (1997) 'Disciplines of organizational learning, contributions and critiques', *Human Relations*, 50.

Kotter, John P. (1982) *The General Manager*. New York: Collier-MacMillan.

Krouwel, Bill and Goodwill, Steve (1994) *Management Development Outdoors*. London: Kogan Page.

Mintzberg, Henry (1973) *The Nature of Managerial Work*. New York: Harper and Row.

Pedler, Mike, Burgoyne, John G. and Boydell, Tom (1991) *The Learning Company: A Strategy for Sustainable Development.* Maidenhead: McGraw-Hill.

Senge, Peter (1990) *The Fifth Discipline. The Art and Practice of the Learning Organization.* New York: Doubleday.

Smith, Peter B. (1980) *Small Groups and Personal Change.* London: Methuen.

Stewart, Rosemary (1976) *Contrasts in Management.* London: McGraw-Hill.

14

Interpreting Action Learning

Mike Pedler

> There can be no learning without action and no (sober and deliberate) action without learning.
>
> (Revans, 1983: 54)

Revans's dictum seeks to heal the split of mind and matter, defining knowing as inseparable from doing, and learning as dependent on action. Through an unflagging exhortation to *action learning*, Revans has become a major influence for many practitioners of adult learning and organizational development. This chapter begins with attempts to define action learning and follows with four criticisms of the idea. Three different interpretations of what action learning may be illustrate some of the roots of these criticisms and the chapter concludes with a suggestion that the third of these interpretations – action learning as social construction – may help us beyond the limitations of individual action and learning towards the learning organization.

What is Action Learning?

Revans is inclined to say that it takes so long to describe action learning, because it is so simple, but anyone who dares a simplicity, for example, 'So, it's learning by doing then?', is soundly admonished and treated to an explanation of 'what action learning is *not*'. It is *not*:

> job rotation . . . project work . . . case studies, business games and other simulations . . . group dynamics and other task-free exercises . . . business consultancy and other expert missions . . . operational research, industrial engineering, work study and related subjects . . . simple commonsense. (Revans 1983: 61–9)

So, what *is* action learning? One attempt by Aspinwall (in Pedler, 1996) is based closely on Revans (see p. 249).

Action learning may be a simple idea, but only at the philosophical level. By resisting any given form or technique, action learning must always re-invent itself – each application is a new accomplishment and a fresh performance. Over the last 20 years action learning has emerged as a creative source of *generative* theory and practice for management and organizational learning. This generative element helps to avoid the

What is action learning?

Action learning was developed by Revans as the best way to educate managers. It is based on his premise that: *'There can be no learning without action and no (sober and deliberate) action without learning.'*

Revans suggests that organizations, (and the individuals in them) cannot flourish unless their rate of learning (L) is equal to, or greater than, the rate of change (C) being experienced:

$$L > C$$

Learning has two elements – traditional instruction or *Programmed knowledge* (P) and critical reflection or *Questioning insight* (Q). This gives the learning equation:

$$L = P + Q$$

He also distinguishes between *puzzles* and *problems*. *Puzzles* have 'best' solutions and can be solved via the application of programmed knowledge with the help of experts. *Problems* have no right answers and are tackled by people in different ways by the exercise of questioning insight. Programmed knowledge can be helpful but it should only be sought after careful reflection on what knowledge is needed and why.

Action learning sets or groups bring people together in order to:

- Work on and through *hitherto intractable problems* of managing and organizing. This must be a voluntary commitment.
- Work on problems which personally engage the set members – situations in which 'I am part of the problem and the problem is part of me'.
- Check individual perceptions of the problem, to clarify and render it more manageable, and to create and explore alternatives for action.
- Take action in the light of new insight. This insight begins to change the situation. An account of the effects of the action is brought back to the set for further shared reflection and exploration.
- Provide the balance of support and challenge (*warmth* and *light*) which will enable each member to act and learn effectively.
- Be aware of group processes and develop effective teamwork. Usually sets have an adviser or facilitator whose role is to help members identify and acquire the skills of action and learning.
- Focus on learning at three levels:
    - about the problem which is being tackled;
    - about what is being learned about oneself; and
    - about the process of learning itself, i.e., 'learning to learn'.

The second and third levels are essential for the transfer of learning to other situations.

(*Source*: K. Aspinwall in Pedler, 1996: 20–2)

vicissitudes of management development fashion and continues to vivify the concept.

After a long pioneering phase, action learning seems increasingly popular. Examples of practice have become commonplace, for example, in UK companies and universities (Pedler, 1991; Weinstein, 1995) and in a wide range of other countries (Pedler, 1991: Chs 15–20). New books appear regularly, usually attempting the Sisyphean task of describing the practice of action learning in simple terms (e.g. Inglis, 1994; Weinstein, 1995). Although this account draws mainly on Revans, there are other versions; Morgan and Ramirez link action learning with many other generic approaches, including group dynamics, T-Groups, co-operatives, Torbert's collaborative enquiry, Korten's social learning, search conferencing, action research, organizational development and networking techniques (Morgan and Ramirez, 1984: 20).

Elsewhere Morgan states that his aim in 'action learning' is '. . . not to produce valid *descriptions* of the world but accounts or "stories" of interventions that may create what I call "generalizable insights"' (1993: 298; original emphasis). These generalizable insights are about 'the *pattern* of one situation that *may*, have relevance for understanding a similar pattern elsewhere' (ibid. 4–5; original emphasis). The concern with pattern recognition is different from Revans's 'questioning insight'. Revans is concerned with the primacy of the question to cast doubt on current perceptions and to create new possibilities for action, which is more akin to Gergen's notion of 'generative theory' (Gergen, 1994: 91).

What's Wrong with Action Learning?

At least four criticisms can be made of the concept and practice of action learning.

1   Despite its basis in questioning, action learning has become increasingly incorporated into unquestioned management agendas

Action learning gives primacy to Q – the naive or critical question which undermines P – the accumulation of 'programmed knowledge'. It works through the deconstructing of the current problem and its reconstruction in a way which allows for new action and learning. The transformative property of the good question is what makes action learning a main contender as a methodology for organizational learning. For example, action learning can critically examine the underpinning assumptions of current practice, which is essential to 'double loop learning' (Argyris and Schon, 1978: Ch. 1) or create the conflict and contention deemed essential for creativity (Pascale, 1990: 262–5).

However, if action learning is incorporated into existing forms of management development, does it still manage to carry the Q function? There are plentiful examples of action learning being suitably tamed to fit current norms. Thus 'action learning' becomes, for example, 'active learning' and . . .

- . . . 'problems' become 'projects';
- . . . 'learning' gives way to 'task-completion';
- . . . 'questioning' becomes 'resolving';
- . . . '(sober and deliberate) action' becomes 'proposing action' and so on.

2 Action learning is atheoretical or 'anti-theory'

Ironically, considering its origins in Revans's abreaction to university and business school teaching methods, action learning is now being reclaimed by academics for the purposes of constructing a 'critical management education' (McLaughlin and Thorpe, 1993; Willmott, 1994). By denying the value of P, action learning is seen as ahistoric and atheoretical. In this view, however strongly managers are encouraged to enquire into their organizational problems, this questioning is likely to be limited to the level of the task rather than encompassing a deeper examination of how these problems come to arise. Managers therefore need some means of leverage against current reality, some basis on which to criticize prevailing norms and assumptions.

This can be done by adding and teaching 'theory'. In the context of university management education, specifically master's degrees, McLaughlin and Thorpe suggest the value of 'some traditional teaching (in the areas of organizational behaviour, problem-solving methodologies, etc.) to ensure that students are able to maximize the benefits of Action Learning' (1993: 26). Similarly, Willmott recommends that 'the cognitive insights of critical theory are fused with the more concrete and embodied process of Action learning' (1994: 130). On a slightly different tack, Beck recommends a combination of 'didactic teaching' and action learning for a 'new paradigm' MBA to help host companies bring about the learning organization (Beck, 1994: 242–6).

3 Action learning is too centred on the individual as agent: as actor and learner

In this criticism, action learning casts the individual manager as heroic 'change agent' in the face of an organized conspiracy of inaction and dysfunctional organizational routines. This is naive, either on the grounds that complex organizations are simply not amenable to one-person change forces, or on the more developed objection that as organizations are defined by multiple interests and realities, and are constructed and re-constructed in a continuous process of negotiation, organizational action is always a collaborative effort. An individualistic focus therefore limits the growth of collective understanding and competence in organizations. For example, the Learning Company, is 'not brought about simply by training individuals; it

can only happen as a result of *learning at the whole organization level'*
(Pedler et al., 1991: 1; original emphasis).

*4 Action learning sets can degenerate into support groups for
individuals*

This criticism notes that sets are social islands or oases which may become
inward-looking or 'ain't it awful' forums to meet the psychological needs of
members rather than deal with 'out there' organizational problems. Such an
inner focus may make members *less* likely to attack the problems in the
organization.

What Action Learning May Be

To attract criticism is perhaps a sign of rude health. All four of these
criticisms can stem from the desire to harness the energetic potential of
action learning for particular causes. A response to the critique demands a
deeper look at action learning. Here is an action learning story with some
alternative readings:

> David Docherty is the 29-year-old director of a small but rapidly expanding
> engineering business. In fact, Harbourne Engineering now employs 60 men and
> has been tripling its turnover in every year of its five-year existence. There are
> three directors, including the MD, who all helped to found the company. David is
> mainly responsible for site work and equipment, while his fellow directors handle
> the manpower and selling aspects. Harbourne Engineering does all its work on
> other people's premises and may be working on 30 or 40 jobs at any one time
> throughout the British Isles and abroad.
>   David Docherty has an engineering background but no formal management
> training. He came to an action learning group because his boss, Bill Harbourne,
> was concerned about two things:
>
> 1   The company's rapid rate of growth was putting pressure on existing
>   management and their 'systems' which were *ad hoc* and depended very much
>   on David and Graham Anderson chasing men and equipment around
>   personally.
> 2   David was spending far too much time on the equipment side of his job. It
>   could take 30 or 40 hours out of a week and he was not infrequently spending
>   12 hours on Sundays checking equipment for safety, loading trucks and
>   generally being at the heart of the action.
>
>   David saw himself as a straight-talker with an open relationship with Bill
> Harbourne. Bill was almost a peer rather than a boss. David had an inbuilt 'crap
> detector' and if he thought the group was wasting his time, he said so. At an early
> meeting he said he would not attend unless he got value out of it.
>   One of the first things he was asked by the group was how many items of
> equipment the company had. 'About 800' was his estimate, as he had been the
> man directly responsible for equipment since the founding of the company. He
> was pushed, a bit unwillingly, into making an inventory for a future group
> meeting. Such a thing had not existed before – to the amazement of the big
> company engineers in the group. His inventory got to over 2,000 items before he
> gave up, admitting that there was other equipment on various sites that he had not
> been able to trace. With items varying from a few pounds for a chock or

sledgehammer and several hundred pounds for a 30 ton chain or block and tackle, there was a lot of money involved.

David then had to go abroad on business for a month and his problem was shelved in his absence. When he returned to the group a number of sessions were devoted to attacking his problem. Numerous suggestions were put forward by the group, involving systems to solve his equipment problem. There was no shortage of ideas but it seemed that none fitted the bill. There was always a good reason from the hard-headed David which effectively meant the system would not work. Eventually the group lost patience. After going round in circles for some time and after five hours of tiring discussion, one member said 'You don't really want to solve this problem do you David?' This was said and meant aggressively. David was not ruffled – he was used to violent arguments. He reiterated all the reasons he had for resolving the problem: it was taking all his time; as the company expanded it would take more time unless a system was instituted; his wife was complaining about him working 60 or 70 hours each week. But the group was not satisfied and he did get ruffled and rather angry, and eventually the meeting broke up.

A few weeks later the problem was resolved. A simple form, a simple filing system, a part-time old-age pensioner and some meetings with the fitters were the components of it. The details are not important – all of them had been thrown up by the group weeks beforehand. Most of the other participants worked with far more complicated paperwork systems. So, why wasn't the problem resolved in week one?

The answer to this is not simple. When individuals begin to tackle a problem in their own company they are often part of the problem themselves, and if they are not personally involved, then their boss usually is. Before it can be resolved they may have to look at the problem and themselves from a new angle. This is what takes the time and, in normal day-to-day managerial routine, rarely happens. David had to see for himself the paradox of his time pressures on the one hand, and his own need to hang on to what made him feel important and indispensible. He had to admit that a paperwork system – 'an alien thing which only happens in big bureaucracies' – could take over *some* aspects of what he did at present all on his own.

Finally, he had to face the consequences of what would happen if he got rid of half his work load – what would he replace it with? If he was selling and meeting clients, could he do it as well as Bill Harbourne? At the end of the action learning group, David was left with some of these questions still unanswered. One problem was resolved, but it had uncovered several more.

How are we to understand what happened in this account? Three interpretations, borrowing generously from Blantern (1992), define action learning differently.

1   Action learning as changing the external world

As one manager puts it, 'To me . . . Revans has a simple message: in action learning real managers share ideas and tackle real problems with their counterparts, which effects change in the real world by helping each other' (Newbould, 1982: vi). There is plenty of support for this perspective in the story of David Docherty and Harbourne Engineering. Not included in the story is the sequel that, as a result of discovering how much equipment it had, scattered all over the country, the company set up a profitable contract hire business. You can't get much more 'real world' than that.

Here action learning confronts the person with a 'stern external reality . . . [which] implies a very "realist" stance and an empiricist/logical positivist faith in sense data breaking through the conceptual frameworks that we use to interpret experience' (Burgoyne, in Blantern, 1992: 14). The world is real; it is the individual's perception of it which needs to change – and for the better – for the problem to be resolved:

> If the generative role of doubt/uncertainty is right . . . then where does uncertainty . . . come from? I guess my understanding of Revans on this is that it comes from the realisation that perceptual constructs – personal or 'received wisdom' – are not adequate to deal with the external reality as it 'pokes through' if honestly faced. Hence my perception that action learning is 'external world' focussed in that it is interested in this kind of uncertainty rather than – immediately – uncertainties found or created in the search for identity. (Burgoyne, in Blantern, 1992: 17)

Much of Revans's own work supports this perspective. As first Director of Education at the Coal Board (1947–55) and then Professor of Industrial Administration at the University of Manchester Institute of Science and Technology (1955–65), Revans worked principally out of an operational research frame. His studies in mines, hospitals, schools and factories measure accident levels, patient length-of-stay rates, childrens' classroom behaviour and the link between communication levels and supervisory satisfaction with work (Revans, 1980: Chs 10–13). The early action learning programmes, notably the Belgian Inter-University Programme, share their theoretical foundations with scientific and operational research models. Thus, 'The system alpha paradigm is the basis of many operational research models' (Revans, 1971: 36), and system beta (survey, decision, action, audit and control) is 'the structure, not only of the negotiation aspects of a decision, but also of the general learning process . . . and of the scientific method' (ibid.: 41).

Claims for action learning as changing the 'real world' reach their peak in Revans's quixotic view of Belgium's manufacturing productivity between 1965 and 1983. Comparing this period with the previous 15 years, he concludes 'Belgium appears in a class by herself. And, perhaps quite incidentally, 1965 was the year Reg Revans left for Belgium to start action learning at the highest level' (Revans, 1985: 42).

2   Action learning as self-development

In contrast to action learning as changing the external world, the story can be read as one of individual *self-development*. In the antepenultimate paragraph, we are told that 'the problem was resolved'. Yet this is the denouement after the dramatic climax in the previous paragraph where David is faced by his actions as seen by other set members – and ultimately by himself. The drama is in the self-development, not in the 'real world', problem-solving.

This is action learning as romantic, humanistic and heroic, in contrast to the modernism, empiricism and positivism of the previous view. Here what matters is the *inner*, rather than the *outer*, in which the aim is to 'help people become more aware of their own processes and their own working models and suchlike' (John Hughes, in Blantern, 1992: 30). This view of action learning accords with the heroic narrative where, after many ups and downs, our hero emerges triumphant at last, the world a backcloth to individual exploits (Gergen, 1994: 197). The outer provides a healthy reality against which individuals, through the questioning of others and through self-questioning, can perturb themselves and reach a healthier self.

By the time he is reporting on his Belgian experiences, Revans is providing plenty of evidence for this interpretation of the action learning idea. Although the scientist/operational researcher is still strongly present in the most formal and 'scientific' account he ever gives of action learning (Revans, 1971: 28–70), Revans is now raising the profile of what has been a lesser theme and looking for 'a general theory of human action, for a science of praxeology' (ibid.: 58). Action learning rests fundamentally upon the discovery and clarification of individuals and of their values:

> To be obliged . . . to answer the question, 'And who do you think you are?' in return for the right to put it to others, is a useful exercise in self-recognition. In a climate of mutual support, it can bring to a man's notice any latent talents that, beneath his defensive disguises, had previously been unknown to him. (ibid.: 132)

and

> Thus it was that the single idea uncovered by the top managers in the First Inter-University Programme of Belgium to be of greatest interest to them was that of the value *system*. What were the standards of integrity against which all final judgements were made by those with whom they worked – including themselves? It was a notion bound to arise out of the set discussions in which the fellows stripped each other naked, an experience which led them to define the most valuable question they had learned as 'What is an honest man, and what need I do to become one?'. (Revans, 1983: 55; original emphasis)

This 'stripping naked', self-questioning and personal change is only achieved after great persistence by other set members. Frustration, conflict and expressions of anger are important in breaking through David's 'defensive disguises' and bringing him to see the self-deceptions which have so far made the many previous sensible suggestions for action unworkable. This self-development process is made critical to action learning in Revans's *Principle of Insufficient Mandate*: 'Those unable to change themselves cannot change what goes on around them' (ibid.: 55).

Action learning as changing the external world and self-development. Yet surely action learning is *both* changing the external world *and* self-development? The flow of consciousness, action and learning between the inner (person) and outer (organizational problem) forms a primary process for many action learning practitioners (e.g., Lessem, 1982: 11–12: Pedler,

Figure 14.1   *'If we want to keep going, one of them will have to go'*
(A. Roff, from M.J. Pedler, 1981: 13)

1996: 60). Yet, despite this, we may find ourselves pulled one way or the other (Figure 14.1).

Drawn from personal experience by an action learning set participant, this picture elicited the response from the visiting Revans: 'Doesn't this young woman know that she has to do both!' (Roff, 1981). In practice it is often difficult to hold the two priorities simultaneously. Individual participants or alliances in a set may urge one view rather than the other; sponsors, managers and the context itself may push one direction rather than another. Recently, in examining some action learning-based MSc dissertations, I noted a common bias to emphasizing learning and self-development at the cost of the external change projects.

We can even talk of the 'early Revans' (as scientist/operational researcher) and the 'later Revans' (as more humanistic and concerned with a general theory of action)[1] reflecting his different concerns at these different times.[2] In terms of a theory of action and learning, we work out of our values and motives at that time, choosing this over that, committing ourselves in the act. It is in this sense that the 'naive' problem-solver *or* the earnest self-developer willing to have a go may accomplish more than those who aim to do a bit of both.

3   Action learning as social construction

To action learning as changing the external world and as self-development, a third possibility can be added: action learning as *social construction*, as a process whereby we collectively construct new social meanings and realities. Here the set is a 'community of practice' of shared activity, shared knowledge and shared ways of knowing (Drath and Palus, 1994: 11). It is not the individual actors and their organizational problems which are important, but the collective relationship of the set, and by extension, the wider context.

David Docherty's action learning set met in 1976/77 and the account presented here is the original one (Pedler, 1983: 57–9). As I saw it then, this was a heroic tale of individuals tackling persistent organizational problems and growing wiser in the process. Now, I notice various embarrassments. Apart from the rather earnest teaching in the penultimate paragraph, there is the dated 'old-age pensioner' label; the invisibility of the (admittedly few) women in the company; and the absence of the work/home dimension – at 29, 'David Docherty' in fact had two failed marriages behind him and was under pressure from his third wife; I knew this at the time but did not include it.

This prompts the general question of what other silences are there in my story of 20 years ago? And what do these signify? For example, little is said about the group itself, the personal relationships between people or the internal thoughts of each person. To tell the story as it was – a persuasive account – much had to be left out, ignored, simply not seen; it now seems more than a bit uncritical. As Gilligan, Ward and Taylor remind us, an important meaning of 're-search' is to look again:

> The stark fact of the all-male research sample, accepted for years as representative by psychologists studying human development, in one sense speaks for itself. . . . The fact that these samples passed the scrutiny of peer review boards, and that studies of adolescence, moral development, and identity formation using all-male samples were repeatedly funded and widely published in professional journals indicates that the psychological research community needs to reexamine its claims to objectivity and dispassion. If the omission of half the human population was not seen, or not seen as significant, or not spoken about as a problem (by women or men) what other omissions are not being seen? (Gilligan et al., 1988: v)

To re-search action learning as social construction we need a new story. Here is a more recent story, told in a different way. A Health Service set of doctors and managers has been discussing with Donald, a consultant physician, the problem of stress in his unit:

> *Donald:*   Nothing we do seems to make it any better. . . . Our length of stay figures are still high, the turnover interval is less than a day, everyone rushes around like headless chickens. . . . Sickness and absence is way up and the

standard of care is just too low. It's a vicious circle. We have tried all sorts of actions, tackling admissions rates, cutting down electives and so on, but it seems to make a marginal difference at best.

Paul: It sounds awful. It reminds me of a story a friend told me when he was working on a newspaper. . . . Every evening at roughly the same time, just when they were due to print, there would be a crisis for an hour or so. It always happened whatever changes they made. Maybe it was the only way they could get the energy together?

Richard: You mean they caused the crisis themselves? Or perhaps there was something about the system they operated that brought it about . . . a systemic reaction formed from a chain of individual actions caused by someone speeding up and it knocking on everyone else?

Shamilla: Systems do have a tendency to persist, because they are dense webs of interconnection with many pathways. . . . You have to make changes to the whole – you can't just act on bits because there are consequences which you can't forsee and which may produce results which you don't want. For example, if one of your colleagues admits less patients, you might predict that this would ease some pressures yet might increase waiting lists and cause managers to put more pressure on the unit . . . but there are all sorts of other possible effects that you would not be able to predict.

Nicki: Donald, are you listening to this? You seem miles away?

Donald: [slowly and hesitantly] I . . . I haven't really given you the whole picture. . . . It's me too . . . I mean, I'm not functioning as well as I usually do. . . . Things at home are not so good and I don't seem to be able to concentrate. Things have run away from me.

[a silence . . . followed by various expressions of surprise, support and sympathy]
I wouldn't normally talk like this. . . . I've not seen the connection before between how I'm seeing things at home and how they are at work . . . it's chaotic . . . hopeless . . .

[more silence]

Lawrence: One thing I've noticed when I've been feeling overwhelmed is that I've assumed others feel the same way – the odds are that they don't. Who else is helping to manage the unit and how do they see it?

Shamilla: You need to get a grip of this, Donald, take a lead . . . that will make you feel stronger . . .

Paul: Hang on, Shamilla, that feeling may be just what is adding to the problem for Donald and the unit . . .

Perhaps the existence of different voices is the most obvious difference about this second story. Secondly, there is less of a beginning, a middle and an end – this is more of an ongoing conversation. Thirdly, although the people and their problems are there, this is not really a story of individual action on intractable organizational problems, nor even of individuals re-framing their issues (Braddick and Casey, 1981); it is about a collective search where everyone contributes their problems and insights to achieve a shared understanding.

A social constructionist perspective invites us to read the story in this way, and in so doing, to question our earlier interpretations. Departing from the strong Western tradition of the independent and self-contained self, what we see now are 'social processes realised on the site of the personal' (Gergen, 1994: 210). The postmodern critique of the notions of absolute truth or of the self' as origin, also highlights the key role of language in sense-making. For Blantern (1992), action learning is 'relational learning' where 'individuals participate in the communal conventions where language and constructs mutually arise and become intelligible through "movement" in relationships' (Blantern, 1992: 88). As in Bohm's notion of dialogue, 'the flow of consciousness (in action learning) is not "outer to inner", nor is it "inner to outer" but in "mutual arising" ' (quoted in Blantern, 1992: 82).

People in action learning sets often say things like 'I don't have anywhere else where I can say things like this' or 'there is a quality of listening here which I have not experienced before'. Braddick and Casey (1981) report how their chief executives were not particularly interested in taking action on their problems. At first they saw this as a failure, but they noticed how these managers greatly valued the set as a place where they could think differently. The case for action learning as social construction is that the value lies not in the action on organizational problems or the learning which might come from this, but in the relationship in the set (and perhaps outside if it can be exported) which allows for new thoughts to be thought, new words to be spoken, new perspectives, possibilities and worlds to be glimpsed.

Evidence for this social constructionist interpretation in Revans's writings is more problematic. Although his vision extends to learning in large organizational systems, learning is seen as coming about through the actions of individuals. It is, however, a social process and he frequently uses the word 'mutual', as in 'The assumptions of managerial mutual development' (Revans, 1982: 613–24) and consistently champions participation as in 'Worker participation as action learning' (ibid.: 546–65). Yet the emphasis is perhaps more on individuals trading ideas and perceptions than on the collective co-creation of new meaning. Again, while Blantern cites Revans's constructive view of language 'as long ago as 1945 Revans himself was alluding to the role of language in learning in the sense that to have a better working knowledge of language is to have more ways of seeing and understanding what is before us' (Blantern, 1992: 88), the sense is that he is referring to language as aiding individual self-expression rather than as the facilitator of 'mutual arising'.

A social constructionist interpretation of action learning extends Revans's work and frees us from the limitations of individual action and learning. Through this lens, action learning can add to our understanding of how to 'do' dialogue or action enquiry or whole systems learning or any of the approaches which seek to link individual with organizational learning.

Re-vision: Four Criticisms of Action Learning

Do these three interpretations of action learning change our view of the four criticisms of action learning outlined earlier? To take the third one first (Action learning is too centred on the individual as agent: as actor and learner), this is the one most likely to be made by social constructionists, the cult of the self and the individual being the focus of the dissent. This becomes a more important criticism because of its impact on the general theory of human action and for designers of action learning interventions in organizations.

However, for action learning as *self-development*, the third criticism is much less relevant, as is the fourth (Action learning sets can degenerate into support groups for individuals). From a self-development standpoint we might see here a necessary therapeutic process in which individuals can reconstruct themselves in a way which better allows them to go on. This fourth criticism is most likely to be made by those who see action learning as *changing the external world*, but a lack of engagement in wider exchange and dialogue might also be a concern for those who take a *social constructionist* perspective.

The second criticism (Action learning is atheoretical or 'anti-theory') is less easily dealt with. Revans's action learning is highly particularistic in this regard; like Kelly's (1970) 'man the scientist', action learners are forever testing their personal constructs against the world, seeking a better fit. However, those who seek to construct a 'critical action learning' argue that the learner's own theories and that of the other set members is usually an inadequate basis on which to critique their own practice. If we only admit the theory which is generated from our own experience of action, how are we to learn, for example, from the great teachers – as Revans himself acknowledges Aristotle and Sophocles, St Matthew and St James?

The issue here is one of power and its distribution. A *social constructionist* perspective makes questions of voice, power and participation a key part of the enquiry. Although even Revans is not against inputs of knowledge – '*We do NOT reject P*; it is the stuff of traditional instruction' – who decides what 'programmed knowledge' is relevant for whom? In the academic setting, relevant questions would include: How is the syllabus decided? Is it a common one for all learners? If so, why? What methods are used for transmitting the knowledge? What is the difference between knowledge passed from tutor to student and that exchanged between peers? and so on. On qualification programmes, there are even tougher questions concerning the power and authority structures of the awarding institutions.

This links with the first criticism (Despite its basis in questioning, action learning has become increasingly incorporated into unquestioned management agendas). Though Revans recognizes that much of what is learned in action learning will be about the 'micropolitics of the organization' and enumerates the blockages which top management may put in the path of the action learner – 'lack of interest, manipulative guidance, tactical procrastination, diagnostic flexibility, evasion and vacillation, directive autocracy, defensive rationalisation' (Revans, 1983: 43–8), he seems remarkably optimistic that these can be overcome.

To those grown more wary of the motives of senior managers, such a view appears heroic at best. Are managers so courageous that they will risk possible 'career limiting events' such as questioning the assumptions of their bosses? The view we now have of power, its ubiquitousness and omnipresence in social life, makes practising the simple versions of action learning far more problematic than they seem in Revans's writings.

Action learning as *social construction* may offer more hope in this respect, the creation of new visions, thoughts and language may be more subversive than simply attempting to change things. Revans has always pointed out the power of conspiracy and the set as a collective 'community of practice' can create new and influential shared realities. The 'set' may have to be larger than usually thought, linking with and extending to, for example, 'search conferencing' or 'whole systems change' methodologies, where 'public learning' can occur as senior managers face and act on questions and challenges from participating members (Weisbord, 1992).

Social Constructionism and the Learning Organization

This perspective on action learning seems to have more to offer than the alternatives, since it is most likely to call into question what Harrison (1995) calls 'the bias to action' in work organizations. Organizations find it easier to act than to learn. The task urgency which besets so many demands decisiveness and quick action, not thought and reflection. At the same time, leaders usually underestimate the extent of negative emotions in the organization – fear, anxiety, anger, resentment and betrayal – which inhibit and limit learning to low risk endeavours at best (Harrison, 1995: 399).

In this context, encouraging individuals to act on problems may make things worse:

> in complex and closely-coupled systems, local problem solving quickly creates many unintended effects in other parts of the system, some of which will become problems for the people involved in those parts. Those people, in turn, engage in more local problem solving, creating more problems elsewhere. (ibid: 403)

This is 'the illusion of taking charge' where 'proactiveness' is actually *re*activeness – 'true proactiveness comes from seeing how we contribute to our own problems' (Senge, 1991: 20–1). And seeing how we contribute to our own problems can only happen at a level beyond the individual actor – in terms of the web of interrelationships or of the whole system. The frenetic action that we are so committed to makes these acts of understanding unlikely. We are more than biased to action and problem-solving; we are addicted (Harrison, 1995: 403). The last thing needed here are actions to change situations which are only partially understood. As organizations become more complex and interconnected, the individual is faced with more and more of those situations. From the notion that action learning is about the individual motivation to act, to influence others, and to change the situation, a social constructionist view of action learning offers a new perspective where the individual participates in a shared process of meaning-making, helping to create frameworks of understanding within which to act. The community of practice is united by shared knowledge and shared ways of knowing which are created by people being involved with each other in action (Drath and Palus, 1994: 11).

In this view, the success of the action learning process is evaluated by the extent to which it facilitates the development of new meanings and under-standings in a given community of practice. The focus is not on individual action and learning – we assume that these happen in such communities – but on collective processes which have a greater capacity to transform the whole.

Conclusion

Action learning has been defined as an idea rather than a method, capable of taking many forms. Four criticisms have been considered and have been shown to have different force when weighed against three interpretations of the idea. Revans's writings show support for all three interpretations, although less so for the third, which reveals the problematic nature of the individual and of individual action in organizations seen as whole systems and as communities of practice. The social constructionist perspective builds on the action learning project and offers some ways forward centred on relationship, on novel social realities and on collective understanding, action and learning. In the light of the current interest in organizational learning, this perspective emerges as the one most likely to be generative of new possibilities and practices.

Notes

My thanks to Chris Blantern, Richard Thorpe, John Burgoyne and Michael Reynolds for their comments and suggestions on earlier drafts of this chapter.

1   Cf. 'early' and 'late' Marx, who in this view moved in the opposite direction from Revans – from the romantic, humanistic poet or dichter who developed the theory of alienation of the human spirit (species-being) to the later more mechanistic, dialectical materialist, who saw humaness as the product of economic and social forces. As in Revans's sketch, Marx did not lose his earlier concerns, but the individual becomes less important in his later preoccupa-tions with economics, politics and for theories as weapons which would change the world (Solomon, 1992: 94–6).

2   Blantern asserts 'the actual words "Action Learning" incidentally, begin to appear in Revans's writings in the late '60s and this is also the period from which he begins to endorse the need to explore aspects of "self" ' (1992: 21–2).

Annotated Bibliography

It is ironic, amusing or tragic, according to your taste, that none of the Founder's books are currently in print. Revans's main texts, *Developing Effective Managers* (1971), *Action Learning: New Techniques for Managers* (1980) and *The ABC of Action Learning* (1983) can now only be found in libraries, especially those at IFAL (International Foundation for Action Learning at 46 Carlton Road, London SW14 7RJ. Telephone and Fax: 0181–878 7358) and the Revans Centre at Salford University, Salford, UK. Depite this, action learning is very much in current usage, both by academics and practitioners. Not all of this usage seems very well informed. In a recent meeting, a very senior organizational development adviser said, 'I use

Action Learning all the time but I've never been in a set.' The current issue of *Management Learning* (27 (1), 1996) has three articles and an editorial which either feature or cite action learning. One of these (endorsed further in the editorial) interprets action learning as a way of teaching via simulation or 'experiential' methods, with no apparant awareness of its origins as an antidote to classroom expertise rooted in tackling problems in organizations and being accountable to clients, sponsors, and so on. Books in print include M. Pedler (1997) *Action Learning in Practice* (3rd edn). Aldershot: Gower, which is a survey of definitions, applications and practice from the UK and around the world. I. McGill and L. Beaty's (1992) *Action Learning: A Practitioner's Guide.* London: Kogan Page, is a lively text which lives up to its name and adds value to Revans's original thesis by bringing in ideas from groupwork and counselling. Krystyna Weinstein's (1995) *Action Learning: A Journey in Discovery and Development.* London: HarperCollins, is also very readable and notable for its contributions from participants. Finally, M. Pedler (1996) *Action Learning for Managers.* London: Lemos and Crawe, is an attempt to strip action learning down to the basics with short text, handout material and activities in response to 10 key questions.

References

Argyris, Chris and Schön, Donald (1978) *Organizational Learning: A Theory of Action Perspective.* Reading, MA: Addison-Wesley.

Beck, J.E. (1994) 'The new paradigm of management education', *Management Learning*, 25 (2): 231–47.

Blantern, Chris (1992) 'Inter-action learning: action learning as a "communal language" for negotiating reality', unpublished research dissertation for the Computer-mediated MA in Management Learning, University of Lancaster, Lancaster.

Braddick, W. and Casey, D. (1981) 'Developing the forgotten army – learning and the top manager', *Management Education and Development*, 12 (3): 169–80.

Drath, W.H. and Palus, C.J. (1994) *Making Common Sense: Leadership as Meaning-making in a Community of Practice.* Greensboro, NC: Center for Creative Leadership.

Gergen, K. (1994) *Realities and Relationships: Soundings in Social Construction.* London: Harvard University Press.

Gilligan, C., Ward, J.V. and Taylor, J.M. (eds) (1988) *Mapping the Moral Domain: A Contribution of Women's Thinking to Psychological Theory and Education.* Cambridge, MA: Harvard University Press.

Harrison, Roger (1995) *The Collected Papers of Roger Harrison.* Maidenhead: McGraw-Hill.

Inglis, S. (1994) *Action Learning.* Aldershot: Gower.

Kelly, G.A. (1970) 'A brief introduction to personal construct theory', in D. Bannister (ed.), *Perspectives in Personal Construct Theory.* New York: Academic Press. pp. 7–31.

Lessem, Ronnie (1982) 'A biography of action learning', in R.W. Revans (ed.), *The Origins and Growth of Action Learning.* Bromley: Chartwell-Bratt. pp. 4–17.

McLaughlin, H. and Thorpe, R. (1993) 'Action learning – a paradigm in emergence: the problems facing a challenge to traditional management education and development', *British Journal of Management*, 4 (1): 19–27.

Morgan, Gareth (1993) *Imaginization: The Art of Creative Management.* London: Sage.

Morgan, G. and Ramirez, R. (1984) 'Action learning: a holographic metaphor for guiding social change', *Human Relations*, 37: 1–28.

Newbould, D.V. (1982) 'Foreword', in R.W. Revans (ed.), *The Origins and Growth of Action Learning.* Bromley: Chartwell-Bratt. pp. vi.

Pascale, R.T. (1990) *Managing on the Edge.* Harmondsworth: Penguin.

Pedler, M.J. (1983) *Action Learning in Practice.* Aldershot: Gower.

Pedler, M.J. (ed.) (1991) *Action Learning in Practice* (2nd edn). Aldershot: Gower.

Pedler, M.J. (1996) *Action Learning for Managers.* London: Lemos and Crawe.

Pedler, M.J., Burgoyne, J.G. and Boydell, T.H. (1991) *The Learning Company: A Strategy for Sustainable Development*. Maidenhead: McGraw-Hill.

Revans, R.W. (1971) *Developing Effective Managers*. New York: Praeger.

Revans, R.W. (1980) *Action Learning: New Techniques for Managers*. London: Blond and Briggs.

Revans, R.W. (1982) *The Origins and Growth of Action Learning*. Bromley: Chartwell-Bratt.

Revans, R.W. (1983) *The ABC of Action Learning*. Bromley: Chartwell-Bratt.

Revans, R.W. (1985) *Confirming Cases*. Manchester: RALI (Revans Action Learning International).

Revans, R.W. (1991) 'Action Learning: its origins and nature', in M.J. Pedler (ed.), *Action Learning in Practice* (2nd edn). Aldershot: Gower. pp. 3–16.

Roff, A. (1981) in M.J. Pedler (ed.), *The Diffusion of Action Learning*. Occasional Paper No. 2. Sheffield: Department of Management Studies, Sheffield City Polytechnic. p. 13.

Senge, P.M. (1990) *The Fifth Discipline: The Art and Practice of the Learning Organization*. New York: Doubleday.

Solomon, R.C. (1992) *Ethics and Excellence: Cooperation and Integrity in Business*. Oxford: Oxford University Press.

Weinstein, K. (1995) *Action Learning: A Journey in Discovery and Development*. London: HarperCollins.

Weisbord, M.R. (1992) *Discovering Common Ground*. San Francisco: Berrett Koehler.

Willmott, H. (1994) 'Management education: provocations to a debate', *Management Learning*, 25 (1): 105–36.

15

The Internationalization of Management Learning: Towards a Radical Perspective

Anna Lorbiecki

There is a widespread view that the growth of multinationals and the upward trend in mergers, acquisitions and joint ventures will inevitably make management more international and, therefore, it will be less easy, as Jackson noted, 'to view management as a parochial activity, based in one country, with no contact with the wider international community' (1995: xi). Such a view has, however, laid a heavy hand on business schools and companies as it has forced them to review their practices and seek ways of 'internationalizing' their management education and development provision. As a result of these reviews, emphasis has been placed mainly on the knowledge, skills and competencies required for international management (see, e.g., Laurent, 1983; Barham and Wills, 1992) or on opportunities for increased international exposure, such as international assignments or study periods abroad (see, e.g., Cova et al., 1993), which give management learners direct experience of what it is like to live, work and learn with people from different countries.

But to my mind this is only part of the picture: learning to become more effective in an international arena also involves understanding the broader, and deeper, political and social processes at work in the way in which international management is talked about, depicted and represented. I argue that the manner in which international management is perceived and discussed reflects deeply embedded assumptions on the nature of truth, people and knowledge. In the first part of this chapter, five perspectives on international management are reviewed and evaluated to demonstrate how differing assumptions on the extent to which people are believed to be 'different', influence international management theory and practice. Four of these perspectives have been drawn from Calas's (1992) classification of management studies on other cultures – universalistic, comparative, relativistic and post-structural/ethnographic. I then extend this range by adding a fifth perspective, labelled radical, which includes (a) critical enquiry, (b) a moral basis for action, and (c) multicentres of discourses.

In the second part of this chapter, I apply this radical perspective to two major issues of international management learning: first, the conceptual issue of overcoming the liability of foreignness, and secondly, the practical issue of educating and developing international managers. In both cases, a radical perspective shows how the traditional rhetoric of international management learning obscures asymmetries of power which may create or perpetuate a disturbing divide between privileged groups of international managers and the rest of the remaining, local workforce, wherever they may be.

Five Perspectives on International Management

Within Western management discourse there is considerable debate on whether international management is merely an extension of domestic management, or whether it is something qualitatively different. As Ralston, Gustafon, Cheung and Terpestra (1993) noted, this debate has become polarized between two positions, convergence and divergence. The convergence position proposes that managers in industrialized nations will embrace the attitudes and behaviours common to managers in other industrialized nations despite cultural differences; that capitalism, technology, structure and the global orientation of many firms will push managers in the direction of adopting a 'one best way' approach to the management of organizations worldwide; that cross-cultural management will ultimately be unnecessary; and that standard management theory does apply and can be transferred to any cultural group. In contrast, the divergence position suggests that for whatever reasons (which might be differing stages of economic development, different systems of government, climactic variations, issues of sovereignty or the extent to which a country has been subject to invasion) there are distinct pockets of humanity where individuals retain diverse, culturally based values, despite any economic and social similarities between nations, which posit the need for differentiated management theory and knowledge.

The above convergence/divergence debate has, however, been reinterpreted and politicized by Calas (1992) who regarded it not so much as an argument on whether standard or diverse theory should be used in international management, but rather on whether the world would be ultimately more similar or dissimilar to Western societies. Under her interpretation, the convergence hypothesis should be regarded instead as an assimilation view of ethnic populations within dominant Western European/Anglo-US populations, with the latter 'worlding the world' (Spivak, quoted in Harasym, 1990) according to their power and influence; and the divergence hypothesis equivalent to a more pluralistic view of ethnic populations, where asymmetrical power relationships between races are identified and contested. Calas substantiated her viewpoint by presenting a matrix based on four categorizations of management studies on other cultures and three modes of rhetorical arguments often used to signify, in Western writings, how 'other people in the world are "different"' (Calas, 1992: 205). Her method of classifying management perspectives – universalistic, comparative, relativistic and post-structural/ethnographic – was determined by the intensity with which she believed any particular study assumed that theory developed in the USA or Western Europe could be transferred to other social/cultural groups. She then placed her classification on to the convergence/divergence continuum (as shown in Table 15.1 below) with a universalistic perspective presenting convergence, a post-structural/ ethnographic perspective assuming divergence, and comparative and relativistic perspectives sharing the middle ground some way between the two views. Calas then analysed the heuristic values of three rhetorical modes – Time, Race and Voice – noting how these changed under each perspective, thus giving rise to different beliefs in the way in which people are regarded, and she summarized how these beliefs influenced resulting knowledge.

Table 15.1   *Calas's framework for rhetorical analysis: summary of arguments*

Research category:	Epistemological base Convergence - Divergence			
	Universalistic	Comparative	Relativistic	Post-structural ethnographic
Rhetorical arguments				
Time	They are behind.	Have they progressed?	Difference should not impede arriving together at the same communication plane.	Time/space used as arbitrary categories: Who is constructing them?
Race	They are inferior.	Eliminate differences once an assessment of similarities indicates such a possibility.	Differences should not create problems as long as they are understood.	Race as the mark of difference and the visible sign to end comparison.
Voice	They cannot represent themselves.	Evaluation of other meanings to assess their progress.	To come to the same plane it is necessary to translate different meanings.	Theorizing? Whose theorizing? For what purposes?
	Convergence hypothesis.	Convergence hypothesis implied.	Divergence hypothesis.	
	One best way.	Contingency views.	Other theories must be developed.	Questions the notion of theory and research as knowledge.
Resulting knowledge	Developed people do knowledge.	Developed people do knowledge. Others will eventually.	Attempts to do 'other's knowledges' result in comparative strategies.	Focus on the construction of knowledge as a core problem.

Each of her four perspectives will now be applied to dominant thinking about international management theory and practice at particular points in time in order to identity different approaches to international management learning.

A universalistic perspective on international management

Universalistic principles are based on two main assumptions: that it is possible to have direct knowledge of reality; and science and reason should be used to find the one, ultimate 'truth' for all. Within a modernist interpretation these assumptions led to the belief that natural and social evils should be identified and conquered, if humanity was to be liberated from ignorance. Calas (1992) identified three rhetorical modes in this interpretation: *time* is used to indicate 'progress' and the distinction between being 'developed' or 'underdeveloped'; *race* (or rather nationality or ethnicity as the term is rarely invoked) as the essential or biological determinant of the capacity for rational thought; and *voice* is used as the idea of 'who speaks the truth here' (Calas, 1992: 208). The use of these discursive modes of argumentation in a modern universalistic perspective results in the premise that only 'developed' people can produce useful knowledge, that 'underdeveloped' people are inferior and incapable, therefore, of representing themselves. This premise of natural superiority or inferiority was reflected in anthropological and social discourses of the 1900s when the term 'culture' was closely associated with socially elite concepts such as refinement of the mind, or tastes and manners based on a superior education and upbringing. As Heller (1985) points out, this definition of culture was also identified with the intellectual side of civilization, and its German spelling *kultur* was used extensively in Europe before the Second World War to support arguments on the social and racial superiority of some groups over others.

When this assumption of natural superiority or inferiority was placed within a modern managerial context, it gave rise to a belief that universally correct managerial approaches existed, that there was 'one best way to manage', and that only developed or educated people were capable of constructing knowledge. The view that only 'developed' races could produce valuable knowledge was confirmed by low adult literacy rates in 'underdeveloped' races and their lack of managerial texts. Since the vast majority of 'scientific management' theories evolved at the same time as cultural discourses on the racial superiority of Western populations, it is, I believe, hard to dispute that early management texts were unaffected, either consciously or subconsciously, by the social arguments in public circulation at that time. Although, as Boyacigiller and Adler (1991) point out, these scientific managerial texts were originally developed by North American academics for the consumption of the US domestic market, they were, due to the USA's dominance in the supply of management education across the world, highly influential on the way in which management was originally conceived and implemented.

Western hegemony in the supply of management education led to a prevailing belief that rationalistic and scientific models of management were universally valid irrespective of the cultural context in which they were applied. This universalistic belief was not, however, seriously questioned until the 1960s when the economic positions of the USA and other European countries in the world economy were repeatedly challenged by inroads into their key domestic markets, such as electronics and automobiles. These inroads, led initially by the Japanese but followed later by China and the 'Four Asian Tigers', forced Western nations to change their economic strategies and learn to compete with countries and trading groups that were at least as successful as those countries which saw themselves as having invented management.

A comparative perspective on international management

Although a comparative perspective on international management still contains the assumption that there is one ultimate 'truth', it contains the philosophical belief that human beings are limited to knowing only what they are historically or culturally ready to know. These assumptions displace prior beliefs in natural laws of superiority or inferiority and replace them with a belief in the principle of social development as signified by changes in the three modes of argumentation. Under a comparative perspective, *time* is used typologically to mark intervals between socioculturally meaningful events (e.g., feudalism, industrialization, postmodernism); *race* is used to separate the more advanced from the less advanced; and *voice* is used as an authoritative device to judge whether what 'the others say' should be afforded credence. The use of these discursive modes in a comparative perspective gave rise to the belief that all humanity could share in the creation of valuable knowledge once it had demonstrated to already advanced races that it too had advanced.

The principle of social development and advanced nation status was epitomized in the Western world's reaction to their declining economies, as characterized by its new-found interest in learning from other countries on how 'they managed over there'. The recognition and acceptance by some that other nations had also advanced was, however, restricted to affluent nations and excluded an examination of management practices in less affluent ones. Early academic responses to the new threat of competition included comparative studies on (principally) US and Japanese management practices to see whether there were lessons to be learnt from the Japanese. These studies were followed by the publication of several best-sellers (Ouchi, 1981; Pascale and Athos, 1981, for example), which attempted to evaluate and translate Japanese management and human resources management (HRM) practices – such as consensual decision-making and high job security – into the American context. These evaluations spawned a spate of domestically focused literature which claimed that many of the apparently superior Japanese practices were already present (again a comparative approach) in the most successful US companies such as Digital, IBM, McDonald's and General Motors. The success of these companies was perceived to be due to highly supportive attitudes towards employees, attention to the management of corporate culture and the creation of a strong, cohesive corporate identity rather than on procedural controls (Deal and Kennedy, 1982; Peters and Waterman, 1982).

A *relativistic perspective on international management*

But over the following years, several factors helped to refocus attention on the knowledge required for international management. Although comparative studies had drawn attention to the importance of considering cultural issues in both national and international management theory and practice, many of the supposedly excellent US companies collapsed. The continued increase in the economic strength of Japan and the emergence of Asian countries, such as India, as significant players in their own right provoked concern over the superficiality of many of the previous studies on national and international modes of management. At this point a relativistic perspective on international management emerged, reflecting more humanistic principles which contained a greater tolerance of the possibility that different beliefs and values could give rise to equally valid, if different, notions of 'truth'. Here rhetorical arguments were used to support pluralistic frames of reference with *time* used contemporaneously to emphasize that 'we all' occupy the same space and can, therefore, speak to one another, even though different; *race* used to categorize differences in national values and beliefs, and *voice* used invitingly to speak to 'the other' which also needed to be listened to.

Hofstede's (1980) work on cultural differences is perhaps the best-known example of a relativistic perspective on international management. His original study proposed a four-part typology of cultural difference and was used by him to demonstrate why US management theories do not apply abroad. Hofstede's model proposes four key dimensions of culture: individualism *versus* collectivism; power distance; masculinity *versus* feminism; and uncertainty avoidance. To this list he has more recently added the idea of 'Confucian dynamism', which is essentially a matter of whether people and businesses take a long or a short view of relationships and investments (dynamism being the former). Hofstede's research then classifies countries in the world on each of these dimensions, and from this it is possible to see how far any one country diverges from another. Other researchers have proposed different classification schema: particularistic *versus* universalistic (Hall, 1995); instrumental *versus* social view of business (Laurent, 1983); and Hampden-Turner and Trompenaars (1993) describe seven different cultures of capitalism.

A relativistic perspective on international management is, however, quite disturbing because its definition of culture depends on the assumption of 'shared' values and beliefs which collude, from a post-structural/ ethnographic perspective discussed below, with dominant prejudices and privileged knowledge. If, for example, Hofstede's analysis of high masculine countries was used in selecting managers for international assignments, women could be excluded from working in Japan or South America.

A post-structural/ethnographic perspective on international management

A post-structural/ethnographic perspective on international management argues, however, that the search for 'truth' is futile on the basis that there are many truths, none of which can be either substantiated or denied. Within this perspective, *time* is to be regarded as an arbitrary category unrelated to any temporal distance, therefore emptying terms such as 'developed' and 'underdeveloped' of their prior meaning; *race* is used as 'a visible sign of contestation' (Calas, 1992: 217) against the use of racial stereotypes frequently found within international management discourses; and *voice* is used paradoxically to question its own ability to construct knowledge.

Relativistic models of culture are severely criticized on the grounds that the concept of culture is used as a 'root' metaphor to attribute national differences in management and culture to racial differences in shared values and beliefs. The notion of shared values and beliefs – an assumption underpinning many conventional interpretations of culture – such as Hofstede's, is also problematic from a post-structuralist/ethnographic perspective. For example, Barth (1989) provides a critique of relativistic models by arguing that views of what are normally called 'culture' often fall into the trap of misconstruing description for explanation. Culture, he argues, is not a hidden code to be deciphered, but rather a relatively unstable product of the way people create meaning. Hence, cultural meanings are not the same for all members of populations: they depend on gender, race and place and the positions of individual actors in society, and their distinctive experiences, knowledge and orientations. This post-structural/ethnographic perspective questions the validity of the popular image of the 'wholeness' and 'sharedness' of values and beliefs, in what is commonly called culture, and in doing so contests the efficacy of the convergence/divergence debate itself since both positions within that debate use a popular image of culture to support their arguments.

Barth, however, may be accused of presenting a Western interpretation of the existing state of social order as other societies may regard themselves as less fragmented in their class divisions, racial conflicts and alienation. On the other hand, his argument may still be valid as disruptive social order does appears to be a world-wide phenomenon with civil unrest and racial/ethnic tensions and conflicts arising in many locations, such as in Africa and in the Middle East, as well as in regions of the USA and Europe.

Towards a radical perspective on international management

The four perspectives (universalistic, comparative, relativistic and post-structural/ethnographic) reviewed above have, as indicated in my introduction, been drawn from Calas's (1992) classification of management studies on other cultures. I now extend her classification by adding a fifth perspective, labelled radical, which critiques the post-structural/ethnographic view. This radical perspective has been influenced by feminist writings (e.g.,

Hubbard and Randall, 1988; Star, 1991; Antal and Izraeli, 1994; and Ferguson, 1996) and the post-colonial debate (e.g., Spivak, 1993; Said, 1995; and Bhabha, 1996) and argues that cognitive acceptance of the existence of multiple truths and the questioning of socially constructed categories does not provide escape from the legacy of these pre-determined categories. As Ferguson points out, 'the opening up of subjugated knowledges to speak' leaves us so pluralistic, fragmented and contextualized that we are left without a generalizable base of solidarity politics or guidance on 'what principles of justice to use to redress unequal distribution of power, property and resources' (Ferguson, 1996: 577).

A radical perspective, therefore, proposes: (a) *a critical stance on all societies* from the premise that they all contain elites and underclasses, and categories of person which privilege the identity and voices of some, while simultaneously disadvantaging and surpressing the identity and voices of others; (b) *a moral basis for action* which includes guidelines on social justice as a means of overthrowing existing systems of exploitation, dependency and dominance; and (c) *multicentres of discourses* which generate inclusive, rather than exclusive, agendas.

In advocating this radical perspective I am aware, however, that I could be accused of promoting, in a universalistic way, the Western liberal ideology which idealizes the virtues of justice, tolerance and equal respect (Bhabha, 1996). As I do not see any escape from this paradox at the moment, I now adopt a pragmatic approach to see whether a radical perspective can be used to shed light on typical international management learning issues. In the second part of this chapter I therefore apply a radical perspective to two major issues: first, the conceptual issue of overcoming the liability of foreignness, and secondly, the practical issue of educating and developing international managers.

Applying a Radical Perspective to International Management Learning

Discussions on international management often present a view that the intensification of competition between nations and firms, reductions in border tariffs and advances in telecommunications and information technology have been major agents in its expansion. Driven by the desire for competitive advantage and sustained business performance, organizations have conducted a strategic search for new markets and business opportunities which has led them further and further away from their domestic bases. Mergers, acquisitions, joint ventures and strategic alliances have emerged as favoured vehicles for international expansion because they provide access to the wider range of resources, knowledge, skills and expertise required for managing internationally. The expansion of management into an international arena is accompanied, however, by a new set of management learning problems – how to manage the liability of foreignness which arises from the increased size, scope and complexity of doing business within and across nations. The way in which companies, business schools and individuals tackle these problems will, as discussed above, differ according to the perspective adopted. A radical perspective will now be used to demonstrate how the strategies used to (1) overcome the liability of foreignness and (2) develop international managers, often ignore asymmetrical power differentials between nations, racial groups and men and women, thereby perpetuating inequalities in the international labour market.

Learning to overcome the liability of foreignness

A major preoccupation for transnational organizations is the identification of solutions to overcome what Zaheer (1995) calls the 'liability of foreignness'. When managing internationally, emotional and economic costs are incurred from the increased size of the firm; from the need for co-ordination across a wider geographical distance; from the unfamiliarity of the environment; and from economic, political and social differences. A popular managerial solution to overcoming the liability of foreignness is for international firms and their managers to adopt the admonition to 'think globally and act locally'. This admonition provides a direct link to the convergence/divergence debate because it attempts to incorporate the two polarized dimensions of that debate within a single frame of reference. Achievement of global thought and local action is problematic in practice because the modern, universalistic principles often assumed in globalization are diametrically opposed to the post-structural/ethnographic concepts required to encourage local action and plural meanings.

The tension arising from attempts to manage simultaneously the duality of globalized thinking and localized activities is highlighted in Sjögren and Janson's analysis (1994) of the strategies which companies and individuals use to overcome the liability of foreignness. Those authors contend that these strategies can be split into two broad types. The first type of strategy is based on *integration* which attempts to reduce the liability of foreignness by standardizing structures, systems and processes across the organization as a means of suppressing deviation from centralized, global ambitions. The main implications for international management learning, under this scenario, is to select individuals who adhere to centralized control and then socialize them by instilling a transnational corporate culture to create a unified workforce all moving towards common goals, beliefs and values, regardless of their place of work. The second type of strategy is based on *differentiation* and attempts to reduce the liability of foreignness by accepting variations in managerial activity which are deemed to be essential to preserving local identity, interests and responsiveness. Under this scenario, the implications for management learning are quite different in that the emphasis is on recruiting a diverse workforce and on creating development processes which help individuals to learn to manage the differences in values and beliefs arising from such diversity.

The 'think global and act local' maxim is, however, problematic from a radical perspective. One such problem arises in critiquing the terms 'global' and 'local' which Latour (1993) maintains are neither empirically observable nor theoretically feasible. As that author puts it, the words 'global' and 'local' offer points of view on networks that by nature are neither global nor local but 'more or less long or more or less connected' (Latour, 1993: 122). The conventional view, however, is to equate the terms global and local with a sense of place, with things global placeless or omnipresent and things local associated with a specific place. The term 'local' is further confused, erroneously and nostalgically, with 'community', thereby giving rise to the false expectation that people who live in proximity to one another are somehow bound together by the traditions of that neighbourhood, or city, or nation state and are, therefore, bound to share a similar mentality. The view that particular customs or thinking exist in a place is fostered, as Massey (1994: 112) noted, by idealized images produced by the tourist industry and the rapidly growing 'heritage industry' which romantically freeze moments of the past of the place in time ('the real Lancashire') and in doing so present a story of the 'true' nature of a place in contradiction to the actual comings and goings of industry and migration. These idealized images of bounded localized identities can also be found in management texts which claim that it is possible to categorize all inhabitants of a particular place as 'truly' Japanese, or British, or even European.

Neighbourhoods, cities and nation states are, as Bammer explains, much more fragmented in their social groupings and multi-racial composition than mythical images would have us believe. 'The separation of people from their native culture either through physical dislocation (as refugees, immigrants, migrants, exiles or expatriates) or the colonising influence of a foreign culture – what I am calling here displacement – is one of the most formative experiences of our century' (Bammer, 1994: xi). The physical and emotional upheaval associated with dislocation and displacement has had far-reaching consequences: it has not only dispersed cultural identities from their place of origin, but also reshaped them as they come into contact with indigenous identities, causing the latter also to be redefined. This nomadic and fluctuating ground of changing identities, therefore, gives an alternative rendering of place and community far different from the unchanging, historical and monotypical view of a local that is fixed in time and space.

Processes of dislocation and displacement have shifted the locus of community interests, which rely on feelings of commonality, of shared visions and commitments, from their traditional, rooted origins and reformed them into communities of interest which are independent of place. If, as has been argued, the fixed nature of the local is an illusion, then the unfixed nature of the global is one too. And in the case of overcoming the liability of foreignness, I would argue that global thinking is more to do with the communal, strategic interests of a select group of powerful players, usually senior managers or parent company policy-makers, than the collective (as opposed to communal) interests of a dispersed and fragmented workforce.

This being the case, the 'think globally and act locally' argument can be reinterpreted as a power struggle between those who are inside the central decision-making process and those who are outside of, or peripheral to it. An integrative strategy, with its emphasis on standardization and homogenization is, therefore, a repetition of a modern universalistic perspective as managing internationally involves the assimilation of less powerful systems, processes and voices into a dominant, colonizing view. Although a differentiation strategy holds more promise, in that diversity appears to accepted, usage of conventional models of culture, rather than complex concepts of place, race gender and position identified by a post-structural/ethnographic perspective, could generate further inequalities in the international labour market, as will be explained in the next section.

Developing international managers

In practice, efforts to educate and develop international managers are conducted through two main channels: business schools which provide formal provision, and companies through career and management development strategies. As explained below, both forms of provision become problematic from a radical perspective. In the case of business schools I concentrate on the use of language and power relations; and in the case of companies I focus on gender and race.

Business schools.   Business schools are influential catalysts in the dissemination of knowledge because they can have a major influence on what future or practising managers learn, and on how they think, about international management. In recent years they have responded to demands from individuals and companies to provide a stronger international orientation (Porter and McKibbin, 1988; Calori and De Woot, 1994). Business schools have focused their efforts on three factors: curriculum, as this provides the knowledge content for international management; composition of faculty and students in terms of ethnic origin and previous exposure to international management; and the choice of teaching methods and recruitment and assessment procedures which best serve international management. Raimond and Halliburton (1995) used two of these factors, curriculum and the composition of faculty and students, to develop a four-stage model of the internationalization of business schools in Europe. Their model is summarized in Table 15.2.

A number of interesting insights can, however, be deduced from this four-stage schema when it is analysed from a radical perspective. Although Raimond and Halliburton term the first stage as 'strictly national' when 'the school, faculty and programmes are predominantly national, and *proud of it*' (1995: 234; my emphasis), this can also be interpreted as a colonial phase in management education when 'less developed' foreign nationals come to learn from 'developed' teachers. Since, according to these authors, few business schools in Europe have reached beyond Stage 2 of their schema, the

Table 15.2 *Stages in the internationalization of business schools in*
Europe (after Raimond and Halliburton, 1995)

Stage	Curriculum	Faculty and students
1 Strictly national/ colonial	Teaching material focuses on context and institutions of local country; teaching methods conform to local norms.	Mainly local nationals with a few foreign students who are there to learn about that country's local methods.
2 Beginning to Europeanize	Course content still mainly national, but optional language courses added, and more case studies from other countries are introduced.	Student intake and faculty mainly national. Links established with foreign institutions and some exchanges take place.
3 European co-operation	Content is deliberately multinational and multicultural. Foreign countries studied in depth, and comparative courses established.	Course based in one country but most students exchange with other foreign students. Hence student body more international. Faculty also do some teaching abroad.
4 Multinational business school	School may have bases in several countries or be part of closely linked network. Teaching material is all multicultural. Two or more languages are mandatory, and used in core management courses.	Faculty chosen for its experience of working in two or more countries. Students will do equal parts of their course in two or more countries.

majority are presumably at a 'national/colonial' or 'beginning to Europeanize' stage where the curriculum and teaching methods are geared primarily to the needs of domestic management with little attention being paid to international management.

Attempts to 'internationalize' courses can, however, backfire as Reiss and Ones's (1995) study of the effect of such courses on undergraduate and postgraduate students at a US business school illustrates. Although these courses attempted to reduce ethnocentricity by including substantial information about the global environment and the significance of cultural differences in a business context, these researchers were surprised (even dismayed) to find that the ethnocentric attitudes of students who took these courses significantly *increased* over the period of the course. Furthermore, this increase was most prominent among students taught by American faculty, whereas those taught by 'international' faculty neither increased nor decreased. While Reiss and Ones concluded that course content might be the cause of the increase in ethnocentrism, they suggested that it had to be examined in combination with teaching style and methods and increasing students' exposure to cross-cultural living.

From a radical perspective, however, the issues raised by Reiss and Ones go deeper than the choice of course content or teaching methods. One view is that deeply embedded ethnocentric assumptions can only be addressed if attention is paid to the subtle use of language commonly used in daily conversations or traditional international/managerial texts. As Cox (1994) argues, language privileges the identities of some members of society, while disadvantaging others, as exemplified by discriminatory discourses which distinguish between foreign, overseas and home students/faculty, and in classifications which afford superior status to advanced/first-world nations and inferior status to underdeveloped/developing/third-world countries. Elias and Scotson point out that 'attaching the label of "lower human value" (ignorant, underdeveloped, lack of progress) to another human group is one of the weapons used in a power struggle by superior [*sic*] groups as a means of maintaining their social superiority' (Elias and Scotson, 1994: xxi). Furthermore, when differences in status are attributed to differences in age, gender, race or occupation, then the use of these categories of person can themselves be considered to be symptomatic of ideological avoidance action. By using them one singles out what is peripheral to these relationships (e.g., differences in age, skin colour, gender, occupation) and turns the eye away from what is central (differences in power ratios) and the exclusion of a power-inferior group from positions with a higher power potential.

In the final section of this chapter I argue that although an international identity is fast becoming a source of superior status for managers, the social and political forces used to develop international managers strengthens or perpetuates existing power differentials on the grounds of gender or race.

Companies.   When thinking about how to develop international managers, companies concentrate on two broad strategies: the management of careers, and on training and development tactics. Although these strategies may be executed separately, their underlying processes are inexorably linked as both include evaluative judgements on who will be selected or developed for privileged, international management status.

In many companies a proven track record of international assignments has become a pre-condition for senior management progression. Antal and Izaeli (1994) have noted, however, that when it comes to being chosen for international assignments or international careers, women face a double set of hurdles. The first set of hurdles relates to entry into management itself, where women face traditional obstacles: the persistent stereotype which associates management with being male; or the myth that management is a full-time job which obligates total dedication and commitment. Although this first set of obstacles has gradually been eroded by women's entry in the labour market over the last two decades, when it comes to international management they now face a second set of hurdles which appears to be closely linked with the concept of risk. Women are perceived to be personally at risk from sexual harassment, in some countries, and they are also being regarded as a commercial risk due to the widespread belief that some societies consider it inappropriate to do business with a women. There is a fear that a female representative might be regarded as an inferior substitute to the man expected and, therefore, her presence could be interpreted as a lack of commitment, on the part of her organization, to the business in hand, which could jeopardize current negotiations and future relations. This risk factor, combined with the lack of clarity on what international managers should do, how they should behave, and the attributes and competencies required, has led to what Antal and Izraeli (1994) call a 'cloning' process in which managers select others most similar to themselves – namely men – in an attempt, albeit subconsciously, to ensure trustworthiness and predictability. The expansion of management into an international arena can, therefore, be regarded as an additional obstruction to women's changes in improving their careers which, if not surmounted, relegates them to a 'domestic' (pun intended) role with an inferior organizational status.

The processes of exclusion which disadvantage women from positions with a higher power potential has not, however, gone unnoticed. For example, during a roundtable discussion on the values, capabilities and leadership required for the year 2010, one CEO commented on the senselessness of 'eight white guys at the top of the organization making decisions for 400,000 people around the world' (*Sloan Management Review*, 1995: 16). Frustration in the narrow, often parochial thinking, of men-only perspectives has given rise to, as remarked on by Dodds (1995), a strategic interest in 'managing diversity' as a releasing mechanism for desperately needed talents which have been suppressed by mono-cultural organizations who label and stereotype on the basis of gender and race. From a radical perspective, however, great care has to be taken in the way in which we think and talk about diversity and Cox (1994) suggests consideration of the following three points:

1 Diversity is a description of the total workforce and not a name for minority groups.
2 Diversity must be distinguished from related concepts such as affirmative action and race research while at the same time preserving the legitimacy of these topics.
3 Diversity is best examined on multiple levels of analysis which include group/intergroup and organizational levels, as well as at the individual level where diversity is normally studied and stops.

Cox's emphasis on a multilateral basis of analysis and the inclusion of all members of the workforce provides a radical approach to managing diversity because it shifts the locus of enquiry. The conventional approach has been to focus on dominant groups as the normative point of reference and to determine the extent to which oppressed groups deviate from their norm. A radical approach, however, avoids the temptation towards comparison by providing a platform for each group to express its own values and beliefs, thereby generating discussion not only on the ways in which some members of society are disadvantaged by their identity, but also how others are advantaged and privileged by theirs.

Conclusion and a Word of Warning

In this chapter I have attempted to demonstrate how extremely powerful networks of business schools, authors, consultants and companies are able to propogate influential views on international management. Views on managing internationally are dominated either by a *universalistic* perspective which assumes that standard systems and procedures of management are valid irrespective of the cultural context in which they are applied, or by a *relativistic* perspective which emphasizes cultural context as the most significant factor. From a critical perspective both of these views are problematic because they contain overarching assumptions and dimensions which are conditioned by Western rationalistic thinking. Relativist attempts to overcome ethnocentricity in universalistic thinking at best only provide crude simplifications of cultural values which are constantly changing and being contested; at their worst, they support national stereotyping and justify discriminatory practices by and within business schools and companies.

The development of a radical perspective on international management learning will, I hope, lead to the critical inspection of power structures which discriminate on the grounds of race and gender. Taking part in that enquiry will not, however, be easy as it involves identifying ourselves with those power structures and taking responsibility for how they behave. If we try to dis-identify ourselves at work and in politics by declaring ourselves outsiders, we jeopardize our effectiveness and eliminate ourselves from the evaluative decision-making processes that we seek to challenge. The role, therefore, of a radical management learner will be complex and ambiguous, and one in which we face, as Hubbard and Randall experienced, 'the tension of being inside and outside at the same time and all times, and not just in the same situation, but in all situations' (1988: 19).

Annotated Bibliography

Angelika Bammer (ed.) (1994) *Displacements*. Bloomington, IN: Indiana University Press, is a delightful book which includes moving accounts of the personal effect of physical dislocation from one's native culture and the consequences of colonizing imposition by a foreign culture. Marta Calas (1992) 'An other silent voice? Representing "Hispanic Woman" in organizational texts', in Albert J. Mills and Peta Tancred (eds), *Gendering Organizational Analysis*. London: Sage, pp. 201–21, is the original source of inspiration which helped me to develop the five perspectives on international management. Ann Ferguson (1996) 'Bridge identity politics: an integrative feminist ethics of international development', *Organization*, 3 (4): 571–87, presents a necessary antidote to the neo-imperialist relationships which exist between countries by offering an empowerment paradigm which tends towards inclusive agendas. Ruth Hubbard and Margaret Randall (1988) *The Shape of Red: Insider/Outsider Reflections*. San Francisco: Cleis Press, is a fascinating collection of letters between two women who explore insider/outsider tensions. Christopher Mabey and Graeme Salaman (1995) *Strategic Human Resource Management*. Oxford: Blackwell, provides a thorough overview of human resource strategy, including chapters on the learning organization and international HRM.

References

Antal, Ariane B. and Izraeli, Dafna N. (1994) 'A global comparison of women in management: women managers in their homelands and as expatriates', in Ellen A. Fagenson (ed.), *Women in Management: Trends, Issues and Challenges in Managerial Diversity*. London: Sage. pp. 52–96.

Bammer, Angelika (ed.) (1994) *Displacements*. Bloomington, IN: Indiana University Press.

Barham, Kevin and Wills, Stefan (1992) *Management across Frontiers: Identifying the Competencies of Successful International Managers*. Berkhamsted: Ashridge Management College; Oxford: Foundation for Management Education.

Barth, Fredrik (1989) 'The analysis of culture in complex societies', *Ethnos*, 54: 120–42.

Bhabha, Homi K. (1996) 'Culture's in-between' in Stuart Hall and Paul du Gay (eds), *Questions of Cultural Identity*. London: Sage.

Boyacigiller, Nakiye A. and Adler, Nancy J. (1991) 'The parochial dinosaur: organizational science in a global context', *Academy of Management Review*, 16 (2): 262–90.

Calas, Marta (1992), 'An other silent voice? Representing "Hispanic Woman" in organizational texts', in Albert J. Mills and Peta Tancred (eds), *Gendering Organizational Analysis*. London: Sage. pp. 201–21.

Calori, Roland and De Woot, Philippe (1994) *A European Management Model*. Eaglewood Cliffs, NJ: Prentice-Hall.

Cova, B., Kassis, J. and Lanoux, V. (1993) 'Back to pedagogy: the EAP's 20 years of European experience', *Management Education and Development*, 24 (1): 33–47.

Cox, Taylor (1994) 'A comment on the language of diversity', *Organization*, 1 (1): 51–7.

Deal, T.E. and Kennedy, A.A. (1982) *Corporate Cultures: The Rites and Rituals of Corporate Life*. London: Addison-Wesley.

Dodds, I. (1995) 'Differences can be strengths', *People Management*, 1 (8): 40–3.

Elias, Norbert and Scotson, John L. (1994) *The Established and the Outsiders*. London: Sage.

Ferguson, Ann (1996) 'Bridge identity politics: an integrative feminist ethics of international development', *Organization*, 3 (4): 571–87.

Hall, K. (1995) 'Worldwide vision in the workplace', *People Management*, May: 20–5.

Hampden-Turner, C. and Trompenaars, F. (1993) *The Seven Cultures of Capitalism*. London: Piatkus.

Harasym, Sarah (ed.) (1990) *Spivak: The Post-Colonial Critic*. London: Routledge.

Heller, F. (1985) 'Some theoretical and practical problems in multinational and cross-cultural research on organizations', in P. Joynt and M. Warner (eds), *Managing in Different Cultures*. Oslo: Oslo University Press.

Hofstede, Geert (1980) *Culture's Consequences: International Differences in Work Values*. London: Sage.

Hubbard, Ruth and Randall, Margaret (1988) *The Shape of Red: Insider/Outsider Reflections*. San Francisco: Cleis Press.

Jackson, Terence (ed.) (1995) *Cross-Cultural Management*. London: Butterworth-Heinemann.

Latour, Bruno (1993) *We Have Never Been Modern*. Hemel Hempstead: Harvester Wheatsheaf.

Laurent, A. (1983) 'The cultural diversity of Western conceptions of management', *International Studies in Management and Organization*, 13 (1, 2): 75–96.

Massey, Doreen (1994) 'Double articulation: a place in the world', in Angelika Bammer (ed.) *Displacements*. Bloomington, IN: Indiana University Press.

Ouchi, W.G. (1981) *Theory Z: How American Business Can Meet the Japanese Challenge*. London: Addison-Wesley.

Pascale, R.T. and Athos, A.G. (1981) *The Art of Japanese Management*. New York: Warner Books.

Peters, T.J. and Waterman, R.H. (1982) *In Search of Excellence: Lessons from America's Best Run Companies*. London and New York: Harper and Row.

Porter, L.W. and McKibbin, L.E. (1988) *Management Education and Development: Drift or Thrust into the 21st Century?* Maidenhead: McGraw-Hill.

Raimond, Paul and Halliburton, Christopher (1995) 'Business school strategies for the Single European Market', *Management Learning*, 26 (2): 231–48.

Ralston, David A., Gustafon, David J., Cheung, Fanny M. and Terpestra, Robert H. (1993) 'Differences in managerial values: a study of US, Hong Kong and PRC managers', *Journal of International Business Studies*, Second Quarter: 250–75.

Reiss, Angelika D. and Ones, Deniz S. (1995) 'Does international management education work? Reduction in ethnocentrism and negative stereotyping', paper presented to Academy of Management Conference, Vancouver, Canada.

Said, Edward (1995) *Orientalism*. Harmondsworth: Penguin.

Sjögren, Annick and Janson, Lena (eds) (1994) *Culture and Management* (vol. 2). Botkyrka: Multicultural Centre; Stockholm: Institute of International Business.

Sloan Management Review (1995) 'CEO Thought Summit', pp. 13–21.

Spivak, Gayatri Chakroavorty (1993) *Outside in the Teaching Machine*. New York: Routledge.

Star, Susan L. (1991), 'Power, technology and the phenomenon of conventions: on being allergic to onions', in John Law (ed.), *A Sociology of Monsters: Essays on Power, Technology and Domination*. London. Routledge. pp. 26–56.

Zaheer, Srilata (1995) 'Overcoming the liability of foreigness', *Academy of Management Journal*, 38 (2) 341–63.

16

Computer Support for Management Learning

David McConnell

One of the major current interests in the use of computers in management learning is the potential for computers and communications technology to bring learners together in 'virtual' environments which support group work. Computer systems designed to support the work of groups can be classified according to several criteria. The terminology applied to these systems is diverse: groupware and computer-supported co-operative work (CSCW) systems are terms often used to mean much the same thing, although it might be argued that CSCW subsumes groupware.

Tom Rodden (1991) suggests a classification of CSCW systems which is useful when considering computer-supported co-operative learning (CSCL). The classification is based on two major characteristics common to all co-operative systems. These are the form of interaction and the geographical nature of the users. Co-operative work can occur in synchronous and asynchronous interactions, and users can be remotely placed, or located in the same room (co-located). These dimensions provide a matrix for describing four classes of co-operative systems (Figure 16.1).

Rodden's classification, however, omits another dimension of CSCW systems, and that is the degree to which they are structured or unstructured. This distinction is important in CSCL environments, where open learning is the predominant method and where, it might be argued, unstructured groupware is more effective.

CSCL relies on the use of computers and electronic communication networks to mediate the work of co-operative learning groups. The use of computers and networks for general communication is often referred to as computer-mediated communications (CMC). The introduction of CMC into organizational and educational life not only broadens the possibility for enhancing the goals of any endeavour, but also introduces a change in the social behaviour of those involved of a kind that has possibly never been experienced before.

Within education, the introduction of CMC into the educational process is partly based on the premis that computer conferencing will support and facilitate groupwork in ways that are not achievable face to face (see, e.g., Harasim, 1989; Mason and Kaye, 1989; McConnell, 1994). The possibility

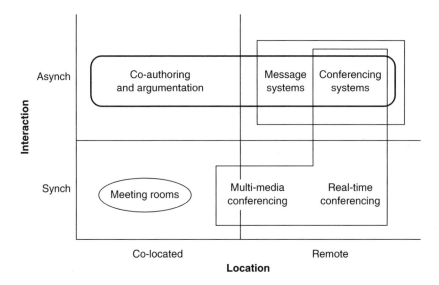

Figure 16.1   *Classification space for CSCW systems (after T. Rodden,*
1991: 320. By permission of the publishers Butterworth-Heinemann Ltd.)

to mediate educational activities through advanced learning technologies such as CMC begins to question many aspects of our educational practice to date. At the core of the use of this technology is the suggestion that tutors and learners need not physically meet in order to take part in group activities (such as seminars and tutorials) where 'presence' and active social participation through discussion is required. This in turn begins to question many of the current assumptions about 'effective' teaching and learning practices.

But to what extent does CMC support educational groupwork? The medium is currently being used as a tool at various levels of education, in the assumption that it does support groups working together. Our research into the potential of the medium for management learning focuses on questions such as the following:

- How do groups with shared educational goals work co-operatively using CSCL?
- What are the problems in working in this way?
- What are the benefits?
- How does CSCL groupwork differ from what we know about groupwork in face-to-face meetings?
- What are the unique characteristics of this medium for groups in education wishing to work together?
- What implications does teaching and learning in this way have for those involved?
- What would a future educational system that uses CSCL as a core medium of activity 'look like'?

The Practice of Computer-supported Management Learning

Clearly, questions such as these relate to our professional practice in running CSCL courses, and offer us the opportunity to examine reflectively what we do in these new learning environments. Making the bridge from traditional forms of learning to co-operative learning requires tutors and learners to re-oriente themselves. Many tutors will have to reconsider much of their existing professional practice. Learners will have to change many of their expectations about learning. This is difficult in itself. Making the link between co-operative learning and computer-supported co-operative learning is perhaps more difficult because few tutors and learners will have the experience of working with technology in this way.

One mechanism for facilitating this re-orientation will be for tutors and learners to learn about successful experiences of CSCL. The Centre for the Study of Management Learning at Lancaster University has been running a CSCL programme for several years, and some discussion of this may be useful in seeing how one design has been implemented.

The computer-mediated MA in management learning

The computer-mediated MA in management learning (CM MAML) is a two-year part-time programme for professionals in management education and development. Participants range in age from mid-twenties to early sixties. We try to get a balance of genders on each cohort, and a spread of public, private and voluntary sector organizations as well as those who are self-employed. The design of the MA is based on educational principles broadly shared by staff, who nevertheless bring influences from different academic backgrounds (including organizational behaviour, educational research, educational technology and linguistics). These principles are:

1   Participants should have as much choice as possible over the direction and content of their learning.
2   They are responsible for 'managing' their own learning and for helping others in theirs. The notion of a 'learning community' is generally used to denote this: a community of course participants and tutors that manages its learning needs through negotiation and discussion (Pedler, 1981; Snell, 1989).
3   The work of the programme integrates the idea of critical perspective in the academic tradition, with participants day-to-day professional experience.
4   The opportunity presented to the students by the MA should be equally for learning about and developing themselves in their professional roles, as for engaging with relevant ideas and concepts in the public domain.
5   That the marked degree of participation inherent in the design assumes a commitment to taking collective responsibility (by participants and tutors alike) for attending to the 'process' of the community – reviewing and modifying the design, procedures and ways of working.

In practice, this means for instance that the staff often, but not always, design in some detail only the first day or so of each one-week residential workshop. Thereafter, activities are planned collectively. Reviewing progress and subsequent planning is also a collective activity. Topics which arise emerge from the interests of staff and participants, as do the choice of methods and the online (CSCL) tutorial groups. The topics for course assignments are the choice of each learner and assessment is 'collaborative' involving peer, self and tutors (McConnell, 1994).

Why CSCL?

We chose to work in this CSCL environment for several reasons. A group of us at Lancaster had just completed a funded project on information technology-based open learning (ITOL). This was a theoretical project looking at the possibilities of extending conventional university teaching and learning through advanced learning technologies to learners outside the university. We developed an ITOL model (see Hodgson et al., 1989) which helped us design our MA programme. In addition, we wanted to try to overcome some of the problems (as we saw them) in running the department's existing part-time MA programme. This is a well-established programme which has a series of workshops over a two-year period, with day-long face-to-face tutorial meetings in between. The underlying educational philosophy is similar to that described here for the computer-mediated MA. It was felt that a computer-supported co-operative learning environment might allow the whole learning community to continue discussions started at workshops (there is little, if any, opportunity for this on the conventional programme); that there might be discussions between different learning sets in the CSCL environment (impossible when they meet in different locations face-to-face); that the opportunity to develop online resources such as databases, bibliographies and the like might enhance learning; and that there might actually be qualitatively better discussions in the electronic learning sets than in the face-to-face ones. These aims have largely been achieved, we think.

The programme design

The programme is structured round two learning environments – a residential one and a CSCL one. The residential learning environment is made up of six intensive residential workshops spread fairly evenly throughout the two years, at which participants examine relevant research and theory, and experiment with and plan alternative strategies for their continuing learning in their normal working contexts.

In the CSCL environment, there is continuation of some of the issues raised in the workshops, and a 'meeting' of tutorial sets. The sets usually consist of between three and five participants and a tutor. Their main purpose is to provide support for each individual in choosing, planning and writing course assignments. Participants also discuss matters arising out of the programme and out of their work experience. These activities are supported by a CSCL environment made up primarily of computer conferencing and electronic mail (we started by using the Caucus system, and now use Lotus Notes), with access to online databases and library catalogues. The whole year group also has the opportunity to 'meet' via the medium. Participants on the programme link into the system from various parts of the UK, the USA and other overseas locations, using a PC (or Mac), modem and communications software. Tutors (usually three per programme) use the local area network on campus, or link in from their homes.

We use the CSCL environment for many different purposes and activities:

- Communication between participants:
  - to keep in touch;
  - to share ideas;
  - as noticeboards; and
  - as resources.
- Formal learning processes:
  - electronic tutorials, seminars and meetings;
  - decision-making about the programme as a whole;
  - discussions and other participatory learning events; and
  - development of ideas about design issues.

Additionally, we are all concerned at one time or another with looking at the role of CSCL in management learning and development. The course concludes with a two-day residential period which is used to review participants' dissertation work and their plans for future development.

Issues Emerging from our Experience

So, what has the experience of working in this way been like? What are the issues that have captured our imagination and posed the most interesting questions for us to consider?

The tutor in CSCL

Despite the focus on a shared learning design, there are some particular functions in CSCL contexts that tutors have actively to work at. The tutors will be the people most knowledgeable about co-operative learning in computer-supported co-operative learning contexts, and they will have the job, initially at least, of helping the learners understand how to work in this new environment. They will have to facilitate the learners' development in the use of CSCL. As time proceeds, the groups themselves will take control of much of this as their understanding of the system and experience of using it develops.

Our experience of working in this medium has indicated that there are certain areas where our role as tutors in a CSCL context could be said to be problematic, as well as areas where we feel the medium offers new possibilities for our practice. Firstly, there is the question of the impact of our interventions. This is not unique to the tutors, but it does have serious implications for our formal role of supportive facilitators. Our position as tutors can carry with it a power and authority which could be abused (Young, 1971; Giroux, 1983; Freire, 1985). We are constantly confronted with the contradiction in playing the dual role of 'tutor-participants'. This is especially so in the assessment process. Any intervention we make has the likelihood of being received differently from interventions made by other participants. Our wish to remove the inequity of power relationships takes some considerable time and active work. As tutors, we have to establish a sense of trust and partnership online with participants. But in this medium it is not always possible to be as aware of our interventions as we might be in a face-to-face situation. Participants may construe our intervention in an unintended way, perhaps reading more into what we say than we intended. There is no way of checking this out (other than constantly asking how an intervention was received, which would get in the way of discussion if done frequently, although it has to be done from time to time).

We can be aware of the ongoing 'climate' of the conference and glean some information about our position in it and how we are being 'received' and perceived. But from time to time it emerges that a tutor's intervention has had some unanticipated affect. Sometimes participants confront us about the issue immediately and we are then able to discuss it (e.g., issues to do with giving and receiving grades). Sometimes its effects are dormant and it is only in time, in discussion over other issues, that we become aware of its significance. This may not appear any different from what a tutor has to confront in a face-to-face situations, but online it does have a different impact on all concerned and seems in practice to be more difficult to manage. It requires self-critical awareness through dialogue with participants.

A second issue is how best to obtain a sense of being effective online. In face-to-face situations we receive information (verbal, body language, and so on) which helps tell us something about our effectiveness as tutors. Online we can only be told (indirectly or directly) about our professional practice. Several tutors have commented on the issue of translating their existing face-to-face practice to the new medium, and the problem of being as 'effective' online as they feel they are face-to-face:

> I have a sense of what I'm trying to do in face-to-face tutorials . . . and I feel that, for better or worse, I've got an approach which I feel fairly comfortable with . . . within CM MAML. I'm wondering whether I can do that effectively in this medium.

> . . . wanting not to be discouraging . . . to get the balance between support and critique . . . difficult to feel that I was getting that balance right when not face-to-face. (Tutors in early stages of using CSCL)

We have to develop an approach we feel comfortable with online. If, however, we are constantly trying to develop honest, trusting and open online learning environments, then we can trust our intuition at times to tell us something of our effectiveness; Polanyi (1958) talks of such commitment saving us from mere subjectivity. Participants will 'say' something about us as tutors in the normal ongoing dialogue, and if the climate is 'correct', we will be able to 'see' ourselves in the process and make judgements about our effectiveness. However, I have found it helpful at times to set up an item in the computer conferences about my role as tutor (the contradiction here of forcing a focus on me as tutor in an environment that tries to by-pass roles is not lost on me, although it might be seen as being no different from the individual items participants set up to focus on themselves). This has been reasonably useful and when it works well participants engage in discussion about 'me as tutor' in a meaningful way.

Thirdly, our role as largely non-directive tutors sometimes feels compromised online. This I think has much to do with the asynchronous nature of CSCL, and with attaching meaning to silences online, and to the nature of our 'voices' online. The medium can have the effect of making what we say stand out more than we would wish. Interventions which, when made face-to-face and supported by non-verbal cues, help to present intention and other meaning beyond the verbal words we use, can only be 'said' online. This sometimes strips the intervention of its richness, so that a comment intended to be non-directive is sometimes 'heard' as direction.

Yet for some tutors, the feeling they have of being forced at times by the medium to be more directive does not necessarily present a major problem:

> I'm enjoying being directive, for example facilitating Moira [a participant] in making her choice about her project essay. That felt good and I wouldn't want to deny being able to do that.

> And that takes us back to the tutor role. . . . I took a firmer line on my first set and forced them effectively to close (their assignment) about two months after the workshop.

> I feel more directive now – both feel obliged to be the one to respond, and want to respond. (Tutors in early stages of using CSCL)

Interpreting a silence online is difficult. With the Caucus conferencing system, everyone can check when anyone else was last online. If someone is frequently online but silent, or if they are online but only silent in particular conferences or items, we can assume that they have actively chosen to be silent, so any intervention on our part to draw attention to their silence may well be seen as directing them in an unhelpful way. This is, of course, a conundrum for tutors. But if the conference participants are being supportive of each other, then it is likely that one of them will offer a way back into the discussion for the silent partner before a tutor has to. Being open and 'able to talk' about one's silences does not always come easy in this medium.

So far I have chosen to highlight areas of our online practice which pose some questions for us, and which we are constantly striving to understand and address. This is not, however, to suggest that working in this medium poses more problems than we might have to attend to in face-to-face contexts. It certainly does not. We are very aware of the positive qualities that working in this environment can offer. We have a strong feeling of being able to do new things using this medium. For example, we can work closely online with participants in planning up-coming face-to-face workshops. This is of considerable benefit in a programme such as ours, and is something which was not really possible before using the medium because we did not have a mechanism for the whole community to engage in planning ahead in between face-to-face workshops:

> One of the best things that has happened for me on CM MAML is that we have actually got a sub-task group designing the next workshop using the computer conference to do so . . . (Course tutor)

> A big plus is the contact with the rest of the community. It enables dialogue about planning and workshops and so on. (Course tutor)

The possibility to take time to reflect on discussions, and to engage with participants at length on topics of common interest over extended periods of time, suits our concern to probe into issues and to develop deep discussion:

> My model of tutoring as 'digging in' is perhaps more suited to CM MAML. (Course tutor)

Although perhaps time-consuming, such discussions can lead to learning relationships which are uncommonly close and highly productive on both sides.

Gender issues

Working in this new medium has highlighted gender differences in online groupwork and the way it sometimes influences learning within the groups. Our research (Hardy et al., 1994; McConnell, 1997) has focused on how this medium can offer new insights into researching issues in gender and learning, and how the dynamics of online learning can be interpreted from a gendered perspective.

We found that some women experience the process of online communication differently when they are communicating with other women than with men. These differences are not, however, peculiar to this medium, nor are they a new phenomenon, as much of the linguistics literature testifies. They are highlighted in this medium by both its written and permanent record, making them more available for individual awareness and more available for research purposes.

Some women often experience some male inputs problematically: male-to-male interactions are sometimes experienced as being difficult to engage with:

> Stephen online and Paul online certainly, I mean as individuals regardless of sex, they have quite different ways of saying things to Helen and Jenny. (Female participant)

Women feel that their own dialogue is qualitatively different and is based on different assumptions (a 'heart and guts' register). If females talk with males in this register, some males will drag the conversation into a highly intellectual form:

> . . . it's perfectly OK in our set conference to talk about how one churns up inside about something, or just life in general. . . . If I put that on to Stephen, Paul, Jed and Alan – I'd tend to think they'd drag it into the intellectual and bring it straight back into their head, and I'm not in my head, I'm in my heart and guts. (Female participant)

However, the dynamics of mixed-sex online groups suggest that the medium may offer new opportunities for female members of groups, especially in terms of their ability to take turns, speak for similar lengths of time to those of male members, and direct the conversation. These are all issues which appear to disadvantage females in face-to-face meetings. It would seem that females appear to be less disadvantaged in this medium, and that there is greater potential for equality of participation.

Our research into gender differences online is, at this stage, tentative and exploratory. The different purposes and contexts of online groups may well have an influence on male-to-female relationships (and indeed relationships between those of the same sex). We feel though that the medium offers new opportunities to analyse these relationships in much more detail and to explore the nature and style of language adopted and the effect it has on both men and women in the learning discussions.

Assessment

The collaborative nature of the assessment process (involving self, peer and tutor assessment) seems to be highlighted online more than in face-to-face contexts. This has proved one of the most difficult areas of our work. In CSCL, learners have a major role in choosing what they work on for their course assignments. They also have an important part to play in assessing their own and other learners' work. Collaborative assessment is a natural corollary of co-operative learning; it supports the co-operative learning process.

This process of collaborative assessment is not trouble-free. There is always scope for the inclusion of personal judgement of a kind that cannot easily be 'defined' or transferred into a grade. Communicating about this is especially difficult in an electronic environment. The group has to work at trying to understand and live with some of the difficulties of assessment. It can be as much an art as it is a science. Dialogue around difficult issues is necessary in order that people can explain their viewpoints and justify their positions. Disagreements do occur, as might be expected. However, we have not been discouraged in the use of this form of assessment. After all, many experienced tutors are not reliable assessors in every situation. And it is not entirely uncommon for different tutors to disagree on their assessment of the same piece of work. It is important to keep in mind some of the wider purposes of triangulated assessment, and to expect and live with disagreements: 'Self assessment can be a valuable learning activity, even in the absence of agreement between student and teacher, and can provide potent feedback to the student about both learning and educational and professional standards' (Falchikov and Boud, 1989: 425).

The assessment process is often concluded with the group examining the whole process of feedback and assessment, once again to see what they did and why, and to imagine how they might go about it next time round. This degree of reflection is important in helping group members learn from the process, and in helping them to be better prepared and skilled for the next assessments.

For us, online collaborative assessment is a central part of the learning process. Assessment is not just something that is tagged on to the end of the course. We think valuable learning emerges from this process. The learning outcomes of collaborative assessment are a feature often commented on by participants, as the following quotations indicate:

> For me, online assessment has been, is, one of the most stimulating aspects of the programme. There seems to be more scope online, compared to the traditional part-time MAML (from what I've heard), for exploring the meaning, legitimacy of assessment criteria which can provoke quite deep and protracted self-examination. (Course participant)

> Online assessment can be very full, rich, time-consuming, and when it comes to marking very confusing. . . . In one of our conferences we spent vast amounts of time grappling with the criteria for marks – that was interesting, but on reflection the struggle to agree marks may have been an alternative to much deeper exploration of our papers. My impression is that the depth of discussion about our papers has been much greater through CM than would be likely, maybe even possible through face to face. (Course participant)

The stripped-down mode of communication online often serves to focus the mind and discussion:

> I also find it much easier to cut through the dross and the bull online. Its much easier to focus on the content of what your assessing and less on the body language of traditional face-to-face meetings. It can also be hard, and frustrating too in making it a more functional approach. (Course participant)

But the mechanics of dealing with the online process can sometimes be daunting:

> I think that for me, there's something about trying to ensure I give everyone feedback on what I think about their work. I'd like to do it so's I'm also commenting on what others have said. But it's difficult for me to do that online when I've been working, initially anyway, from their work in isolation, and then uploading a file of comment. To refer to others means I either have to refer to print-outs of people's responses AND the piece of work, so that I'm preparing my response from several documents perhaps, or I have to remember what others have said. It's the sheer difficulty of trying to do all that, that for the moment defeats me. (Course participant)

However, the general experience of the online processes and outcomes are very positive:

> Greg – Your comments I find similarly helpful. What I found with both your comments on my p.e [project essay] and on my seminar paper . . . is that

sometimes you're really looking at something in entirely different ways from me. It's like having light thrown from a different angle so that something new and previously hidden to me is illuminated – it's great! (Course participant)

I guess my view is similar to yours Cathy – I love the assessment process and in some cases have achieved (for myself) learning as powerful, maybe more so, than the preparation and writing bits. (Course participant)

Information overload

We have found that another potential drawback is the possibility of CSCL users to become overloaded with information. When users are participating frequently this is less likely to occur, but when there are periods of absence from the groups' work, then it is often the case that large amounts of information accumulate, which are presented to the members on their return. This can have several effects. The members may feel overwhelmed by the amount of communications to be read, and may either choose to ignore it all (thus missing out on the groups' actions), try to read and digest it (which can be extremely time-consuming), or skim over it in an attempt to get a rough understanding of what has been happening during their absence.

Even when users are participating frequently, there are times when the groups' activities are so involving that the amount of information piles up day by day. This can be exciting and challenging for members of the groups, and if they feel connected to the interactions, the high level of activity does not become a problem of information overload. But of course there are always times when it is just not possible to read everything, and users sift through the material using online tools.

Written dialogue

Working in these kinds of CSCL environments means that all communications are made via a keyboard, in textual form. Research suggests that typing skills are not important for the success of online group communications (Hiltz, 1986; McConnell, 1988). Nevertheless, when asked if they ever felt constrained in the type of contributions they could make, many students do say that they feel constrained at some time (McConnell, 1988). It could well be that, for some at least, having to present their thoughts publicly in typewritten form acts as a barrier to full participation. However, most students say they are usually able to express their views during the online meetings.

Summary

In this chapter, I have tried to outline the potential of computers and communication technologies, and the potential of computer-supported co-operative learning, in management learning. This has been achieved largely by reference to the research into our professional practice which we have carried out while running the computer-mediated MA in management learning. Issues concerning the tutor role online, gender differences in online groupwork, collaborative assessment, the possibility of information overload and the need for a written form of communication have all been considered.

Conclusion

In a programme such as the MA in management learning which carries certain assumptions concerning the process of learning, the introduction of information technologies raises some important questions: will the technology determine the nature of the programme, as often seems to happen elsewhere? Will the learning philosophy and the relationships between learners, and between staff and learners, be affected detrimentally? These were legitimate fears of staff prior to the introduction of CMC. But our experience of running the programme using these new technologies suggests that the fears were largely unfounded. We have been able to introduce new ways of facilitating learning via CMC at no real loss to our professional and educational values. Indeed, for some of us this new form of 'virtual' learning has offered opportunities beyond our expectations.

Annotated Bibliography

Very little has been written specifically about information and communication technologies and management learning. My own book on computer-supported co-operative learning, mentioned in this chapter, is based largely on my (and others') experiences of, and research into, the use of computer conferences to support management trainers and developers studying for their Masters degree.

New information and communication technologies have drawn the attention of those interested in distance learning. R. Mason and A.R. Kaye's book *Mindweave* (1989) is a highly informative collection of papers looking at the the role of computer-mediated communications in distance learning. A.R. Kaye (ed.) (1991) *Collaborative Learning Through Computer Conferencing*. Berlin: Springer Verlag, is another excellent collection of papers by world experts on the educational uses of these media. G. Davies and B. Samways (eds), *Teleteaching*. IFIP North Holland: International Federation for Information Processing, is a massive collection of conference papers on the topic, while Betty Collis (1996) *Tele-Teaching in a Digital World*. London: International Thomson Computer Press is a comprehensive look at the future of online distance learning, with many useful references and Web locations (see www.itcpmedia.com). Dale Spender's (1995) *Nattering on the Net: Women, Power and Cyberspace*. Melbourne: Spinifex, is a highly engaging, and at times provocative, assessment of the Internet in education and publishing. Looking a little further afield, I have enjoyed the collection of readings in I. Grief (ed.) (1988) *Computer-supported Cooperative Work: A Book of Readings*. San Mateo, CA: Morgan Kofmann. This book offers a collection of classic papers which have helped shape the views of many social scientists interested in this area of research. The potential of these media for professional development generally has been the subject of several research projects, among them the JITOL (Just in Time Open Learning) EU Delta Project. A special edition of the *Journal of Computer Assisted Learning* (8 (3)) is devoted to this project. If you have access to the Internet and the World Wide Web, additional sources can be found, such as:

- Models of European Collaboration and Pedagogy in Open Learning (MECPOL), an EU Socrates funded project: www.idb.hist.no/mecpol/

- Dissemination of Open and Distance Learning (Do ODL), another EU Socrates funded project: www.idb.hist.no/DoODL/
- Just in Time Open Learning (JITOL), a professional development project at Sheffield University: www.shef.ac.uk/uni/projects/jitol/

References

Falchikov, N. and Boud, D. (1989) 'Student self assessment in higher education: a meta-analysis', *Review of Educational Research*, 59 (4): 395–430.

Freire, P. (1985) *The Politics of Education: Culture, Power and Liberation*. Basingstoke: Macmillan.

Giroux, H.A. (1983) *Theory and Resistance in Education: A Pedagogy for the Opposition*. London: Heinemann.

Harasim, L. (1989) 'On-line education: a new domain', in R. Mason and A.R. Kaye (eds), *Mindweave: Communication, Computers and Distance Education*. Oxford: Pergamon. pp. 40–9.

Hardy, V., Hodgson, V. and McConnell, D. (1994) 'Computer conferencing: a new medium for investigating issues in gender and learning', *Higher Education*, 28: 403–18.

Hiltz, S.R. (1986) 'The virtual classroom: using computer-mediated communication for university teaching', *Journal of Communication*, 36 (2): 95–104.

Hodgson, V., Lewis, R. and McConnell, D. (1989) 'Information technology-based open learning: a study report', Occasional Paper: InTER/12/89, Lancaster University, Lancaster.

Mason, R. and Kaye, A.R. (1989) *Mindweave: Communication, Computers and Distance Education*. Oxford: Pergamon.

McConnell, D. (1988) 'Computer conferencing in teacher inservice education: a case study', in D. Harris (ed.), *World Yearbook of Education 1988: Education for the New Technologies*. London: Kogan Page.

McConnell, D. (1990) 'A case study: the educational use of computer conferencing', *Educational and Training Technology International*, 27 (2): 211–23.

McConnell, D. (1994) *Implementing Computer Supported Cooperative Learning*. London: Kogan Page.

McConnell, D. (1997) 'Interaction patterns in mixed sex groups in educational computer tele-conferences: part 1, empirical findings', in *Gender and Education*, 1997 (3).

Pedler, M. (1981) 'Developing the learning community', in T. Boydell and M. Pedler (eds), *Management Self-Development: Concepts and Practices*. Aldershot: Gower.

Polanyi, M. (1958) *Personal Knowledge: Towards a Postcritical Philosophy*. London: Routledge and Kegan Paul.

Rodden, T. (1991) 'A Survey of CSCW Systems', *Interacting With Computers*, 3 (3): 319–53.

Snell, R. (1989) 'Learning to work in a peer learning community', *Group Relations Training Association Bulletin*. (Also mimeo, CSML, Lancaster University, Lancaster, UK.)

Young, M.F.D. (1971) *Knowledge and Control: New Directions for the Sociology of Education*. London: Macmillan.

17

Lessons from Informal and Incidental Learning

Victoria J. Marsick and Karen E. Watkins

Recent work has refocused attention in management development on the process of 'natural learning' (Burgoyne and Hodgson, 1983), which takes place on the job and may not always be planned. We call this 'informal and incidental learning' (Marsick and Watkins, 1990). The value of this kind of learning is underscored today by interest in high-performing and learning organizations in which managers are challenged to take more responsibility for learning: their own and that of subordinates, the teams which they lead and in which they increasingly work, and the organization's learning. In this chapter we explore lessons from informal and incidental learning. We first examine informal and incidental learning through the lens of a model which we have developed, and in comparison to other theories. We then look at how an awareness of informal learning can enhance learning in organizational settings – with the consequent paradox of managing the unmanaged. We conclude with lessons from application of theory and a critique.

Our Theory of Informal and Incidental Learning

We have defined informal and incidental learning by contrasting them with formal learning:

> Formal learning is typically institutionally-sponsored, classroom-based, and highly structured. Informal learning, a category that includes incidental learning, may occur in institutions, but it is not typically classroom-based or highly structured, and control of learning rests primarily in the hands of the learner. Incidental learning, a subcategory of informal learning, is defined by Watkins as a byproduct of some other activity, such as task accomplishment, interpersonal interaction, sensing the organizational culture, trial-and-error experimentation, or even formal learning. Informal learning can be deliberately encouraged by an organization or it can take place despite an environment not highly conducive to learning. Incidental learning, on the other hand, almost always takes place although people are not always conscious of it. (Marsick and Watkins, 1990: 12)

We base our model on the action science perspective of Argyris and Schön (1978) that, in turn, has roots in John Dewey's (1938) theories of learning from experience and in Kurt Lewin's understanding of the interaction of individuals and their environment. The problem-solving cycle proposes that people learn from their experience when they face a new challenge or problem. This triggers a fresh look at the situation, followed by a search for alternative responses, action, and evaluation of results. Alan Mumford (1994) proposes that this problem-solving cycle is essentially equivalent to the work that managers do, and that at each stage, opportunities exist to identify learning opportunities, expand one's repertoire of possible solutions, and learn from mistakes.

Kolb (1984) and other experiential learning theorists have translated Dewey's work into a problem-solving cycle, but Dewey's interest in the scientific method as a basis for learning from experience was more integrated than these models imply. He feared that some might interpret his focus on scientific method too narrowly as 'the special technique of laboratory research' (Dewey, 1938: 87). Dewey conceived the scientific method more broadly as 'the only authentic means at our command for getting at the significance of our everyday experiences of the world in which we live. It . . . provides a working pattern of the way in which and the conditions under which experiences are used to lead ever onward and outward' (ibid.: 88). For Dewey, experience was not educational unless it was purposive. Purpose guides the use of the scientific method:

> It involves (1) observation of surrounding conditions; (2) knowledge of what has happened in similar situations in the past, a knowledge obtained partly by recollection and partly from the information, advice, and warning of those who have had a wider experience; and (3) judgment which puts together what is observed and what is recalled to see what they signify. (ibid.: 69)

Dewey emphasized two interactive, related principles that he called 'the longitudinal and lateral aspects of experience' (ibid.: 44), and that reflect a teleological emphasis on growth towards a more integrative level of being as a result of being purposeful in one's learning: the continuity principle and the interaction principle. By the continuity principle, he meant that experience has a lasting impact on biological habit, the formation of attitudes that lead a person to new experiences. By the interaction principle, Dewey meant that experience involves both 'objective and internal conditions', that they interact one with the other in any given situation, and that both must be equally attended to. Prior forms of education paid too much attention to external conditions that were considered objective, and not enough to internal meanings ascribed to a situation by the learner.

Our theory of informal and incidental learning is closer to the original Dewey interpretation of the scientific method, broadly conceived, than it is to a tool or method. Insights gleaned from action science (Argyris and Schön, 1978) reinforce insights gained from Dewey's thinking, that is, that problem-solving is not straightforward. Our model is not straightforward nor prescriptive: steps such as observation and reflection are interwoven throughout various phases of the model, and the learning process varies because of the situation in which people find themselves. The problem-solving cycle is embedded within a sub-surface cycle comprising the beliefs,

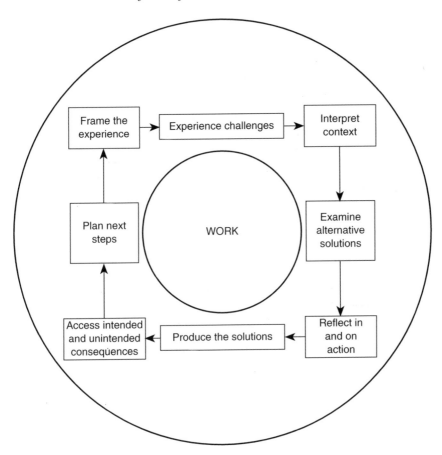

Figure 17.1 *Informal and incidental learning model*

values and assumptions that guide action at each stage. The sub-surface cycle is not readily accessible. So, as learners move around the problem-solving cycle, they need to work hard to identify and acknowledge tacit beliefs, values, assumptions, contextual factors and unintended outcomes that might shape their understanding of the situation (see Figure 17.1).

An example illustrates how people learn from experience (see p. 298).

Notice that the move to self-directed work teams provided the group members with a new challenge, which they thought they had handled by looking at alternatives, deciding on a way of working, and planning for their daily work based on their limited perceptions of what was or was not working. It was only when an external disruption occurred that they chose to dig beneath the surface and look at other assumptions, values and beliefs that they could not know were brewing in the hearts and minds of their team mates.

Recent work on cognition and communication helps us to understand that people do not simply translate 100 per cent of what they see or hear into 100

Illustrating our model of learning from experience

Consider the experience of a small group of professionals in a company that has adopted self-directed work teams. Guidelines for work teams have been announced. The man who was formerly the supervisor is part of the team. Team members say they are pleased with the new structure because it gives them more autonomy. Looking at our model, the work experience offers new challenges to all parties involved. Members assumed that they all agreed on what it meant to work in self-directed teams because they all heard the guidelines. However, each person framed his/her experience of self-direction based on prior experience of work in teams which, while somewhat similar, was also different in fundamental ways. In addition, members carried into the new situation different perceptions of how their relationship should change towards the member who had been the supervisor. The supervisor thought, with a mixture of humorous relief and disappointment, that his job now was to ask people if they wanted milk or sugar with their coffee! One team member was totally confused by the idea that he should now decide his own work objectives and schedule, while another member interpreted the shift as freedom to work autonomously and felt relieved to spend less time communicating with others. The culture of the company in the past did not encourage members to question the supervisor, so they simply took this set of norms into the new self-directed work teams and made judgements about what was expected, assumed that everyone clearly understood what these judgements were without discussion, acted on these judgements, and held others accountable to personal judgements which were, at times, contradictory.

Some team members were not even aware that new learning was needed until a crisis erupted several months later when they received complaints by internal customers about a perceived lack of service. Team members could have simply blamed one another for the problem, which would have led them to continue in their cycle of misinterpretations. However, the supervisor decided to tell people what he was thinking about the nature of their experience in the last few months, and his questioning about whether he had contributed to the problem because, feeling unappreciated, he had held back information about what he thought they ought to be doing to meet customer demands. His candor led others on the team to examine their perceptions and feelings, and to look frankly at the fact that their relationships with their customers had dropped significantly even though they had been meeting production quotas. This led the group to several decisions: a desire to get more training in communication skills, the development of an agreed upon procedure for deciding who would take on which tasks, and a decision to seek clarification from the management committee about some responsibilities that they thought would be better carried out by a central staff group. The team was not yet ready to deal with all of the feelings they held about how they wanted to be supported by one another, but they were on the road to working more effectively because they had stopped to learn from their experience.

per cent of the meaning that they attribute to the situation (Varela et al., 1995). About 20 per cent of their interpretation comes from sensory stimuli; 80 per cent of the meaning they make is a result of the way in which they use accumulated meaning schemes to interpret what they see or hear. It is not surprising, then, that informal and incidental learning is unique to individuals, and that because it is seldom consciously or critically examined, it is subject to a high degree of misinterpretation.

Misinterpretation easily leads to error. Error is a surprising outcome, in the Dewey sense, that can have positive or negative results. Errors are self-defined as 'a mismatch of outcomes to expectations' that 'are not in themselves mistakes; rather they signify the presence of mistakes' (Argyris and Schön, 1996: 32). Feedback about mistakes can help people learn if they are willing to identify the reasons for errors. Nevis et al. (1995) cite Electricité de France (EDF) as the best example of the openness needed to learn from errors. Abnormalities or deviations are reported throughout 57

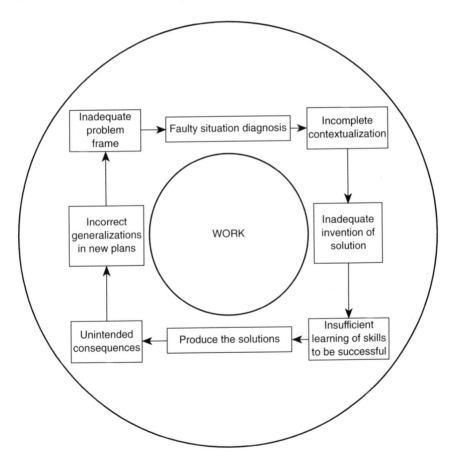

Figure 17.2   *Potential sources of error in the informal and incidental learning model*

nuclear power plants and each mistake is treated as a researchable event. EDF follows up with an investigation to determine if the problem exists anywhere else and disseminates the knowledge of what eliminated the problem to all plants.

Many factors make it difficult to recognize and correct errors. We can locate potential sources of error in each step of our model, as illustrated in Figure 17.2.

Turning back to the self-directed work team example, members of the team framed their task inadequately because of different perceptions that were not shared. They did not fully understand the issues they needed to resolve and, as a result, their performance met targets but did not satisfy customers. They had not learned adequately how to communicate well and to make decisions in this new mode. They learned when consequences became too obvious to be disregarded, which made it possible to break the cycle of inaccurate generalizations from their experience. It is important to underscore that they learned from feedback from outside the team – from observations of their effectiveness from an outsider's perspective. This outsider perspective is critical to breaking the error cycle, and can be created within the team through guided reflective learning processes.

In the next section, we compare our model to other theories relevant to informal and incidental learning.

Definitions and Models Compared

Authors writing about 'incidental learning' agree that incidental learning is unintentional and occurs as a by-product of something else. Jost Reischmann (1986) describes unintentional adult learning as learning 'en passant', a planned event in which learning is not the main purpose, but rather an offshoot of life routines. Learning 'en passant', may lead to intentional learning, but it always has unintended learning consequences. It is integrated, holistic, not compulsory, and individualized, builds on previous learning, can be a basis for further intentional learning, and is identified by looking back, that is, by reflection.

People often accept the value of incidental learning simply because it occurs naturally. We question this perspective because when learners do not analyse their interpretations, their false assumptions can lead them to inaccurate conclusions (Watkins and Wiswell, 1987). Jarvis (1987) likewise critiques incidental learning as non-reflective and reactive. He concludes that 'this is a major part of the process whereby people learn and acquire their culture and by which it is maintained through taken-for-granted behavior' (Jarvis, 1987: vi). We see the taken-for-granted aspect of incidental learning in what is often called the 'hidden curriculum' in which students 'psych out' teachers and learn unstated values through the interpersonal actions, climate and classroom practices of teachers. Students have been said to have 'built-in crap detectors' (Postman and Weingartner, 1971). Ironically, the students' largely tacit, incidental learnings are based on largely tacit, taken-for-granted behaviours by teachers.

We define incidental learning as a specialized category of informal learning. Because informal learning generally takes place outside the classroom, it is often equated with self-directed learning. However, as Candy (1991) points out, there is a difference between self-directed learning as a method – that is, self-management of learning activities – and self-directed learning as a goal – that is, becoming an autonomous, independent owner of choices about learning. It is sometimes assumed that people will be less exploited if they are more self-directed in their learning. In organizations, however, the organization always controls the goals towards which people learn, even though they may have more choice over the means of learning.

Mocker and Spear (1982) suggest that the learner's environment is key to enhancing informal learning; it is the 'organizing circumstance'. Self-directed learning takes place in natural, everyday settings. The individual's perceptions of the environment give meaning to experience. The organizational context is a powerful mediator of an individual's learning. In organizations, learning typically occurs in groups which have a life together outside the classroom, one which is continuous over a long period of time. These people share norms, a culture, and meanings that are so mutually reinforced that individuals may not recognize other meanings. The relationships between people in organizations are role-bound and hierarchical. An unspoken exchange process operates that asks individuals to perform and silently threatens to let them go if they do not perform. This unspoken exchange deeply affects what is learned.

Our model differs somewhat from the self-directed, informal learning described by Tough (1979, 1982), who studied adult learning projects. Tough emphasizes intentionality of design more than do we: 'episodes in which a certain intention (gaining and retaining certain knowledge and skill) accounts for more than half the person's motivation to learn' (1979: 13). Tough's focus was on a self-defined, successful series of activities to achieve a goal that excluded situations such as self-initiated change processes that were not successful or which, after a period of thought and experimentation, were abandoned. For example, on a trip to India he conducted a learning project about poverty, but did not include his own learning about how important his family became to him because of their absence. Tough's definition effectively excludes much of the learning that we talk about here.

Managers may not set out intentionally and explicitly to learn something through preplanned means. Often, their choices evolve from their interaction with others. Sometimes they become fully conscious of these choices; at other times, they remain unaware. Informal learning can be planned, but includes learning that is not designed or expected. Incidental learning, by definition, includes the unexpected. For example, an individual may decide to create a document using a new word processing programme. On the toolbar across the top of the screen are a number of unfamiliar symbols. The individual may elect to read the manual to learn what each symbol means, or they may click on the symbol while creating a document and discover that their document is suddenly in two columns. This accidental or trial-and-error discovery learning has potential side effects as well. In some instances, the individual may feel more competent for having discovered a new way to present information. In others, individuals may be frustrated by their inability to work with the new tool without further instruction.

Incidental learning shares theoretical roots with transformative learning in which an individual experiences a transformation of perspective as a result of reflection following some triggering event. Table 17.1 compares the transformative learning theories of six writers, including action science (Argyris, 1970; Argyris and Schön, 1978, 1996) and Mezirow (1978, 1991) on whom we draw in developing our model.

The first four of these models – those developed by Boyd and Fales (1983), Mezirow (1978), Chene (1988), and Boud et al. (1985) – describe theories of learning based on data collected from the retrospective reflections of learners. Following an event defined as significant or transformative by the learner, these authors interviewed respondents about the experience of transforming their perspectives and coming to new insights. In each of these models, there is an evolutionary shift from having a triggering experience, to some sense that how one understood the situation before is no longer adequate, followed by re-evaluating and reconstruing the event. This leads to new insights and sometimes to new behaviours. These researchers note that it is difficult to translate new insights into new behaviours because people are surrounded by social systems that expect them to act as before, so reintegration may be more cognitive than behavioural. Organizations do pose limits to informal learning, especially when questions challenge prevailing views.

By contrast, in other models (Argyris, 1970; Argyris and Schön, 1978, 1996) – through the active agency of a facilitator and/or a group – individuals use reflection to redefine or reconstrue a triggering experience. They then may experience a transformative process which is similar to those in each of the other theories. Triggering situations among the first authors may have been self-chosen, but might as likely be accidental, such as the death of a loved one. By contrast, in the change models, trigger events are constructed which are potentially catalytic. In all six models, individuals must be open to the possibility of alternative world-views or frames. We note that, whether learning is provoked by events or by others, the process is similar, and involves the following:

1 Proactive learners remain open to alternative frames on a problem, seek competing explanations, and adopt an attitude of experimentation, trying on new behaviours and working at the process of their own development.

Table 17.1   *Reflective and transformative learning theories*

Stages of reflective learning (Boyd and Fales, 1983)	Stages of transformative learning (Mezirow, 1978)	Reflective learning phases (Chene, 1988)	Components of experience (Boud, Keough and Walker, 1985)	Transformation (Boyd and Myers, 1988)	Model II skills and transformation (Argyris, 1970)
A sense of inner discomfort requires a trigger	1. A disorienting dilemma	*Phase 1 – Precedes commitment to learning*	*Stage 1 – Returning to experience*	*Discernment*	OWNING
	2. Self-examination with feelings of guilt or shame	1. Reaction to destabilizing event is decision to learn		1. Receptivity – to symbols, images, meanings from the shadow, animus/a, archetypes	*Unfreezing*
Identification/clarification of the concern, with a sense that something is missing	3. Critical assessment of epistemic or psycho-cultural presuppositions	2. Objective is unfocused	*Stage 3 – Re-evaluating experience*	*Recognition*	Recognizing dysfunctional control-oriented theories of action
	4. Recognizing that one's discontent and the process of transformation is shared	3. Situation is global		2. Ownership – acknowledgement that experience is authentic and connected to inner history	
		Phase 2 – Period of doubt, clash of ideal and real			
Openness to new information	5. Exploring new roles, relationships, actions		*Stage 2 – Attending to feelings*	3. Grieving	OPENNESS
	6. Planning a course of action	4. With resolution of problems comes a commitment to the project and new action		an open dialogue is experienced as a loss and moves through four grief stages:	Reframing theories-in-use to a learning orientation
Resolution – 'aha' stage, change in experience, learning, closure	7. Acquiring knowledge and skills for implementing one's plans	5. Learner acquires knowledge, skills, feels challenged	a. Using positive feelings	a. numbness and panic	*Changing*
Establishing continuity of self with past, present, and future self	8. Provisional efforts to try new roles	*Phase 3 – Performance*	b. Removing obstructing feelings	b. pining and protest	EXPERIMENTATION
	9. Building competence, self-confidence in new roles and relationships	6. Diffuse interpretation of actions, facts and global learning outcomes		c. disorganization and despair	Redesigning action
Deciding whether to take action	10. Reintegration	*Phase 4 – Judgement*		d. restabilization and reintegration	*Refreezing*
		7. Learner judges new state as more stable			

2 Reflection is the primary tool to trigger learning from experience. Disciplined reflection, challenging one's assumptions and comfortable ways of thinking, leads to deeper learning.
3 Insight alone is not enough. Creating a support system which encourages all individuals to grow, and accepts individuals who have changed, promotes retention of new behaviours.
4 Transformative learning may be catalysed through expert facilitation.

Most learning is intentional and the task of the facilitators under these conditions is primarily to help self-directed learners be more productive in their learning projects. When learning is unintentional, facilitators have added tasks: to deal with the emotions generated by this surprise and to behave ethically. The facilitator of unintentional learning enters deep territory where the potential for harm is great. While our work suggests that important learning can come from these processes, caution is in order.

Managing the Unmanaged: Managers as Models and Coaches for Informal and Incidental Learning

Increasingly, individuals must learn continuously in order to be competitive. There is a push towards self-reliance, self-development and self-directed learning (Tough, 1979, 1982; Pedler et al., 1994), with managers and employees being held more accountable for performance. From a positive view, this means that people can actualize themselves and develop portable skills that open doors to new jobs at a time when cradle-to-the-grave employment seldom exists. However, companies may simply wish to divest themselves of responsibility for employee development in an era when supply of human resources is greater than demand. In addition, people do not always want to take control of their learning.

Assuming that managers want to facilitate informal learning, what can they do? Strategies include: planning for learning, creating mechanisms for learning in teams, and developing an environment conducive to learning.

Planning for learning

Learning is enhanced by planning – before the fact, or by looking back retrospectively to learn from past experience. One of the more systematic of the approaches to planning for self-learning has been created by Alan Mumford (1994), writing alone and in collaboration with Honey (Honey and Mumford, 1989, 1992). The centerpiece of Mumford's work includes taking the 'learning styles questionnaire' and 'learning diagnostic questionnaire' which Honey and Mumford have created, and the creation of 'personal development plans' which are developed in concert between managers, their managers and/or staff, and often an external learning facilitator. Personal development plans emphasize natural learning opportunities outside the classroom, along with more structured courses or activities. In the USA, many organization-wide systems to plan for learning begin with competency assessments to identify accurately what is expected of managers and employees in the new roles they find themselves assuming.

Planning makes learning more conscious, better focuses effort and increases measures of accountability. O'Brien with Shook (1995), for example, describe 21 exercises that build learning habits and skills. However, planning strategies can be artificial; learning becomes an end in itself, and as such, can also be separated from experiences. To counteract this problem, learning is often tied to real-life problems and experiences. Learning takes place 'just-in-time' while struggling with a challenge. This cannot happen, however, without time to learn, honest feedback and, at times, other forms of assistance. Real-life challenges are also woven consciously into classroom training. Computer-based technology is often used as well to aid in problem-solving, self-directed learning and interactive online dialogue. Sometimes, broad-brush development is used to stimulate new thinking and exchange of ideas. In Land O'Lakes, for example, a book club stimulates new ideas, and one division has sponsored 'brown bag' lunch discussions to hear colleagues discuss initiatives or studies they have undertaken (Watkins and Marsick, 1996).

Some tools have been created to enhance planning for learning that is tied to job challenges (Dechant, 1994). Denny and Weldon (1993) used our informal and incidental learning model to design a learning cycle tool for managers in Ernst and Young to use in their own learning and when coaching or mentoring others. The cycle involves mental rehearsal of anticipated challenges in order to identify contextual factors that might influence one's understanding of the challenge and one's learning needs. Reframing of the challenge in this light might then lead to gaining knowledge and skills that are more effective in meeting the challenge, planning for seeking and using feedback to improve performance, documentation of the experience and its effects, and analysing results to examine lessons learned.

Planning enables people to nurture learning strategically and to take advantage of a wider range of learning strategies that might otherwise be overlooked. However, factors such as the following make it difficult to plan for informal learning:

- Organizations do not always let people follow their natural inclinations to learn in different ways, and may value credentials over informal learning.
- People differ in their capacity to seek needed information and skills, which speaks to readiness for learning, access to learning opportunities, and information search skills.
- There is disagreement as to what learning to learn means and, therefore, as to how to help people to better learn how to learn – compare, for example, Kolb's (1984) Learning Style Theory with Heinman's (1987) approach to study skills.
- The topic of learning might require the assistance of outside experts, which is especially true for highly technical topics.

- Organizations may not provide clear guidance regarding what people must know and how this will assist them in their career paths.
- Resources may not be available for learning: time, funding and learning materials.

Some organizations do not give people a choice as to whether or not they wish to learn. In Johnsonville Foods (Watkins and Marsick, 1996), for example, individuals are expected continuously to stretch themselves, regardless of their interest in learning. They are rewarded for performance based on measurement against contracts that they negotiate with their customers. They are rewarded for learning only when they exceed normal day-to-day requirements, a demand that might actually discourage learning for some people.

Learning in teams

Managers increasingly work together in intact, self-directed or cross-functional teams. Sometimes these teams are also characterized as 'virtual' in that they are dispersed geographically, and communicate through electronic technology. The challenges for learning in teams are even greater than for individual learning. Needs must be negotiated, conflicts addressed and ideas brought together. At the same time, learning in teams forces people to confront multiple viewpoints that they might otherwise ignore. Action Reflection Learning[TM] and action science are strategies that promote group and organizational learning.[1]

Action Reflection Learning is a variant of action learning, originally developed by Revans (1982), in which peers help one another to learn by asking questions in order to generate new insights. People work on real problems, and as they do, they get feedback from others about their thinking and actions. Action learning involves an iterative cycle of taking action to address the problem, and then reflecting on what was learned with the assistance of others, which typically leads to a new cycle of action and reflection. The effectiveness of action learning depends on people's willingness to admit mistakes and to subject themselves and their experience to constructive criticism by their peers.

Action science provides a method for constructive criticism. Managers analyse cases in groups that lay out the dialogue they might have had in a situation which they would have liked to handle more effectively. They develop maps of their behaviour which identify the assumptions they brought to the situation and the way assumptions lead them to jump to inferences without testing their thinking from one step to another. Because managers are prone to quick action, these inferences often escalate into other unnecessary complications and generate self-fulfilling prophecies and defensive routines (Watkins, 1995). Action science helps managers to recognize values that make learning difficult, such as unilateral control of a situation, or a desire that events seem predictable and rational even if they are not so.

Enacting an environment supportive to informal and incidental learning

Informal learning theory is focused primarily on the learning of individuals. Yet in today's organizations, the focus must also be on learning systems. Managers are challenged to create conditions where information flows freely and knowledge is valued wherever it emerges. It is not enough that people learn; informal learning theory must jump from the individual level to the systems level in order to show how knowledge gained by individuals can be captured and used by others. How can informal learning theory enable managers to track information as part of routine accounting systems? How can theory help managers to find new measures for return on knowledge or information investments? How can theory assist managers in enhancing the speed with which the organization translates new ideas into products and market share?

Managers might critique the feasibility of enacting informal and incidental learning because they feel they cannot change the environment to support learning. Managers are stewards of the organization's vision; they can influence systems and culture even though they might also see themselves as prisoners of those systems. It does help, however, if top leadership supports such a shift, or at least, if managers can collectively influence top leadership. Many change consultants believe that you can change the brain of the firm by changing a top management team. Middle managers, however, often hold sway in making or breaking change efforts. They are guardians of embedded norms, structures and goals which define how individuals in the organization relate and share meaning.

Major shifts in organizations signal additional sources of incidental learning. Before, we could anticipate that the presence of a title next to a person's name on an organizational chart would define how others in the organization would relate to that person, who would relate to them, and the scope of their influence. Now, individuals' access to information, expertise, interpersonal network and interpersonal skills are more likely to define who they will relate to and with what scope of influence. Managing the largely tacit incidental learning attendant on such widespread cultural and environmental change, paradoxically, asks managers to learn how to manage the unmanaged.

We might readily ask if it is reasonable to ask managers to attempt to create cultures which support surfacing these hidden sources of knowledge or to promote more informal means of learning. Aren't there costs? Perhaps there are good reasons that some things are undiscussible or hidden. More informal learning is also less well-controlled and predictable. How, then, can we continue to hold managers accountable for the performance outcomes of their employees? There may be costs to employees as well. Managers may expect them to learn on their own at a rate that exceeds their capabilities and the time available. What is now tacit knowledge may be painful or embarrassing to individuals if surfaced and made public. Like any process, informal and incidental learning may be more or less effective, and can lead to preferred or undesirable, unintended outcomes.

Critique of Our Model

Our model has been empirically tested both in our research (Marsick and Watkins, 1990) and that of our doctoral students. Over 20 studies have used this model to explore the informal and/or incidental learning of managers and human resource professionals, teachers, higher education administrators, co-operative education directors, stroke survivors, caregivers, multiple sclerosis victims and families, paramedics, nurses and nurse educators. McCall et al. (1988) studied the lessons from experience of managers, as have others using models similar to ours. Most of these studies involved retrospective reflection on critical incidents. Burgoyne and Hodgson (1983) studied reflection in real time. Rogers (1989) used action science cases to intervene with a group of adult children of alcoholics. She then studied both what facilitated transformative learning and the process of reflective learning within individuals and groups. More studies are needed that focus on real-time reflection and the reflective learning/intervention relationship.

Our model is primarily defined situationally as non-classroom-based learning. The model would be enhanced by incorporating the intrinsic characteristics identified in the reflective and transformative learning models presented in Table 17.1, such as integrating learning with past learning and attending to feelings. We have added to Argyris and Schön's work on action science a deeper elaboration of the cognitive processes undergirding error detection (Figure 17.2). A more explicit empirical test of this aspect of our work would further deepen our understanding of the cumulative effect of misinterpretations in problem-solving.

Finally, our model – as is true for most other models of informal and incidental learning – does not attend to the key role of emotions. While most mention their importance, only Boud et al. (1985) and Boyd and Myers (1988) actually incorporate a stage which explicitly addresses emotion. Research and theory building which elaborate the language of emotions, the preverbal message that feelings are trying to convey, will lead to more robust and holistic models of informal and incidental learning.

Summary and Conclusion

In summary, then, managers who want to enhance informal learning can build on the internal circle of the model we have described. They can, for example, plan more consciously to turn challenges into learning opportun-ities, seek alternative viewpoints and perspectives to compensate for blind spots and limitations, and draw out lessons more explicitly that are relevant for similar circumstances. Enhancing incidental learning is more difficult, given that it is, by definition, unplanned. Lessons here focus on the potential sources of error identified in Figure 17.2. Managers can surface assumptions and tacit beliefs, clarify the way in which context influences understandings, and pay attention to triggers that set off patterns of behaviour that continually produce undesired results.

Effective managers of the future will have to attend to the more subtle, implicit learnings which drive behaviour. By learning to surface tacit meanings, they will be able to achieve shared meaning and to engage in dialogue. This will enable the organization to learn and possibly to innovate. On the other hand, we acknowledge that this requires great skill and may exact its own hidden costs.

We have observed that incidental learning is more coincidental than incidental, less accidental than intuitive, and must almost always be surfaced. It is coincident with other organizational and individual actions, events or prior experiences. This situatedness affects how people understand the event. Incidental learning exists as unstated or even subconscious beliefs, assumptions, attributions and evaluations. These are not at all accidental, even though they are often arrived at intuitively and may cause 'accidents' in the form of unintended consequences. When incidental learning is not surfaced, it is subject to ever-deepening cycles of individual and organizational error, misinterpretation and unintended consequences. We don't know what we don't know. Surfacing these implicit meanings requires an intentional and guided reflection process such as action research, action science, or Action Reflection Learning™. Sometimes, this process leads to individual and organizational transformation. In an era of continuous change and transformation, managers can ill afford to ignore this potent form of learning in the workplace.

Note

1   Action Reflection Learning™ is a trademark of Leadership in International Management.

Annotated Bibliography

V.J. Marsick and K. Watkins (1990) *Informal and Incidental Learning in the Workplace.* London and New York: Routledge, presents our theory of informal and incidental learning and the results of six studies which illustrate the theory. Two studies involve managers: action learning projects in Sweden depict the process of learning through facilitated reflection, and higher educational managers' roles in managing change illustrate the way attributions about role influence action. M. McCall, M. Lombardo and A. Morrison (1988) *The Lessons of Experience: How Successful Executives Develop on the Job.* Lexington, MA: Lexington Books, is based on extensive interviews with managers. The authors demonstrate that critical learning for managerial mobility is obtained through three key experiences: learning from challenging assignments, learning from difficult bosses, and learning from hardships. A. Mumford (1994) *How Managers Can Develop Managers.* Aldershot: Gower, looks at how managers can use day-to-day contact, including learning from experience, from problems and challenges, and from others, to develop managers. Topics included in the book are recognizing learning opportunities, and understanding the learning process, the skills required to develop others, and the idea of reciprocity in helping.

References

Argyris, C. (1970) *Intervention Theory and Method*. Reading, MA: Addison-Wesley.

Argyris, C. and Schön, D. (1978) *Organizational Learning: A Theory of Action Perspective*. San Francisco: Jossey-Bass.

Argyris, C. and Schön, D. (1996) *Organizational Learning II: Theory, Method, and Practice*. Reading, MA: Addison-Wesley.

Boyd, E.M. and Fales, A.W. (1983) 'Reflective learning: key to learning from experience', *Journal of Humanistic Psychology*, 23: 99–117.

Boyd, R.D. and Myers, J.G. (1988) 'Transformative education', *International Journal of Lifelong Education*, 7 (4): 261–84.

Boud, D., Keogh, R. and Walker, D. (1985) 'Promoting reflection in learning: a model', in D. Boud, R. Keogh and D. Walker (eds), *Reflection: Turning Experience into Learning*. New York: Nichols. pp. 18–40.

Burgoyne, J.G. and Hodgson, V.E. (1983) 'Natural learning and managerial action: a phenomenological study in the field setting', *Journal of Management Studies*, 20 (3): 387–99.

Candy, P. (1991) *Self-Direction for Lifelong Learning*. San Francisco: Jossey-Bass.

Chene, A. (1988) 'From the text to the adult learning trajectory', in C. Warren (ed.), *Proceedings of the 29th Annual Adult Education Research Conference, Calgary, Canada*. Calgary: University of Calgary. pp. 43–54.

Dechant, K. (1994) 'Making the most of job assignments: an exercise in planning for learning', *Journal of Management Education*, 18 (2): 198–211.

Denny, M. and Weldon, K. (1993) 'Continuous workplace learning model', unpublished manuscript, Vienna, VA, Ernst and Young.

Dewey, J. (1938) *Experience and Education*. New York: Collier Books.

Heiman, M. (1987) 'Learning to learn: a behavioral approach to improving thinking', in D.N. Perkins, J. Lochhead and J. Bishop (eds), *Thinking: The Second International Conference*. Hillsdale, NJ: Erlbaum.

Honey, P. and Mumford, A. (1989) *Capitalizing on Your Learning Style* (2nd edn). King of Prussia, PA: Organization Design and Development.

Honey, P. and Mumford, A. (1992) *Capitalizing on Your Learning Opportunities*. King of Prussia, PA: Organization Design and Development.

Jarvis, P. (1987) *Adult Learning in the Social Context*. London: Croom Helm.

Kolb, D.A. (1984) *Experiential Learning*. Englewood Cliffs, NJ: Prentice-Hall.

Marsick, V.J. (1994) 'Trends in managerial reinvention: creating a learning map', *Management Learning*, 25 (1): 11–33.

Marsick, V.J. and Watkins, K. (1990) *Informal and Incidental Learning in the Workplace*. London and New York: Routledge.

McCall, M., Lombardo, M. and Morrison, A. (1988) *The Lessons of Experience: How Successful Executives Develop on the Job*. Lexington, MA: Lexington Books.

Mezirow, J. (1978) 'Perspective transformation', *Adult Education Quarterly*, 28: 100–10.

Mezirow, J.D. (1991) *Transformative Dimensions of Adult Learning*. San Francisco: Jossey-Bass.

Mocker, D.W. and Spear, G.E. (1982) *Lifelong Learning: Formal, Non-Formal, Informal and Self-Directed*. Columbus, OH: ERIC Clearinghouse on Adult, Career and Vocational Education.

Mumford, A. (1994) *How Managers Can Develop Managers*. Aldershot: Gower.

Nevis, E.C., DiBella, A.J. and Gould, J.M. (1995, Winter) 'Understanding organizations as learning systems', *Sloan Management Review*, 36 (2): 73–85.

O'Brien, M.J. with Shook, L. (1995) *Profit from Experience: How to Make the Most of Your Learning and Your Life*. Austin, TX: Bard and Stephen.

O'Neil, J. and Marsick, V.J. (1994) 'Becoming critically reflective through action reflection learning', in A. Brooks and K.E. Watkins (eds), 'The emerging power of action inquiry technologies', *New Directions in Adult and Continuing Education*, 63: 17–30.

Pedler, M., Burgoyne, J. and Boydell, T. (1994) *A Manager's Guide to Self-Development* (3rd edn). London: McGraw-Hill.

Postman, N. and Weingartner, L. (1971) *Teaching as a Subversive Activity*. New York: Penguin.

Reischmann, J. (1986, October) 'Learning "en passant": the forgotten dimension', paper presented at the annual conference of the American Association of Adult and Continuing Education, Miami, FL.

Resnick, L. (1987) 'Learning in school and out', *Educational Researcher*, 16 (9): 13–20.

Revans, R.W. (1982) *The Origins and Growth of Action Learning*. Bickly, Kent: Chartwell-Bratt (and Lund, Sweden: Studenlitteratur).

Rogers, R.P. (1989) 'Reflective learning about the workplace: an action science study with adult children of alcoholics', PhD dissertation, University of Texas, Austin.

Tough, A. (1979) *The Adult's Learning Projects* (2nd edn). *Research in Education Series, No. 1. Toronto*. Ontario: Ontario Institute for Studies in Education.

Tough, A. (1982) *Intentional Changes: A Fresh Approach to Helping People Change*. Chicago, IL: Follett.

Varela, F.J., Thompson, E. and Rosch, E. (1995) *The Embodied Mind: Cognitive Science and Human Experience*. Cambridge, MA: MIT Press.

Watkins, K. (1995) 'Changing managers' defensive reasoning about work/family conflicts', *Journal of Management Development*, 14 (2): 77–88.

Watkins, K. and Marsick, V.J. (1993) *Sculpting the Learning Organization*. San Francisco: Jossey-Bass.

Watkins, K. and Marsick, V.J. (1996) *In Action: The Learning Organization*. Alexandria, VA: American Society for Training and Development.

Watkins, K. and Wiswell, B. (1987) 'Incidental learning in the workplace', in H. Copar (ed.), *Proceedings of the Human Resources Management and Organizational Behavior Western Regional Conference, Virginia*. Virginia: Association of Human Resources Management and Organization Behavior.

18

Towards a Critical Management Pedagogy

Michael Reynolds

In their critique of management education, Reed and Anthony observe:

> All too often, the educational community has retreated into a narrow vocationalism in which the overriding emphasis is given to functional and technical skills which crowds out any sustained concern with the social, moral, political and ideological ingredients of managerial work and the form of educational experience most appropriate to their enhancement and development. (1992: 601)

These concerns are echoed by other writers (see, e.g., Willmott, 1994, and Chapter 9 of this volume), who also draw attention to the lack of a 'critical' perspective in management education, one which would involve managers in thinking questioningly about their roles and responsibilities and the purposes and social consequences of the organizations they work for. The critical perspective called for by these authors is qualitatively different from concepts of critical thinking which can be found in management education: making discerning choices between various options; evaluating alternative courses of action; making judgements about other people in the course of their work (see e.g., McCormick, 1994); or, in adult education generally, the development of understanding through scepticism and through questioning of ideas and concepts in ways which encourage more creative and satisfactory solutions to problems (Garrison, 1991).

An additional problem, however, is that while concerns for a critical perspective address the *content* of management education, little is said as to how educational *methodology* should equally reflect a critical position. Indeed, alternative methodologies in use in management education and development, such as experiential learning and self-directed learning, are generally dismissed by critical theorists for reasons which will be covered later. A critical management pedagogy should be reflected in both content and methodology.[1] This would offer an advance on current practice in academia in which critical content, as for example in the dissemination of organizational sociology, is invariably delivered through methodologies which reflect little of the position advocated by Reed and Anthony (1992).

Addressing the domain of educational generally, Giroux (1981) makes a distinction between two schools of theory and practice which is applicable to the current situation in management learning. The two positions he identifies are 'content focused radicals', whose emphasis is on presenting more

Traditional Education	Content-focused Radicals
Traditional content Traditional method	Radical content Traditional method
Strategy-based Radicals	**Critical Pedagogy**
Radical method Traditional content	Radical method Radical content

Figure 18.1   *Alternative pedagogies (based on Giroux, 1981)*

politicized ideas through the curriculum, and 'strategy based radicals', for example such exponents of student-centred learning as Knowles (1975), whose concern has been to counter the intrusion into education of hierarchy and authoritarianism with methods based on more humanistic values.

While each position attempts to provide a critical alternative to traditional educational principles, neither does so completely. The content radicals have not addressed the contradictory values embedded in the traditional methods and classroom relationships they use to disseminate their subject matter. The process radicals have developed an alternative, non-hierarchical pedagogy but supported this with a conceptual vocabulary which is inadequate to the task of analysing the complexities of social relationships. These positions and the alternatives are summarized in Figure 18.1.

The purpose of this chapter is to define an educational approach whose content *and* methodology demonstrate a critical perspective. First, however, it is necessary to outline a working definition of what it means to be 'critical' in this context, to argue for the significance of educational methodology as a learning medium, and to consider the possibilities and limitations of alternative methodologies in current use.

The Basis of a Critical Perspective

Of the different critical perspectives possible (critical theory, Marxist, postmodern, phenomenological), I have drawn particularly on the ideas of radical educationalists such as Giroux (1981), and on the work of Hindmarsh (1993) and Kemmis (1985), who have applied the critical theory of Jurgen Habermas in the context of adult education (Habermas, 1972). Central to Habermas's approach is the idea that reflecting on the social and political forces which affect and often distort communication between people can lead to more authentically democratic relationships. Hindmarsh and Kemmis have developed Habermas's ideas in relation to educational practice, and the types of reflection they distinguish can be adapted to provide the basis of a

Instrumental	using knowledge in order to control the environment knowledge assumed to be dispassionate, objective, value-free. finding the most effective and efficient solutions to material and social problems.
Consensual	identifying the values and assumptions underlying actions. developing shared norms and common values. alignment: seeking goodness of fit between individual and institutional values and beliefs. shared commitment to common purpose.

Critical	questioning taking-for-granteds, both about practice and its
	    social and institutional context.
	identifying and questioning relevant purposes, and conflicts of
	    power and interest.
	relating the experience of work to wider social, political and
	    culural processes with the prospect of changing them.

Figure 18.2   *Modes of reflection (based on Hindmarsh (1993) and Kemmis (1985))*

critical perspective for theory and practice in management learning (see Figure 18.2).

In essence, a distinction can be made between *instrumental reflection*, which is concerned with practical questions about what courses of action can best lead to the achievement of goals or to solutions of specific problems; *consensual reflection*, which raises questions about ends as well as means but within the context of what has been prescribed as 'good practice', illustrated in an organizational context in the promotion by senior management of values chosen by them to epitomize its 'culture' – as in culture change programmes, for example, and *critical reflection*, which confronts underlying assumptions, in particular about the context and its 'institutionalized relationships of class, gender, race and power' (Hindmarsh, 1993: 111).

Critical reflection, the least familiar mode in both adult and management education, is more than a theoretical exercise. It involves engaging with individual, organizational or social problems with the aim of changing the conditions which gave rise to them, as well as providing the basis for personal change. Alvesson and Willmott, in their account of critical theory, describe its goal similarly as: 'The emancipatory potential of reason to *reflect critically* on how the reality of the social world, including the construction of the self, is socially produced and, therefore, open to transformation' (1992b: 435; my emphasis).

The overriding implication of a critical perspective is that the concern with *means* should not be allowed to obscure questions about *ends*. In management learning, examining educational purposes and the values on which they are based, is no less important than developing the methods, techniques and tools of measurement employed in furthering them. It is this characteristic which distinguishes critical reflection from less politicized versions. It embodies both the language of *critique* and the language of *possibility* (Giroux, 1988) in that questioning of assumptions provides the basis for changes in practice. Before considering the application of critical reflection to educational design, it is important to identify its character-istics.[2]

Characteristics of a critical perspective

1 Questioning assumptions. The purpose of critical reflection is to iden-tify, question and, if necessary, change the 'invisible' assumptions and taken-for-granteds which have become incorporated in received knowledge and practice (Wilson, 1994). Giroux emphasizes the importance of asking the questions which are usually *not* asked, and makes a useful distinction between apparently coherent sets of values, beliefs and practices which are constructed and disseminated by majorities to explain and sustain their position, and the assumptions and taken-for-granteds which are concealed during that process. He draws attention to questions which are suppressed, as well as to those which are raised. Appeals to 'common sense' or 'the right way to do things' may be based on assumptions which no longer hold good, or which reflect sectional interests but which have acquired the status of unspoken 'truth' and are no longer questioned. So, for example, the familiar assertion that 'people resist change' obscures the possibility that there are good reasons why the changes in question *should* be resisted.

2 Analysing power relations. Relationships in education, as at work generally, are invariably based on asymmetries of power. Knowledge and professional practice can be constructed in ways which support and maintain those arrangements. The work of critical reflection is to make clear the relationships between power, knowledge and its social consequences. So, for example, in their application of critical reflection to education, Brah and Hoy (1989) are concerned with the way hierarchies of power are expressed in relation to gender, class, age and race, and how such sources of inequality might be confronted through an approach to learning based on critical reflection.

> We may or may not challenge dominant ideologies. Whether we do is mediated by the specificity of historical and social conditions, including what goes on in the classroom and what is included in the curriculum. Empowerment means identify-ing and acknowledging where power lies and the structures which uphold it and challenging those structures in struggles toward a more equal society. (Brah and Hoy, 1989: 76)

This aspect of critical theory underlines its relevance for management educators. Managing is not neutral or disinterested. Managers affect other people's lives and their future through the agency of the power held by them. Management educators, in turn, play their part in the construction and dissemination of knowledge for professional use. If reflection is to be critical, these processes should be examined, and the sectional interests concealed in the 'truths' which are offered as the rationale for our own and others' actions revealed (Gibson, 1986).

3 Critical reflection has a collective focus. This sense of acting in concert with others contrasts with the discourse of individualism inherent in much formal education and experiential learning in particular. The experience on which each of us reflects is inevitably social and this must be taken into account for reflection to have any meaning. Wilson makes this point in a critique of adult education in the USA when he writes: '. . . our theory and practice are situated within and emanate from historical traditions; we don't practice as individuals but as members of those communities whose values, beliefs and norms about the means and ends of practice are reflected in and constitutive of our daily educational work' (Wilson, 1994: 188).

Underlying these three characteristics of critical reflection are the goals of personal development and of betterment of society through reason based on the application of historical and contextual perspectives. Rather than providing the means of fitting people into work or society as it exists, education from a critical perspective is intended to further the creation of a society based on non-exploitative relationships (Giroux, 1983). It is this emancipatory element of critical reflection which seems most vulnerable in the educational domain, where preoccupation with technique and measurement often seems at the expense of moral and social considerations (Wilson, 1994).

Critical reflection in practice: applying an example from management learning

The familiar 'learning styles' approach provides a useful vehicle for illustrating the difference a critical perspective makes to theory and practice in management learning. Thinking through the options of using 'learning styles' in the context of a management training programme, different interpretations of what it means to be critical, and different degrees of importance attached to the idea of being critical, can be identified. The level of criticality shown in deciding whether or not to use 'learning styles' can range from unquestioned acceptance, with no consideration of the assumptions underlying the approach or its validity, through informed choice amongst alternative versions of 'learning style', to an examination of the basic concept or the possible social consequences of its application. Neglecting to question the concept of 'learning style' would, for example, miss its individualizing properties. Critical reflection would be more likely to reveal them.

These distinctions in levels of criticality can be illustrated by the following statements (modes of reflection from Figure 18.2 in parenthesis):

Unquestioning acceptance (instrumental)
'Before we get into the detailed design of this course I think we should find out what range of learning styles they're bringing with them.'

Selection of alternatives on a pragmatic or instrumental basis (instrumental)
'We should use a learning-styles instrument people can relate to. Some are off-putting for participants and the analysis is complicated. And preferably one we can get hold of without too much fuss.'

'In-house' critique: evaluating and discriminating between alternatives without questioning shared assumptions (consensual)
'I don't see why we stick to the idea of style, the validity of the questionnaires used to measure "learning strategies" is more convincing.'
'We need to select a version of learning style which highlights how readily participants learn from experience. That fits well with the learning organization programme we'll be starting later in the year.'

Questioning assumptions and taken-for-granteds (critical)
'What do we mean by learning style? Whose definition are we using? What theory of learning is it based on and is it one we can go along with? For example, does it allow for the conscious choices people make in learning? We need to find a way of helping participants reflect on how they learn which draws on their own ideas and experience.'

Questioning of social, political, ecological or cultural assumptions: exposing vested interests (critical)
'I'm not happy with using learning styles in any form. The concept seems to blow a smokescreen over the way some approaches to learning are gendered, privileging ways men think and talk, for example. And just as worrying, it seems to encourage people in labelling themselves. It's too close to discrimination for my liking. Who benefits from that?'

Similar distinctions could be made in relation to choices of educational method. For example, a particular experiential approach might be used because it fits the time available or the number of participants on a course, or because it matches the trainer's skills (instrumental). Or it could be chosen because of its capability of accelerating participants' familiarity with each other, or because it generates the level of team spirit expected within the organization as a whole (consensual). Alternatively, some methods might be rejected because they encourage inappropriate levels of self-disclosure, or depend on absolute but covert trainer control (critical).

The Importance of Educational Methodology from a Critical Perspective

There is reason to believe that critical reflection should be applied to education method as well as content. Even in formal and conventional educational processes there is more to learning than engaging with the spoken or written word and there are more potential sources of learning than teachers, the literature and course materials. The learning setting more generally, its structures, relationships and methods are also implicated, not only through their effect on the learning process, but directly, as an additional source of learning.

Students' experience is of both content and process. Process includes: the tutor or trainer's approach to the event; the methods used; the influence students can exercise over both the structural and the conceptual aspects of the course design; the relationships which develop; the reflection of institutional or organizational values and constraints; and participants' own ideas and their reactions and responses to the course design as it unfolds.

These aspects of the learning environment not only affect how people learn and how much or how deeply they learn (Marton and Saljo, 1976), they are also a *source of learning*, in as much as they reflect systems of values and beliefs which are acceptable within the institution, organization, profession or society more generally (Reynolds, 1982). Parlett and Hamilton (1972) used the idea of the 'learning milieu' to describe this complexity. They saw it as representing:

> . . . a network or nexus of cultural, social, institutional and psychological variables. These interact in complicated ways to produce . . . a unique pattern of circumstances, pressures, customs, opinions and work-styles which suffuse the teaching and learning that occur there. (Parlett and Hamilton, 1972: 11)

Remembering also the work of Snyder (1971) in articulating the 'hidden curriculum' and Bernstein's (1971) proposition that cultural values are transmitted even through the way a curriculum is hierarchically organized and compartmentalized, it seems reasonable to suppose that course participants learn through the medium of the milieu, as well as from explicitly transmitted content. From the educational environment as a complex whole, they find out about the behaviour which is expected of them as students or employees, and they are exposed to the social, political and cultural values which underlie these expectations (Hodgson and Reynolds, 1981).

Unless management educators apply a critical perspective to all aspects of a course, informing the design of both content *and* process, it could be that they encourage a reflexivity in their students that they have not applied to their own practice. MBA classes might be introduced to principles of critical theory conveyed by teaching staff who are in total control of the course methodology, its structure and content – yet seem unaware of the contradiction. The students for their part assimilate received – if critical – wisdom while subordinating themselves to an educational setting they have played no part in constructing or managing. Critically reflective management education should involve an examination of these processes as well as of curricular content.

In some respects, alternative approaches, such as experiential learning and student-centred learning, would seem to reflect a critical perspective. Its proponents have taken the position that traditional, hierarchical social relationships are replicated in most educational settings through values communicated by the structures of the institution, its methods and the relationships engendered by them. As Giroux observes, the most significant contribution of these 'strategy-based radicals' is that they have 'called into question the political and normative underpinnings of traditional classroom pedagogical styles' (Giroux, 1981: 65).

The problem with student-centred learning and related pedagogies, however, is that they are based on a humanist perspective which isolates educational experience from its history and context. As a consequence, the social, political and cultural forces which make up the formative context of learning are reduced to mere background. The primary focus is the development of the individual with scant concern for connections between power, difference and social relations (Usher, 1991). Attention is focused on such concerns as 'understanding how people learn', elaborating differences in approaches to learning, and on the development of an array of alternative teaching methods, rather than on providing the conceptual frameworks necessary for any analysis of the ideological content of policy and institutional practice.

Management development and to a lesser extent management education, have been strongly influenced by the humanist perspective. Concepts of self-directed learning have evolved in which organizational constraints are accepted as 'common sense' parameters, fragmentary technologies proliferate in the form of 'competencies' and psychometrics (Edwards, 1991; Hyland, 1994) and, as in education generally, cultural differences are translated into 'learning styles' (Popkewitz, 1988; Reynolds, 1997). At worst, humanistic education replaces traditional hierarchical structures with radical alternatives which, while 'parading under the banner of self-actualization, warmth, and personal autonomy – may appear more palatable, but . . . may be no less "oppressive"' (Giroux, 1981: 66).

Despite these limitations, however, experiential and student-centred learning should not be totally rejected in a search for a critical management pedagogy, precisely because of the possibilities of alternative, non-hierarchical relations which they provide. What is additionally required is that these methods are informed by broader theoretical perspectives which enable understanding of social and political, as well as individual or organizational, processes.

Towards a Critical Management Pedagogy

In her postmodern critique of emancipatory practice in education, Lather's definition of pedagogy is consistent with the idea of an educational 'milieu' and underlines the importance of applying critical reflection more generally than to the curriculum alone.

> By pedagogy, I mean that which addresses the transformation of consciousness that takes place in the intersection of the teacher, the learner and the knowledge they together produce . . . It furthermore, denies the teacher as neutral transmitter, the student as passive, and knowledge as immutable material to impart. Instead, the concept of pedagogy focuses attention on the conditions and means through which knowledge is produced. (Lather, 1994: 104)

But ways need to be found of translating these principles into practice, or management learning will be prone to the same criticism levelled at adult educators as having failed to move beyond the language of critique (Giroux and McClaren, 1987), for demonstrating more vision than practical recommendations (Gore, 1993).

A critical perspective should at least lead to questioning the intentions, beliefs and values which underlie programme design and the methods used within it. For example:

- What assumptions about how people learn is this design based on?
- What social and educational values are reflected in the structures, procedures, roles and relationships adopted within the programme design and the methods it incorporates?
- Does the design of the course or the tutors' approach imply that theirs are the only ideas, information or experience worth learning about?
- Does the design support critical reflection and dialogue?
- Are teachers or trainers aware of the assumptions implicit in the way they work with course participants?
- Do the methods used develop participants' abilities to work with others and to develop confidence in their abilities to convey ideas?
- Do participants have an opportunity to question the assumptions implicit in the design or to influence its design and content?

The proposal which follows is based on the premise that there already are participative methods consistent with a critical approach, but needing to be strengthened by the incorporation of theoretical frameworks whose focus is not limited to personal and interpersonal process, and by an element of reflexivity which both content and process radicals have so far lacked.[3]

Characteristics in practice

Based on the argument so far, a critical pedagogy might be expected to demonstrate the following features, the first in relation to 'content', and the rest in relation to 'process'.

1 *The curriculum*: access to critical treatment of management theory and practice in various disciplines (accounting, organizational theory, and so forth).
2 *Structures, procedures and methods*: teaching/learning methods and procedures which are non-hierarchical, providing choice, opportunities for dialogue and influence over the programme's design and content.
3 *Introduction to critical perspectives*: some of which may be included in the curriculum (gender, ideas on the practice of critical reflection) but are applied to the learning process (together with ideas on pedagogy and the analysis of social dynamics).
4 *Reflexivity*: applying critical perspectives to understanding one's own position in relation to the educational process, and to understanding and managing the learning milieu jointly with participants.

1 The curriculum. The curriculum might be expected to be less imposed than is usually the case in management education, and ideas and material made available to participants should include applications of critical theory to different topic areas (see Alvesson and Willmott (1992a) as an example of a source of critical writing in a range of management disciplines). Fundamentally, the purpose of the course content should be to stimulate questioning and dialogue in relation to professional problems, rather than to disseminate and reinforce a particular managerial or academic discourse.

One indication as to whether the course is informed from a critical perspective is the positions reflected in reading lists and departmental libraries. Is the bulk of the available literature in the form of descriptive texts, instruction manuals and the best-sellers of 'corporate dreamers' (Welton, 1994: 288)? Are there sources available which will help illuminate the practice of management through language, history and culture (Giroux and McClaren, 1987)? Does the literature include the experiences and ideas of managers, management students and trainers as well as academic research? Is reading encouraged outside the mainstream of management thinking, such as novels and short stories, which might draw attention in a different but more forceful way to personal and socio-economic conditions (Nord and Jermier, 1992)?

2   Structures, procedures and methods.   The second task for the critical pedagogist is to create the foundations of a learning milieu which will support student choice, and the opportunity to select, critique and construct ideas through dialogue with others, including tutors. The participation this would involve is not limited to the discussion of ideas, important as this is, and it is certainly more significant than the busyness that characterizes involvement in many experiential activities. Responsibility for the management of the programme, reviews of the design, and control over procedures for determining the agenda would also involve course members as well as tutors.

It is commonly assumed that certain methods are, by their nature, participative, and others are not. This is misleading. For example, an experiential activity might appear to be participative yet its structure and theoretical framework may be in the total control of the tutor or trainer. A lecture, on the other hand, usually signifies tutor control over method and content but need not, if it is given at the request of course participants in relation to *their* interests rather than as a curricular inevitability.

The argument for participation is both pedagogical and ideological. It enhances the probability of the content being relevant to the students' interests, and it reinforces educational and organizational values which are democratic. Above all, participation supports the aim of collectively 'producing' knowledge rather than the more familiar process of receiving wisdom 'within the asymmetric relations of power that structure teacher–student relations' (Giroux, 1992: 98).

3   Introduction to critical perspectives.   To benefit from participative educational methods and avoid the decontextualizing nature of conventional androgogy, it is necessary to incorporate a 'curriculum of perspectives', through which students can critically examine theory, practice and their individual and collective experiences of education and work. Perhaps this is the nearest we should get to imposing anything. Brah and Hoy (1989), in arguing for a more critical pedagogy, describe this as a responsibility for tutors. They emphasize that experiential learning approaches – increasingly applied in management education and development – usually fail to draw on the social and political concepts which would help students make sense of their experience from a contextualized perspective.

> Can experience ever be constituted outside of social relations? We do not think so. Each of us, though unique as individuals, are positioned within society alongside hierarchies of power constructed around such factors as class, caste, racism, gender, age and sexuality. Social encounters, as for instance in a classroom, are therefore mediated within the parameters set by this broader social context. (Brah and Hoy, 1989: 71)

Perspectives offered could also include internationalism and race, a conceptual language for understanding social relations which takes account of cultural and political processes and not only personal or interpersonal dynamics, theoretical frameworks with which to analyse power and its relation to social control as reflected in organizational practices, and an introduction to the principles and methods of discourse analysis. These are all examples not so much of chosen topics, but of perspectives used to ensure critical reflection in the study of them, perspectives which can also be applied to the educational process itself.

4 Reflexivity. A critical pedagogy would be characterized by an application of the ideas and perspectives described above in a critique of the course itself, its pedagogical assumptions and methods, and the social relations which developed within it, not least between tutors and participants. Reflexivity might, for example, entail a critique of the tutor's role generally and a deconstruction of authority and its expression in social relations in the classroom (Lather, 1994), as well as students reflecting on their orientation to the course. It could also involve an examination of the social and political assumptions embedded in the institutional context (Gore, 1993). Even in a programme designed for participation, students' relationships with tutors differ depending on whether or not they are sympathetic to or 'reciprocate' their tutors preferred mode of working (Keddy, 1971).

Choices are made over all aspects of the learning design, its methods, material, groupings and roles, as well as over content and direction. The origins of the content and methods which are selected and the values they incorporate can also be questioned (Zeichner, 1981). How is the power to influence these decisions distributed between staff and participants? How much are design decisions determined from positions of authority within the department, institution or profession? Which discourses are expressed in these educational practices, whether humanist, individualist, or the traditions of professional management or academia?

In particular, assessment and accreditation are arguably the most important manifestations of institutionalized power within educational institutions and professional bodies and must affect the social relations which develop as part of the learning milieu. How is assessment or appraisal taken into account? Are criteria negotiable? Are they made explicit? Tutors or trainers cannot lightly make assertions about participants having freedom of choice or control over what they say or do in the context of, for example, an experiential activity. Are participants encouraged to disclose personal material (feelings, opinions, history) against a background of assessment over which they have little or no control? The description of a course as 'self-directed' when it involves conventional assessment, takes no account of the imbalance of power with which the procedures is inevitably associated (Hearn, 1983).

To work reflexively is to enquire as to who is enabled to speak by the educational milieu and who is silenced by it? Who asks the questions and who gives the answers, and how do these patterns relate to role, gender, experience or age? Is confidence generally enhanced or undermined through the experience of learning? Do tutors change their views as a result of working with students through the substance of content or process? Of course reflexivity does not necessarily mean immobilizing introspection. Perhaps the overriding question is *where* these questions are discussed – in the privacy of staff rooms or within the learning community as the basis of negotiation and change.

Possibilities and Problems

Reed and Anthony (1992) advocate three propositions on which a 'critical response' in management education should be based:

(i)   that the negotiation of organizational order is the abode of the actual but often unrecognized concerns and problems of practising managers in the real world – it is practical rather than abstracted;

(ii)   that management practice is about moral issues and requires ethical examination because these are fundamentals upon which any organizational reality rests;

(iii)   that any educational process must develop and encourage critical and sceptical responses. Failure of management education to support this will contribute to its own redundancy. (Reed and Anthony, 1992: 603)

The purpose of this chapter has been to identify the basis of a comprehensive learning environment to support the quality of enquiry and learning Reed and Anthony argue for. Management education designed from a more critical perspective is likely to be significantly different from much current practice. In some respects there is more similarity with the practice of management development in organizations in which methods such as action learning can involve more participative roles and relationships, with shared control and more active involvement. So, for example, action learning, like experiential methods generally, does at least privilege experience over recieved academic wisdom.

Pedagogy based on these principles, even in the relatively privileged domain of management education and development, parallels a social order in which people influence decisions which affect them. It encourages the confidence born of 'taking part' in the social and political process of the learning environment rather than of being made subject to them. A critical perspective therefore is enacted both directly, by facilitation of dialogue, and indirectly, by mirroring a social order which is non-hierarchical.

What implications does this have for the educator, whether in an organization or educational institution? It certainly does not imply a passive 'facilitatory' role. Indeed, Garrison's concern is that introducing critical theory results in more guidance than is appropriate for a participative educational process (Garrison, 1991). Some see the tutor's role as more of critical theorist than manager (Giroux and Mclaren, 1987), sharing in management and design with participants and at the same time providing access to ideas and perspectives which inform them in their sense-making. Brah and Hoy's summary of the tutor's role reflects this position:

> One implication is that we must develop non-hierarchical modes of teaching and learning, but this does not mean that the tutor becomes simply a facilitator of student experience. The tutor must play an active role in constructing and presenting well-integrated and coherent frameworks within which to locate and understand individual as well as group experience. (Brah and Hoy, 1989: 75)

There are currently educational designs which offer a potential fit with these principles. Gibson (1986) and Gore (1993) are among authors who have emphasized the compatibility of action research with the principles of critical theory, and Willmott (1994) has put a similar case for action learning in the context of management education, a proposal which he elaborates in this volume. A further example of an existing approach suitable as the basis of a critical management pedagogy, is the learning community (Pedler, 1994), a brief account of which follows.

The *learning community* is a participative methodology with the aim of supporting dialogue through its design and educational philosophy. The structures, procedures and methods, including assessment of the learning community, are, ideally, jointly designed and managed by tutors and students. There is choice over both the direction and focus of participants' learning and of the ideas, concepts and theoretical frameworks used to make sense of their organizational situations. As much as possible, students' choices of direction or focus should be free from either academic or professional coercion.

For the prospect of choice to be realistic, however, there should be access to a wide range of sources of material relevant to participants' interests, at least some of which written from a critical perspective. And perhaps the most important characteristic, which will ensure a *critical* learning community and not another variant of individualizing androgogy, is the availability of analytical perspectives through which students are able to critique the ideas, theories and research they encounter, *and* examine and influence the social structures and relations of the community as it develops.

Conclusion

How realistic is this or any other critically based proposition? It is character-istic and understandable that managers' predominant concern is that educa-tion and training should provide solutions for the problems which beset them. The value of continually questioning ideas and practices may be less apparent. In addition, the dominant discourse of individualism in manage-ment education and particularly management development has obscured social and cultural considerations. Radical ideas which do find their way into the domain of management learning risk incorporation in weakened or distorted forms into the vocabulary of 'human resource development', itself a product of de-personalizing thought. 'Empowerment', 'reflection' and 'praxis' are notable casualties of this process.

The application of a critical perspective is not without problems either. Brookfield (1994) describes possible consequences of introducing student professionals to critical enquiry, such as self-doubt, alienation from col-leagues and fears of having begun a process of 'cultural suicide'. Similarly, Willmott (1994) observes that a critical approach can fuel cynicism and guilt, and Brittan and Maynard (1985: 87), writing in the context of gender and race awareness, comment that increased reflexivity 'could conceivably be the grounds for inactivity and a debilitating pessimism'. These con-sequences must apply equally to managers on postgraduate programmes which are designed from a similar perspective. Arguably, management educators should understand and address these consequences if they are to work from a more critical perspective.

Nevertheless the value of encouraging reflexivity and participation within approaches such as action learning or the learning community is that individuals are supported intellectually and emotionally in understanding their experience of the educational method used as well as making sense of theory in relation to their professional work. Educational designs with this element of practical reflexivity are more likely to lead beyond the language of critique to the real possibilities of change in working conditions and working relationships.

Notes

1   The term 'pedagogy' is used throughout in the sense of the whole approach or educational practice – content, methods, etc. – and the values and beliefs on which it is based. In this sense, androgogy or self-directed learning are examples of pedagogy. The term has its limitations but is common currency in the writings of adult educators and radical educational-ists on which this chapter draws.

2   Critical theory and its derivatives are not without criticism. Critical pedagogy in particular has been criticized as elitist (Welton, 1994), patriarchal (Luke and Gore, 1992), and for creating a 'masterful' discourse (Usher, 1992) in which there is a privileged 'we' who understand what is good for the less privileged 'them' (Simons, 1994). Furthermore, the origins of critical pedagogy are characterized as eurocentric (Giroux, 1992), implicitly excluding those who are not intellectual, white, male or middle class (Wildermeersch, 1992).

3 I have abbreviated Giroux's terms 'content-focused radicals' and 'strategy-based radicals' to 'content radicals' and 'process radicals', respectively, to use language more familiar in a management learning context. Throughout the argument in this chapter, I am also concerned that distinguishing between content and process should not obscure their interconnectedness.

Annotated Bibliography

For an introduction to Habermas, Gibson (1986) is particularly accessible and the articles by Hart (1990), Hindmarsh (1993) and Kemmis (1985) apply critical theory – including Habermas – to an adult education setting. It is more difficult to find references to the notion of learning from method and process but there are related ideas in Young (1971), especially the chapters by Bernstein and Keddy. For applications of these ideas to a management education context, see Hodgson and Reynolds (1981) and Reynolds (1982). Giroux (1981) provides a readable introduction to radical pedagogy, including explanations of 'content-focused radicalism' and 'strategy-based radicalism', and the collection of readings edited by Luke and Gore (1992) contain critiques of radical pedagogy from a feminist perspective.

References

Alvesson, M. and Willmott, H. (eds) (1992a) *Critical Management Studies*. London: Sage.

Alvesson, M. and Willmott, H. (1992b) 'On the idea of emancipation in management and organization studies', *Acadamy of Management Review*, 17 (3): 432–64.

Bernstein, B. (1971) 'On the classification and framing of educational knowledge', in M.F.D. Young (ed.), *Knowledge and Control*. New York: Collier-Macmillan. pp. 47–69.

Brah, A. and Hoy, J. (1989) 'Experiential learning: a new orthodoxy', in S.W. Weil and I. McGill (eds), *Making Sense of Experiential Learning*. Milton Keynes: Society for Research into Higher Education/Open University Press. pp. 70–7.

Brittan, A. and Maynard, M. (1985) *Sexism, Racism and Oppression*. Oxford: Blackwell.

Brookfield, S. (1994) 'Tales from the dark side: a phenomenography of adult critical reflection', *International Journal of Lifelong Education*, 13 (3): 203–16.

Edwards, R. (1991) 'The politics of meeting learner needs: power, subject, subjection', *Studies in the Education of Adults*, 23 (1) April: 85–97.

Garrison, R. (1991) 'Critical thinking and adult education: a conceptual model for developing critical thinking in adult learners', *International Journal of Lifelong Education*, 10 (4): 287–303.

Gibson, R. (1986) *Critical Theory and Education*. London: Hodder and Stoughton.

Giroux, H.A. (1981) *Ideology, Culture, and the Process of Schooling*. Philadelphia, PA: Temple University Press.

Giroux, H.A. (1983) *Theory and Resistance in Education*. London: Heinemann.

Giroux, H.A. (1988) 'Postmodernism and the discourse of educational criticism', *Journal of Education*, 170 (3): 5–30.

Giroux, H.A. (1992) *Border Crossings*. New York: Routledge.

Giroux, H.A. and McClaren, P. (1987) 'Teacher education as a counter-public sphere: notes towards redefinition', in T.S. Popkewitz (ed.), *Critical Studies in Teacher Education*. London: Falmer Press. pp. 266–97.

Gore, J.M. (1993) *The Struggle for Pedagogies*. New York: Routledge.

Habermas, J. (1972) *Knowledge and Human Interests*. London: Heinemann.

Hart, M.U. (1990) 'Critical theory and beyond: further perspectives on emancipatory education', *Adult Education Quarterly*, 40 (3) Spring: 125–38.

Hearn, J. (1983) 'Issues of control in simulations and games: a reconsideration', *Simulation/Games for Learning*, 13 (3) Autumn: 120–5.

Hindmarsh, J.H. (1993) 'Tensions and dichotomies between theory and practice: a study of alternative formulations', *International Journal of Lifelong Education*, 12 (2): 101–15.

Hodgson, V. and Reynolds, M. (1981) 'The hidden experience of learning events: illusions of involvement', *Personnel Review*, 10 (1): 26–9.

Hodgson, V. and Reynolds, M. (1987) 'The dynamics of the learning community: staff intention and student experience', in D. Boud and V. Griffin (eds), *Appreciating Adults Learning*. London: Kogan Page. pp. 147–58.

Hyland, T. (1994) 'Experiential learning, competence and critical practice in higher education', *Studies in Higher Education*, 19 (3): 327–39.

Keddy, N. (1971) 'Classroom knowledge', in M.F.D. Young (ed.), *Knowledge and Control*. New York: Collier-Macmillan. pp. 133–60.

Kemmis, S. (1985) 'Action research and the politics of reflection', in D. Boud, R. Keogh and D. Walker (eds), *Reflection: Turning Experience into Learning*. London: Kogan Page. pp. 139–63.

Knowles, M. (1975) *Self-Directed Learning: A guide for Learners and Teachers*. Chicago: Association Press.

Lather, P. (1994) 'Staying dumb? Feminist research and pedagogy with/in the postmodern', in M. Billig and H.W. Simons (eds), *After Postmodernism*. London: Sage. pp. 101–32.

Luke, C. and Gore, J.M. (eds) (1992) *Feminisms and Critical Pedagogy*. New York: Routledge.

Marton, F. and Saljo, R. (1976) 'On qualitative differences in learning: I – outcome and process', *British Journal of Educational Psychology*, 46: 4–11.

McCormick, D.W. (1994) 'Critical thinking and credit for prior experiential learning', *Journal of Management Education*, 18 (3) August: 342–50.

Nord, W.R. and Jermier, J.M. (1992) 'Critical social science for managers? Promising and perverse possibilities', in M. Alvesson and H. Willmott (eds), *Critical Management Studies*. London: Sage. pp. 202–22.

Parlett, M. and Hamilton, D. (1972) *Evaluation as Illumination: A New Approach to the Study of Innovatory Programmes*. Occasional Paper No. 9, Centre for Research in the Educational Sciences, University of Edinburgh, Edinburgh.

Pedler, M. (1994) 'Developing the learning community', in M. Pedler and T. Boydell (eds), *Management Self-Development: Concepts and Practices*. Aldershot: Gower. pp. 68–84.

Popkewitz, T.S. (1988) 'Culture, pedagogy, and power: issues in the production of values and colonialization', *Journal of Education*, 170 (2): 77–90.

Reed, M. and Anthony, P. (1992) 'Professionalizing management and managing professionalization: British management in the 1980s', *Journal of Management Studies*, 29 (September): 591–613.

Reynolds, M. (1982) 'Learning the ropes', *Transaction, Social Science and Modern Society*, 19 (6) September/October: 30–4.

Reynolds, M. (1997) 'Learning styles: a critique', *Management Learning*, 28 (2): 115–33.

Simons, H.W. (1994) 'Teaching the pedagogies: a dialectical approach to an ideological dilemma', in M. Billig and H.W. Simons (eds), *After Postmodernism*. London: Sage. pp. 133–49.

Snyder, B. (1971) *The Hidden Curriculum*. New York: Knopf.

Usher, R. (1991) 'Theory and metatheory in the adult education curriculum', *International Journal of Lifelong Education*, 10 (4) October/December: 305–15.

Usher, R.S. (1992) 'Experience in adult education: a post-modern critique', *Journal of Philosophy of Education*, 26 (2): 201–15.

Welton, M.R. (1994) 'Cathedrals and doghouses: a conversation', *International Journal of Lifelong Education*, 13 (4) July/August: 281–9.

Wildermeersch, D. (1992) 'Ambiguities of experiential learning and critical pedagogy', in D. Wildermeersch and T. Jansen (eds), *Adult Education, Experiential Learning and Social Change*. Uitgeverij B.V.: 's-Growenhage.

Willmott, H. (1994) 'Management education, provocations to a debate', *Management Learning*, 25 (1): 105–36.

Wilson, A.L. (1994) 'To a middle ground: praxis and ideology in adult education', *International Journal of Lifelong Education*, 13 (3): 187–202.

Young, Michael F.D. (ed.) (1971) *Knowledge and Control*. New York: Collier-Macmillan.

Zeichner, K.M. (1981) 'Reflective teaching and field-based experience in teacher education', *Interchange*, 12 (4): 1–22.

Reconstruction: Looking Forward

In our opening chapter we argued that the field of management education, training and development, despite having become a sizable 'industry' in itself, has not in any obvious or clear-cut way revolutionized the social and economic benefits that are derived from managed organizations. The major growth of these activities, starting from the 1960s, and the initiative to redirect it through the study and teaching of management learning from the mid-1970s were based on such utopian aspirations. In this circumstance, the thrust of this volume has been to dig deep and wide into what management learning might be, the underlying theoretical, philosophical and moral ideas relevant to its interpretation, the more fundamental values and purposes that it might serve, and the implications of this for the design of management learning activities.

Management learning has been strongly committed to relating theory to practice, and the view that the detachment of these two domains is one of the main problems in realizing the benefits of management education, training and development. However, probing deeper into areas of theory and philosophy has been a key emphasis in this volume. Many readers may have expected a more straightforward and instrumental set of proposals about what is involved in 'doing' management development. But our interpretation of the current situation is that such formulations simply do not exist in workable form, and that the necessary way forward is to encourage critically reflective practice by critically reflective practitioners, supported by academic enquiry and teaching which examines the normative and descriptive theory of the field in terms of more interpretative and critical perspectives. Our working assumption is that, despite all the efforts to the contrary, the actual practices of management education, training and development have remained too superficial, have lacked the power to reformulate the managerial and organizational practices at which they are targeted, and have themselves absorbed the problems and dilemmas which characterize management and organization. In this circumstance the only way to improve practice is to dig deeper into theory, to try to establish the grounds for a more fundamental basis on which to found practice. This is the aim that has been pursued in this volume. It has to be acknowledged, however, that the intellectual debate that this implies has become, perhaps necessarily, esoteric and at least temporarily detached from teaching and training practice. Making the esoteric debate more accessible, and sophisticating the degree and nature of the articulation of practitioner working theories so that the two can fruitfully interact should be a priority in developing the theory and practice of management learning.

Our tentative conclusions from putting together this volume, and considering the overall picture that it produces, can be summarized under the headings of *'what* might be done?', *'how* might it be done?', *'who* might do it?', and 'what are the main *challenges* to be faced in doing all this?'.

What Might be Done?

We can discern three broad ways forward for management learning and the world of organized and managed activity that it seeks to influence.

1 From humanism to emancipation

Much of the practice of management learning still has a basis in humanistic developmental psychology, which, while well meaning, has turned out to be naive at best, based on a too simple idea of the individual self and unable to cope with the dynamics of power in organizations, conflicts of purpose, the more collective nature of learning and practical meaning making, and the social and possibly material constraints on the achievements of aspirations. At worst, humanistic approaches play an active part in the exploitation and control of people under the disguise of offering help. The field of management learning has a long way to go in coming to terms with this insight, finding a more appropriate approach and finding ways of implementing it in practice. However, it does look as though, in the broadest sense, an *emancipatory* agenda is the most promising way forward. In this, the development and sharing of knowledge and the ability to use it gives the best chance of defining life-enchancing purposes and achieving them through management and organization. The development of applied critical theory, critically reflective practice, critical action learning, collaborative and reflective enquiry begin to suggest ways forward on this agenda.

2 New collectivism, stakeholder society, communitarianism, organizational learning

Shifts in our understanding of learning as a more collective and social process, and of managing and organizing as arranging things in a pluralistic context contribute to a new and much more collective vision of the future consistent with the emancipatory agenda. Facilitating collective learning that recognizes multiple stakeholders, addresses the development and fulfilment of their interests and helps this process become self-perpetuating looks like a promising way forward, demanding a whole new set of methods and approaches to practice.

3 From instrumentalism to social concern

It is clear from a variety of arguments in this volume that management learning has been historically, and is still currently, unbalanced in its concerns with instrumental, 'how to', means–ends issues, at the expense of developing ways to address the issues of moral, ethical and social responsibility in working out how to agree and how to determine what to do. Although 'values' are much discussed, it is usually in the context of their dissemination, sharing or reconciliation, rather than their legitimation and justification. Management learning as an arena for the moral and ethical debate about organization, management and the learning process itself can be promoted with some confidence as a priority for the future. This must be as well as, rather than instead of, a rigorous addressing of instrumental issues, since these must be crucial to the implementation of ethical decisions. However, concentration on the instrumental must not be allowed to obscure the moral and ethical issues of purpose.

How Might it be Done?

A number of broad approaches to pursue these agendas can be identified. First, new technology, particularly information technology, creates a whole new set of possibilities for management learning work that are as yet only partially understood. In principle, the potential of information technology to share and disseminate knowledge and enable its co-creation to contribute to the emancipatory agenda is clear, as is its opposite potential to standardize, control, inspect, monitor and normalize variety and experimentation. The potential of information technology to affect substantially the economics and logistics of management learning practice means that it is certain to be an exciting domain of experimentation and development which is creating and will continue to create opportunities for innovation and change, and shake up many of the customs and practices that inhibit them.

Secondly, management learning has a unique opportunity to contribute to the development of new social and economic orderings through innovations in the *processes* by which learning is engendered, as opposed to, or as well as, its *content*. Critical management pedagogy is an area of possibility unique to management learning and, to the extent that 'the medium is the message', a crucial one.

Thirdly, management learning, through its practices, creates special arenas within and between organizations through which new perspectives can be brought to bear, and experiences shared and examined. This arena constitutes a special opportunity to raise collective consciousness, and conscience, about managerial and organizational practice. Finally, to the extent to which management learning both creates a more theoretical debate about its practice, and keeps this debate in touch with the practice, its very existence creates the opportunity to challenge otherwise unquestioned working assumptions and to find alternatives. This should provide an alternative to the common trend for management learning practices to be copied between organizations as uncritically examined habits which are implemented without regard to context and history.

Who Might Do It?

This volume envisages practice and practitioners as having to become more critically reflective as the practical justification of their work continues to be problematical, and sees theory and theorists as having to become not only more sophisticated, but also more able to be accessible to those outside their specialist debates, and more willing to engage with their ideas in action. Although this is likely to be a struggle, as this book exemplifies, these two interests, in principle, coincide and could and should converge. New media of journals, books, conferences, consortia, networks are needed to enable this.

What Are the Challenges?

As we see it, there are three major challenges to be faced in management learning. The first is to enrich the theoretical debate without detaching theory from practice. The second is to create a common language amongst the communities involved. The third is to lever management learning, and the field of management education, training and development, out of the situation in which it is trapped by its current ideas, customs and practices. This is the reform needed if it is to live up to the aspirations we have for it.

Our explanation for the failure of this relatively young field to live up to the grander expectations that have existed for it is in these terms, and we hope that this volume may mark the beginning of a turning-point in which, as the field matures, it reaches a new level of engaged *and* detached involvement from which it can have a significant impact on the social and economic contribution of managing and organizing.

Author Index

Subject Index